CHURCH DOGI

For further resources, including the forewords to the original 14-volume edition of the *Church Dogmatics*, log on to our website and sign up for the resources webpage: http://www.continuumbooks.com/dogmatics/

KARL BARTH

CHURCH DOGMATICS

VOLUME I

THE DOCTRINE
OF THE WORD OF GOD

§ 19–21

HOLY SCRIPTURE

EDITED BY
G. W. BROMILEY
T. F. TORRANCE

t&t clark

Published by T&T Clark
A Continuum Imprint
The Tower Building, 11 York Road, London, SE1 7NX
80 Maiden Lane, Suite 704, New York, NY 10038

www.continuumbooks.com

Translated by G. W. Bromiley, G. T. Thomson, Harold Knight

Authorised translation of Karl Barth, *Die Kirchliche Dogmatik I*
Copyright © Theologischer Verlag Zürich, 1932–1938
All revisions to the original English translation and all translations of Greek, Latin and French
© Princeton Theological Seminary, 2009

British Library Cataloguing-in-Publication Data
A catalogue record for this book is available from the British Library

ISBN13: 978-0-567-34651-3

Typeset by Interactive Sciences Ltd, Gloucester, and Newgen Imaging Systems Pvt Ltd, Chennai
Printed and bound in Great Britain by CPI Antony Rowe, Chippenham, Wiltshire

PUBLISHER'S PREFACE TO THE STUDY EDITION

Since the publication of the first English translation of *Church Dogmatics I.1* by Professor Thomson in 1936, T&T Clark has been closely linked with Karl Barth. An authorised translation of the whole of the *Kirchliche Dogmatik* was begun in the 1950s under the editorship of G. W. Bromiley and T. F. Torrance, a work which eventually replaced Professor Thomson's initial translation of *CD I.1*.

T&T Clark is now happy to present to the academic community this new *Study Edition* of the *Church Dogmatics*. Its aim is mainly to make this major work available to a generation of students and scholars with less familiarity with Latin, Greek, and French. For the first time this edition therefore presents the classic text of the translation edited by G. W. Bromiley and T. F. Torrance incorporating translations of the foreign language passages in Editorial Notes on each page.

The main body of the text remains unchanged. Only minor corrections with regard to grammar or spelling have been introduced. The text is presented in a new reader friendly format. We hope that the breakdown of the *Church Dogmatics* into 31 shorter fascicles will make this edition easier to use than its predecessors.

Completely new indexes of names, subjects and scriptural indexes have been created for the individual volumes of the *Study Edition*.

The publishers would like to thank the Center for Barth Studies at Princeton Theological Seminary for supplying a digital edition of the text of the *Church Dogmatics* and translations of the Greek and Latin quotations in the original T&T Clark edition made by Simon Gathercole and Ian McFarland.

London, April 2010

HOW TO USE THIS
STUDY EDITION

The *Study Edition* follows Barth's original volume structure. Individual paragraphs and sections should be easy to locate. A synopsis of the old and new edition can be found on the back cover of each fascicle.

All secondary literature on the *Church Dogmatics* currently refers to the classic 14-volume set (e.g. II.2 p. 520). In order to avoid confusion, we recommend that this practice should be kept for references to this *Study Edition*. The page numbers of the old edition can be found in the margins of this edition.

CONTENTS

§ 19–21

THE WORD OF GOD FOR THE CHURCH

The Word of God is God Himself in Holy Scripture. For God once spoke as Lord to Moses and the prophets, to the Evangelists and apostles. And now through their written word He speaks as the same Lord to His Church. Scripture is holy and the Word of God, because by the Holy Spirit it became and will become to the Church a witness to divine revelation.

1. SCRIPTURE AS A WITNESS TO DIVINE REVELATION

The theme of dogmatics (cf. *Dogm.* I, 1, §7, 1) is the question of the Word of God in the proclamation of the Christian Church, or, concretely, the question of the agreement of this proclamation with Holy Scripture as the Word of God. To answer this question as such we had first to investigate that form of the Word of God which precedes both proclamation and Holy Scripture, i.e., the revelation of God. It is because God has revealed Himself, and as He has done so, that there is a Word of God, and therefore Holy Scripture and proclamation as the Word of God, and therefore a relation and correspondence between the two, and therefore the possibility and necessity of this question of their agreement. We have already answered the question of the concept of revelation presupposed in both these other forms of the Word of God. We have not sought or found this answer at random. We have taken it from the Bible. For the Bible is a sign which, it cannot be contested, does at least point to a superior authority confronting the proclamation of the Church. In contrast to Roman Catholicism and Protestant modernism, we felt that we ought to take this sign seriously. For that reason, at every decisive point we took our answer to the question of revelation from the Bible. And the Bible has given us the answer. It has attested to us the lordship of the triune God in the incarnate Word by the Holy Spirit.

But in so doing it has answered that question concerning itself which we have not yet asked. We now know to what extent it points to a superior authority confronting the proclamation of the Church: obviously to the extent that it is a witness of divine revelation. It is not in vain that we have taken notice of [458] this sign. It has proved itself a true sign. It has shown us something. It has in fact indicated a higher, judicial, decisive authority superior to all the proclamation which takes place in the Church and can claim the authority of the Church. Does the Church recognise this authority? Does it, therefore, recognise the concrete significance of the Bible as the sign which points to this authority? Does it recognise that the question of dogmatics must also be its question? the question of the agreement of its proclamation with this sign, because in, with and under this sign that proclamation is confronted by the Word of God with which it must be in agreement if it would itself be the Word of God? Dogmatics cannot answer this question for the Church. It can do so only at its own specific place in the Church. But if it is a Church dogmatics, how can it give any but a positive answer?

Now that the content of the biblical witness is before us, we see better than we did that the actual recognition of this witness and the willingness to follow it will always be something which takes place miraculously and very simply, without any special claim. If the biblical witness is obeyed in the Church, it happens quite unassumingly, without the adornment of special grounds and reasons, or any appeal to a prophetic mission or experience or illumination. Looking back on the content of this witness, we can now say that the lordship of the triune God has shown itself to be a fact. If this is so, if therefore obedience to this witness is also a fact, if therefore the proclamation of the Church is actually subjected to and measured by and executed according to this witness, then we will not ask: why the Bible? and look for external or internal grounds and reasons. We will leave it to the Bible itself, if we are to be obedient to it, to vindicate itself by what takes place, i.e., to vindicate the witness to divine revelation which we have heard in it, to repeat itself in such a way that it can again be apprehended by the obedient man and everyone else. If the obedient man tries to base his obedience on some other calling, as though that were necessary, then at once his obedience is called in question as obedience. Where the lordship of the triune God is a fact, it is itself the basis, and a sufficient basis, for obedience.

Presupposing this obedience, what it means for the proclamation of the Church to be subjected to and measured by and executed according to the biblical witness, is, of course, a very necessary topic of discussion, and we shall take up the question in the last chapter of these prolegomena, when we give the theme and task of dogmatics its final, concrete formulation. Before we come to this question, there is an obvious need—again presupposing that tacit obedience—to think about the Bible as such: its nature as sign, its relation to the thing which it signifies, its normative and critical character in relation to the Church's proclamation, its limiting and determinative significance for the

[459] life of the Church both as a whole and in each of its members. We have to be quite clear about this: that in that tacit obedience in face of the biblical witness, expressed or unexpressed, there is a quite definite perception with regard to that witness. Even the statement we have made already, that it is the witness of revelation, is of itself important and full of content. But it needs to be elaborated and explained. And it must not be the only statement. If it is a witness of revelation, and if, however tacit, there is a genuine and necessary obedience to it, then the witness itself and as such—as well as the revelation which it attests—is necessarily in the power of the revelation of the Word of

2

1. *Scripture as a Witness to Divine Revelation*

God attested by it, and it necessarily acquires in the Church, as distinct from all other words and signs, the dignity and validity of the Word of God. It is not superfluous to think this through and to state it, for the very reason that our attitude to this witness has constantly to be re-tested, whether it really is that tacit but genuine and necessary obedience. The presupposition of this obedience—which we cannot create, but can only presuppose as a fact—will have to be clarified by answering the later question of the concrete task of dogmatics in relation to proclamation. But this clarification is only possible as we try to bring out the perception with regard to the character and basic significance of the witness which is contained in a genuine and necessary obedience to the biblical witness. It is therefore to the doctrine of Holy Scripture that we must turn.

We have now reached the point which, confessionally and doctrinally, the Reformation Churches of the 16th century found it so important according to their own conscience and experience expressly to fix and emphasise, as against the Roman Church on the one hand, and fanatics on the other, that it soon became the rule, and an increasingly strict rule, to introduce the official explanations of the Confession, and then theological expositions of Evangelical teaching, with an exposition of this very perception: the perception with regard to the character and significance of Holy Scripture. *Fallitur quisquis aliunde christianismi formam petit, quam e sacra scriptura*[EN1], Melanchthon had already written in the Preface to his *Loci* of 1521. And the invitation, which at the beginning of 1523 the Council of the city of Zürich issued to the decisive disputation, was significant for the development of this doctrine. It not only says that "divine Scripture" ought almost as a matter of form to be the decisive and wholly decisive general presupposition of the proposed discussion of the division which has arisen in the Church. But rather threateningly in view of the expected results of this discussion, it also lays down that "when we have found according to divine Scripture and truth, we will send everyone home, with the injunction to proceed or abstain, that none may henceforth preach what is right in his own eyes, without foundation in divine Scripture. … And if any is contumacious in this, and does not come with true divine teaching, we will deal further with him according to our perception, enjoining that which we will should be maintained." In the same way the theses which Zwingli drew up for the disputation of Berne in 1528 begin with the clear-cut statement that "the holy Christian Church, whose one Head is Christ, is born of the Word of God, is incorporated in the same, and heareth not the voice of a stranger." It has often been remarked that the 1530 Lutheran *Augustana*, as opposed to the contemporary *Confessio tetrapolitana* with its Zwinglian orientation, does not expressly mention, but only tacitly assumes this Scripture principle. It must be noted, however, that the memorial which Zwingli himself then directed to the Emperor (*Fidei ratio*[EN2]) did not contain it either, and that there was no emphatic assertion of the principle in the Zürich [460] "*Introduction*" of 1523, the Synod of Berne of 1532 and the Confession of Basel of 1534. If Luther omitted it in his catechisms of 1529, the same must also be said of Calvin's catechism of 1545. We are not dealing, therefore, with something which is specifically Reformed: this becomes clear later, when insistence on the Scripture principle came to be more generally adopted. Since the *Conf. Helv. prior* and the Genevan *Confession de la foy* (both of 1536) it has been the typical introductory article of Reformed confessional writings. And the famous

---

[EN1] Anyone who seeks the form of Christianity anywhere other than from sacred Scripture, is in error

[EN2] The basis of Faith

opening of Calvin's *Institutio* can only be understood if we see that its bearing is to assert the Scripture principle in opposition to all those other sources of the knowledge of God which have been destroyed by the fall. But it also comes right at the beginning of Melanchthon's *Examen ordinandorum* (1559), of the *Examen concilii Tridentini* of Martin Chemnitz (1565) and of the two parts of the Formula of Concord (1579). And if we compare the older orthodox dogmatics, e.g., on the one side the *Loci* of J. Gerhard (1610 f.) and the *Compendium* of Leonard Hutter (1610), and on the other the *Loci* of Peter Martyr (1576), the *Institutiones theologicae* of W. Bucan (1602), the *Syntagma* of Polan (1609) and the *Compendium* of J. Wolleb (1626), we shall find that if possible the Lutherans put the Scripture principle at the very peak of their theological system even more ardently and obviously than did the Reformed. It maintained this role as formally the basic doctrine of the Evangelical Church until it was first challenged, then replaced in fact and finally in theory, by the new dogma *De religione*EN3. For the theology of the 18th and 19th centuries it was generally a respected historical survival and something of an embarrassment. But we must not overlook the latent continuity of its existence even at that time. The Bible has always remained in the Church as the regular textual basis of proclamation. Biblical criticism and later biblical scholarship, which were now the main interest of theology, bore indirect, but for that reason all the more impressive, witness to its authority. And when more recently German Protestantism especially was forced to examine and give account and defend itself by an internal danger which threatened to bring to a head the creeping sickness of the previous centuries, it was neither accident nor caprice that in May 1933 at the head of the so-called Dusseldorf theses we again find word for word the statement made by Zwingli in 1528. Again, it was neither accident nor caprice that the Free Reformed Synod of Barmen-Gemarke in January 1934, the first of the free Synods in which the Confessional Church was constituted, and then once more and with a definite polemical delimitation at the Reich Synod of Barmen in May 1934, the Scripture principle of the Reformation was affirmed and confessionally stated with almost automatic necessity. It seems to be the case that whether the principle is expressly formulated or not the *dixit*EN4 and *contradixit*EN5 contained in it, the attitude of obedience which answers to it, is essential to Protestantism as such. If there was no longer the same reaction as at the time of the Counter-Reformation and again in our own days, if the Church dared simply to abandon the sign of the Bible dominating its worship and instruction, it would be the end of Protestantism. For in so doing it would cease to protest—the only protest which concerns it. In the measure that it must and will protest, according to the law of the concrete twofold antithesis which it has followed, the formulation of this principle is always unavoidable.

The doctrine of Holy Scripture as such involves therefore the confession in which the Church clarifies that perception which corresponds to a right and necessary attitude of obedience to the witness of revelation, and in that way adopts and maintains such a position. It is important to be on our guard at once against the view that we have to prove and justify this position. When the [461] Bible has spoken as a witness to divine revelation, and when it has been recognised and acknowledged as such, we are forced into this position; we have our work cut out to do what we have to do in this position; we have neither room nor time to ask whether and why we can and will maintain it in the future; we are neither able to find reasons nor justifications for our attitude. Therefore

---

EN3 On religion
EN4 statement
EN5 counter-statement

4

the doctrine of Holy Scripture can only confirm that we are placed in this position by the witness of revelation. We admit the fact and therefore the necessity of all that that position involves.

We might ask: Is such a confession necessary? Is it not enough that we are put in this position? Is not the obedience which we have to give in it itself enough? Is not every doctrine of Holy Scripture as such a superfluous saying of "Lord, Lord"? Might we not ask whether such a confession is not even dangerous as a confirmation of our attitude, whether it will not lead again to an attempted defence and justification which will jeopardise our obedience?

To the first of these questions our answer is that confession of Holy Scripture as a witness to divine revelation is necessary, whenever and to the extent that we are questioned concerning our attitude to it. But in fact we are always being questioned concerning it: by Scripture itself, which always wants us to know what we are doing when we obey it; by other men, who propose that we should take up some other attitude, and sincerely or insincerely want to know whether we are aware or not of the meaning and the consequences of what we are doing; and finally by ourselves, inasmuch as obedience and disobedience are constantly at war with each other especially in ourselves. Therefore since the boundary has to be marked out between obedience and disobedience, the confession of Scripture is itself a necessary part of obedience to Scripture.

When in Mt. 7[21f.] Jesus said that not all who say to Him Lord, Lord shall enter into the kingdom of Heaven, but those who do the will of His Father in Heaven, He did not say that where the will of the Father is done we can or should omit to say Lord, Lord. The fact that confession can be only the confession of obedience does not alter the fact that obedience must still confess itself to be obedience as against the disobedience of ourselves and others, recognising and overcoming the temptation which constantly threatens.

Our answer to the second question is that a confession of Holy Scripture only involves a defence of our position to the extent that in our attitude to it we order ourselves by this confession, i.e., by the clarifying and expressing of the character and value peculiar to the witness of revelation as such. When we do this rightly, when we ground and maintain ourselves in it, there can be no question of a defence and justification of our attitude, but only of a constant indication of its necessity. The content of a true doctrine of Holy Scripture will simply be a development of our knowledge of that law which has its basis and [462] justification in itself, the law under which we stand when we really have to do with the witness of revelation. If our obedience is called in question by a knowledge of this law, this is something which it needs, for we are summoned by it to an obedience which is pure and not confused by defences and justifications.

But as the genuine content of these two questions, we gladly accept the reminder that confession of Holy Scripture, i.e., the explication of the knowledge of its reality and nature contained in obedience to it, is in fact a superfluous and dangerous and in spite of its exactness and completeness an incredible protestation, if the obedience which it presupposes is itself alien to us. On the other hand, if the doctrine of Holy Scripture is simply the necessary exponent of its correct exegesis, we do not forget that the right doctrine of Holy Scripture cannot claim abstract validity, but its confirmation must always be sought and found in exegesis and therefore in Holy Scripture itself.

The basic statement of this doctrine, the statement that the Bible is the witness of divine revelation, is itself based simply on the fact that the Bible has in fact answered our question about the revelation of God, bringing before us the lordship of the triune God. Of course, we could not have received this answer, if as members of the Church we had not listened continually to the voice of the Church, i.e., if we had not respected, and as far as possible applied the exposition of the Bible by those who before and with us were and are members of the Church. About this important definition of true obedience to Scripture, in which there emerges a definition of Scripture itself, we will have to speak explicitly in § 20. And, of course, even then we could not have received this answer if we had not also read and searched and pondered the Bible with our own eyes, if we had not ourselves accepted the responsibility for its correct exposition. That is the second definition of obedience to Scripture, which again points back to a definition of Scripture itself, with which we shall have to deal in § 21. But just as we should ask Holy Scripture in vain about the revelation of God, if we were to sidetrack the exposition of the Church, or to try to spare ourselves the trouble of individual exposition, what is equally necessary, and even more so, is that it should be Scripture which actually does and alone can answer us. The Church can expound, and we can expound, and there is authority and freedom in the Church, only because Scripture has already told us what we are asking about when we ask about God's revelation. The statement that the Bible is the witness of divine revelation is not, therefore, limited by the fact that there is also a witness of the Church which we have to hear, and in addition witness is also demanded of us. The possibility both of the witness of the Church and of our own witness is founded upon the reality of which that statement speaks. Yet all statements which we have still to formulate about those secondary definitions of our obedience to Scripture, all the statements about the necessary authority and equally necessary freedom in the Church itself, can only be expositions of the basic statement that there is a Word of God for the Church: in that it receives in the Bible the witness of divine revelation. Therefore it is the truth of this basic statement which has been tested and proved in the fact that seeking in the Bible we have found in the Bible the answer to our question about God's revelation.

[463]

When we examine this statement more closely, we shall do well to pay attention to the particular determination in the fact that we have to call the Bible a witness of divine revelation. We have here an undoubted limitation: we distinguish the Bible as such from revelation. A witness is not absolutely identical with that to which it witnesses. This corresponds with the facts upon which the truth of the whole proposition is based. In the Bible we meet with human words written in human speech, and in these words, and therefore by means of them, we hear of the lordship of the triune God. Therefore when we have to

6

do with the Bible, we have to do primarily with this means, with these words, with the witness which as such is not itself revelation, but only—and this is the limitation—the witness to it. But the concept of witness, especially when we bear clearly in mind its limiting sense, has still something very positive to say. In this limitation the Bible is not distinguished from revelation. It is simply revelation as it comes to us, mediating and therefore accommodating itself to us—to us who are not ourselves prophets and apostles, and therefore not the immediate and direct recipients of the one revelation, witnesses of the resurrection of Jesus Christ. Yet it is for us revelation by means of the words of the prophets and apostles written in the Bible, in which they are still alive for us as the immediate and direct recipients of revelation, and by which they speak to us. A real witness is not identical with that to which it witnesses, but it sets it before us. Again this corresponds with the facts on which the truth of the whole proposition is founded. If we have really listened to the biblical words in all their humanity, if we have accepted them as witness, we have obviously not only heard of the lordship of the triune God, but by this means it has become for us an actual presence and event. If we want to think of the Bible as a real witness of divine revelation, then clearly we have to keep two things constantly before us and give them their due weight: the limitation and the positive element, its distinctiveness from revelation, in so far as it is only a human word about it, and its unity with it, in so far as revelation is the basis, object and content of this word.

To avoid this, there is no point in ignoring the writtenness of Holy Writ for the sake of its holiness, its humanity for the sake of its divinity. We must not ignore it any more than we do the humanity of Jesus Christ Himself. We must study it, for it is here or nowhere that we shall find its divinity. The Bible is a witness of revelation which is really given and really applies and is really received by us just because it is a written word, and in fact a word written by men like ourselves, which we can read and hear and understand as such. And [464] it is as such that we must read and hear and understand it if this is to happen at all and there is to be any apprehension of revelation.

The demand that the Bible should be read and understood and expounded historically is, therefore, obviously justified and can never be taken too seriously. The Bible itself posits this demand: even where it appeals expressly to divine commissionings and promptings, in its actual composition it is everywhere a human word, and this human word is obviously intended to be taken seriously and read and understood and expounded as such. To do anything else would be to miss the reality of the Bible and therefore the Bible itself as the witness of revelation. The demand for a "historical" understanding of the Bible necessarily means, in content, that we have to take it for what it undoubtedly is and is meant to be: the human speech uttered by specific men at specific times in a specific situation, in a specific language and with a specific intention. It means that the understanding of it has honestly and unreservedly been one which is guided by all these considerations. If the word "historical" is a modern word, the thing itself was not really invented in modern times. And if the more exact definition of what is "historical" in this sense is liable to change and has actually changed at times, it is still quite clear that when and wherever the Bible has been really read and expounded, in this sense it has been read "historically" and not unhistorically, i.e., its concrete humanity has not been ignored. To the extent that it has been ignored, it has not been read at all. We have, therefore, not only no cause to retract from this demand, but every cause to accept it strictly on theological grounds.

But when we do take the humanity of the Bible quite seriously, we must also take quite definitely the fact that as a human word it does say something specific, that as a human word it points away from itself, that as a word it points towards a fact, an object. In this respect, too, it is a genuine human word. What human word is there which does not do the same? We do not speak for the sake of speaking, but for the sake of the indication which is to be made by our speaking. We speak for the sake of what we denote or intend by our speaking. To listen to a human word spoken to us does not mean only that we have cognition of the word as such. The understanding of it cannot consist merely in discovering on what presuppositions, in what situation, in what linguistic sense and with what intention, in what actual context, and in this sense with what meaning the other has said this or that. And the exposition of his word cannot possibly consist only in the exposition which, as I listen to him, involuntarily or even consciously I try to give of the speaker himself. These things do not mean that I penetrate to his word as such. At best, they mean only that I am prepared to listen and understand and expound. If I were to confuse this preparation with the listening, understanding and expounding, and concern myself only with the word as such and the one who speaks it, how I should deceive myself! As far as I am concerned, he would have spoken in vain. We can speak meaningfully of hearing a human utterance only when it is clear to us in its function of indicating something that is described or intended by the [465] word, and also when this function has become an event confronting us, when therefore by means of the human word we ourselves in some degree perceive the thing described or intended. It is only then that anyone has told me anything and I have heard it from him. We may call other things speaking and hearing, but in the strict sense they are only unsuccessful attempts at speaking and hearing. If a human word spoken to me does not show me anything, or if I myself cannot perceive what the word shows me, we have an unsuccessful attempt of this kind. Understanding of a human word presupposes that the attempt to speak and hear has succeeded. Then I know what is being said. On the basis and in the light of the word I understand what is said to me. Now understanding is, of course, a return to the word, an inquiry into the word itself: the word with all its linguistic and factual presuppositions; an inquiry in which even as I turn afresh to the word and speaker, I take up a standpoint outside the word and speaker, that is, in that perception of the thing described or intended in the word which is mediated to me by my hearing of the word. Again, if the word does mediate any such perception, if the thing described or intended by the word is still not known by me even when it has been spoken, then I have not heard that word at all, and in that case how can I understand it? But if I have heard it, how can I understand it except in the light of what it says

8

to me, i.e., of the matter, the perception, which it mediates to me? Of course, concretely this understanding can consist only in my returning from the matter to the word and its presuppositions, to the speaking subject in its concrete form. But it is only in the light of what is said to me and heard by me, and not of myself, that I try to inquire of the word and the speaking subject. The result of my inquiry in this form will be my interpretation of this human word. My exposition cannot possibly consist in an interpretation of the speaker. Did he say something to me only to display himself? I should be guilty of a shameless violence against him, if the only result of my encounter with him were that I now knew him or knew him better than before. What lack of love! Did he not say anything to me at all? Did he not therefore desire that I should see him not *in abstracto*[EN6] but in his specific and concrete relationship to the thing described or intended in his word, that I should see him from the standpoint and in the light of this thing? How much wrong is being continually perpetrated, how much intolerable obstruction of human relationships, how much isolation and impoverishment forced upon individuals has its only basis in the fact that we do not take seriously a claim which in itself is as clear as the day, the claim which arises whenever one person addresses a word to another.

At this point the question arises: What is the source of the hermeneutic teaching which we have just sketched? Well, the fact that in spite of its inherent clarity it still does not enjoy general recognition is in itself an indication that it does not arise out of any general considerations on the nature of human language, etc., and therefore out of a general anthropology. Why is it that, as a rule, general considerations on the nature of human language do not lead to the propositions indicated? My reply would be: because the hermeneutic principles are not dictated by Holy Scripture, as they are in our case. If we ask ourselves, and as readers of Holy Scripture we have to ask ourselves, what is meant by hearing and understanding and expounding when we presuppose that that which is described or intended by the word of man is the revelation of God, the answer we have given forces itself upon us. Hearing undoubtedly means perceiving revelation by the word of man—understanding, investigating the humanly concrete word in the light of revelation—expounding, clarifying the word in its relation to revelation. It is in view of the only possible explanation of Holy Scripture that we have laid the principles of exposition indicated—not, of course, believing that they apply only to biblical exposition, but believing always that because they are valid for biblical exposition they are valid for the exposition of every human word, and can therefore lay claim to universal recognition. It is not at all that the word of man in the Bible has an abnormal significance and function. We see from the Bible what its normal significance and function is. It is from the word of man in the Bible that we must learn what has to be learned concerning the word of man in general. This is not generally recognised. It is more usual blindly to apply to the Bible false ideas taken from some other source concerning the significance and function of the human word. But this must not confuse us into thinking that the very opposite way is the right one. There is no such thing as a special biblical hermeneutics. But we have to learn that hermeneutics which is alone and generally valid by means of the Bible as the witness of revelation. We therefore arrive at the suggested rule, not from a general anthropology, but from the Bible, and obviously, as the rule which is alone and generally valid, we must apply it first to the Bible.

[466]

[EN6] in the abstract

9

The fact that we have to understand and expound the Bible as a human word can now be explained rather more exactly in this way: that we have to listen to what it says to us as a human word. We have to understand it as a human word in the light of what it says.

Under the caption of a truly "historical" understanding of the Bible we cannot allow ourselves to commend an understanding which does not correspond to the rule suggested: a hearing in which attention is paid to the biblical expressions but not to what the words signify, in which what is said is not heard or overheard; an understanding of the biblical words from their immanent linguistic and factual context, instead of from what they say and what we hear them say in this context; an exposition of the biblical words which in the last resort consists only in an exposition of the biblical men in their historical reality. To this we must say that it is not an honest and unreserved understanding of the biblical word as a human word, and it is not therefore a historical understanding of the Bible. In an understanding of this kind the Bible cannot be witness. In this type of understanding, in which it is taken so little seriously, indeed not at all, as a human word, the possibility of its being witness is taken away from the very outset. The philosophy which lies behind this kind of understanding and would force us to accept it as the only true historical understanding is not of course a very profound or respectable one. But even if we value it more highly, or highest of all, and are therefore disposed to place great confidence in its dictates, knowing what is involved in the understanding of the Bible, we can only describe this kind of understanding of the reality of a human word as one which cannot possibly do justice to its object. Necessarily, therefore, we have to reject most decisively the intention of even the most profound and respectable philosophy to subject any human word and especially the biblical word to this understanding. The Bible cannot be read unbiblically. And in this case that means that it cannot be read with such a disregard for its character even as a human word. It cannot be read so unhistorically.

[467]

Even the best and finest results, which were to be and have actually been achieved by the methods based on this understanding, will not prevent us from making this rejection, but only strengthen us in it. In accordance with the only remaining possibility of exposition, the best and finest results of this method usually consist in a certain clear knowledge of the biblical men in their concrete state, of their personality and piety in relation to their position and role in the historical circumstances in which they lived, their specific speech and being, greatness and limitation, significance and weakness as microcosmically or macrocosmically determined. We certainly cannot despise such knowledge as worthless. When their word is heard, and in the hearing attention is paid to what is signified and intended in this word, and there is an understanding of the full meaning and scope of their humanity in the light of this object of their word, then a proper exposition of their word can take account of their humanity in all its scope and meaning—not, however, *in abstracto*EN7 but in its connexion with the object revealed in their word as it is heard and understood. An exposition of their humanity *in abstracto*EN8 may be very full historically. It may be informed and penetrated by a very great understanding for their religion. It may be carried out with the greatest possible zeal. But we still have to reject it as an interpretation of the Bible—and on the very ground that it does not take the human word of the Bible as seriously as according to the Bible itself it ought to be taken. Therefore Calvin is really right from this, the historical point of view (let alone any other), when he believes that the Bible itself excludes any interpretation of the Bible which puts biblical man in the centre of consideration. And he is probably also right

---

EN7 in the abstract
EN8 in the abstract

when he brings such an interpretation of the Bible into connexion with the false intentions of the doctrine of the Papal Church. *Retenons bien que saint Paul en ce passage, pour monstrer que nous devons tenir l'Escriture saincte indubitable, ne dit pas, Moyse a esté un homme excellent: il ne dit pas, Isaie avoit une eloquence admirable: il n'allegue rien des hommes pour les faire valoir en leur personnes: mais il dit qu'ils ont esté organes de l'Esprit de Dieu, que leurs langues ont esté conduites en sorte qu'ils n'ont rien advancé de leur propre, mais que c'est Dieu qui a parlé par leur bouche, qu'il ne faut point que nous les estimions comme creatures mortelles, mais que nous sachions que le Dieu vivant s'en est servi, et que nous ayons cela pour tout conclu, qu'ils ont esté fideles dispensateurs du thrésor qui leur estoit commis. Or si cela eust esté bien observé, on ne fust pas venu en telle et si horrible confusion comme encores sont tous les povres Papistes. Car sur quoy est fondee leur foy, sinon sur les hommes? ... Il est vray qu'ils alleguerons bien le nom de Dieu: mais cependant ils mettront en avant leurs songes et resveries, et puis c'est tout. Or au contraire, voici sainct Paul qui nous dit qu'il nous faut tenir à l'Escriture saincte. Voilà pour un item. Et à quelles enseignes? Pource que Dieu parle là, et non point les hommes. Nous voyons donc comme il exclud toute authorité humaine, qu'il faut que Dieu ait sa pre-eminence par dessus toutes ses creatures, et que grans et petis s'assuiettissent à luy, et que nul ne presume de s'ingerer pour dire, Je parleray*[EN9] ... (*Serm. on 2 Tim.* 3[16f.], *C.R.* 54, 286). And Luther was no less right when he drew attention to the fact that in his well-known saying: "If any man preach any other Gospel unto you than that ye have received," Paul undoubtedly subordin-ates himself completely to the Word which he preached: Paul *simpliciter seipsum, Angelum e coelo, doctores in terra et quicquid est Magistrorum, hoc totum rapit et subiicit sacrae scripturae. Haec Regina debet dominari, huic omnes obedire et subiacere debent. Non eius Magistri, Judices seu Arbitri, sed simplices testes, discipuli et confessores esse debent, sive sit Papa, sive Lutherus, sive Augustinus, sive Paulus, sive Angelus e coelo. Neque alia doctrina in Ecclesia tradi et audiri debet quam purum verbum Dei, vel doctores et auditores cum sua doctrina Anathema sunto*[EN10] (*Comm. on Gal.* 1[9], 1535, W.A. 40[1.] 120, 18). For *hoc vitium insitum est nobis, quod personas admiramur et plus respicimus quam verbum, cum Deus velit nos inhaerentes et affixos esse tantum in ipsum verbum. Vult, ut nucleum, non testam eligamus, ut plus curemus patremfamilias quam domum. In Petro et Paulo non vult nos admirari vel adorare Apostolatum, sed Christum in eis loquentem et ipsum verbum Dei, quod de* [468]

[EN] 9 Let us note well that in the passage, St Paul does not say, in order to demonstrate that we must hold Holy Scripture to be indubitable, that Moses was an excellent man. He does not say that Isaiah had admirable eloquence. He claims nothing about men in order to legitimate them in their persons. Rather, he says that they have been instruments of the Spirit of God, that their tongues have been conducted in such a way that they have done nothing on their own. In fact, it is God who has spoken through their mouths; he says that we must not reckon them as mortal creatures, but that we should know that the living God is using them, and that finally we should conclude that they have been faithful stewards of the treasure which has been committed to them. And if that had been well noted, one would not have fallen into such a terrible confusion as those poor papists are still in. For what is their faith founded upon, if not upon men? ... Granted, they certainly claim the name of God. And yet they give priority to their dreams and fantasies, and then that is all. Against them, St Paul tells us that it is neces-sary to hold to Holy Scripture. So much for that. On what grounds? Because it is there that God speaks, and not men. We see then as he excludes all human authority, that it is necessary that God have His pre-eminence above all His creatures, and that large and small alike must subject themselves to Him, and that no-one should presume to interfere by saying, 'I will declare that ... '

[EN10] takes himself, an angel from heaven, earthly teachers and whatever other teachers: he takes all these together and subjects them to sacred Scripture. This queen must rule, and all must obey and prostrate themselves before her. They must not be her masters, judges or arbiters, but simply witnesses, disciples and confessors, be they the Pope, or Luther, or Augustine, or Paul, or an angel from heaven. No other teaching should be passed down or heard in the Church than the pure word of God: otherwise the teachers and hearers should be anathema along with their teaching

11

ore ipsorum egreditur[EN11] (*on Gal.* 2⁶, *ib.*, 173, 18). All the care and love which we may apply to the biblical text within the framework of that other understanding cannot alter the fact that the understanding as such is inadequate. Luther and Calvin, on the other hand, have at this very point shown a real historical understanding for the Bible.

It is not only not an abuse or violation either of the human word of the Bible in particular or of human words in general, but it has importance as an example when the Christian Church bases its understanding of this word, or of the two humanly composed and selected collections which we call the Bible, not only in relation to the hearing but also in relation to the exposition of it, upon what is said in this word. That it derives this hermeneutic principle from the Bible itself, i.e., that the Bible itself, because of the unusual preponderance of what is said in it over the word as such, enforces this principle upon it, does not alter the fact that this principle is necessarily the principle of all hermeneutics, and that therefore the principle of the Church's doctrine of Holy Scripture, that the Bible is the witness of divine revelation, is simply the special form of that universally valid hermeneutic principle. The Church not only has to hold this in respect of the understanding of the Bible itself. In demanding a historical appreciation of the Bible, it must also require—and self-evidently of every reader of the Bible—that his understanding of it should be based on what is said in the Bible and therefore on God's revelation. It cannot, therefore, be conceded that side by side with this there is another legitimate understanding of the Bible, that, e.g., in its own way it is right and possible when we hear and understand and expound the Bible not to go beyond the humanity as such which is expressed in it. There is indeed a very definite humanity expressed in it, as, for example, that of the apostle Paul. But as the Reformers felt and saw with true historicism, as it is expressed and as the reader of the Bible honestly and unreservedly accepts it, it does not speak of itself, but of God's revelation, and no honest and unprejudiced reader of the Bible can ignore this historical definiteness of the word. No one, of course, has ever dared to say that from their own standpoint—and that is what we have to take into account in understanding this word as a human word—the biblical writers said nothing, and that therefore the problem of what is intended or signified in their word, the problem of the matter or object of it, simply does not exist. And similarly there can hardly be any controversy concerning the fact that what is said by them, that what at least from their standpoint has the character of matter or object, on a closer consideration, is simply God's revelation. It has to be conceded, of course, as in relation to every human word, that there might be a slip somewhere between the word and the reader, whether in the

---

[EN11] this evil has taken hold among us, that we marvel at and respect people more than the word, while God wills that we cling and be anchored only to the word itself. He wants us to choose the kernel, and not the husk, so that we might care more for the father than for the house. In Peter and Paul, he does not want us to admire or adore the apostolate, but the Christ who speaks in them, and the very word of God which proceeds from their mouths

attempt to speak or the attempt to hear: that what is said does not appear to   [469]
the hearer or reader in its factuality, that it cannot do anything with him, and
that he for his part does not know how to make anything of it. If that is the
case, he will, as it were, be left in the air in relation to the word. He will certainly not be able to understand it, because he has no *locus*[EN12] from which he
can understand it. Self-evidently, therefore, he will not be able to expound it
either. But this possibility of failure cannot alter or destroy the validity of the
general hermeneutic principle. If it is really the case that a reader of the biblical Scriptures is quite helpless in face of the problem of what these Scriptures
say and intend and denote in respect of divine revelation, that he sees only an
empty spot at the place to which the biblical writers point, then in a singular
way this does set in relief the extraordinary nature of the content of what these
writers say on the one hand, and on the other the state and status of the reader.
But all that it actually proves is that there can be no question of a legitimate
understanding of the Bible by this reader, that for the time being, i.e., until his
relation to what is said in the Bible changes, this reader cannot be regarded as
a serious reader and exegete. There can be no question of his exegesis being
equally justified with one which is based upon the real substance of the Bible,
divine revelation.

There is a notion that complete impartiality is the most fitting and indeed the normal
disposition for true exegesis, because it guarantees a complete absence of prejudice. For a
short time, around 1910, this idea threatened to achieve almost canonical status in Protestant theology. But now we can quite calmly describe it as merely comical.

Now this does not mean that the hermeneutic principle is destroyed or
altered. For it is characteristic of what is said and intended and denoted in the
Bible, again in the sense of those who said it, that if it is to reveal and establish
itself at all as substance and object, it must do so of itself. How can it be otherwise, when what is said is God's revelation, the lordship of the triune God in
His Word by the Holy Ghost? To what is said—and even as they say it, and the
biblical witnesses themselves attest it—there belongs a sovereign freedom in
face of both speaker and hearer alike. The fact that it can be said and heard
does not mean that it is put at the power and disposal of those who say and
hear it. What it does mean is that as it is said and heard by them it can make
itself said and heard. It is only by revelation that revelation can be spoken in
the Bible and that it can be heard as the real substance of the Bible. If it is to be
witness at all, and to be apprehended as such, the biblical witness must itself be
attested by what it attests. We shall have to return expressly to this peculiarity of
the biblical witness in the second section of this chapter under the title "Scripture as the Word of God." But at this point already we can and must lay down
that even this property of biblical witness does not give us permission to depart
from the historical understanding of the text as we have described it, or to   [470]
accept the possibility and legitimacy of any understanding which deviates from

---

[EN12] place

13

it. In exegesis, too—and especially in exegesis—there is only one truth. In face of it, the unfortunate possibility that the matter of which the word speaks may be alien to us does not excuse us. Nor does it permit us, instead of proceeding from the substance to the word, to go first to the word, i.e., to the humanity of the speakers as such. But if that is the case, we are obviously not excused or permitted by the mystery which is the obvious source of this fatal possibility: the mystery of the sovereign freedom of the substance. On the contrary, the knowledge of this mystery, even when it is only a matter of hearing as such, will summon us as readers of the Bible to hear, really to give ear, in a way in which we would probably never do otherwise. Not knowing this mystery, we will, of course, hear as we always do, as though we know already, and can partly tell ourselves what we are to hear. Our supposed listening is in fact a strange mixture of hearing and our own speaking, and, in accordance with the usual rule, it is most likely that our own speaking will be the really decisive event. We have to know the mystery of the substance if we are really to meet it, if we are really to be open and ready, really to give ourselves to it, when we are told it, that it may really meet us as the substance. And when it is a matter of understanding, the knowledge of this mystery will create in us a peculiar fear and reserve which is not at all usual to us. We will then know that in the face of this subject-matter there can be no question of our achieving, as we do in others, the confident approach which masters and subdues the matter. It is rather a question of our being gripped by the subject-matter—not gripped physically, not making an experience of it and the like, although (ironically) that can happen—but really gripped, so that it is only as those who are mastered by the subject-matter, who are subdued by it, that we can investigate the humanity of the word by which it is told us. The sovereign freedom of this subject-matter to speak of itself imposes on us in face of the word as such and its historicity an ἐποχή[EN13], of which there can be no inkling if we presuppose the comical doctrine that the true exegete has no presuppositions, and against which we consistently and most flagrantly offend if we presuppose that doctrine. And the knowledge of this mystery will see to it that the work of exposition, which is the goal of all hearing and understanding, at least enters the stage of convalescence from the sickness with which all exposition is almost incurably afflicted, the sickness of an insolent and arbitrary reading in. If the exposition of a human word consists in the relating of this word to what it intends or denotes, and if we know the sovereign freedom, the independent glory of this subject-matter in relation both to the word which is before us and to ourselves, we will be wholesomely restrained at the very least in our usual self-assured mastery of

[471] the relationship, as though we already knew its content and our exposition could give something more than hints in its direction. We shall be at least restrained in our evil domination of the text (even though in this age we can as little rid ourselves of it as we can of our old Adam generally). And then the way

---

[EN13] suspension of judgment

14

will no longer be radically closed to a real relating of the word and subject-matter. It is not, then, that by a knowledge of the mystery of what is said in the Bible we acquire the right to turn to some other understanding of the Bible than that which is based upon this subject-matter and therefore upon God's revelation. It is rather that knowledge itself brings this understanding before us and makes it possible to us as the only possible one. It is as the sovereign freedom of the subject-matter of the Bible is presented to us that its character as a subject-matter becomes unshakably and unequivocally certain, so that we can no longer confuse it with the word or the humanity of those who speak, and even less with ourselves. Characterised as the matter which speaks of itself, it will be respected by us as that which claims our interest for its own sake.

We have described the mystery which we have to recognise at this point as the peculiarity of the biblical word, i.e., of the subject-matter of the biblical word. But we must now add that there is no question of a peculiarity of the biblical word or its subject-matter, beside which we have normally to ascribe to other human words and their subject-matter a different peculiarity. It is rather that the peculiarity of the Bible has the force of an example, i.e., that we learn from it what is to be learned concerning the peculiarity of the human word in general. Everything that is said in a human word is as such always wrapped in a mystery, in this mystery, even when it is not divine revelation. But it is because what is said in the biblical word of man is divine revelation, and as such the *analogia fidei*[EN14], that everything which is said by human word is drawn into the darkness and light of its mystery. Is it not the case that whatever is said to us by men obviously wants—and it is with this claim that it confronts us with something said to us—to make itself said and heard? It wants in this way to become to us a subject-matter. It wants us for our part to bring it a true objectivity, i.e., interest for its own sake. Therefore the human word, by means of which it is told us, wants to be heard openly and not with that mixture of hearing and our own speaking and interrupting. In order to be understood by us, it wants not to be mastered by us, but to lay hold of us. It wants to be evaluated in its relation to what is said in it, when this has been spoken to us and made itself intelligible to us. In short, whatever is said to us by men always demands of us what God's revelation in the human word of Holy Scripture— but that alone—can actually achieve in relation to us. God's revelation in the human word of Holy Scripture not only wants but can make itself said and heard. It can become for us real subject-matter, and it can force us to treat it objectively. And as it does so, the human word in which it is told to us is heard [472] openly and understood without being mastered, and expounded rightly, i.e., in relation to its subject-matter. God's revelation in the human word of Holy Scripture is distinguished from everything else that is said to us by men by the fact that a majesty belongs to the one which obviously is radically lacking in the other, a majesty without which the latter would be meaningless if the former

---

[EN14] analogy of faith

15

were only an exception and not the law and the promise and the sign of redemption which has been set up in the sphere of all other human words, and of all that is said by them. How can we deny or ignore the distinction between what merely wants to be the thing said by other men, and what can be God's revelation in the human word of Holy Scripture? We have to accept this distinction. But knowing this distinction, how can we regard the false hearing and understanding and expounding of the human word, and therefore the meaninglessness with which it is delivered, as the norm and law of our words, just because it is the rule under which they labour, and the power of the revelation of God in the human word of Holy Scripture only as an outside exception? Even though as an exception it may confirm the rule, it necessarily breaks through it and reveals itself to be the norm and law in the light of which all human words now actually stand. Their aim and intention cannot possibly be concealed if we start with the hearing and understanding and expounding of the human word of the Bible. They cannot themselves become witnesses of revelation. Good care is seen to that. But when we start with the witnesses of revelation, we have to approach all other human words with at least the question what it is that however feebly and ineffectively they want to say, and what would make itself said and heard in them. There will then be no question of the assurance of a hermeneutics which is based on the necessity of irrelevance, nor of the meaninglessness to which human words generally would in fact be condemned, were it not that they had with them with all its promise the human word of Holy Scripture, and their own future was revealed by this human word. In view of the future of every human word which is already present in Holy Scripture, we will, of course, read Homer and Goethe and even the newspaper rather differently than if we did not know the future. It is not our present task to pursue this line. Our present concern is to establish that when we have to do with revelation as the content of the biblical word and with the hermeneutics prescribed by this content, we are not dealing with a mysterious thing apart which applies only to the Bible. Biblical hermeneutics must be guarded against the totalitarian claim of a general hermeneutics. It is a special hermeneutics only because hermeneutics generally has been mortally sick for so long that it has not let the special problem of biblical hermeneutics force its attention upon its own problem. For the sake of better general hermeneutics it must therefore dare to be this special hermeneutics.

2. SCRIPTURE AS THE WORD OF GOD

If what we hear in Holy Scripture is witness, a human expression of God's revelation, then from what we have already said, what we hear in the witness itself is more than witness, what we hear in the human expression is more than a human expression. What we hear is revelation, and therefore the very Word of God. But is this really the case? How can it be? How does it come about that it is? We will postpone the answer to this question—the two succeeding sections of the chapter will be devoted to it—in order first of all to clarify by rather more exact definitions the meaning and scope of the question itself, the meaning and scope of the positive side of our basic principle, that Scripture is the witness of divine revelation.

1. If we say that Scripture is this witness, or if we say that this witness is Scripture, we say this in the Church and with the Church, i.e., we say it of that Scripture which the Church has discovered and acknowledged as Holy Scripture, of canonical Scripture. When we say it with this qualification and restriction, we say that it is not for us or for any man to constitute this or that writing as Holy Writ, as the witness of God's revelation, to choose it as such out of many others, but that if there is such a witness and the acceptance of such a witness, it can only mean that it has already been constituted and chosen, and that its acceptance is only the discovery and acknowledgment of this fact. If in respect of what we regard as Holy Scripture we accept the qualification and restriction made in the Church's Canon, this does not mean that although it is not for the individual Christian to-day to constitute or choose Holy Scripture, it was once the task of the Church to do it, round about the year 400. "Canon" means "rule," i.e., the "rule of truth," and most significantly this conception was originally connected with the dogma as well as the constitution of the texts which are recognised to be holy. In no sense of the concept could or can the Church give the Canon to itself. The Church cannot "form" it, as historians have occasionally said without being aware of the theological implications. The Church can only confirm or establish it as something which has already been formed and given. And it can do so only to the best of its knowledge and judgment, in the venture and obedience of faith, but also in all the relativity of a human knowledge of the truth which God has opened up to men. This establishment of the Canon is the work of the Church, both in those matters which relate to the constitution of Holy Scripture and in those which relate to dogma.

As is well known, the establishment of the Canon has had a long and complicated history. Basically, we cannot yet say that that history is closed. In evaluating the history we have, of course, to discriminate the means and motives and criteria from the establishment itself. It is quite true that in this question of the rule of truth the Church was always affected *in*   [474]
concreto[EN15] by historical, theological and even ecclesiastico-political considerations. This fact marks its judgment as a human judgment in the same way as it does its judgments with regard to dogma. But the question actually discussed from these various angles and finally decided at various stages was simply a question of faith in relation to those Scriptures in which we can recognise the rule of truth. This object as such the Church could neither form nor reveal by means of the discussions conducted according to those considerations. In discussions of that kind it could not see either the fact or the extent to which the rule of truth has already been created and already revealed to it. For the obvious core of the history of the Canon is this, that within the various churches, and with all kinds of vacillations,

---

[EN15] concretely

particular parts of the oldest tradition have gradually been distinguished and set apart from others in the appreciation and acceptance of Christendom, a process which proper and formal canonisation by synodic resolutions and the like could only subsequently confirm. At some time and in some measure (with all the chance features which this appreciation and acceptance may have strengthened) these very writings, by the very fact that they were canonical, saw to it that they in particular were later recognised and proclaimed to be canonical.

Therefore we hear the judgment of the Church, but we do not obey its judgment, when we accept the settlement which the Church has, of course, made. In and with the Church we obey the judgment which was already pronounced, before the Church could pronounce its judgment and which the Church's judgment could only confirm. Just as the question of the witness of revelation can only be a question of faith, so too the answering of that question can only be a knowledge of faith. When we adopt the Canon of the Church we do not say that the Church itself, but that the revelation which underlies and controls the Church, attests these witnesses and not others as the witnesses of revelation and therefore as canonical for the Church.

Nous cognoissons ces livres estre canoniques et reigle trescertaine de nostre foy: non tant par le commun accord et consentement de l'eglise, que par le tesmoignage et interieure persuasion du sainct esprit, qui les nous faict discerner d'avec Us autres livres Ecclesiastiques. Sur lesquels (encores qu'ilz soyent utiles) on ne peut fonder aucun article de foy[EN16] (*Conf. Gallic.* 1559, Art. 4). *Non potest ecclesia ex libris non canonicis canonicos facere, sed efficit tantum ut ii libri pro canonicis recipiantur, qui revera et in sese sunt canonici. Ecclesia inquam, non facit scripturam authenticam, sed tantum declarat. Illud enim authenticum dicitur, quod se commendat, sustinet, probat et ex se fidem et autoritatem habet*[EN17] (W. Bucan, *Instit. theol.*, 1602, *loc.* 43, *qu.* 15). *Divino instinctu ... (hi libri) accepti sunt, idque non libero aliquo actu ecclesiae sed necessaria susceptione*[EN18] (*Syn. pur. Theol.*, Leiden, 1624, *disp.* 3, 13). Is this also the Roman Catholic doctrine of the Canon? In the Vatican Council it was indeed decreed that *Eos* (*libros*) *vere ecclesia pro rectis et canonicis habet ... propterea quod Spiritu sancto inspirante conscripti Deum habent autorem atque ut tales ipsi ecclesiae traditi sunt*[EN19] (*Const. dogm. de fide cath.* cap. 2). And B. Bartmann (*Lehrb. d. Dogm.*[7], 1928, I, 14) writes as follows: "The books are canonical *in actu primo*[EN20] and *quoad se*[EN21] because they are inspired, *in actu secundo*[EN22] and *quoad nos*[EN23] because they were adopted into the

---

[EN16] We know these books to be canonical, the most certain rule of our faith: not so much by the common accord and agreement of the church, as by the witness and inward persuasion of the Holy Spirit, who causes us to distinguish them from other ecclesiastical works. Upon these others (even though they be useful) one cannot establish any article of faith

[EN17] The church cannot make canonical books out of non-canonical ones, but merely causes those books which are truly and intrinsically canonical to be accepted as canonical. I say that the church does not make authentic Scripture, but merely declares such. For that which commends itself, which sustains, which proves, and which intrinsically is trustworthy and authoritative, is called authentic

[EN18] By divine instigation (these books) have been accepted, and that not by any free act of the church, but out of necessary responsibility

[EN19] The church truly considers these (books) to be correct and canonical ... on the grounds that they were written by the inspiration of the Holy Spirit, have God as their author, and have themselves been passed down to the church as such

[EN20] in the first instance

[EN21] as they are in themselves

[EN22] in the second instance

[EN23] as they are to us

canon as inspired. By the divine act they were adapted to canonicity, by the Church's act this was formally accorded to them." Now the meaning may well be that this "according" of the Church can consist only in a recognition of that property, that when the Church adopts this or that Scripture into the Canon all that it does is, in the light of its inspiration and in deference to it (otherwise might it not just as well omit it?), to confirm that it already belongs to the Canon. We cannot think that the Church can give authority to a sacred writing, but only that it can establish its authority. Yet at the time of the Reformation Sylvester Prierias (in the *Dialogus de potestate Papae*, 1517, 15, which he wrote against Luther) could say that the doctrine of the Roman Church and of the Roman Pope is the *regula fidei infallibilis, a qua etiam sacra scriptura robur trahit et auctoritatem*[EN24]. And John Eck (*Enchir.*, 1529, *De ecclesia, c. objecta* 3) could boldly declare, and he was not for long the only one, that *Scriptura non est authentica sine autoritate ecclesiae*[EN25]. And there were controversialists who actually expressed the opinion that Aesop's Fables would have just as much or even more weight than a Bible which did not have the authority lent it by the Church. The saying of Augustine was constantly appealed to in this sense: *Ego vero evangelio non crederem, nisi me catholicae ecclesiae eommoveret auctoritas*[EN26] (*C. ep. Manich.* 5, 6). Now even at that time there were some Roman Catholic writers who did not share this view, so that it would not be right to see in these utterances the doctrine of the Roman Catholic Church. However that may be, the true doctrine of the canon can be re-stated in the words of John Gerhard: *Non est duplex, sed una scripturae auctoritas, eademque divina, non dependens ab ecclesiae auctoritate, sed a solo Deo. Auctoritas scripturae quoad nos nihil aliud est quam manifestatio et cognitio unicae illius divinae et summae auctoritatis, quae scripturae est interna atque insita. Ecclesia igitur non confert scripturae novam aliquam auctoritatem quoad nos, sed testificatione sua ad agnitionem illius veritatis nos deducit. Concedimus ecclesiam esse scripturae sacrae (1) testem, (2) custodem, (3) vindicem, (4) praeconem, (5) interpretem, sed negamus ex eo effici, quod auctoritas scripturae sive simpliciter sive quoadnos ab ecclesia pendeat*[EN27] (*Loci theol.*, 1610 f., LI c. 3, 39). Or in the words of Joh. Wolleb: *Ecclesiae testimonium prius est tempore; Spiritus sancti vero prius est natura et efficacia. Ecclesiae credimus, sed non propter ecclesiam; Spiritui autem sancto creditur propter seipsum. Ecclesia testimonium τὸ ὅτι demonstrat, Spiritus sancti vero testimonium τὸ διότι demonstrat. Ecclesia suadet, Spiritus sanctus persuadet. Ecclesiae testimonium opinionem, Spiritus sancti vero testimonium scientiam ac fidem firmam parit*[EN28] (*Comp. Christ. Theol.*, 1620, *Praecogn.* 9). As the Protestant theologians of the time liked to expound it, the Church may be compared with the Samaritan woman, of whom it first says in Jn. 4[39] that many of that city believed in Christ because of

---

[EN24] infallible rule of faith, from which even sacred Scripture draws its strength and authority

[EN25] Scripture is not authentic without the authority of the church

[EN26] But I would not have believed the Gospel, had the authority of the Catholic church not compelled me

[EN27] There is not a double authority of Scripture, but a single authority, and that is divine: it does not depend on the authority of the church, but on God alone. The authority of Scripture as far as we are concerned is nothing other than the manifestation and the knowledge of that single divine and supreme authority, which is internal and intrinsic to Scripture. Therefore, the church does not confer a new authority, as far as we are concerned, upon Scripture, but rather by its own testimony it leads us to the acknowledgement of that truth. We admit that of sacred Scripture the church is (1) the witness; (2) the guardian; (3) protector (4) the herald; (5) the interpreter. But let us not conclude from this that the authority of Scripture, whether in itself or in relation to us, depends upon the church

[EN28] The testimony of the church is prior in time, but the testimony of the Holy Spirit is prior in nature and causality. We believe that the testimony is of the church, not on account of the church. It is to be ascribed to the Holy Spirit on His own account. The testimony of the church demonstrates the fact 'that', but the testimony of the Holy Spirit demonstrates the 'because'. The church advises, the Holy Spirit convinces. The testimony of the church provides opinion, but the testimony of the Holy Spirit provides knowledge and firm trustworthiness

her saying, but then in v. 42 that they say unto her: "Now we believe, not because of thy saying: we have heard him ourselves, that this is indeed the Christ, the Saviour of the world." We cannot suppose, of course, that this is the doctrine of the Canon held by the Catholic Church.

Holy Scripture is the Word of God to the Church and for the Church. We are, therefore, ready to know what Holy Scripture is in the Church and with the Church. We do not regard ourselves as unrestrained in this matter or restrained only by our own direct knowledge of the rule of truth. Therefore we know that we have to listen to the Church in matters of the Canon, as we have also to listen to it at all points in matters of the exposition of Holy Scripture and faith and order. But even though it is in and with the Church that we ask what is that Holy Scripture which is the Canon given in the Church and forcing itself upon it by its own inspiration, we cannot take our answer from the Church but from Holy Scripture itself. We will not be obedient to the Church but to the Word of God, and therefore in the true sense to the Church.

[476]   This answer is in itself a divine and therefore an infallible and definitive answer. But the human hearing of this answer, whether that of the Church or our own to-day, is a human hearing, and therefore not outside the possibility of error, or incapable of being improved. This is true of our answers to the question of faith and order; it is also true of our answer to the question of the Canon. As we give this answer, believing in and with the Church, as we recognise certain Scriptures (e.g., the sixty-six of our Authorised Version) to be canonical in and with the Church, we have the right and duty to accept this answer as good and sufficient, and with the help of these Holy Scriptures seriously to ask concerning the witness of God's revelation and the Word of God itself. Every bit of real witness of God's revelation—we cannot without error deny the presence of such witness among the sixty-six books—is also a portion of God's Word and is all-sufficient for the life of the Church and for our own life in time and in eternity. An absolute guarantee that the history of the Canon is closed, and therefore that what we know as the Canon is also closed, cannot be given either by the Church or by individuals in the Church according to the best and most satisfactory answers to this question. In the past there has already been more than one proposal to narrow or broaden the human perception of what ought to count as canonical Scripture, and if the proposals never came to anything they were at least seriously considered. The insight that the concrete form of the Canon is not closed absolutely, but only very relatively, cannot be denied even with a view to the future.

Even if we ignore the considerable variations in the first four centuries, it is worth noting that the Council of Florence in 1441—a thousand years after our present-day New Testament had gained general acceptance—for the purpose of the understanding which was then sought with the Eastern Churches, could still think it necessary to put out an express list of the Old and New Testament writings recognised to be canonical (*Denz*. No. 706). This act had to be repeated in 1546 by the Council of Trent (*Sess*. IV *Denz*. No. 784), the problem of the Canon having meanwhile been reopened by the Reformation. The Protestant Churches—the Reformed very definitely, and at bottom too the Lutheran quite decidedly—thought it right to exclude from the Canon as "Apocrypha" a whole series of Old Testament writings which had been recognised as wholly canonical for a thousand years (the books of Judith, the Wisdom of Solomon, Tobias, Sirach and the two Maccabees). But even the question of the New Testament Canon seemed to be reopened at that time. It is well known what Luther thought about Hebrews, James, Jude and Revelation. He did not wish to deprive anyone of them, but for his own part he could not number them with the "right, sure, principal books." What is not so well known is that in the table of contents of his September Bible of 1522 he openly separated them from the other twenty-three and according to him true New Testament writings, thus characterising them at once as deutero-canonical. And Luther did not stand alone. Before the Council of Trent with its new tradition, not only Erasmus but even Cardinal Cajetan expressed open doubts concerning the authenticity and authority of Hebrews, James and Jude as well as 2 and 3 John. Zwingli thought especially that the Apocalypse should be rejected. And it is at least noteworthy that Calvin omitted the Apocalypse in what was otherwise a complete exposition of the New Testament. From his introductions to the commentaries it emerges clearly that he had doubts not only concerning the books mentioned by Luther but also concerning 2 Peter and 2 and 3 John. In the *Apol. Conf. Württ.*, 1555, J. Brenz dismissed these seven writings in the same gentle but decisive way as Luther had done the Old Testament Apocrypha in his well-known formula. They were edifying and wholesome, but not normative. Among the Reformed the same view was held and taught by the Bernese W. Musculus (cf. H. Heppe, *Dogm. d. ev. ref. Kirche*, new edn., 1935, 15). It seemed for a moment as though the separation of the Old Testament Apocrypha might be paralleled in the New Testament sphere by a return to the Eusebian Canon with its distinction between the homologoumena and the antilegomena, the seven books in question being reckoned with the latter. J. Gerhard (*Loci theol.*, 1610 f.) can still speak (in chap. 9 and 10 of his *Locus de Scriptura*) quite openly *De libris Novi Testamenti canonicis primi et secundi ordinis*[EN29], meaning by the *libri secundi ordinis*[EN30] precisely the seven Eusebian antilegomena. But in spite of the authority of Luther himself, this was still only a private opinion. And in the debate with the Roman Church and theology this private opinion soon proved embarrassing and was therefore rejected on internal grounds. Even J. Gerhard had reasons to show that all the books which he described as *libri canonici secundi ordinis*[EN31] must still be counted *canonici*[EN32]. This meant that the older objections had to be contested, and it was obvious that the distinction made by Eusebius could not be sustained. That is how it turned out. Already in 1545 the Confession of Zurich had attacked Luther's view: In the aforesaid books of the New Testament we are not misled by any stubborn fool, nor do we believe that any among them are strawy, or have been inserted wrongly. And although the mind of man may not agree to Revelation or other books, we set no store by such agreement. For we know that we men ought to be judged by Scripture and not Scripture by us (in K. Müller, *Bek. Schr. der ref. Kirche*, 155). The *Conf. Gallic.* (1559, Art. 3) and the *Conf. Belgica* (1561, Art. 4) follow the example of the Tridentinum and give a solemn list of all the sixty-six canonical Scriptures, not trying to make any distinction between the New Testament books. And J. Gerhard's Reformed contemporary, Polanus, declares concisely and authoritatively that *Novi Testamenti (libri) omnes sunt vere, univoce et proprie divini et canonici, nullo excepto*[EN33]. Of course there were some (*quidam*) Evangelicals who disputed the canonicity of

[477]

EN29 On the canonical books of the New Testament, of first and second rank
EN30 books of the second rank
EN31 canonical books of the second rank
EN32 canonical
EN33 all the books of the New Testament are truly, univocally, and strictly divine and canonical, without exception

the seven books. But their opinion was now felt to be a *pudendum: Horum opinio erronea, quia paucorum est, communitati ecclesiae evangelicae seu reformatae impingi non debet*EN34 (*Synt. Theol. chr.*, 1609, 283 and 307). All the same even Polanus still took the trouble to give an explicit counter-proof in relation to each of the contested books. By the end of the 17th century the matter had passed to the stage of historical reminiscence in Reformed circles. It was not mentioned at all, for example, by F. Turrettini (*Instit. Theol. el.*, 1679, *Loc.* 2, *qu.* 9, 13). On the other hand, Quenstedt among the Lutherans was still conscious of the distinction between *libri primi et secundi ordinis*EN35 in the New Testament (he also calls them *protocanonici*EN36 and *deuterocanonici*EN37). And he still accepts the distinction, although not so obviously as J. Gerhard had done. The point which he tries to make with regard to the latter is that there has for a time been doubt concerning their human author—not their divine. And he goes to great lengths to try to conceal as much as possible certain hints in Luther's works which point quite definitely in a different direction (*Theol. did. pol.*, 1685, P I *cap.* 4, *sect.* 2, *qu.* 23, *th.* 2, *dist.* 5 and *font. sol. obs.* 23 f.). For practical purposes the whole process was only an interlude. But that it was possible at all is of fundamental significance: for the later writers, who did not share the doubts of the earlier ones, never formally disputed that questions may be raised concerning the constitution of the Canon as they had in fact been raised in the 16th century. On the contrary, by the express numbering of those books which must be recognised as authentic, both the Church of Rome (in the Confession of Trent) and the Reformed Churches (in the *Gallicana* and *Belgica*) accepted the legitimacy of the question. And we can see something of the same in the tenacious maintaining of a formal distinction between the protocanonical and the deuterocanonical writings by the later Lutherans.

[478]

At this point we must not forget, of course, a general phenomenon which points in the same direction. And that is that even where there is no question of a direct attack on the traditional constitution of the Canon, not only the individual readers of the Bible, but the Church as a whole, as it has made its mind known in its symbols, confessional writings, its theology, preaching and devotional literature, does not in fact and practice treat all parts of the Bible alike, or without tacit questions in relation to one or other of them. Holy Scripture has always been defined in the Church with varying degrees of emphasis on the constituent parts. The well-known criterion of Luther was to test every Scripture by whether "it sets forth Christ or not." "What teacheth not Christ is not apostolic, even though Peter or Paul teacheth it. Again what preacheth Christ is apostolic, even though Judas, Annas, Pilate and Herod doth it" (*Preface to the Epistles of St. James and St. Jude*, 1522). And with a varying insight into what can be called Christ, this is the criterion which in all ages the Church has in its own way applied to the Canon. Yet in so doing it has not reached any conclusions or made any demands concerning an alteration in its public constitution. In spite of its 1000 years and in spite of the Florentinum and the Tridentinum, the Roman Church was the very last (we have only to think of its flagrant exalting of the Gospels above the prophets and apostles in the *Missale*) actually to treat all parts of the traditional Canon alike. The Church, even the Roman Church, even Luther, has always had to ask concerning the traditional Canon as a whole whether we are not right to value some parts more and others less highly, whether in so doing we do not neglect essential parts of the witness of revelation to the detriment of our knowledge of the Word of God. But if that is true, it is also true that on the basis of the

---

EN34 embarrassment: the erroneous opinion of these, since they are few, ought not to influence the community of the evangelical, or reformed, church
EN35 books of the first and second rank
EN36 protocanonical
EN37 deuterocanonical

knowledge of the Word of God, which it has perhaps gained from some parts of the witness of revelation as distinct from others, the Church can and must continually ask concerning the legitimacy of the traditional Canon. But if it can and must do this, as in fact it always does, then we cannot rule out a consideration of the possibility of an open alteration in its constitution, either a narrowing as in the 16th century or an extension. We know that there once existed an unknown letter of Paul to the Laodicaeans, and two letters of Paul to the Corinthians no longer extant. There are also some known but "unrecorded" sayings of Jesus, unrecorded, that is, only in the canonical Gospels. And for all we know—and certain recent discoveries ought to prepare us for any eventuality—there may be things awaiting us in the sands of Egypt, in the light of which not even the Roman Church will, perhaps, one day—i.e., the day of their discovery—be able to accept responsibility for dogmatically insisting upon the concept of a closed Canon. Yet it is not the consideration of possibilities such as these, but the basic consideration of the positive nature and meaning of the Canon, which forces us to re-accustom ourselves to the thought that the Canon is not closed absolutely.

Clearly a change in the constitution of the Canon, if it arises as a practical question, can take place meaningfully and legitimately only as an action of the Church, i.e., in the form of an orderly and responsible decision by an ecclesiastical body capable of tackling it. Individuals can think and say what they like on theological and historical grounds. But what they think and say can have only the character of a private and non-binding anticipation of the Church's action. Whether it is genuinely of the Church will again depend entirely on the question whether it is a matter now as before of a *necessaria susceptio*[EN38], i.e., an [479] actual instruction of the Church by writings which either prove or do not prove themselves to be canonical. As long as no decision is publicly reached in the Church, we have steadfastly to accept the force and validity of decisions already taken both in respect of the faith and also of the Canon. In the decisions already taken, the Church still tells us that this or that, this particular *corpus*[EN39], is Holy Scripture. The individual in the Church certainly cannot and ought not to accept it as Holy Scripture just because the Church does. He can and should himself be obedient only to Holy Scripture as it reveals itself to him and in that way forces itself upon him, as it compels him to accept it. But he still has to remember that Scripture is the Word of God for and to the Church, and that therefore it is only in the Church that he can meaningfully and legitimately take up an attitude to Scripture. Whatever his private judgment may be, even his private judgment of faith, however much it may diverge, he must always listen to the Church. The so far unaltered judgment of the Church radically precedes as such the judgment of the individual, even if it is the judgment of quite a number of individuals who have to be reckoned with seriously in the Church. It is not, of course, the absolute judgment of God, but the judgment of the *majores*[EN40], the πρεσβύτεροι[EN41] (Irenaeus), the judgment of those who were called and believed before us. As such, so long as the

---

[EN38] necessary responsibility
[EN39] collection
[EN40] greater ones
[EN41] elders

Church does not revise it, i.e., restrict or widen it, we have to respect it. As such, it has the character of a direction which no one can simply ignore. Until the Church itself is better instructed, we must expect to find Holy Scripture, Scripture as the witness of divine revelation, Scripture as the Word of God, where the Church itself has found it in virtue of its own decision. We must expect it there and only there, i.e., we have no authority on the basis of our own decision to proclaim in the Church any other Scripture but this. We personally may accept it. But we cannot act as though we speak in any way but in and with the Church, as though we have a right to speak without first listening to the Church. It is where the Church declares that it has found Holy Scripture that we have actually to expect Holy Scripture. That is, whatever may or may not be our own experiences of this or that part of it, we have always to approach the Scripture which the Church calls holy, the witness of revelation, with instructions to see whether what has been heard by the *majores*[EN42], although not perhaps by us, may not have something to say to us.

We have to accept the concept of the Canon in a more guarded way than was actually the case in 17th-century Protestantism. That is, we cannot definitely reject the fact that the Church does establish the divine authority of the Scripture contained within this or that limit. In this question of the Canon we cannot ascribe to the Church the role of a mere witness and spectator, however honourable. We cannot attribute the true and binding divine authority, which decides upon the Canon, so entirely to Scripture itself as the Word of God,

[480]

as the older Protestant orthodoxy rightly did, and then say to individuals in the Church—as though Luther and Calvin had never had any doubts on the question—that in certain Scriptures, for the limit of which they are still primarily referred to the testimony of the Church, they will hear in equal measure as the Word of God. If that is so, then it will be so, i.e., the Word of God will really speak to them in just these Scriptures. But if the negative and positive presuppositions are true, if the Church really takes seriously its assurance that only the Word of God itself can dispose and decide in relation to the revelation of the Word of God, the Church cannot speak of its Canon as though in its decision it had made the decision of the Holy Ghost Himself, and therefore decided in its own power for all ages and as against all individuals in the Church. The Church can only regard and proclaim its decision as a direction—an indication seriously meant and therefore to be taken seriously. If it is not to call in question the lordship of Jesus Christ and of the Holy Spirit, and therefore revelation and its own being—it cannot regard and proclaim it as a divine law. In respect of the Canon, it will always be open to further instruction. Towards individuals within it it will show patience in respect of their practical relationship to the Canon. It can and must require of them respect for its indication. To the fluctuations of time and temporal movements, to particular gifts and illuminations, but also to the dangerous caprices of individuals and individual groups, it can and must attest the totality of the Canon, and of the Canon which it itself recognises to be such. It can and must see to it that in the name and applying of Luther's criterion, there does not arise a neglect of specific aspects of the biblical witness, a heretical one-sidedness and overemphasis. It can and must in its own sphere prevent the attempting of arbitrary alterations of the Canon in the limit entrusted to it, or the treatment of some of its parts as alone truly canonical in opposition to others. But even in respect of the limit of the Canon

---

[EN42] greater ones

entrusted to it, it cannot and must not be closed *a priori*[EN43] to further instruction. By its witness in respect of this limit it cannot and must not anticipate the witness of the Holy Spirit to the individual within it. All that it can and must say to him is that in the limit attested by it he has to expect the witness of the Holy Spirit, and with Him to expect that the promise which it has the right and duty to give him will be confirmed. This is the distinction in respect of the truth of the biblical Canon which the doctrine of the Canon held by Protestant orthodoxy has obscured. It had every right actually to contend for the seven antilegomena in opposition to Luther and others when on inward grounds, and decidedly in obedience to Holy Scripture itself, it had the consciousness that it ought to do so. But it had no right to overlook and suppress the basic significance of the fact that in the 16th century the Canon had proved to be an uncertain quantity as far as its constitution was concerned. It claimed too much, and plunged too far, when it equated the Canon which it recognised with the Canon revealed by God. It had no right to make the Church take up any other position in relation to the Canon (in flagrant contradiction with its own accusation of the Roman Church) than that of a witness and spectator, i.e., that of a guarantor of its divine authority. To the extent that it did this, the orthodox doctrine of Scripture, as we shall see again when we discuss the concept of inspiration, simply prepared the way for Neo-Protestantism. It gave to the Church, that is, to men in the Church, power and assurance, which, according to its own presuppositions, could only be the power and assurance of God as opposed to all men, and therefore men in the Church. Had they not said that the divine authority of Scripture must speak for itself, and therefore alone be listened to as itself speaking for itself? Why were they not content to attest its spiritual authority? Instead, they arbitrarily made a divine law out of the Church's decision of faith. They did not proclaim it in faith, as the law of the Church and therefore the law of the Spirit. They made it a divine law, which ended the possibility of any further instruction, and which it was believed could be laid on the neck like a yoke. But in so doing they brought out its contradiction to the real law of Christ and of the Holy Ghost—indeed they were themselves unwittingly enmeshed in the contradiction. They cast their pearls before swine. They had, therefore, no reason to be surprised if for long periods the Church's direction in regard to the Canon was not even accepted as the spiritual law of the Church, if the doctrine of Scripture was forced and dissolved by the far more prominent doctrine of religion. Therefore for the sake of the real authority of the biblical Canon we must again learn to regard its establishment as a witness of faith, its recognition as the obedience of faith, and therefore its actual constitution, even if we have no reason to oppose it, as not finally closed. [481]

2. When we have to do with Scripture, i.e., canonical Scripture, the Scripture which the Church has defined and we in and with the Church have recognised as canonical, when we have to do with Holy Scripture as a witness, in fact the witness of divine revelation, we have to do with the witness of Moses and the prophets, the Evangelists and the apostles. What is meant (and in this formulation we are merely repeating certain biblical passages) is the witness of the Old and New Testament, the witness of the expectation and the recollection, the witness of the preparation and the accomplishment of the revelation achieved in Jesus Christ. Concerning revelation as time and between these two times we have already spoken explicitly in the doctrine of revelation itself (§ 14). We are speaking now of its attestation, of the records of it as such. And in the light of what we have already said about their content, of these we

---

[EN43] unconditionally

25

have to say that in the content created by their context, and in the variety conditioned by their varied relationship to that content, they all belong together in the sense that they are all equally Holy Scripture and have this content. The Old and the New Testament both have as their distinctive feature to attest in the one case the Messiah who is to come, and in the other the Messiah who has already come. In the Old Testament the Law is distinguished from the prophets by the fact that in the Law it is the calling of Israel, in the prophets the direction and instruction of Israel already called by the Word of Yahweh, which constitutes the material of the prophecy inherent in both. Similarly in the New Testament the Gospels are distinguished from the apostolic writings by the fact that the Gospels look back to the words and acts of Jesus as they point us to the resurrection, whereas the apostolic writings look back from the resurrection to the human situation as illumined and altered by it. But the two lines, of the Old Testament witness on the one hand and of the New Testament witness on the other, always intersect at a single point. The same is true of the Old Testament and New Testament lines as a whole. In detail we shall often find that the distinctions disappear. There is a legal element in the prophets and a prophetic element in the Law, an evangelical element in the apostolic writings and an apostolic element in the Gospels. Only two distinctions really remain: the first consists in the fact that in the Old Testa-

[482] ment Christ is not attested as the One who has already appeared, whereas in the New Testament He is not attested as the One who has not yet appeared. Yet we have to allow an exception to this rule in the early chapters of the Gospels of Matthew and Luke and the Baptist and Mary episodes, where the New Testament still uses the terminology of the Old. And the on the whole irreversible distinction between the two witnesses is again completely relativised by the unity of its object. Within all the groups there is a second irreversible distinction, the distinction between the various individualities of the known and unknown writers with whom we have to do in the biblical witness. Isaiah is not Qoheleth, and Paul is not James. Yet although this is obviously a permanent distinction, it too is relativised by the unity of what is said by all these individuals. When we speak of the biblical witness, we mean this witness as a whole. The distinctions in the content of the witness do not mean a distinction in the witness itself. The Church arose when the witness as a whole was to hand. For the Church arose through the record of Jesus Christ and the message of the power of His resurrection. These two, the record and the message, even before they were fixed in writing, and more especially when they were, were from first to last an exposition of the Law and the prophets. The one necessarily belongs to the other. We cannot separate either the Law and the prophets, or the Gospels and apostolic writings, or the Old and New Testaments as a whole, without at each point emptying and destroying both. If the Church had not from the very first heard this whole, it could not have heard what it did hear. It would not have arisen as the Church. It is only in this unity that the biblical witness is the witness of divine revelation. And remembering this unity, the Church

holds fast to this witness. In it it recognises the ruling, divine authority. It busies itself with its exposition. It exists by itself attesting what it finds attested in it. The Church has no control over the unity of this witness. It has it, but it is not of its power that it is the witness of divine revelation. How can it control this unity? How can it be of its power that this witness, although it has it, is in its totality the witness of divine revelation? Apart from the witness itself, all that it can have is the recollection and therefore again the expectation bound up with it. It is in its recollection and expectation that it is the witness of divine revelation, and Scripture is Holy Scripture. The Church has no control or power over what may lie between, over the event that this witness is the witness of divine revelation not only in recollection and expectation, but here and now. This is also true of the totality, the unity of this witness. But as the recollection is generally enough to awaken, confirm and justify the expectation, it allows the Church no expectation but that of the totality, the unity of this witness. This is what the Church means when it teaches the holiness and therefore the unity of Scripture. It means the holiness and unity of God in His revelation, as revealed and confirmed first of all in the founding of the Church and then again and again in the human variety of this witness. Again, it means [483] the holiness and unity of God in His revelation, which in possession of this witness, it is summoned and authorised to expect of Him. Therefore bound by past and future, its present can be only a very humble and claimless, but unbroken, assent to this witness, and therefore to the fulness of this witness in its unity. It does not in this way anticipate what only God Himself in His revelation can create and give, the event of the perception of this unity. But it affirms that God in His revelation can create and give this perception, as He has created and given it already. In this sense it will lay hold of the whole biblical evidence, the Law and the prophets, the Gospels and the apostolic writings, the Old and New Testaments. In this sense it will have a concern for the exposition and proclamation of the whole. In this sense it will confront each of her members with the promise and task of listening to the Word of God in this totality. In this sense, as we have already seen when investigating the concept of the Canon, it will be on its guard not only against any exclusions, but also against preferences of this or that part which may compromise the unity of the witness, against devaluations which may isolate the part from the whole. Even if only in recollection and expectation, it knows of the peace in which this witness has its origin and its goal. It is in its willingness to participate in this peace that it subjects itself to this witness and therefore to the whole of this witness.

Rightly understood, the unity of Holy Scripture gives rise to a conclusion and demand to which the Church must pay good heed. But this conclusion and demand is not that we should abstract from the Bible some concealed historical or conceptual system, an economy of salvation or a Christian view of things. There can be no biblical theology in this sense, either of the Old or New Testament, or of the Bible as a whole. The presupposition and the organising centre of such a system would have to be the object of the biblical witness, that is, revelation. Now revelation is no more and no less than the life of God Himself turned to us, the Word of God coming to us by the Holy Spirit, Jesus Christ. But in our thinking, even in our meditation on the biblical texts, it is only improperly, i.e., only in the form of our recollection and expectation, that we can "presuppose" Jesus Christ and then add to this presupposition other thoughts, even those which are derived from our exposition of those texts. Properly, and that means, in living fact, revelation can only be presupposed to our thoughts, even to those based on exposition, that is, it can only be their organising centre, by revelation itself. Therefore a biblical theology can never consist in more than a series of attempted approximations, a collection of individual exegeses. There can never be any question of a system in the sense of Platonic, Aristotelian or Hegelian philosophy. For the basic thought essential to such a system is not only, as even the philosophers say, the thought of an ultimate, inconceivable reality, but as such—and it is here that the inconceivability of the theologian differs from that of the philosopher—it is not at our disposal. We cannot attain to it as the thought of a true, i.e., a present reality, or we can do so only improperly, i.e., in the form of recollection and expectation. Even the biblical witnesses themselves cannot and do not try to introduce revelation of themselves. They show themselves to be genuine witnesses of it by the fact that they only speak of it by looking forward to it and by looking back at it.

[484] How can we wish to complete the totality of their witness by treating revelation as a presupposition which we can control? How can we expound it except by surrendering ourselves with them to the recollection, their recollection, and to the expectation, their expectation? It is only in this surrender—and not in an arbitrary doing of what they omitted to do—that our exposition of that witness will be kept pure and will become our own witness. Biblical theology (and self-evidently dogmatics too) can consist only in an exercise in this surrender, not in an attempt to introduce the totality of the biblical witness.

At this point we must ask whether the older Protestant theology of the 17th century did not do too much, and therefore too little. Intrinsically, there can be no objection to the fact that in its exposition it made such active use of the instruments of Aristotelian and later Cartesian philosophy. How can we find fault, and not take as a model, the comprehensive thoroughness and accuracy which it obviously sought and in such surprising measure revealed? If only it had kept itself freer from the temptation to be inspired to go further and to seek that which is theologically impossible, a systematics of revelation, a system in which revelation can be used as a presupposition! It attempted to bring in the witness of revelation as such in its unity and entirety. But in so doing it did violence to it. And it was on this that it foundered when the Philistines came upon it in the 18th century as once they had come upon Samson. We must leave it to revelation itself to introduce itself either in its unity and entirety or indeed at all. Revelation is never behind us: always we can only follow it. We cannot think it: we can only contemplate it. We cannot assert and prove it: we can only believe it, believe it in recollection and expectation, so that if our faith is right and well-pleasing to God in what we then think and say, it can assert and prove itself. This, then, is the conclusion and demand to which we are led by a right understanding of the unity of Holy Scripture. And the Church must see to it that we never forget that by virtue of the content and object of canonical Scripture, which are not at our disposal, we have to do with a single witness, i.e., a witness which points in a single direction and attests a single truth. If we accept it in and with the Church to which it was given, then that is the recollection and it is also the expectation in which we have to read it. In this direction the surrender, the following, the contemplation, the believing, can never cease. They cannot and must not be replaced by an arbitrary questing and searching and striving for all other possible directions. Luther once spoke about the unity of Holy Scripture in this way: "For Holy Scripture is the garment which our Lord Christ has put on and in which He lets Himself be seen and found. This garment is woven throughout and so wrought together into one that it cannot be cut or parted. But the soldiers take it from Christ crucified, i.e., heretics and schismatics. It is their particular mischief to want to have the coat entire, persuading everyone that all Scripture agrees with them and is of their opinion ... they fashion another meaning, apart from and without the Word, this meaning is continually before their eyes, and like a blue glass through which they see everything blue and of their meaning. But they are rogues, as Paul calls them, in Eph. 4, when he warns them not to be driven about by every wind of doctrine through the sleight of men. In Greek this little word "sleight" is *kybia*, in German dicing or cheating. For just as rogues are masters of dicing, and it yields them whatever they desire, so the schismatics and sectarians deal with Scripture, each of them wanting it all and dicing for it" (*Pred. üb. Mt. 26*[33f], *Hauspostille*, 1545, W.A. 52, 802, 1). Now the question raised is one which with all due respect we must put to Luther himself. For instance, in his doctrine of the Law and the Gospel, ought he not to have mastered dicing in the best sense and not parted the robe of Christ? We can also put it to the later doctrine of a redemptive history working itself out in many different and ascending stages. We can put it to the idea of a development of revelation, which can and necessarily does so easily become that of a development of biblical [485] religion. We can put it to the exalting of the Synoptists over John, or the Gospels over the apostolic writings, or in the Old Testament to the customary exalting of the prophets in the narrower sense: all of which correspond to the one-sidedness of Luther. In all these cases the failure to recognise the unity of Scripture involved sooner or later, and inevitably, a failure to recognise that it is Holy Scripture. For when we have such arbitrary preferences, we do not read even the parts which we prefer as Holy Scripture. The same is true of any preference, even the most detailed. This criterion ought to be applied to the most commonly accepted doctrine of the Church, even that which we find in the confessional documents. And particularly should it be applied to individual teachers, even the greatest of them. For fundamentally, whenever anything which is "written" is overlooked in the exposition of Scripture, whenever for the sake of the exposition we are forced to weaken or even omit what is written, there is always the possibility that the exposition has really missed the one thing which Scripture as a whole attests, even when it thinks that it has found it. An exposition is trustworthy to the extent that it not only expounds the text in front of it, but implicitly at least expounds all other texts, to the extent that it at any rate clears the way for the exposition of all other texts. Among the older Protestant theologians there were some (e.g., B. Bucan, *Inst. theol.*, 1602, *Loc.* 4, 11; *Syn. pur. Theol.*, Leiden 1624, *Disp.* 3, 20), who argued that when the prophets were added to the Law, which alone constituted Holy Scripture in the first instance, they did not make it more complete as such, i.e., as the Word of God, but as the expounding and confirming of the first witness by a second they made it clearer. But the same can also be said of the adding of the New Testament to the Old. Salvation is in fact already proclaimed and can be accepted in the Pentateuch as such. We can say that this is too bold a view. In any case it is gratuitous, for we do not have to do now only with the Pentateuch. But I cannot see where it is actually wrong. If all Scripture does in fact attest one thing, it cannot be denied that if we only know one part of it, it attests it perfectly even in that part. It does not consist only of such a part, but of the whole. Therefore this consideration does not absolve us from taking it seriously as a whole. But it is a constant reminder that, instructed and restrained by the whole, we have in fact to seek the one thing in the individual part as well.

3. It has often been asked whether and to what extent the doctrine of Holy Scripture, and especially the proposition that of all the literature of the world, ancient and modern, we must recognise in these writings Holy Writings, is based on the Bible itself?

That this statement does correspond with what Holy Scripture teaches about itself rests first of all, and generally and indirectly, upon the uniqueness and contingency of the revelation attested in it. We can put it even more simply and say that it rests on the true humanity of the person of Jesus Christ as the object of its testimony. What else is the Bible but the proof of the existence of the historical environment of this reality and, to that extent, of the historicity of the reality itself? But of all world literature it is only the Bible which offers this proof: or other literature offers it only because it has first been offered by the Bible. In general, therefore, the witness of Holy Scripture to itself consists simply in the fact that it is witness to Jesus Christ. And the knowledge of the truth of this self-witness, the knowledge of its unique authority, stands or falls with the knowledge that Jesus Christ is the incarnate Son of God.

[486]   But because this knowledge coincides with the knowledge of faith in His resurrection from the dead, we must say that Scripture attests itself in the fact that at its decisive centre it attests the resurrection of Jesus Christ from the dead. But the attestation of the resurrection of Jesus, which awakens faith and its knowledge, is itself again only the self-attestation of God by the Holy Spirit. In the final analysis, therefore, we have to say that Holy Scripture testifies to and for itself by the fact that the Holy Spirit testifies to the resurrection of Christ and therefore that He is the incarnate Son of God.

To this general and implicit self-witness, however, there corresponds a specific and explicit. Everywhere the Bible speaks not only of the revelation of God in Jesus Christ as opposed to all men, man and humanity generally. It does, of course, do that. In fact, we must say that this is the real content of the Bible. We have seen earlier that the man addressed and claimed in revelation belongs as such to its content, is taken into revelation itself. But now we must go further and say more concretely that the content of the Bible, as understood in this setting, has a definite form, which cannot be separated from it as this content. The Bible as witness of divine revelation comes to every man, all men, and in a measure includes them in itself. Rightly understood, all humanity, whether it is aware of it or not, does actually stand in the Bible, and is therefore itself posited as a witness of divine revelation. But that this is the case is made possible and conditioned by the fact that in the first instance not all men but certain specific men stand in the Bible: that is, the men who in face of the unique and contingent revelation had the no less unique and contingent function of being the first witnesses. Because there were and still are those first witnesses, there could and can be second and third witnesses. We cannot speak about Yahweh's covenant with Israel without at once speaking of Moses and the prophets. Similarly in the New Testament, indissolubly bound up with Jesus Christ, there are the figures of His disciples, His followers, His apostles, those who are called by Him, the witnesses of His resurrection, those to whom He Himself has directly promised and given His Holy Spirit. The Church can say anything at all about the event of God and man only because something unique has taken place between God and these specific men, and because in what they wrote, or what was written by them, they confront us as living documents of that unique event. To try to ignore them is to ignore that unique event. The existence of these specific men is the existence of Jesus Christ for us and for all men. It is in this function that they are distinguished from us and from all other men, whom they resemble in everything else. Therefore the specific and explicit self-witness of Scripture consists in the fact that, from the standpoint of the form in which its content is offered and alone offered to us, it is the witness of the existence of these specific men.

It is the unique and contingent fact of the New Testament apostolate from which we may   [487] best begin if we are to hear and understand what the Bible means by this witness. (Cf. for what follows: E. Fuchs, *"Die Auferstehung Jesu Christi und der Anfang der Kirche," Zeitschr. für Kirchengesch.*, 1932, vol. I–II 1 f.) Jesus Christ as the revelation of God does not remain alone and therefore unhistorical. He can therefore come to us and to all men. He has primary witnesses, who can be succeeded by secondary and tertiary witnesses. This fact, which is just as unique as revelation itself, is expressly described as a special creation of Jesus Christ: καὶ ἐποίησεν δώδεκα ἵνα ὦσιν μετ᾽ αὐτοῦ καὶ ἵνα ἀποστέλλῃ αὐτοὺς κηρύσσειν EN44 (Mk. 3¹⁴). Like so many evangelical passages embedded in the passion narrative, we have to regard this saying as proleptic, i.e., it acquires its proper sense only through the message of the resurrection. Another creative word, but the real content of which can again only be understood in the light of Easter, is that when Jesus (e.g., Mk. 2¹⁴) challenges a man with His ἀκολούθει μοι EN45. Eph. 4¹¹ also speaks of a creation of the resurrected Christ when it says: αὐτὸς ἔδωκεν τοὺς μὲν ἀποστόλους, τοὺς δὲ προφήτας, τοὺς δὲ εὐαγγελιστάς ... EN46. It is "by Jesus Christ, indeed by God the Father, who raised him from the dead" that Paul is an apostle and was "set apart from his mother's womb" (Gal. 1¹ ¹⁵, cf. Jer. 1⁵). Apostles are those who were chosen as such by Jesus "through the Holy Spirit" (Ac. 1²). In this light we can understand the unusual characteristics in which not only Paul spoke of his aposto-late, but which are everywhere peculiar to the evangelical part of the New Testament. "Whoso heareth you heareth me" (Lk. 10¹⁶). "He that receiveth you receiveth me" (Mt. 10⁴⁰). We must not weaken this. It does not say: "also heareth me" or "also receiveth me." The meaning already is that to hear and receive the disciples is to hear and receive Christ. There is no hearing or receiving of Christ which does not have the form of a hearing and receiving of His disciples. For "as the Father hath sent me (ἀπέσταλκεν), even so send (πέμπω) I you" (Jn. 20²¹). "The words which thou gavest me I have given unto them; and they received them and knew of a truth that I came forth from thee, and they believed that thou didst send me" (Jn. 17⁸). In the relationship between Jesus Christ and the apostles there is therefore repeated or reflected in some degree the economy of the incarnation of the Word. That is why in the one breath Jesus prays for them, and yet not only for them, but for them that believe on Him through their word (Jn. 17²⁰). That is why He spoke to Peter as He did. Peter by the confession revealed to him by the Father in heaven showed himself to be the rock on which Jesus would build His Church, the man to whom He would give the keys of the kingdom of heaven for a human binding and loosing on earth, with which the divine binding and loosing in heaven would be utterly identical (Mt. 16¹⁸ᶠ·)—a power which we know from Mt. 18¹⁸ and Jn. 20²³ is not only (as the well-known Roman Catholic expos-ition has it) ascribed and attributed to Peter, but in the person of Peter to the whole apos-tolic band, to the primary witnesses as such. That is why these primary witnesses are told that, when challenged by the world to give an account of themselves, they should not be anxious how and what they should speak: " ... For it shall be given yon in that same hour

---

EN44 and He appointed twelve to be with Him, in order to send them out to preach
EN45 'follow me'
EN46 he gave some to be apostles, some to be prophets, some to be evangelists

what ye shall speak. For it is not ye that speak but the Spirit of your Father which speaketh in you" (Mt. $10^{19f.}$). "Ye shall receive the power of the Holy Ghost which shall come upon you; and ye shall be my witnesses" (Ac. 1^8). For "the Comforter, which is the Holy Ghost, whom the Father will send in my name, he shall teach you all things and bring all things to your remembrance whatsoever I have said unto you" (Jn. 14^{26}). As the Spirit of truth He "will guide you into all truth" (Jn. 16^{13}). The fulfilment of this promise is the specific theme of the story of Whitsunday in Ac. $2^{1f.}$, and it is the presupposition of all the apostolic activity and proclamation which begins there. "Look on us," is what Peter can and must now say to the lame man before the beautiful gate of the Temple, although he has nothing to give him

[488] other than the Word in the name of Jesus Christ of Nazareth (Ac. $3^{4f.}$). It is the fact that they have to speak this Word, that is, therefore, that they have to speak in fulfilment of the revelation accomplished in Jesus Christ of Nazareth, in such a way that He Himself is with them always (Mt. 28^{20}); it is this which marks them out, so that now we have to look at them. In the light of these passages we cannot speak of Paul's sense of his office and mission as extraordinary. It was in keeping with the New Testament as a whole when in 2 Cor. 5^{18} he described the reconciliation accomplished in Jesus Christ, and the "gift" of the "ministry of reconciliation," as two sides of one and the same thing. In the *analogia fidei*[EN47] there is again a similarity between God and man, between the heavenly and the earthly reality. "We are ambassadors for Christ, as though God did beseech by us: we pray you in Christ's stead, be ye reconciled to God" (2 Cor. 5^{20}). In this saying we could easily find the whole biblical basis of the Scripture principle.

And it was not the case that the early Church arbitrarily expanded the evangelical-apostolic witness to Jesus Christ, when out of a pious regard for the sacred records of God's former people, or a need to vindicate itself by an attachment to this tradition, it added as a preface the Canon of the Synagogue. Both in the early days and more recently there have been many proposals and attempts to shake off the so-called Old Testament altogether or to reduce it to the level of a deutero-canonical introduction to the real Bible (i.e., the New Testament), which is good and profitable for reading. In face of such attempts we cannot be too clear that for the most primitive Church, not only for Jews but also for the Gentiles, the New and not the Old Testament was the addition, the enlargement and the extension of the Canon, and that not the Gospels and the apostolic writings, but the Canon of the Synagogue, Moses, the prophets and the psalms (Lk. 24^{44}) constituted the self-evident basis of Holy Scripture. Neither in the New Testament nor in the documents of the 2nd-century post-apostolic period do we find the slightest trace of anyone seriously and responsibly trying to replace the Holy Scriptures of Israel by other traditions of other nations, all those nations within which the first Churches sprang up, or to proclaim those traditions as prophecies of Christ and therefore as a more suitable introduction to the New Testament Bible. Yet this would have meant a great easing of the missionary task, and apologetics often tended in this direction, although hardly ever with reference to the problem of the Canon. Even Marcion never plunged in this direction, although he was near enough to it. We cannot plunge in this direction, we cannot even try to do what Marcion and after him the Socinians and Schleiermacher and Ritschl and Harnack tried to do, without substituting another foundation for the foundation on which the Christian Church is built. The Old Testament is not an introduction to the real New Testament Bible, which we can dispense with or replace. We cannot eliminate the Old Testament or substitute for it the records of the early religious history of other peoples, as R. Wilhelm has suggested in the case of China, B. Gutmann in some sense in that of Africa, and many recent fools in the case of Germany. If we do, we are not merely opposing a questionable accessory, but the very institution and existence of the Christian

---

[EN47] analogy of faith

Church. We are founding a new Church, which is not a Christian Church. For not only is the canonicity of the Old Testament no arbitrary expansion of the evangelical-apostolical witness to Christ. It existed before and when the first Church arose, even in the evangelical-apostolical witness to Christ, which as the witness of recollection has rightly been placed alongside the original Canon, the witness of expectation. It was so embedded in the New Testament Bible itself that only if we wanted to make the latter unreadable could we try to assess and understand it as the witness of divine revelation apart from the original Canon. Whether we like it or not, the Christ of the New Testament is the Christ of the Old Testament, the Christ of Israel. The man who will not accept this merely shows that in fact he has already substituted another Christ for the Christ of the New Testament. It was not to dissolve   [489] the Law and the prophets but to fulfil them that the real Christ of the New Testament came (Mt. 5^{17}; cf. Jn. 10^{35}). Let us remember what is said on this score by that Gospel of Luke, which Marcion preferred but also assiduously corrected. "This day," says Jesus when He first appears, "is the scripture fulfilled in your ears" (Lk. 4^{21}). In the suffering of Jesus "all things that are written by the prophets concerning the Son of man shall be accomplished" (Lk. 18^{31}). The revelation of the risen Christ in the episode of the walk to Emmaus (Lk. 24$^{13f.}$) consists in nothing but the opening, expounding and confirming of what Moses, the prophets and all the Scriptures have prophesied. That is why it says in Jn. 1^{45}: "We have found him, of whom Moses in the law, and the prophets, did write." That is why the Jews are reproached in Jn. 5^{39}, "Ye search the scriptures; for in them ye (rightly) think ye have eternal life: and they are they which testify of me." "For had ye believed Moses, ye would have believed me; for he wrote of me" (Jn. 5^{46}). The tenor of the New Testament witness to Christ can really be seen from the verse of the Psalm quoted in Heb. 10^{7}: "Lo, I come (in the volume of the book it is written of me) to do thy will, O God." The "Gospel of God," which Paul too, and especially Paul, proclaims, is none other than that which God "promised afore by his prophets in the holy scriptures" (Rom. 1^{2}, 3^{21}, 16^{26}). Again and again Paul stresses (Rom. 4$^{23f.}$, 15^{4}; 1 Cor. 9^{10}, 10^{11}) that what happened and was recorded in the Old Testament was "for our sakes," and therefore that it takes place and is recorded in an actuality which does not diminish but is only now fully demonstrated. It is decisive for Paul that the death and resurrection of Christ took place κατὰ τὰς γραφάς^{EN48} (1 Cor. 15$^{3f.}$). At the very points where we might expect the word "God," he uses "Scripture": "the scripture saith unto Pharaoh ... " (Rom. 9^{17}), "the scripture hath concluded all under sin" (Gal. 3^{22}, cf. Rom. 11^{32}). It is evident, therefore, that the desire of the Evangelists and apostles themselves was simply to be expositors of the former Scriptures. According to Ac. 26^{22}, Paul will say nothing (οὐδὲν ἐκτός) but what the prophets and Moses had said in relation to the future. And they obviously instructed their followers to do the same, as we see from the story of the Christians of Beroea (Ac. 17^{11}) or of the conversion of the Jew Apollos (Ac. 18$^{24f.}$), or from passages like 1 Tim. 4^{13}, 2 Tim. 3$^{15f.}$ We have "the sure word of prophecy." And "ye do well that ye take heed thereunto as unto a light that shineth in a dark place, until the day dawn, and the day star arise in your hearts" (2 Pet. 1^{19}).

And now we have only to answer the question whether the Old Testament witnesses understood themselves in the same way, i.e., as called and separated witnesses of the one revelation of the one God in Jesus Christ, as they undoubtedly came to be understood by the men of the New Testament. This is the decisive issue between the Church and the Synagogue. In denying Christ, the Synagogue denies the one revelation of the one God. Its answer is therefore in the negative. But the Church gives an affirmative answer, as does also the New Testament: Christ has risen from the dead, and has revealed the fulfilment of Scripture and therefore its real meaning. In the light of this, how can the Church understand the Old

---

EN48 according to the Scriptures

Testament witnesses except as witnesses to Christ? A religio-historical understanding of the Old Testament in abstraction from the revelation of the risen Christ is simply an abandonment of the New Testament and of the sphere of the Church in favour of that of the Synagogue, and therefore in favour of an Old Testament which is understood apart from its true object, and content. Already, in an earlier context, we have stated the basic considerations which have to be stated in this regard, and all that we can now do is to say once more that this question of the self-understanding of the Old Testament witnesses is ultimately identical with the question of faith. If Christ has risen from the dead, then the understanding of the Old Testament as a witness to Christ is not a later interpretation, but an understanding of its [490] original and only legitimate sense. Moses and the prophets do not belong only because the New Testament undoubtedly says so, but—when the New Testament has undoubtedly said so on the basis of the resurrection of Jesus—they belong, not as the representatives of an earlier religion prior to the Evangelists and apostles, but as the prophetic heralds of Jesus Christ side by side with them. Therefore the Church cannot be released from its task of expounding and applying the Old Testament witness too, and of respecting its authority as the Word of God.

Scripture not only attests to us the objective fact of the revelation which has taken place, its expectation and recollection. It also attests itself in the existence of these specific men, Moses and the prophets, the Evangelists and apostles. And in so doing—and this is what we now have to emphasise—it has in view the function in which passively and actively these men were what they were, and in their writings are what they are. Passively, as distinct from us and all other men, they were those who have seen and heard the unique revelation as such, and seen and heard therefore in a unique way, fashioning their historical environment.

"That which was from the beginning, which we have heard, which we have seen with our eyes, which we have looked upon and our hands have handled, περὶ τοῦ λόγου τῆς ζωῆς [EN49] (perhaps: surrounding the word of life) ... For the life was manifested, and we have seen it" (1 Jn. 1[1f.]). But we must also remember the remarkable passage in Num. 12[1-16], which tells us of a rebellion of Miriam and Aaron against Moses: "Hath the Lord indeed spoken only by Moses? hath he not spoken also by us?" The following is the answer given to them: "If there be a prophet among you, I the Lord will make myself known unto him in a vision, and will speak unto him in a dream. My servant Moses is not so, who is faithful in all mine house. With him will I speak mouth to mouth, even manifestly, and not in dark speeches; and the form of the Lord shall he behold: wherefore then were ye not afraid to speak against my servant Moses?" But there is another rather stronger view of the idea of prophecy, and in some contexts the same directness of meeting with God is ascribed to the prophets as well. With all other Israelites the prophets are witnesses to the internal and external history of Israel. But at the same time—and it is this that raises them out of the mass of the nation—they are witnesses to the will of God concealed in this history, challenging and ruling, promising and threatening. "The Lord God doeth nothing, but he revealeth his secret unto his servants the prophets" (Amos 3[7]). To that extent they, too, are obviously amongst those who see and hear according to 1 Jn. 1[1f.].

But the function of these men has also and necessarily another and active side. As distinct from us and all other men, they were those who have to pro-

---

[EN49] concerning the word of life

claim to others, and therefore to us and all other men, revelation as they encounter it.

Reading on in 1 Jn. 1 [3f.]: "That which we have seen and heard declare we unto you, that ye also may have fellowship with us: and truly our fellowship is with the Father, and with his Son Jesus Christ. And these things write we unto you, that our joy may be fulfilled." We are now reminded that right throughout the Old Testament, to those to whom He speaks, and by the very fact that He does speak, Yahweh gives a mission and authority, a commission and command, that they too should speak. We are reminded that everywhere the Old Testament claims to speak with authority, because it repeats in human words what has first been said by Yahweh Himself. Not every man can do this. Not every man can speak God's Word. For not [491] every man has heard it. But those who have heard it can and must repeat it. This speaking the Word of God is the second thing which makes prophets prophets. And at this point we have striking evidence of the unity between the Old Testament and the New. For as Yahweh does with His prophets, so Jesus calls and sends and commissions His disciples, to speak of the kingdom of God, i.e., of His own presence as the presence of the Messiah. No Old Testament witness had spoken of it. Therefore no one in the Old Testament, not even Moses, exercised such a mission. All of them, even Moses himself and the greatest prophets, are themselves sent. Yahweh alone is the subject of this sending. In the New Testament only Jesus is the subject of the sending, and compared with Him the others are all sent by Him. Apart from this unheard-of innovation everything is exactly as it was in the Old Testament. It is part of the concept of εὐαγγελιστής [EN50], and ἀπόστολος [EN51], as it is also of that of prophet, that they do not have to speak in their own name but only in the name, i.e., in fulfilment of the revelation of Jesus: to speak of Him, to speak by His commission, to speak according to His ordering, to speak of the ability which is to be expected from Him. If we interpret these men as free religious thinkers, from the very outset we are guilty of an interpretation which the texts not only do not substantiate but openly contradict: at a decisive point we are understanding them in a way in which they did not understand themselves and did not wish to be understood at any price. "And such trust have we through Christ to Godward: not that we are sufficient of ourselves, to think anything as of ourselves: but our sufficiency is of God, who also hath made us able ministers of the new covenant" (2 Cor. 3 [4f.]). "I will not dare to speak of any things save those which Christ hath wrought by me, to make the Gentiles obedient by word and deed" (Rom. 15 [18]). In fact: "Christ ... speaketh in me ... " (2 Cor. 13 [3]). That is why Paul has to say: "Woe is unto me, if I preach not the Gospel" (1 Cor. 9 [16]). That is why in the Acts and Epistles the preaching of the apostles is often regarded as equivalent to the Word of God itself. The active side of the function of these men has to be understood wholly and utterly in the light of the passive.

And now a necessary and self-evident delimitation: these men are holy men and the authors of Holy Scripture in this function, but only in this function, only in the exercise of this office. Not therefore as thinkers, not as religious personalities or geniuses, not as moral heroes, although they were these things too in the right sense and in varying degrees. What they were as witnesses to revelation, and therefore as those who saw and heard and were sent on a commission and empowered, was neither the greater nor smaller, the better nor the worse, for what they were from the intellectual or religious or moral standpoint.

[EN50] evangelist
[EN51] apostle

In relation to many of these spokesmen, the Bible itself has unintentionally and often enough intentionally made it clear that it holds out little reward for those who try to find its meaning at this kind of level. At this level they are only like us and all men. Perhaps there have been much more pious men and cleverer and better men than these prophets and apostles. Indeed, J. Wichelhaus ventured to say rather morosely that "as men Paul and Peter do not deserve our confidence at all" (*Die Lehre der Heiligen Schrift³*, 1892, 221). Now, there is no reason why as men they should not deserve as much faith as we usually give to other men—but no more, and of no other kind.

[492] The decisive confidence, i.e., a confidence in what they say, is something which they certainly cannot create by the incidental glimpses of their humanity. On the contrary, it is only what they say that by its own credibility can create confidence in their humanity. But necessarily this means—and it applies to all of them—a judgment on their humanity. To look on them, as we are requested to do in Ac. 3⁴, always means, to look on Him who has sent them.

4. As the witness of divine revelation the Bible also attests the institution and function of prophets and apostles. And in so doing it attests itself as Holy Scripture, as the indispensable form of that content. But because this is the case, in this question of divine revelation the Church, and in and with it theology, has to hold fast to this unity of content and form. The distinction of form and content must not involve any separation. Even on the basis of the biblical witness we cannot have revelation except through this witness. We cannot have revelation "in itself." The purpose of the biblical witness is not to help us achieve this, so that its usefulness is outlived when it is achieved. Revelation is, of course, the theme of the biblical witness. And we have already seen that the perception of it is absolutely decisive for the reading and understanding and expounding of this biblical witness. But it always, is the theme of this, the biblical witness. We have no witness to it but this. There are, therefore, no points of comparison to make it possible for us even in part to free ourselves from this witness, to put ourselves into direct relationship to the theme of it. And it is in keeping with the nature of this theme that (in the form of the calling and enlightening and empowering of these specific men) it has been indissolubly linked with its witness, i.e., their witness. In this question of revelation we cannot, therefore, free ourselves from the texts in which its expectation and recollection is attested to us. We are tied to these texts. And we can only ask about revelation when we surrender to the expectation and recollection attested in these texts.

"It holdeth God's word," is what Luther once said about the Bible (*Pred. üb. Rom.* 15⁴ᶠ·, 1522, *W.A.* 10ᴵ· ², 75, 6). It only "holds," encloses, limits and surrounds it: that is the indirectness of the identity of revelation and the Bible. But it and it alone does really "hold" it: it comprehends and encloses it in itself, so that we cannot have the one without the other; that is why we have to speak about an indirect *identity.* The idea against which we have to safeguard ourselves at this point is one which has tacitly developed in connexion with modern theological historicism. It is to the effect that in the reading and understanding and expounding of the Bible the main concern can and must be to penetrate past the biblical texts to the facts which lie behind the texts. Revelation is then found in these facts as such

36

(which in their factuality are independent of the texts). Thus a history of Israel and of Old Testament religion is found behind the canonical Old Testament, a history of the life of Jesus, and later of course a Christ-myth, behind the canonical Gospels, a history of the apostolic age, i.e., of primitive Christianity behind the canonical Acts and Epistles. The intention is to subject the biblical Canon to the question of truth as formulated in the sense of modern historicism. The Bible is to be read as a collection of sources. In the first instance this was all done in all good faith even from the ecclesiastical and theological standpoint. There was such confidence in the rightness and utility of the question of truth formulated in the sense [493] of modern historicism that it could be thought the highest honour for the Bible and the greatest benefit for oneself, i.e., for Christendom, to proceed from a study of the texts to the formation, with the help of observations gained from them, of a conception or conceptions of what is true and proper in them, of a form of the spirit apart from the letter. Now we must not overlook the human significance not only of the genuine scientific concern but also of the religious earnestness which went to the making of these pictures, or of the enthusiasm with which it was thought they should be presented to the Church: "These be thy gods, O Israel." But at the same time we cannot ignore the fact that in substance it was a mistake from the very first. From the very first: not therefore from the moment when the Canon was approached critically as a collection of sources; not from the moment when it was read with caution, with actual doubt whether things did take place exactly as we read, with an assessment of the varying so-called "values" of the different sources, with the disqualification of this or that constituent part, with conjectures on the true connexions of what actually took place instead of those given or omitted in the texts, with a more or less comprehensive correction of the biblical in favour of an "historical" truth, and finally with a partial or total reconstruction of reality as it is thought to be better seen over the heads and shoulders of the biblical authors. It was a long way from Zacharias to Gunkel and Reimarus to Wrede. But once the way was entered we need not be surprised if the eventual results were so radical that they caused pain in the Church. And they could not be prescribed or suppressed. But it is not because of the results, which were, of course, opposed by other more harmless, i.e., conservative ones, that this road must be called the wrong one. It is so, because at bottom it means succumbing to the temptation to read the Canon differently from what it is intended to be and can be read—which is the same thing. The universal rule of interpretation is that a text can be read and understood and expounded only with reference to and in the light of its theme. But if this is the case, then in the light of the theme—not *a priori*, but from the text itself—the relationship between theme and text must be accepted as essential and indissoluble. The form cannot therefore be separated from the content, and there can be no question of a consideration of the content apart from the form. We cannot therefore put the question of truth in the direct way that it was arbitrarily thought it should be put. It is not that, when we have consulted Genesis and the Synoptics as unfortunately our only sources, the real question concerning the early history of Israel or the life of Jesus is a question of history, i.e., the history of the world of culture, of religion, somewhere behind Genesis and the Synoptics. Except in historical terms—in terms of the history of literature—these writings cannot be read merely as sources. If we have a particular interest in antiquities, we can read them in this way at our own risk, at the risk of failing to serve even our own interest and missing the real nature and character of the writings. Why should there not be occasional items of this kind in the Bible? But by obstinately putting this question of truth, by acting as though the interest in antiquities is the only legitimate interest, the true nature and character of the writings has been missed for over a hundred years. And that this should be so— even if there were more agreement than there actually is on the validity of this hermeneutic principle—we can only describe as a scandal even from the celebrated standpoint of "pure scholarship." At any rate it was a scandal in the Church; not, of course, that D. F. Strauss and

Wellhausen came to all sorts of extreme results, but that theology allowed itself to be decoyed into this trap (without even being able to advance in excuse the pretext of being nominally a non-theological discipline). Theology at least, even and especially historical theology, which applies itself particularly to the biblical texts, ought to have (let us say it at once) the tact and taste, in face of the linking of form and content in those texts of which it

[494] must still be aware, to resist this temptation, to leave the curious question of what is perhaps behind the texts, and to turn with all the more attentiveness, accuracy and love to the texts as such. In its arbitrary attempt to sketch and create those pictures, it largely failed to do the work really laid upon it. It is only to-day that we can see how little we have really gained from that intensive and extensive ploughing of the field of New Testament literature to help us to explain even the simplest individual concepts, not to speak of commenting on the texts both as they stand and in relation one to another. It is no accident that, when about 1920 Protestant theology made a kind of rediscovery of the objectivity of the New Testament and of the biblical witness generally, at almost the same time—with the emergence of the so-called "*formgeschichtlich*" method introduced by M. Dibelius, R. Bultmann and K. L. Schmidt (F. Overbeck was, of course, a forerunner)—in the case of the New Testament at least it came to a consciousness of the form of the witness corresponding to that objectivity. And it is also no accident that in our days it is to the preparation of a biblico-theological dictionary that the most powerful forces of biblical research are applied, although unfortunately we cannot say that the advance which we must now make is equally clear to all those who are co-operating in this enterprise. The real decision whether in this field we are going to make a move for the better will depend on two things. The first is whether there will be the rekindling of a similar interest in Old Testament scholarship. But the second is whether in both fields the time has not passed when we can select arbitrary themes, whether the exegesis of canonical Scripture as such, the coherent exposition of Genesis, Isaiah, the Gospel of Matthew, etc., according to their present status and compass is again recognised and undertaken as in the last resort the only possible goal of biblical scholarship. As material for the carrying out of this true and long neglected task, we must not and cannot ignore the insights won under the perverted sign of the earlier source-investigation of the Bible. There cannot, therefore, be any question of sealing off or abandoning so-called "criticism," as it has been so significant for this investigation. All relevant, historical questions must be put to the biblical texts, considered as witnesses in accordance with their literary form. And the differences in exposition which result when we answer them can only be to the good, so long as criticism is clearly made to serve this task, so long as it no longer has to serve the foolish end of mediating a historical truth lying behind the texts. The historical truth which in its own way biblical scholarship does have to mediate is the true meaning and context of the biblical texts as such. Therefore it is not different from the biblical truth which has to be mediated. When that is seen and understood, when the foolish pursuit of a historical truth *supra scripturam*[EN52] is on all sides abandoned in favour of a circumscribed investigation of the *veritas scripturae ipsius*[EN53], then we can and must give the freest possible course to critical questions and answers as demanded by the character of the biblical witness as a human document, and therefore a historical quantity. For in these circumstances the questions and answers can and will indicate only that Scripture is taken seriously as it actually is before us. And the questions and answers can and will help to safeguard our reading and understanding and expounding of Scripture from the arbitrary desire, by which it was continually threatened in the earlier days of the Church, which knew nothing of these questions and answers, to express its concrete form plastically, and in that way to direct and hold in definite lines the question of its object-

---

[EN52] above Scripture
[EN53] truth of Scripture itself

ive content, the question of God's revelation. As I see it, this does not mean an annulling of the results of biblical scholarship in the last centuries, nor does it mean a breaking off and neglect of efforts in this direction. What it does mean is a radical re-orientation concerning the goal to be pursued, on the basis of the recognition that the biblical texts must be investigated for their own sake to the extent that the revelation which they attest does not stand or occur, and is not to be sought, behind or above them but in them. If in reply it is asked whether Christianity is really a book-religion, the answer is that strangely enough Christianity has always been and only been a living religion when it is not ashamed to be actually and seriously a book-religion. Expounding the saying in 2 Cor. 5[7] ("We walk by faith, not by sight") and linking it up with 1 Cor. 13[12], Calvin coined the statement, *videmus enim, sed in speculo et aenigmate; hoc est loco rei in verbo acquiescimus*[EN54] (*C.R.* 50, 63). Biblical theology can be as critical as it will and must—but if it carries out the programme outlined in this statement, it will always do good work as ecclesiastical scholarship: better than that done in recent centuries in spite of all the seriousness and industry applied to it. And it will have an honourable place as scholarship in the general sense. [495]

5. When we regard the prophets and apostles as witnesses of divine revelation, in this their function as witnesses we ascribe to them, as under 3, a very definite separation from us and all other men, a singular and unique position and significance. The thought of this separation is obviously sharpened when it is clear to us that we cannot separate between the form and content of this witness, that in order to arrive at revelation we should not and cannot go beyond the prophets and apostles, and their expectation and recollection, to the pseudo-presence of revelation in itself. Among the many other quantities and factors, which together constitute our human-historical cosmos, the Church sees that these men, this collection of Scriptures (not in the first instance and directly in opposition to the so-called world, but very definitely and in the first instance in opposition to the Church itself) are underlined and singled out and appointed to a role and dignity peculiar to themselves alone.

"They have received the gift of miracles and instruction as distinct from us, to whom it can only belong to speak what has been delivered to us by this declaration of grace" (John Damascene, *Ekd.* 1, 3). *Hoc esse*[EN55], writes Calvin, *rectae intelligentiae initium, cum fidem, quae Deo debetur, tribuimus sanctis eius prophetis*[EN56]. They can be described as "holy men of God" because they *iniunctum sibi munus fideliter exsequentes, divinam in suo ministerio personam sustinuerunt*[EN57] (*Comm. on 2 Pet.* 1[20] *C.R.* 55, 458).

But this setting apart and singling out are ascribed to them by the Church because it belongs to them, and because they have shown and proved themselves to be singled out and set apart, as we have seen already in our discussion of the concept of the Canon. It lies in the nature of this separation and differentiation that it has a limit. Scripture is Holy Scripture as the witness of divine

---

[EN54] for we see, but in a glass darkly; that is, in place of the thing, we rest content with the word
[EN55] This is
[EN56] the beginning of correct understanding, when we direct the faith which is owed to God to his holy prophets
[EN57] faithfully carry out the office entrusted to them and hold up the person of God in their ministry

revelation, in the passive and active function of the men who speak in it, in the event of this function, i.e., in such a way that the revelation of God is manifest in its witness demanding and receiving obedience as the Word of God. But only in this way. We have already indicated that the intellectual and moral and religious qualities of these men can neither confirm nor compromise their differentiation. We must now go on to say that between the Bible and the other quantities and factors of our human cosmos there is no difference in so far as the Bible is incidentally a historical document for the history of ancient Israel and its religion, in so far as it is also a document for one aspect of the religious history of Hellenism and can therefore be used as a collection of historical sources—although with little prospect of success in view of its peculiar literary form. Again, as a timeless document of the human longing and seeking for the unconditioned, the Bible can, if we like, be read alongside documents of a similar kind. And we shall find that fundamentally at any rate it is not different from other documents of this kind. Therefore we need not be surprised if we have to say that in other documents of this kind we may perhaps find more edification, i.e., a stronger impulse to this longing and seeking, that in Goethe's *Faust* or even in the sacred books of other religions we can better attain this end. On our own account and at our own risk we can go further and widen the concept of man of God, or prophet, or perhaps even apostle. And on all sorts of pretexts (not without approximation to the Catholic principle of tradition, and even perhaps assimilation to it) we can extend the concept of the witness of revelation to all the realities in which we think we can see an actual mediation of Christ, or more generally a divine impulse from man to man.

[496]

For the sake of clarity I will quote what Horst Stephan (*Glaubenslehre²*, 1928) wrote about "gradation" within that sum of the sources of Christian doctrine which is for him the "Word of God": "If we give Jesus the special place due to Him, the first rank is taken by the God-sent figures whom we call prophets. They are the leaders from the great days of Israel to Paul and the founding of Protestantism. We can provisionally describe Luther as the last of the prophets. Even this series of prophets demands in detail a more exact differentiation in type and importance. But the second rank stands in even greater need of grouping and individuation. It comprises all the pious who have had influence at particular periods, especially those who have given classical formulation to the Christian faith in definite cultural epochs: figures like Origen and Augustine in late antiquity; Saint (!) Thomas or Meister Eckart in the Middle Ages; Melanchthon, Zwingli and Calvin in the older Protestantism (together with Luther, who in the main motifs of his activity rose to the height of prophecy ...), Herder and Schleiermacher in German Neo-Protestantism. In the third place we might mention those who are children of their age in their Christianity, but who transcend it in certain aspects, e.g.. Saint (!) Francis in the Middle Ages, and more recently a Zinzendorf or John Wesley or even (at a considerable remove) a Wichern and Kierkegaard. It is only after the figures of the second and third groups that we encounter all those other spirits whose achievements are only small or preparatory, but who do at times formulate items of knowledge with particular clarity and impressiveness; as for example the many religious poets or great theologians" (p. 28). In a later passage of the book (p. 217) we find that "the skill of a Paul Gerhardt, Bach or Dürer" comes "under consideration" in this sense, and we are told that "living faith is conscious that not only in the Bible is it touched by God's address" (p. 216). "The living God addresses His men where and how He will; therefore many a word can become 'God's Word,' which at a first glance seems to be purely of the world. If the present congregation leads to Jesus Christ, if a man of the present can become Christ to another man, and win a part in the divine nature, every kind of human speech, of proclamation but also of concept or visible sign or action, can bear within itself the divine speech. In short, the story of faith must be full of the Word of God" (p. 217). Indeed, there can be no question of a separation of the Bible if we take it on ourselves to introduce all kinds of gradations and to call that revelation and the Word of God in which according to individual taste and judg- [497] ment we think we see revelation and the Word of the so-called "living" God for a so-called "living" faith. We can only ask whether the representatives of this view seriously deny that in the sphere of the Christian Church there can only be revelation and the Word of God, the living God and a living faith, where it is a matter not of an arbitrary human valuation and selection, but of a divine command and on our part obedience? Or do they regard all these voices of the peoples and centuries as commands enjoining obedience? And if so, will they seriously claim that there is only a distinction of degree between the divine command heard in the "prophet" Luther or "Saint" Thomas and "Saint" Francis and that heard in the apostle Paul and, "in the special place which belongs to Him," in Jesus. If they do seriously deny the former or assert the latter, and think that they can rightly read and understand and explain the Bible on this presupposition, then we shall have to grant that there is no differentiation of the Bible. It is only rhetorically that we call it "holy" Scripture.

If we ascribe to it the character of Holy Scripture, we can do so only because we remember at least its witness to revelation and the event of its prophetic-apostolic function. We can do so only because we reconcile ourselves to its effective power of command, as we ourselves recognise and acknowledge it to be effective. We can do so only as we reconcile ourselves to it, not as one of the living powers and forces of Christian history, but as the one power and force which has created and bears and rules the Church and with it all Christian history, which therefore confronts as the critical norm the Church and all the forces active in the sphere of the Church—all that we might regard as the witness of revelation and the Word of God according to our individual taste and judgment. It is only in virtue of this separation of itself that the Bible can be set apart. But in virtue of it, it is actually and truly and radically set apart. The objection is to hand: To what extent after all can and should a historical quantity like the Bible be given this basic priority over against all other historical quantities? When the Christian Church makes the act of remembrance and the corresponding self-reconciliation, in which it gives to the Bible the authority of Holy Scripture, and expects to hear in the Bible and only in the Bible the Word of God, does there not take place something which cannot be squared with the majesty of God: the absolutising of a relative, that is, of a word which is always human, and which cannot stand side by side with the One who Himself is and wills to be God alone? And if it cannot do that, as a relative does it not belong to the other relativities of our human cosmos? Does it not belong, in fact, as something which can be compared although it has not yet perhaps been excelled, to that series in which Neo-Protestantism and in another way Roman Catholicism can see it? Does not the Protestant principle

41

attribute too much to the Bible, and too little to God Himself on the one hand, and to all other witnesses of His revelation on the other? The answer is that there is indeed only one single absolute fundamental and indestructible priority, and that is the priority of God as Creator over the totality of His creatures and each of them without exception. Yet how strange it is that we learn of this very priority (in the serious sense, in all the compass and power of the concept) only through the Bible, and only through the Bible as it is read and understood and expounded as witness of revelation and therefore as itself the Word of God. We learn of it only through the Bible as it is itself apparently absolutised. The distinction between absolute and relative seems so easy, and it seems childishly easy to say that God alone is absolute and everything else relative, and that there can be no mixture of the two and no third thing between God and everything else. But we have to ask ourselves how we ever come to make this distinction, how human thinking can achieve the thought of the priority of the absolute over against the relative, without either positing the alleged absolute relatively or the relative as quite unreal over against the absolute? We have also to ask how we succeed not only in thinking this distinction, i.e. achieving it as an idea and concept, but—and this is what makes it a serious thought—in so making it our own that it is not merely a *theoria*[EN58], a drama played out in front of us, but that we ourselves achieve it with our lives, in our existence, and the drama of it is our drama? For what sort of a knowledge of the priority of the absolute would that be which did not mean our acknowledgment of it, which did not include the authority of the absolute and our obedience to it, which was not in fact based on this obviously not self-evident acknowledgment, authority and obedience? And we have also to ask how after all we can achieve this distinction without coming up against the reality of the judgment in which our existence and with it our thinking are destroyed? Who then can see the priority of God the Creator and live? Who or what can be drawn into this drama and not inevitably perish? It is not, therefore, quite so easy to achieve the distinction on the basis of which we can and must query the differentiation and separateness of the Bible. Even if it is actually achieved in the Bible, with a clear answer to these three questions, this must make us think concerning the nature and status of the Bible itself. According to the Bible, the in itself unthinkable co-existence of absolute and relative is made possible by the fact that it does not speak of the absolute but of the goodness and patience of the Creator of all things revealed to us in Jesus Christ, nor does it speak of the relative, but of the creatures of this Creator. This God is always the Lord of a creation which genuinely exists after its kind. Further, the Bible certainly does not offer us any mere *theoria*[EN59], but what takes place in it as a proclamation of the divine Law is the attack on our existence, the act in which we have to recognise the priority of God, in which His

[EN58] spectacle
[EN59] spectacle

42

authority is set up and our obedience to it becomes an event, and in all these things this distinction becomes reality. Yet according to the Bible this attack is not simply and of itself the judgment on our existence; but as the proclamation of the Gospel in the Law it is mercy even in judgment, the promise that [499] we can live and shall live, our preservation in the death which encompasses us for the resurrection of the body and eternal life. The knowledge of the priority of God as achieved in the Bible is the knowledge of the divine benefit, again— and here the circle closes—permitting and commanding us in the thought of Creator and creature to achieve calmly and clearly the unthinkable thought of the co-existence of absolute and relative, no, of the gracious God and of the men saved by His grace. But how can we use this knowledge which we owe to the Bible to query the peculiar status and significance of the Bible? It is certainly impossible for us to ascribe to it this status and significance arbitrarily, i.e., in any act of free valuation. For that reason, for the serious representatives of the Evangelical Scripture principle there was not the remotest question of the "absolutising" of a strictly relative quantity, of the divinisation or quasi-divinisation of men. On this principle nothing was absolutised and no one divinised. Rather the absolute, no, God was present in His Word as the Lord, as the One who commands and the One who shows mercy, as in the human word of the Bible. And the achievement—for the first time seriously—of the distinction between absolute and relative did not mean that the Bible only came later and arbitrarily, with a knowledge of its nature, to stand on the former side. It was there already. It spoke from that side. The distinction could only seriously be made from that side as it was already made. And the so-called Scripture principle, by which it does stand singly and uniquely on this former side, by which it is the Word of God, can only try to be the later statement of an existing content. Again it is quite impossible that there should be a direct identity between the human word of Holy Scripture and the Word of God, and therefore between the creaturely reality in itself and as such and the reality of God the Creator. It is impossible that there should have been a transmutation of the one into the other or an admixture of the one with the other. This is not the case even in the person of Christ where the identity between God and man, in all the originality and indissolubility in which it confronts us, is an assumed identity, one specially willed, created and effected by God, and to that extent indirect, i.e., resting neither in the essence of God nor in that of man, but in a decision and act of God to man. When we necessarily allow for inherent differences, it is exactly the same with the unity of the divine and human word in Holy Scripture.

What Calvin said of the presence of God in the flesh of Christ can, *mutatis mutandis*[EN60], be applied to the presence of God in the word of the prophets and apostles: *Sacramenta … iustitiae et salutis materiam in eius canne residere docent, non quod a se ipso iustificet aut vivificet*

EN60 in different circumstances

merus homo, sed quia Deo placuit, quod in se absconditum et incomprehensibile erat, in mediatore palam facere[EN61] (*Instit.* III, II, 9).

[500]   Even here the human element does not cease to be human, and as such and in itself it is certainly not divine. And it is quite certain that God does not cease to be God. In contrast to the humanity of Jesus Christ, there is no unity of person between God and the humanity of the prophets and apostles. Again, in contrast to the humanity of Jesus Christ, the humanity of the prophets and apostles is not taken up into the glory of God. It cannot independently reveal, but only attest, the revelation which did and does take place in the humanity of Jesus Christ. But at this remove and with this difference, as this word of testimony, as the sign of the revelation which has taken place and does take place, and indeed, as we saw, as the sign posited in and with revelation itself, as the witness of witnesses directly called in and with revelation itself, Scripture, too, stands in that indirect identity of human existence with God Himself, which is conditioned neither by the nature of God nor that of man, but brought about by the decision and act of God. It too can and must—not as though it were Jesus Christ, but in the same serious sense as Jesus Christ—be called the Word of God: the Word of God in the sign of the word of man, if we are going to put it accurately.

There is still a third quantity of which we have to say the same thing in its relation to Holy Scripture as we now say of Holy Scripture in its relation to Jesus Christ: the proclamation of the Christian Church by word and sacrament. And there are other signs of revelation of which we cannot say that they are the Word of God, at any rate in the strict and proper sense. The Church as such, e.g., is one great sign of revelation. But it is not the Word of God. On the contrary—and this is something different—it is created by the Word of God and it lives by it. Again, the dogmas of the Church, the constitution of the Canon as recurrently recognised and accepted, the existence of teachers of the Church and their doctrine, the actions and experiences of the Church or of Christians in the world: all these are indeed signs of revelation, but they cannot on that account be called the Word of God in the true and autonomous sense. They are, to the extent that they are proclamation, and to the extent that as proclamation they attest the witness of Holy Scripture and therefore revelation. On the other hand, Holy Scripture is marked off as a sign of revelation from the sign of the true humanity of Christ by the fact that because of the uniqueness and therefore the temporal limitation of revelation, because it has terminated in the ascension of Christ, the latter is hidden from us, i.e., it can be seen only as it is attested by Scripture and the proclamation of the Church and in faith. But since Holy Scripture is the original form of its attestation, since, unlike the proclamation of the Church, it attests revelation in its uniqueness and temporal limitation, it belongs to the first and original sign, the true humanity of Christ. That the Word has become Scripture is not one and the same thing as its becoming flesh. But the uniqueness and at the same time general relevance of its becoming flesh necessarily involved its becoming Scripture. The divine Word became the word of the prophets and apostles by becoming flesh. Because the man Jesus became for these men the Word of God and there-

---

[EN61] The sacraments ... teach that the substance of righteousness and salvation are present in his flesh, not that a man on his own could justify or make alive by himself. Rather, it is because God decides to make plain in the mediator what was hidden and incomprehensible in Himself

fore said to these men, "Receive ye the Holy Ghost," and "He that heareth you heareth me," and "Behold I am with you alway, even unto the end of the world," they have entered into the gap created through the uniqueness and temporal limitation of revelation. To the Church founded by Him, but *in concreto*^{EN62} by their Word—as mediators, as those who bear His commission, as heralds of His lordship—they now stand in the originality which is proper to Him. They share *ministerialiter*^{EN63} the honour which *principaliter*^{EN64} is proper to Him. It is decided by them whether the proclamation of the Church, which corresponds to the original Word of God entrusted by them to the Church, will be the actual Word of God. If the [501] Church really wishes to live by the Word of God and therefore really to be the Church, it can as little overlook and ignore them as it can Jesus Christ Himself. We again recall Calvin's *loco rei in verbo acquiescimus*^{EN65}. Calvin also formulated the same perception in this way: *Mysteria Dei enim, cuiusmodi sunt, quae ad salutem nostram pertinent, in se, suaque (ut dicitur) natura cerni non possunt: verum ipsa in eius verbo duntaxat intuemur: cuius veritas sic persuasa esse nobis debet, ut pro facto impletoque habendum sit quicquid loquitur*^{EN66} (*Instit.* III, 2, 41). It should now be clear that the word (i.e., the word of Scripture) takes the place of the thing itself (i.e., the Word of God). This does not mean that it is "only" the word of Scripture and not the Word of God which now confronts us. What it does mean is that the Word of God is now the word of Scripture which is its sign; or more generally, that the thing itself is present and active in the Word.

As the Word of God in the sign of this prophetic-apostolic word of man Holy Scripture is like the unity of God and man in Jesus Christ. It is neither divine only nor human only. Nor is it a mixture of the two nor a *tertium quid*^{EN67} between them. But in its own way and degree it is very God and very man, i.e., a witness of revelation which itself belongs to revelation, and historically a very human literary document. As such it does not violate the majesty of the one God in His distinctness from all that is not Himself. On the contrary, in its existence, i.e., even in its form (which is, of course, entirely grounded in its content) as the only word of man distinguished and separated in this way, it attests the uniqueness of the divine Majesty. The fear that the holiness of Scripture might prejudice the holiness of God will always prove superfluous where the holiness of Scripture is believed in and respected. But in its uniqueness Scripture does not violate the dignity and significance of the other signs and witnesses of revelation. This is primarily because apart from Jesus Christ Himself there is still this other form of the Word of God, which Scripture needs to be the Word of God, just as it needs Scripture. Preaching and the sacrament of the Church do indeed need the basis and authority and authenticity of the original Word of God in Scripture to be the Word of God. But Scripture also needs proclamation by preaching and sacrament, for it wills to be read and

---

^{EN62} concretely

^{EN63} ministerially

^{EN64} magisterially

^{EN65} in place of the things, we rest content with the word

^{EN66} For the mysteries of God which relate to our salvation are of such a kind that they cannot be discerned in themselves, and in their own nature, so to speak. Rather, we can intuit them only in His Word. The truth of this should have been so forced upon us that whatever He speaks should be considered as done and complete

^{EN67} third option

understood and expounded and the Word of God attested in it wills to have actuality. Therefore Holy Scripture cannot stand alone as the Word of God in the Church. And far from the voice and the voices of the Church and its teachers and its experiences and decisions and its history and tradition in the manifoldness of its various epochs and gifts being suppressed by the existence of Scripture as the basic and normative and regulative form of the Word of God, it is the very existence of this original form of the Word of God which sees to it that the voice of the Church and all these voices in the Church are heard as voices and have something to say, and have sufficient reason and cause to rise up again and again, receiving a stable direction and order calculated to keep them from chaos and cacophony in spite of all the aberrations and follies of man, so that as the Church is reminded of its existence in Jesus Christ, there is

[502]   held out to it in concrete reality the promise under which it lives. When the Church has suffered seriously, i.e., not from without but inwardly and essentially, it is never because it has lived too much but too little under the Word of Scripture. But the Church has become increasingly strong and self-conscious and bold, and produced heroes and geniuses and benefactors, and been able to establish comfort and hope for all people, not only within but without its walls, and gained genuine respect for itself, even in the world, when it has had a humble mind, and been prepared to live not above or alongside but under the Word. The existence in all ages of a Church which is really alive is therefore a concrete answer to the objection that an acknowledgment of the priority of the Bible in the Church will be detrimental to the living God and a living faith. The very opposite is the truth. Death usually reigns in the Church when it is thought that this acknowledgment should not be made.

6. We believe in and with the Church that Holy Scripture has this priority over all other writings and authorities, even those of the Church. We believe in and with the Church that Holy Scripture as the original and legitimate witness of divine revelation is itself the Word of God. The words "has" and "is" in these two sentences proclaim the same truth. But they need to be explained and delimited rather more exactly. For the sake of perspicuity we must anticipate the result: the "has" and "is" speak about a divine disposing, action and decision, to which when we make these statements we have on the one hand to look back as something which has already taken place, and on the other to look forward as something which has yet to do so. They do not speak, therefore, about a content which we can see clearly or control. They do not say that we have the capacity and competence to ascribe to the Bible this priority, this character as the Word of God, and that this priority and character of the Bible are immediately clear to us. If we venture to make them, we do so in obedience and therefore not on the basis and according to the measure of an *a priori*[EN68] understanding and judgment made by us and applied to this object (as though its holiness were a quality open to our observation and judgment), but in

---

[EN68] independent

46

obedience to a judgment of God already made in the light of the object, and in preparation for one which has again and again to be made in the light of it. We venture to do so in thankfulness for what we remember we have already heard in Scripture and in hope of what we may expect to hear again. If we say: the Bible has this priority, it is the Word of God, we must first replace the "has" by a "had" and "will have," and the "is" by a "was" and "will be." It is only as expounded in this way that the two words correspond to what we can actually know and say: we who are not in a position to carry through that divine disposing, action and decision or to handle them as though they were ours. But again when we expound the saying in this way—and it does say "has" and "is"—we must not lose sight of, or forget, or (in a superiority and power which demand   [503] this exposition but scoff at all exposition) weaken the fact that the truth of this "has" and "is" cannot be denied by dissolving it into a past and future. The life of the "had" and "was" and "will have" and "will be" derives entirely from the centre, the present "has" and "is." And our explanatory statements about the recollection and expectation, in which alone we can know and say anything about this present, can be genuine exposition only when they are related entirely to this centre, to the present which we do not know, for which we have no word, over which we have no power, of which as such we cannot say anything except this extravagant "has" and "is," because it is the event of what God Himself decides and wills and does in divine freedom and superiority and power. In the reality and truth of this event nothing is past or only future, nothing is only recollection and nothing only expectation, nothing is doubtful and nothing uncertain, nothing is after or before, nothing has to be repeated and nothing confirmed. It is round this event that the whole doctrine of Holy Scripture circles, and with it all Church dogmatics, and with it, too, preaching and the sacrament of Church proclamation. If our thinking and speaking cease to circle round this event, if we begin to think and speak about the Word of God in Holy Scripture only historically or only eschatologically even, and therefore in one way or another with doubt and uncertainty, we do not think and speak in and with the Church, in faith, we do not think and speak at all about the Word of God in Holy Scripture, but about something else which has consciously or unconsciously taken its place. But when we try to avoid this, we have to be clear that we can only circle round this event; we cannot attain to it of ourselves any more than we can—as we saw earlier—to the unity of Scripture. If it desires and wills to come, taking place within our own encircling exposition—well, it will simply do so, and it will do so the more strongly and gloriously the less we interfere with our clumsy and insolent attempts to attain to it. It is when we are clear that in all our exposition we can only think and explain this event, that we are equally clear that for our part we can never do more than think and explain it. All the possible denials and dissolutions of this present into all kinds of pasts and futures have their source in the fact that this present is not respected as the divine present. It is thought that we can and should turn everything upside down and treat this present as a created human

47

present which we can seize and control. There is no patience to continue circling round that centre, to stick to that faithful exposition and therefore that recollection and expectation which in face of this present—because it is this present—is our place and portion, our task and yet also our comfort. This is the insight which we must now consider and defend in detail.

[504]
It will be in place for us to remember first at this point the two important and always much noted statements in which in the New Testament itself there is explicit mention of the priority and character of Holy Scripture as such. Both passages refer primarily to the Old Testament, but according to the fundamental meaning of the two authors in whom they are found, the expressions can and ought and must be applied to all the witness of revelation and therefore to the New Testament witness as well.

The first passage is in 2 Tim. 3¹⁴⁻¹⁷, where Paul orders Timothy—it is noted that we are almost on the edge of the Canon—to "continue" in the things which he has learned, and received in faith (ἔμαθες καὶ ἐπιστώθης). He is to remember those of whom he has learned them, and that from a child he has known the Holy Scriptures (the ἱερὰ γράμματα) which have the power (τὰ δυνάμενα ...) to make him "wise unto salvation through faith in Christ Jesus." All that he has said so far has been said in clear and express remembrance of the fact that the Scriptures have already played a definite, decisive role in the life of his reader, that they have already given the proof of what they claim to be, that they have already shown their power, the specific power of instruction in the faith which saves him, and, concretely, in the faith which is founded on Jesus Christ, directed to Him, and actual through Him. But then Paul goes on to give the assurance that these same Scriptures will also be profitable to thee "for doctrine, for reproof, for correction, for instruction in righteousness" (all obviously as much for himself as through him for others), "that the man of God may be perfect, thoroughly furnished unto all good works." The same Scriptures have now become the object of expectation. The content of the expectation does not differ from that of the recollection of which he spoke earlier, but all that was previously represented as a gift now acquires the character of a task which has still to be taken up and executed. But the ὠφέλιμος EN69 corresponds exactly with the δυνάμενα EN70: Scripture was able and it will be able for what is said about its meaning for the life and activity of the reader both before and after. In the middle of these two statements, throwing light both backwards and forwards, there stands the sentence: πᾶσα γραφὴ θεόπνευστος EN71, all, that is the whole Scripture is—literally: "of the Spirit of God," i.e., given and filled and ruled by the Spirit of God, and actively outbreathing and spreading abroad and making known the Spirit of God. It is clear that this statement is decisive for the whole. It is because of this, i.e., in the power of the truth of the fact that the Spirit of God is before and above and in Scripture, that it was able and will be able for what is said of it both before and after. But it is equally clear that at the centre of the passage a statement is made about the relationship between God and Scripture, which can be understood only as a disposing act and decision of God Himself, which cannot therefore be expanded but to which only a—necessarily brief—reference can be made. At the decisive point all that we have to say about it can consist only in an underlining and delimiting of the inaccessible mystery of the free grace in which the Spirit of God is present and active before and above and in the Bible.

The other passage which calls for consideration is 2 Pet. 1¹⁹⁻²¹. The author had been speaking (vv. 16–18) about the visual witness to the "greatness" (μεγαλειότης) of Jesus

---

EN69 useful
EN70 powerful
EN71 all Scripture is God-breathed

Christ. Side by side with this—and he uses a most remarkable comparative (βεβαιότερον EN72)—he places the "prophetic word," calling it "a light that shineth in a dark place, until the day dawn, and the daystar arise in your hearts." It is said of this word that we have (ἔχομεν) it and that in the future we must take heed thereto (προσέχοντες). Here too, therefore, although not quite so clearly in relation to the "prophetic word" as such, we stand between the two times. The pointing to the coming dawn, which corresponds to the recollection of the visual witness, undoubtedly puts what is said into this framework. And here again, and in fact more clearly than in 2 Tim. 3, the centre is revealed from which we have to look backwards and forwards. The "prophecy of Scripture" is rightly read in the sense of what precedes, it is our light in a dark place, when it is not made the object of an ἰδία ἐπίλυσις EN73: i.e., when we allow it to expound itself, or when we allow it to control and [505] determine our exposition. This is because, as the text goes on, it is not given "by the will of man," but in it men spoke as they were "moved by the Holy Ghost," ὑπὸ πνεύματος ἁγίου φερόμενοι, they spoke "from God" (ἀπὸ θεοῦ).

The decisive centre to which the two passages point is in both instances indicated by a reference to the Holy Spirit, and indeed in such a way that He is described as the real author of what is stated or written in Scripture. It should be noted that the expressions used in these passages merely confirm what we have already seen concerning the sending and authorising of the prophets and apostles. In their function as witnesses to revelation they speak in the place and under the commission of Him who sent them, that is, Yahweh or Jesus Christ. They speak as *auctores secundarii* EN74. But there can be no question of any ignoring or violating of their *auctoritas* EN75 and therefore of their humanity. Moreover what we experience elsewhere of the work of the Holy Spirit on man in general and on such witnesses in particular, and our recollection of the *conceptus de Spiritu sancto* EN76 in Christology, does not allow us to suppose that we have to understand what we are told here about the authors of the Holy Scriptures, as though they were not real *auctores* EN77, as though in what they spoke or wrote they did not make full use of their human capacities throughout the whole range of what is contained in this idea and concept. Exegetically Calvin was right when in his note on 2 Pet. 1²¹ he wrote: *Impulsos fuisse dicit, non quod mente alienati fuerint (qualem in suis prophetis ἐνθουσιασμὸν fingunt gentiles), sed quia nihil a se ipsis ausi fuerint: tantum obedienter sequuti sint Spiritum ducem, qui in ipsorum ore tanquam in suo sacrario regnabat* EN78 (*C.R.* 55, 458). *Theopneustia* EN79 in the bounds of biblical thinking cannot mean anything but the special attitude of obedience in those who are elected and called to this obviously special service. The special element in this attitude of obedience lay in the particularity, i.e., the immediacy of its relationship to the revelation which is unique by restriction in time, and therefore in the particular nature of what they had to say and write as eye-witnesses and ear-witnesses, the first-fruits of the Church. But in nature and bearing their attitude of obedience was of itself—both outwardly and inwardly—only that of true and upright men. In particular, it did

---

EN72 more certain
EN73 private interpretation
EN74 secondary authors
EN75 authorship
EN76 conceived by the Holy Spirit
EN77 authors
EN78 He says that they were driven on, not because they were given the minds of others (as the pagans talk of 'enthusiasm' in their prophets), but since they had not ventured anything of themselves. They merely obediently followed the leading of the Spirit, who reigns as much in their mouths as in His own sanctuary
EN79 Divine inspiration

not mean any abolition of their freedom, their self-determination. How could their obedience be obedience unless it was rendered freely? But if it was rendered freely, we can only say that they themselves and of themselves thought and spoke and wrote what they did think and speak and write as genuine *auctores*[EN80]. They did so individually, each within his own psychological, biographical and historical possibilities, and therefore within the limits set by those possibilities. Their action was their own, and like every human action, an act conditioned by and itself conditioning its temporal and spatial environment. That as such it acquired this special function, was placed under the *auctoritas primaria*[EN81], the lordship of God, was surrounded and controlled and impelled by the Holy Spirit, and became an attitude of obedience in virtue of its direct relationship to divine revelation—that was their *theopneustia*[EN82]. In order to understand this biblical concept we cannot make any essential distinction between the thinking and speaking of the prophets and apostles and their writing, either in the sense in which many attempts have been made recently to limit inspiration to their thinking and speaking, or even to the prophetic experience which precedes and underlies their thinking and speaking, or in the sense that it rests distinctly in their writing. What we are told of it in the Old and New Testaments generally, and especially in 2 Tim. 3 and 2 Pet. 1, gives us no cause to adopt either of these explanations. As men, who lived then and there and not here and now, the prophets and apostles do, of course, exist for us only in what they have written. But in what they have written it is they themselves who do exist for us. In what they have written they exist visibly and audibly before us in all their humanity, chosen and called as witnesses of revelation, claimed by God and obedient to God, true men,

[506] speaking in the name of the true God, because they have heard His voice as we cannot hear it, as we can hear it only through their voices. And that is their *theopneustia*[EN83]. That is the mystery of the centre before which we always stand when we hear and read them: remembering that it was once the case (the recollection of the Church and our own recollection attest it) that their voice reproduced the voice of God, and therefore expecting that it will be so again. The biblical concept of *theopneustia*[EN84] points us therefore to the present, to the event which occurs for us: Scripture has this priority, it is the Word of God. But it only points us to it. It is not a substitute for it. It does not create it. How can it, seeing it is only a description of what God does in the humanity of His witnesses? But as it occurs in these two passages, it points us to what Holy Scripture was and will be. Yet even by this circuitous route it points to what it is. Therefore if we are to read and understand and expound Holy Scripture as the Word of God, it will always have to be a matter of taking the road which Scripture itself lays down for us.

In the statement: we believe that the the Bible is the Word of God, we must first emphasise and consider the word "believe." Believing does, of course, involve recognising and knowing. Believing is not an obscure and indeterminate feeling. It is a clear hearing, apperceiving, thinking and then speaking and doing. Believing is also a free human act, i.e., one which is not destroyed or disturbed by any magic; but, of course, a free act which as such is conditioned and determined by an encounter, a challenge, an act of lordship which confronts man, which man cannot bring about himself, which exists either as an event or not at all. Therefore believing is not something arbitrary. It does not

---

[EN80] authors
[EN81] primary authorship
[EN82] divine inspiration
[EN83] divine inspiration
[EN84] divine inspiration

control its object. It is a recognising, knowing, hearing, apperceiving, thinking, speaking and doing which is over-mastered by its object. Belief that the Bible is the Word of God presupposes, therefore, that this over-mastering has already taken place, that the Bible has already proved itself to be the Word of God, so that we can and must recognise it to be such. But when and where there is this proof, it must be a matter of the Word of God itself. We must say at once, that of itself the mere presence of the Bible and our own presence with our capacities for knowing an object does not mean and never will mean the reality or even the possibility of the proof that the Bible is the Word of God. On the contrary, we have to recognise that this situation as such, i.e., apart from faith, only means the impossibility of this proof. We have to recognise that faith as an irruption into this reality and possibility means the removing of a barrier in which we can only see and again and again see a miracle. And it is a miracle which we cannot explain apart from faith, or rather apart from the Word of God in which faith believes. Therefore the reality and possibility of it cannot be maintained or defended at all apart from faith and the Word. Nor can there be any assurances of it apart from faith and the Word. It is not only that we cannot attribute to ourselves any capacity or instrument for recognising the Word of God either in the Bible or elsewhere. It is also that if we are serious about the true humanity of the Bible, we obviously cannot attribute to the [507] Bible as such the capacity—and in this it is distinguished, as we have seen, from the exalted and glorified humanity of Jesus Christ—in such a way to reveal God to us that by its very presence, by the fact that we can read it, it gives us a hearty faith in the Word of God spoken in it. It is there and always there as a sign, as a human and temporal word—and therefore also as a word which is conditioned and limited. It witnesses to God's revelation, but that does not mean that God's revelation is now before us in any kind of divine revealedness. The Bible is not a book of oracles; it is not an instrument of direct impartation. It is genuine witness. And how can it be witness of divine revelation, if the actual purpose, act and decision of God in His only-begotten Son, as seen and heard by the prophets and apostles in that Son, is dissolved in the Bible into a sum total of truths abstracted from that decision—and those truths are then propounded to us as truths of faith, salvation and revelation? If it tries to be more than witness, to be direct impartation, will it not keep from us the best, the one real thing, which God intends to tell and give us and which we ourselves need? But if it does not try to do this, if it is really witness, we must understand clearly what it means and involves that in itself it is only witness. It means the existence of those barriers which can be broken down only by miracle. The men whom we hear as witnesses speak as fallible, erring men like ourselves. What they say, and what we read as their word, can of itself lay claim to be the Word of God, but never sustain that claim. We can read and try to assess their word as a purely human word. It can be subjected to all kinds of immanent criticism, not only in respect of its philosophical, historical and ethical content, but even of its religious and theological. We can establish lacunæ, inconsistencies and overemphases. We may be alienated by a figure like that of Moses. We may quarrel with James or with Paul. We may have to admit that we can make little or nothing of large tracts of the Bible, as is often the case with the records of other men. We can take offence at the Bible. And in the light of the claim or the assertion that the Bible is the Word of God—granting that the miracle of faith and the Word does not intervene—we are bound to take offence at it. But this is a miracle which we cannot presuppose. We can remember it. We can wait for it. But we cannot set it up like one chessman with others, which we can "move" at the right moment. Therefore we are bound to take offence at the Bible in the light of that claim. If we do not, we have not yet realised the importance of that claim. Only the miracle of faith and the Word can genuinely and seriously prevent us from taking offence at the Bible. But the *theopneustia*[EN85] of the Bible, the attitude of obedience in which it is written, the compelling fact that in it true men speak to us in the name of the true God: this—and here is the miracle of it—is not simply before us because the

[508] Bible is before us and we read the Bible. The *theopneustia*[EN86] is the act of revelation in which the prophets and apostles in their humanity became what they were, and in which alone in their humanity they can become to us what they are.

In the *De servo arbitrio* Luther made the important assertion: *Duae res sunt Deus et scriptura Dei, non minus quam duae res sunt creator et creatura Dei*[EN87] (*W.A.* 18, 606, 11). And again: "Thus Scripture is a book, to which there belongeth not only reading but also the right Expositor and Revealer, to wit, the Holy Spirit. Where He openeth not Scripture, it is not understood" (*Pred. üb. Lk.* 24[13f.], 1534, according to Rörer, *E.A.* 3, 334). But whoso knoweth not Christ, may hear the Gospel or hold the book in his hands, but its import he doth not have, for to have the Gospel without understanding is to have no Gospel. And to have the Scripture without knowledge of Christ is to have no Scripture, and is none other than to let these stars shine and yet not to perceive them (*Pred. üb. Mt.* 2[1-12], *Kirchenpostille*, 1522, *W.A.* 10[1], 1, 628, 3). According to Augustine there is only one reason why Scripture is not understood: *Nam dicere ut est, quis potest? Audeo dicere fratres mei, forsitan nec ipse Joannes dixit ut est, sed et ipse ut potuit! quia de Deo homo dixit: et quidem inspiratus a Deo sed tamen homo. Quia inspiratus, dixit aliquid; si non inspiratus esset, dixisset nihil; quia vero homo inspiratus, non totum quod est, dixit, sed quod potuit homo dixit*[EN88] (*In Joann. tract.* 1, 1). Augustine was here pointing to something which the older Protestant orthodoxy almost completely overlooked, especially with its doctrine of the *perspicuitas*[EN89] and *perfectio*[EN90] of Holy Scripture. We know what we say when we call the Bible the Word of God only when we recognise its human imperfection

---

[EN85] divine inspiration
[EN86] divine inspiration
[EN87] There are two entities: God and the Scripture of God, which are no less than two entities, creator and creature of God
[EN88] For who can speak (the truth) as it is? I venture to say, my brothers, perhaps not even John himself spoke it as it is, but rather as he was able! Since man has said of God, and indeed has been inspired of God, but he is nevertheless still man. Since he has been inspired, he has said something; if he had not been inspired, he would have said nothing. But since man has been inspired, he has not said everything there is to say; rather, man has said what he could
[EN89] perspicuity
[EN90] perfection

in face of its divine perfection, and its divine perfection in spite of its human imperfection. In relation to the obvious uncertainty of the traditional Canon, whether in respect of its compass or of its textual form, this could be conceded by many writers. F. Burmann, for instance, could say in this respect: *Doctrina ipsa et hoc verbum Dei vivum sese ipsum ostendit et cordibus electorum per operationem Spiritus sancti potenter insinuat, non obstante defectu vel vitio quocunque in organis istis externis. Non enim ab illis fides vel salus nostra pendet sed a doctrina ipsa iis contenta .... Doctrina sacra vi sua propria pollet et defectum organorum superat et licet per homines fallibiles praedicata, tamen plenam sui fidem in cordibus fidelium facit*[EN91] (*Syn. Theol.*, 1678, I, 5, 21). This very distinction between inspiration and therefore the divine infallibility of the Bible and its human fallibility has now to be carried through more radically.

First, there is the truism that we cannot expect or demand a compendium of solomonic or even divine knowledge of all things in heaven and earth, natural, historical and human, to be mediated to the prophets and apostles in and with their encounter with divine revelation, possessing which they have to be differentiated not only from their own but from every age as the bearers and representatives of an ideal culture and therefore as the inerrant proclaimers of all and every truth. They did not in fact possess any such compendium. Each in his own way and degree, they shared the culture of their age and environment, whose form and content could be contested by other ages and environments, and at certain points can still appear debatable to us. *Quod potuit homo dixit*[EN92]. This means that we cannot overlook or deny it or even alter it. In the biblical view of the world and man we are constantly coming up against presuppositions which are not ours, and statements and judgments which we cannot accept. Therefore at bottom we cannot avoid the tensions which arise at this point. We must reckon with the fact that this may be possible in points of detail, and we must always be ready for it. Instead of talking about the "errors" of the biblical authors in this sphere, if we want to go to the heart of things it is better to speak only about their "capacity for errors." For in the last resort even in relation to the general view of the world and man the insight and knowledge of our age can be neither divine nor even solomonic. But fundamentally we certainly have to face the objection and believe in spite of it! [509]

Not for all ages and countries, but certainly for our own, it is part of the stumbling-block that like all ancient literature the Old and New Testaments know nothing of the distinction of fact and value which is so important to us, between history, on the one hand, and saga and legend on the other. We must be clear that we cannot attach any final seriousness to this distinction and therefore any final difficulty to the objections to which it gives rise. But if we cannot deny that this distinction is now part of our apparatus of apperception, we cannot try to suppress or artificially to remove the doubts arising from it. We have to face up to them and to be clear that in the Bible it may be a matter of simply believing the Word of God, even though it meets us, not in the form of what we call history, but in the form of what we think must be called saga or legend.

But the vulnerability of the Bible, i.e., its capacity for error, also extends to its religious or theological content. The significance of a fact which was known to the early antiquity weighs on us more heavily to-day than formerly: that in their attestation of divine revelation (from the standpoint of the history of religion) the biblical authors shared the outlook and spoke the language of their own day—and, therefore, whether we like it or not, they did not speak

---

EN91 the teaching itself and that Word of God shows itself to be living and works powerfully in the hearts of the elect by the operation of the Holy Spirit, and any defect or fault of any kind in its external parts will not stand in the way. For our faith and salvation do not depend on those, but upon the teaching itself contained in them ... Sacred teaching will be strong in its own power and will overcome the defect of its parts, and though it has been proclaimed by fallible men, nevertheless it makes in the hearts of the faithful full confidence in itself

EN92 Man has said what he could

a special language of revelation radically different from that of their time. On the contrary, at point after point we find them echoing contemporaries in time and space who did not share their experience and witness, often resembling them so closely that it is impossible to distinguish between them. Not only part but all that they say is historically related and conditioned. It seems to be weakened, and therefore robbed of its character as witness to revelation, by the fact that it has so many "parallels." That they speak of Yahweh and of Jesus Christ, and not of other entities, is something we have laboriously to work out and prove from their usage as compared with that of their environment—and we can never do it with unimpeachable evidence, but in the last resort only on the presupposition of our faith. It amounts to this, that, as we see it, many parts, especially of the Old Testament, cannot be accepted as religious and theological literature, but only as documents of secular legislation and history and practical wisdom and poetry, although the Synagogue and later the Church claimed to find in them witness of revelation. It amounts to this, that not one of the biblical authors has done the Church and us the pleasure of giving his witness to divine revelation the form of a more or less complete and thorough-going theological system, that even in relation to the theology of a St. Paul and St. John we can only arrive later and by dint of much laborious construction at a certain hypothetical scheme. It amounts to this, that the biblical authors wrote with all the limitations imposed by their most varied possible historical and individual standpoints and outlooks, so that the content of their writing as a whole, for all the "harmony" upon which we touched earlier, does not in any sense constitute a system. But depending on how we can and want to look on them, there are distinctions of higher and lower, of utterances which are more central and peripheral, of witnesses which have to be understood literally and symbolically. There are obvious overlappings and contradictions—e.g., between the Law and the prophets, between John and the Synoptists, between Paul and James. But nowhere are we given a single rule by which to make a common order, perhaps an order of precedence, but at any rate a synthesis, of what is in itself such a varied whole. Nowhere do we find a rule which enables us to grasp it in such a way that we can make organic parts of the distinctions and evade the contradictions as such. We are led now one way, now another—each of the biblical authors obviously speaking only *quod potuit homo*[EN93]—and in both ways, and whoever is the author, we are always confronted with the question of faith. Again, we must be careful not to be betrayed into taking sides into playing off the one biblical man against the other, into pronouncing that this one or that has "erred." From what standpoint can we make any such pronouncement? For within certain limits and therefore relatively they are all vulnerable and therefore capable of error even in respect of religion and theology. In view of the actual constitution of the Old and New Testaments this is something which we cannot possibly deny if we are not to take away their humanity, if we are not to be guilty of Docetism. How can they be witnesses, if this is not the case? But if it is, even from this angle we come up against the stumbling-block which cannot be avoided or can be avoided only in faith.

[510]

To all this, however, we must still add as an independent matter something the importance of which the Church has only begun to recognise in our own day, although it has actually exercised a definite effect in every age. The Bible as the witness of divine revelation is in its humanity a product of the Israelitish, or to put it more clearly, the Jewish spirit. The man who in these Scriptures has said *quod potuit*[EN94] is *homo Judaeus*[EN95]. This is true—and no devices can avail us, for it is so closely bound up with the content—of the whole of the Bible, even of the whole of the New Testament Bible. It is once and for all the case that the

---

[EN93] what man could
[EN94] what he could
[EN95] Jewish man

content of these writings is the story of the divine election and calling and ruling of Israel, the story of the founding of the Church as the true Israel. And it is Israelites—and since, as we were told, the witnesses of revelation belong to the revelation themselves, it is necessarily Israelites—who attest all this to us in these Scriptures. If we want it otherwise, we will have to strike out not only the Old but all the New Testament as well, replacing them by something else, which is no longer a witness of divine revelation. The cry of dismay which is heard so strongly to-day is quite justified: we and the men of all nations are expected by Jews not only to interest ourselves in things Jewish, but in a certain and ultimately decisive sense actually to become Jews. And we may well ask whether all the other offences which we may take at the Bible, and will necessarily take if we are without faith, are not trifles compared with this offence. We may well ask whether there is any harder test of faith than the one which we see here. For the Bible itself does not hide the fact, but shows relentlessly that this is a hard demand, that the Jewish people is a hard and stiff-necked people, because it is a people which resists its God, the living God. It is characterised as the people which in its own Messiah finally rejected and crucified the Saviour of the world and therefore denied the revelation of God. It is in this way that the Bible is a Jewish book, the Jewish book. What has later Anti-Semitism to say compared with the accusation here levelled against the Jews? And what can it do compared with the judgment under which they have been put at the hand of God Himself long ago? But in all its folly and wickedness Anti-Semitism, which is as old as the Jewish nation itself, is not based, as its liberal critics think, upon an invincible and therefore recurrent arbitrariness and caprice, which can be kept in bounds by occasional pleas for humanity. Anti-Semitism is so strong to-day that it can hammer out a whole racial theory which claims to be a science, but in the last resort is naively directed against the Jews. And on this basis, which is ultimately an anti-Jewish basis, it can fashion a state. But this Anti-Semitism sees and intends something real which liberalism has never actually seen. This real thing is not, of course, identical with what it accuses and attacks. If it knew what it is, it would not accuse and attack it, for it would know—this is not the only reason, but one reason—that no power in the world can match what confronts it here. Modern German Anti-Semitism is concerned about Jewish blood and Jewish race. At best, these are signs of the real thing which encounters humanity unperceived and uncomprehended. But the real thing itself is the one natural proof of God adduced by God in the existence of the Jewish nation amongst other nations. It is hardly seen by Anti-Semites and liberals, but here a part of world-history gives the most direct witness to the biblical witness of revelation, and therefore to the God who is attested in the Bible. To this very day Israel confronts us as the people of God rejected [511] by God. To this very day Israel shows us that it is only in judgment that God exercises grace and that it is His free decision that He exercises grace in judgment. Israel reminds the world that it is the world, and it reminds the Church from what it has been taken. And because it is this people, the other nations are constantly enraged by its existence, revolting against it and wishing its destruction. Because it is this people, something hostile arises in all non-Jews against every Jew without exception, even the best and finest and noblest of Jews—and this quite apart from ethical or biological feelings and considerations. We cannot attribute the hostility simply to foreign blood and the like. If all the foreign blood which meets us every day in the welter of nations in the modern Western world were to give rise to this hostility, we could never escape it. By being hostile to Jewish blood, the world simply proves that it is the world: blind and deaf and stupid to the ways of God, as they are visibly before it in the existence of this people. And if the Church tries to co-operate in this hostility to Jewish blood, it simply proves that it too has become blind and deaf and stupid. In fact in the Jew, the non-Jew has to recognise himself, his own apostasy, his own sin, which he himself cannot forgive. And in the Jew he has to recognise Christ, the Messiah of Israel, who alone has made good his apostasy and pardoned his sin. Confronted in this way by the divine severity and

55

goodness, he is necessarily alienated by the existence of the Jew, and it is devilish madness if instead he abandons himself to a biological and moral alienation, working out his perverted hostility—as all perversions necessarily work themselves out—in accusations and attacks upon the Jews because of their national alienation. In this way he persists in his own apostasy. He acts as though he could forgive his own sins. In rejecting the Jew he rejects God. But that means that in this perversion we have to do not only with a real thing, but with the most real thing of all. And it is no accident if at the point where we have to do with this most real thing, in the Bible, we are asked point blank whether we are guilty of this perversion or not. For the Bible as the witness of divine revelation in Jesus Christ is a Jewish book. It cannot be read and understood and expounded unless we openly accept the language and thought and history of the Jews, unless we are prepared to become Jews with the Jews. But that means that we have to ask ourselves what is our attitude to the natural proof of God adduced in world-history by the continuing existence of the Jews, whether we are ready to accept it or to join the wolves in howling against it. And once we are clear that the liberal solution, i.e., the liberal evasion of the Jewish problem cannot help us, this question will necessarily be a very hard one. We may not always be alienated by the goodness and severity of God. But the Jew brings this alienation right into national and social life to-day, even in the Bible. Salvation means alienation, and "salvation is of the Jews" (Jn. 4^{22}). And because man will not be alienated, even for his own salvation, he rolls away the alienation on to the Jew. In that way it all becomes so simple. We can find so many grievances against the Jew. Once we have raised even our little finger in Anti-Semitism, we can produce such vital and profound reasons in favour of it, and they will all apply equally well to the Bible, not only to the Old but also to the New Testament, not only to the Rabbi Paul but also to the Rabbi Jesus of Nazareth of the first three Gospels. And we have to ask: What offence that we can take at the Bible is more pressing and goes deeper and is more general than the offence which it offers here? For if the liberal solution, which is no solution, collapses, how can we not be Anti-Semitic? At this point we need the miracle of the Word and faith if the offence is to cease, the perversion to be overcome, the Anti-Semitism in us all eliminated, the word of man, the Jewish word of the Bible, heard and accepted as the Word of God.

[512]   We started with Luther's saying: *Duae res sunt, Deus et scriptura Dei*[EN96]. We have learned from Augustine the one reason why this is the case. Luther is right, because the Bible is vulnerable. At every point it is the vulnerable word of man. Luther did not stop at this saying. For faith, God and Holy Scripture are not two things but one. We believe that Scripture is the Word of God. But when we say that, we say more than we can say in view of our own present: in recollection and expectation we look to the present of an event which God alone can bring about. It is not only in regard to the ultimately harmless question of tradition, but at every point, that the saying is true which points us to the miracle of God which we cannot bring about: *Doctrina sacra vi sua propria pollet et defectum organorum superat el licet per homines fallibiles praedicata, tamen plenam sui fidem in cordibus fidelium facit*[EN97]. Nothing else, or less, can lead to the decision which has to be made here.

But now in order to see the full acuteness of the problem, we must also emphasise and consider the concept "Word of God" in the statement: We believe that the Bible is the Word of God. What we have said so far cannot mean that the miracle just mentioned consists in our having to believe in a sort

---

[EN96] There are two entities: God and the Scripture of God

[EN97] Sacred teaching will be strong in its own power and will overcome the defect of its parts, and though it has been proclaimed by fallible men, nevertheless it makes in the hearts of the faithful full confidence in itself

of enthusiastic rapture which penetrates the barriers of offence by which the Bible is surrounded. Of course, the whole mystery of this statement rests on the fact that faith is not for everybody, and that even if we have it, it is a small and weak and inadequate because not a true faith. Therefore the miracle which has to take place if the Bible is to rise up and speak to us as the Word of God has always to consist in an awakening and strengthening of our faith. But the real difficulty of the statement does not rest in the side which concerns us men, but in that which concerns God Himself. It does not rest, therefore, in the severity of the offences caused by the humanity of the Bible. Although the question of faith of which we have just been speaking is central, it is only the secondary form of the question which has to be decided at this centre. Faith can in fact only be obedience and cling to the Word as a free human decision. And it can do so only because the Word has come to it and made and introduced it as faith. Therefore faith cannot simply grasp at the Bible, as though by the energy of its grasping, perhaps that highest energy which may even rise to enthusiasm, the Word of God would come to it in spite of all the offences (which are therefore overcome by the enthusiasm). Rather, the energy of this grasping itself rests on the prior coming of the Word of God. Faith does not live by its own energy and therefore not even by its arousing and strengthening by the Word of God. It lives by the energy of the movement in which the Word of God in Holy Scripture has come to us in spite of all the offences which we might take at it, and has first created our faith. Whether this has happened or not is the objective mystery which confronts and precedes the question of faith, the mystery of the statement that "the Bible is the Word of God." In the statement that "the Bible is the Word of God," we cannot suddenly mean a lesser, less potent, less ineffable and majestic Word of God, than that which has occupied us in the doctrine of the Trinity and in the doctrine of Christ and of the Holy Spirit. There is only one Word of God and that is the eternal Word of [513] the Father which for our reconciliation became flesh like us and has now returned to the Father, to be present to His Church by the Holy Spirit. In Holy Scripture, too, in the human word of His witnesses, it is a matter of this Word and its presence. That means that in this equation it is a matter of the miracle of the divine Majesty in its condescension and mercy. If we take this equation on our lips, it can only be as an appeal to the promise in virtue of which this miracle was real in Jesus Christ and will again be real in the word of His witnesses. In this equation we have to do with the free grace and the gracious freedom of God. That the Bible is the Word of God cannot mean that with other attributes the Bible has the attribute of being the Word of God. To say that would be to violate the Word of God which is God Himself—to violate the freedom and the sovereignty of God. God is not an attribute of something else, even if this something else is the Bible. God is the Subject, God is Lord. He is Lord even over the Bible and in the Bible. The statement that the Bible is the Word of God cannot therefore say that the Word of God is tied to the Bible. On the contrary, what it must say is that the Bible is tied to the Word of God. But

57

that means that in this statement we contemplate a free decision of God—not in uncertainty but in certainty, not without basis but on the basis of the promise which the Bible itself proclaims and which we receive in and with the Church. But its content is always a free decision of God, which we cannot anticipate by grasping at the Bible—even if we do it with the greatest faith of which we are capable, but the freedom of which we will have to recognise when we grasp at the Bible in the right way. The Bible is not the Word of God on earth in the same way as Jesus Christ, very God and very man, is that Word in heaven. The being of Jesus Christ as the Word of God even in His humanity requires neither promise nor faith. The act in which He became the Word of God in His humanity requires neither repetition nor confirmation. But in His eternal presence as the Word of God He is concealed from us who now live on earth and in time. He is revealed only in the sign of His humanity, and especially in the witness of His prophets and apostles. But by nature these signs are not heavenly-human, but earthly- and temporal-human. Therefore the act of their institution as signs requires repetition and confirmation. Their being as the Word of God requires promise and faith—just because they are signs of the eternal presence of Christ. For if they are to act as signs, if the eternal presence of Christ is to be revealed to us in time, there is a constant need of that continuing work of the Holy Spirit in the Church and to its members which is always taking place in new acts. If the Church lives by the Bible because it is the Word of God, that means that it lives by the fact that Christ is revealed in the Bible by the work of the Holy Spirit. That means that it has no power or control

[514]   over this work. It can grasp at the Bible. It can honour it. It can accept its promise. It can be ready and open to read and understand and expound it. All these things it can and should do. The human side of the life of the Church with the Bible rightly consists in all these things. But apart from these things, the human side of its life with the Bible can consist only in the fact that it prays that the Bible may be the Word of God here and now, that there may take place that work of the Holy Spirit, and therefore a free applying of the free grace of God. Over and above that: the fulfilment of this prayer, that the Bible is the Word of God here and now in virtue of the eternal, hidden, heavenly presence of Christ—that is the divine side of the life of the Church. Its reality cannot be doubted: the fulness of the reality of the life of the Church with the Bible lies in this its divine aspect. Also the certainty of the perception of it cannot be doubted: it is mediated to us in the promise, it can be grasped in faith. But the very fact that this happens, that the promise speaks to us and that we are obedient in faith, is always before us as the question which has to be answered again and again by the work of the Holy Spirit. This is the event we look to, if—here on earth in the Church non-triumphant, but militant—we confess that the Bible is God's Word. For in doing so we acknowledge God and His grace, and the freedom of His grace.

By means of this criterion we must now test what the Church has said about the inspiration of Holy Scripture in relation to the sayings in 2 Tim. 3[16] and 2 Pet. 1[20f.] In the so-called doctrine of inspiration the point at issue was and is how far, i.e., on the basis of what relationship between the Holy Spirit as God opening up man's ears and mouth for His Word and the Bible, the latter can be read and understood and expounded as a human witness of His revelation as the Word of God and therefore in the strict sense as Holy Scripture. On the basis of our latest consideration the criterion will necessarily be this: that the doctrine of inspiration will always have to describe the relation between the Holy Spirit and the Bible in such a way that the whole reality of the unity between the two is safeguarded no less than the fact that this unity is a free act of the grace of God, and therefore for us its content is always a promise.

Now first we will show the need for this criterion from two New Testament passages.

In 2 Cor. 3[4–18] Paul made it clear how he primarily wanted the reading of the Old Testament as a witness of the revelation of Jesus Christ to be understood by the Christian congregation. The Old Testament Scripture as such is described by Paul (v. 6) as γράμμα[EN98], i.e., as that which is simply written and indeed prescribed as holy and necessary for salvation. There is *per se*[EN99] no disqualification of Scripture in this designation. Nor is there when Paul goes on to say that the γράμμα[EN100] kills but the Spirit gives life. This is said in favour of the Spirit but not against Scripture, or only against a Scripture received and read without the Spirit. From this standpoint we ought calmly to reflect on Mt. 5[17f.], where it says that not one jot or tittle can pass from the law until it is completely fulfilled, and that therefore even the least of its commandments must not be "broken." Paul claims for himself the ministry of the new covenant (v. 6), the ministry of the Spirit (v. 8), the ministry which has an incomparably greater "glory" (v. 9). Yet he does not contest, but expressly presupposes, that even the ministry of the γράμμα[EN101] as such has its "glory" (v. 9f.). And Paul does not exclude the ministry of Scripture when he contrasts it with his own ministry, the spiritual ministry of the new [515] covenant. On the contrary, he regards his own ministry as the true ministry of Scripture, i.e., its fulfilment. This is proved by the fact that in this very section he is commenting on Ex. 34. It makes no difference that as such and apart from the work of the Holy Spirit the written not only does not minister life, but ministers death; indeed, in its own way it proves that it is and remains that which is prescribed by divine authority. Paul must have known the theories of Talmudic and Alexandrian Jewry concerning the divine-human origin of the Torah, i.e., all the Old Testament Canon. If, as we can certainly assume, he for his part affirmed a special inspiration of Scripture by God, it was obviously only in connexion with his view of the present attestation of the same God by the work of the Holy Spirit. For in 2 Cor. 3 everything depends on the fact that without this work of the Spirit Scripture is veiled, however great its glory may be and whatever its origin. This is the case in that reading of the Scripture by the Synagogue, which is foreshadowed by the veiling of Moses' countenance (Ex. 34). What God has prescribed is there and the men who read it are also there, but over their hearts there hangs a veil. Their thinking is rebellious. For them the open book is in fact a closed book. Only a return to the Lord could set aside the curtain and open up for them access to Scripture. But the Lord, by whose presence the freedom which has already been objectively created "in Christ" (v. 14) can now be achieved, is the Spirit (v. 17). All we who are Christians, and as such, are an unveiled mirror of the glory of the Lord. We know how to read and receive what the Jews read but do not know how to read and receive. But we do so, not by virtue of any capacity of our own as distinct from them, but only of the Lord who is the

---

EN 98 letter
EN 99 in itself
EN100 letter
EN101 letter

Spirit—or from the Lord the Spirit (v. 18). We do so, not as though we had made ourselves capable of it, but because God makes us capable of it, as it tells us in vv. 4–6 with a primary reference to the personal ministry of Paul. We could hardly say more clearly that the holy and redemptive nature of Scripture is only a preliminary. The Christian community cannot stop at this preliminary. It is as little helped by the reality of it as the world or the Synagogue. Indeed, like the world or the Synagogue, it is brought under judgment by this reality. But of itself it cannot go on to fulfil and complete this preliminary. If it finds life where the Synagogue can only meet its condemnation, it is the grace of the Holy Spirit, an event for whose occurrence only God can be praised.

We have an interesting parallel in 1 Cor. 2⁶⁻¹⁶ to the extent that Paul here speaks of his own addresses and therefore of what he has written as an apostle from exactly the same standpoint. Paul is conscious of speaking wisdom, "the wisdom of God in a mystery," the hidden wisdom which was predetermined by God before all times to our glory, the wisdom which was not recognised by the powerful of this aeon and therefore smitten on the cross: that which in itself is not accessible to the eye or ear or heart of man, but "which God hath prepared for them that love him" (vv. 6–9). Of this "wisdom in a mystery," i.e., of the revelation of God which took place in Jesus Christ, he says no more and no less than that he, Paul, speaks or says or expresses it. *Λαλοῦμεν σοφίαν* EN102. How can he ever come to do this unless God opens up the way to it, unless it is first of all revealed, and indeed revealed by the Spirit? As the human spirit knows human things, so it is the divine Spirit—He alone, but He perfectly and without doubt—who knows divine things. This Spirit he, Paul, has received, that he may know as such the divine benefits of the divine wisdom *(τὰ ὑπὸ τοῦ θεοῦ χαρισθέντα ἡμῖν* EN103 vv. 10–12). But as he sees it, this does not exhaust the work of the Holy Ghost. In exact correspondence with this knowledge of the benefits indicated to us by God's wisdom he now believes he can and must express them: *οὐκ ἐν διδακτοῖς ἀνθρωπίνης σοφίας λόγοις, αλλ' ἐν διδακτοῖς πνεύατος* EN104: not in the words which man's wisdom teacheth but which the Spirit teacheth: *πνευματικοῖς πνευματικὰ συγκρίνοντες* EN105: measuring and embracing in spiritual words that spiritual reality (v. 13). [516] In face of this self-utterance we cannot assume that Paul did not take account of an inspiration, even a real and verbal inspiration, of the Old Testament hagiographa. We have therefore no reason to think that the *θεόπνευστος* EN106 of 2 Tim. 3¹⁶ is non-Pauline. At all events Paul distinctly describes himself, not merely as a witness of the divine benefits, so that his statements about them have the value of a historical record, but more than that, as one who by the Spirit is enabled and led to know these benefits, and even more, as one who by the same Spirit is authorised and taught to speak about them. There now follows the expression which is decisive in this connexion. Paul is aware that man in himself and as such, the living creature man, the *ψυχικὸς ἄνθρωπος* EN107, does not receive what on the basis of the work of the Spirit is said in this way about the benefits of God *(τὰ τοῦ πνεύματος τοῦ θεοῦ* EN108). It is foolishness to him, because he cannot know it. It is only spiritually, i.e., on the basis of the same work of the same Spirit, by which he can know and therefore speak about these benefits, that they can be known and therefore received: *πνευματικῶς ἀνακρίνεται* EN109 (v. 14). There is therefore a state of man which is radically different from that of the

---

EN102 We speak wisdom
EN103 the things given to us by God
EN104 not in the teachings of human wisdom, but in the teachings of the Spirit
EN105 assessing spiritual things by spiritual means
EN106 'divinely inspired'
EN107 carnal man
EN108 the things of the Spirit of God
EN109 spiritually discerned

ψυχικὸς ἄνθρωπος EN110. This is the state of the πνευματικός EN111, of the man who is endowed with the Spirit and enlightened and led by the Spirit. But what is the particular feature of this state? Simply and yet very strongly this, that as a man he sees and understands what that other who is himself taught and led by the Spirit says: ἀνακρίνει τὰ πάντα EN112. The circle which led from the divine benefits to the apostle instructed by the Spirit and authorised to speak by the Spirit now closes at the hearer of the apostle, who again by the Spirit is enabled to receive as is necessary. The hearer, too, in his existence as such is part of the miracle which takes place at this point. No less than the apostle, indeed no less than the wisdom which is not known by this aeon but revealed to the apostle, the hearer of the apostolic word is himself a mystery to everyone (and as Paul sees it especially to himself). As a hearer, he is understood by no one. αὐτὸς δέ ὑπ᾽ οὐδενός ἀνακρίνεται EN113 (v. 15). At every point, Paul concludes, we have to do with the thoughts of the Lord, to whom no one can give counsel, i.e., who has no equal, no one therefore who is able to think with Him and to know His thoughts: τίς γὰρ ἔγνω νοῦν κυρίου, ὃς συμβιβάσει αὐτόν EN114. To know Him three keys are necessary. Paul is conscious that he has two of them, indeed that he himself represents them in his existence as an apostle—between the hidden wisdom of God, i.e., the benefit of its revelation, and the spiritual man, there stands the man who has the "thoughts of Christ," the apostle, who himself is empowered by the Spirit to know and declare that which is hidden: ἡμεῖς δέ νοῦν χριστοῦ ἔχομεν EN115 (v. 16); faced by it—and here the question arises whether the third key is available—the hearer has to decide whether as a ψυχικὸς ἄνθρωπος EN116 he will not receive or recognise it but regard it as foolishness— whether by the help of the same Spirit, who has spoken to and through the apostle, he will himself be a spiritual man who will listen to what the apostle has to say to him?

If we keep the two parts side by side, we get a fairly complete picture of how the function of a witness to revelation appeared on both sides at any rate to Paul according to its true character and limits. With all other men the witness stands before the mystery of God and the benefit of His revelation. That this mystery is disclosed to him is the first thing, and that he can speak of it the second, in the miracle of his existence as a witness. But the mystery of God, now entrusted to the human witness, will still remain a mystery, as it encounters the Synagogue, which only has and reads the γράμμα EN117, and as it encounters the living creature, man, for whom the word of the apostle is always foolishness, if its self-disclosure does not go a step further, even in its form as human witness, if the same Spirit who has created the witness does not bear witness of its truth to men, to those who hear and read. This self-disclosure in its totality is *theopneustia* EN118, the inspiration of the word of the prophets and apostles. It is justifiable to regard the content of these two passages as a commentary on the brief data which we have on this matter in 2 Tim. 3[16f.] and 2 Pet. 1[19f.] And it is justifiable to [517] measure by the content of these passages what was later said about it in the Church.

But already in the literature of the early Church we must be struck by three things.

1. There is soon displayed a striking inclination to concentrate interest in the inspiration of Scripture upon one particular point in that circle, and to limit it to it: namely, to the work

---

EN110 carnal man
EN111 spiritual man
EN112 he understands all things
EN113 but he himself is judged by no one
EN114 for who has known the mind of the Lord that he may instruct Him?
EN115 we have the mind of Christ
EN116 carnal man
EN117 letter
EN118 divinely inspired

of the Spirit in the emergence of the spoken or written prophetic and apostolic word as such. We have seen that Paul, too, does take serious cognisance of a holy γράμμα[EN119], of something prescribed by divine authority in the Canon of the Old Covenant. We have seen that he also considers even his own words to be "taught of the Spirit." Now this point in the circle of the work of the Spirit cannot be denied or regarded as unimportant. The way of inspiration does actually go through this phase. But what was the significance of the one-sided concentration of the Church's interest on this particular point? Can we understand what it means that the prophets and apostles spoke and wrote by the Holy Spirit, if we do not keep equally before us that that of which they spoke and wrote, the object of their witness, the beneficent revelation of the mystery of God, was mediated to them only by the Spirit, and that the hearers and readers of what they spoke and wrote have need of the work of the same Spirit if they are really to read and hear it? Paul is clearly speaking about an act of the free grace of God. But is not the contemplation of this act necessarily obscured to the extent that the one aspect is, as it were, pushed into the forefront as a conclusion and datum which we can easily grasp; that it was and still is the case that these men spoke and wrote what they did by the Holy Spirit? Of course, they did speak and write in that way and in no other. We cannot possibly reject this truth which comes from Paul himself. But is the grace and the mystery of God, which we rightly see in it, really the grace and mystery of the Word of God in the full biblical sense of the concept, if we think of it as reduced to this act of speaking? To what sphere do we now belong? Is it an accident that we find the apologists of the 2nd century pushed in this direction? Is it not the attempt to make the miracle of God in the witness of His revelation perspicuous to everybody, conceivable in its inconceivability, natural for all the emphasising of its supernatural character, a factor with which we can reckon even though we do ascribe it to the Holy Spirit, just as in the last resort the Jews could reckon as given factors with their inspired Torah and the heathen with their Sibylline and similar books? What are we to think of Theophilus of Antioch (*Ad. Autol.* 2, 9) and Pseudo-Justin (*Coh. ad Graecos* 37) when they did actually ascribe the same inspiredness to the prophets and the Sibyllines?

2. Already in the early Church we see a tendency to insist that the operation of the Holy Spirit in the inspiration of the biblical writers extended to the individual phraseology used by them in the grammatical sense of the concept. If I am right, the first express statement along these lines is to be found in the *Protrepticus* of *Clement of Alexandria* (IX, 82, 1): that the fact that according to Mt. 5^{18} not even the slightest jot or tittle of Scripture can be destroyed is based on the truth that it has all been spoken by the mouth of the Lord, the Holy Spirit. And a hundred years later Gregory Nazianzus (*Orat.* 2, 105) writes that every slightest line and stroke of Scripture is due to the minute care of the Spirit and that even the slenderest nuance of the writers is not in vain or displayed to us in vain. Here, too, in the light of Mt. $5^{17f.}$ we must be on our guard against trying to say anything different. If in their concrete existence and therefore in their concrete speaking and writing the witnesses of revelation belong to revelation, if they spoke by the Spirit what they knew by the Spirit, and if we really have to hear them and therefore their words—then self-evidently we have to hear all their words with the same measure of respect. It would be arbitrary to relate their inspiration only to such parts of their witness as perhaps appear important to us, or not to their words as such but only to the views and thoughts which evoke them. If inspiration is co-ordinated into that circle of God's manifestation by the Spirit only for our illumination by the same Spirit, the inspiration of the biblical witnesses which is the link between the two, between God and us, can and must be regarded quite definitely not merely as real but as verbal inspiration. But

[518]

[EN119] letter

the question is whether it has not been taken out of the circle and regarded as verbal-inspiredness, something for which we give thanks to the grace of God, but which is itself no longer understood as grace but as a bit of higher nature? What those Church fathers said was in itself correct. But where do we find in them the context in which Paul certainly did speak implicitly of verbal inspiration? He did not speak of verbal inspiredness—otherwise he would have spoken very differently of the Old Testament in 2 Cor. 3 and of his own word in 1 Cor. 2. And we must not speak of verbal inspiredness in the sphere of the Church if the Church is not to have that false assurance of the Word of God which the Jews and heathen have betrayed by the very fact that the real Word of God is strange to them.

3. Already we find a tendency to explain the event of the inspiration of the biblical authors in a way which suggests that there is a secret desire to evade the asserted mystery of this matter: that here a real human word is the real Word of God, the real humanity of it being more or less compromised by a foolish conception of its divinity. Again we cannot object but only approve when Irenaeus (*C.o.h.* II, 28, 2) bases the perfection of the Holy Scriptures on the fact that they are *a verbo Dei et Spiritu eius dictae*[EN120]. That God Himself says what His witnesses say, that those who hear them hear Him, is something that we often read in the Bible itself and quite patently: in itself it is the right expression for the mystery of its speech. But it is obviously going too far, or, in view of the magnitude of the mystery, not far enough, when Gregory the Great (*Moralia praef.* 1, 2) will not let the human writers of Holy Scripture weigh at all as the authors of it, or allow them to be considered as such: it being all one to the recipient of the letter of a great man, in whose hand he has actually dictated the letter. *Ipse igitur haec scripsit, qui scribenda dictavit*[EN121]. Where there is this idea of a "dictation" of Holy Scripture through Christ or the Holy Spirit, is not the doctrine of inspiration slipping into Docetism? If I am right, it was Augustine (*De consensu evang.* I, 35, 54) who first spoke clearly about a divine dictation, or the encountering of it through the biblical writers: *Quidquid enim ille (Christus) de suis factis et dictis nos legere voluit hoc scribendum illis tamquam suis manibus imperavit*[EN122]. Of course this could and can be regarded non-docetically as a picture of the strictness of the control under which the hagiographers stood and the strictness of their obedience. But if it was not intended docetically, how else can we think of it except—again on the Jewish and heathen model—as a mantically-mechanical operation? And if it is not to be regarded as mantically-mechanical, how can it not be docetic? The same choice is even more stringently imposed when we are told by the 2nd century Athenagoras (*Leg. pro Chr.* 7 and 9) that the Holy Spirit moved the mouths of the prophets as His organs, snatching away from them their own thoughts (κατ' ἔκτασιν τῶν ἐν αὐτοῖς λογισμῶν), and using them as a flute-player blows on his flute; or by Pseudo-Justin (*Coh. ad. Graecos* 8) and later by Hippolytus (*De Antichristo* 2), that the Logos was the plectrum, by means of which the Holy Spirit played on them as on a zither or harp. The obvious aim in all these passages was a stabilising of the word of man as the Word of God and an accompanying assurance in respect of the Word of God. But the price which had to be paid for this apparent gain was far too high. By, as it were, damping down the word of man as such, by transmuting it into a word of man which is real only in appearance, a Word of God which can be grasped in human speech, the whole mystery was lost, the mystery of the freedom of its presence both in the mouths of the biblical witnesses and also in our ears and hearts. And the miracle which took its place,

---

[EN120] dictated by the Word of God and His Spirit
[EN121] Therefore, he who dictated these things to be written, himself wrote these things
[EN122] For whatever He (Christ) wills us to read concerning His deeds and words, he has commanded to be written, as much by them as by His own hands

[519]   which was recounted in various forms about the biblical writers and the result of which was admired in the Bible, has only the name in common with the miracle of the presence of the Word of God.

Already the doctrines of inspiration of the early Church were leading to a rather naive secularisation of the whole conception of revelation. Certainly the existence of the prophets and apostles, the existence of the Bible, is a very surprising and praiseworthy phenomenon. But instead of being placed at once into the circle of the mystery which proceeds without a break from the revelation of the triune God to the present illumination of our hearts, this fact was incorporated into a view of things in which inspirations and inspired men and states have a place with all kinds of other things: have their place, that is, in the Bible, to which in a more or less well-fenced circle there may be added what we accept of saints recognised by the Church and the teaching office of the Church itself. From this standpoint we understand at once how it was possible for the unique authority of Scripture to be so relativised in relation to Church tradition as it actually was in the doctrine of Catholicism and as it was officially recognised to be at the Council of Trent. In the secular compression of inspiration on which it rests, as opposed to the inspiration in which it is known, it obviously cannot be regarded as a unique reality compared with similar phenomena both outside and inside the Church. Probably the struggle and reaction against Montanism had already contributed quite early to this secular compression of inspiration to an objective inspiredness and its continuations as authorised by the Church. But however it took place, in this compression, in the change to an objective inspiredness, even the doctrine of an objective inspiration of the Bible necessarily lost its meaning as one moment in the doctrine of the Word of God, i.e., the doctrine of the Word of God itself necessarily lost its original and comprehensive meaning. The doctrine of Scripture acquired the character of a description of a phenomenon of history and nature which is certainly remarkable, but which can still be established and studied neutrally, which as such could in the last resort be the phenomenon of the origin of the documents of any sort of religious foundation. This is the doubtful element in what is usually accepted as the standard doctrine of inspiration. On this point read the very acute and cautious but in their purely phenomenological character very disturbing expositions of Thomas Aquinas on the nature of prophecy (*S. Theol.* II 2, *qu.* 171 ff.). How obscure it now is that it is the Holy Spirit of God who in the revelation of Jesus Christ has made prophets prophets, and who alone can guide and enlighten us to recognise them as such. We can and certainly should take comfort in the fact that the Bible was actually read in the early and mediaeval Churches, even though on other presuppositions than those we find in the teaching of the Bible as such. We can come across the fine thought in Augustine (*De civ. Dei* XI, 4) that the author of Gen. 1[1] at once proved himself to be a true witness of God by the fact that, by the same Spirit in which he himself knew the revelation of God, he also prophesied our future faith. And we can hear him pray (*Conf.* XI, 3, 5): *Qui illi servo tuo dedisti haec dicere, da et mihi haec intelligere*[EN123]. Obviously, a recollection of the actual setting of the inspiration of the Bible was never completely lost. But this being the case, we must anxiously ask why it was not strong enough to win recognition in the doctrine of the Bible and in that way to exert an influence upon the actual relationship of the Bible and the Church.

What took place in the 16th century proved itself a Reformation of the Church by the fact that with the restoration of the authority and lordship of the Bible in the Church there now arose a new reading and understanding and expounding of Scripture in accordance with

---

[EN123] You who have granted to this servant of yours to say these things, grant also that I may understand them

this authority and lordship. On the same lines there grew up a new doctrine of Scripture, and especially of the inspiration of Scripture, corresponding to Scripture itself (cf. for what follows Paul Schempp, *Luthers Stellung z. heiligen Schrift*, 1928. The teaching of Luther really ought to be taken together with that of Calvin, but so far the latter has not been expounded on the basis of these essential insights.) In the Reformation doctrine of inspiration the following points must be decisive. [520]

1. The Reformers took over unquestioningly and unreservedly the statement on the inspiration, and indeed the verbal inspiration, of the Bible, as it is explicitly and implicitly contained in those Pauline passages which we have taken as our basis, even including the formula that God is the author of the Bible, and occasionally making use of the idea of a dictation through the biblical writers. How could it be otherwise? Not with less but with greater and more radical seriousness they wanted to proclaim the subjection of the Church to the Bible as the Word of God and its authority as such. Even in his early period Luther demanded, *ut omne verbum vocale, per quemcunque dicatur, velut Domino ipso dicente suscipiamus, credamus, cedamus et humiliter subiiciamus nostrum sensum. Sic enim iustificabimur et non aliter*[EN124] (*Comm. on Rom.* 3²², 1515–16, *Fi.* II, 89, 31). And on the same passage (obviously appealing to Jas. 2¹⁰, *Fi.* II, 86, 10): *Fides enim consistit in indivisibili, aut ergo tota est et omnia credenda credit aut nulla, si unum non credit*[EN125]. At least, therefore, Luther is not inconsistent when we hear him thundering polemically at the end of his life: "Therefore, we either believe roundly and wholly and utterly, or we believe nothing: the Holy Ghost doth not let Himself be severed or parted, that He should let one part be taught or believed truly and the other part falsely .... For it is the fashion of all heretics, that they begin first with a single article, but they must then all be denied and altogether, like a ring which is of no further value when it has a break or cut, or a bell which when it is cracked in one place will not ring any more and is quite useless" (*Kurzes Bekenntnis vom heiligen Sakrament*, 1544, *W.A.* 54, 158, 28). Therefore Calvin is not guilty of any disloyalty to the Reformation tendency when he says of Holy Scripture that its authority is recognised only when it is realised that it *e caelo fluxisse acsi vivae ipsae Dei voces illic exaudirentur*[EN126] (*Instit.* I, 7, 1), when it is realised that *autorem eius esse Deum. Itaque summa Scripturae probatio passim a Dei loquentis persona sumilur*[EN127] (*ib.*, 7, 4). *Constituimus* (*non secus acsi ipsius Dei numen illic intueremur*) *hominum ministerio ab ipsissimo Dei ore ad nos fluxisse*[EN128] (*ib.*, 7, 5). In Calvin's sermon on 2 Tim. 3¹⁶ᶠ· (*C.R.* 54, 283 f.) God is constantly described as the *autheur*[EN129] of Holy Scripture and in his commentary on the same passage we seem to hear a perfect echo of the voice of the early Church, when we read: *Hoc principium est, quod religionem nostram ab aliis omnibus discernit, quod scimus Deum nobis loquutum esse, certoque persuasi simus, non ex suo sensu loquutos esse prophetas, sed, ut erant Spiritus sancti organa tantum protulisse, quae coelitus mandata fuerunt; quisquis ergo vult in scripturis proficere, hoc secum inprimis constituat, legem et prophetas non esse*

[EN124] that we accept, believe, yield to, and humbly subject our reason to every single word through whomever it is spoken as spoken by God Himself

[EN125] For faith is indivisible: so either it is whole and it believes everything it should believe, or it is nothing if it fails to believe at one point

[EN126] has flowed from heaven and the very living words of God can be heard from it

[EN127] its author is God. Therefore the supreme proof of Scripture is found in the person of God speaking everywhere in it

[EN128] We have established (just as if we see the presence of God Himself there) that it has flowed to us through man's service from the very mouth of God Himself

[EN129] author

doctrinam hominum arbitrio proditam, sed a Spiritu sancto dictatam[EN130] (*C.R.* 52, 383). It is clear that in themselves the questions we raised in relation to the corresponding statements of Augustine and Gregory the Great could also be raised here. But it is no less clear that here they are set in a context which in fact makes them innocuous. In spite of the use of these concepts neither a mantico-mechanical nor a docetic conception of biblical inspiration is in the actual sphere of Calvin's thinking. This does not mean, of course, that these statements, like Luther's, could not later lose this context and give fresh rise to the questions.

2. The Reformers saw and stated once more the fact that the inspiration of the Bible as inspiration by the Holy Spirit is not any kind of miracle, nor is it comparable with any other alleged or real inspiration. For it rests on the relationship of the biblical witnesses to the very definite content of their witness. It is indeed this content which inspires them, i.e., which in their speaking and writing gives them a part in the Holy Spirit and therefore makes their writing Holy Scripture. It is not of itself, but—as Luther especially always insisted—of Christ as its Lord and King that Scripture has and again and again acquires for us its clarity as the divine Word: Others have strange thoughts and remove themselves from Christ, and want something new. But Holy Scripture refuses to know or put before us anything but Christ. And whoso therefore goes to Scripture or is led by Scripture to Christ, it is well with him and he is on the right path (*Pred. üb.* 2. *Buch Mose* 1524 on *Ex.* 7³, *W.A.* 16, 113, 22). All Scripture has its light from the resurrection: *Quid enim potest in scripturis augustius latere reliquum, postquam fractis signaculis et voluto ab hostio sepulchri lapide, illud summum mysterium proditum est, Christum filium Dei factum hominem, Esse Deum trinum et unum, Christum pro nobis passum et regiturum aeternaliter? ... Tolle Christum e scripturis, quid amplius in illis invenies?*[EN131] (*De servo arb.*, 1525, *W.A.* 18, 606, 24). But in this way the doctrine of the inspiration of the Bible is restored as the doctrine of a divine mystery which we cannot grasp and which is therefore true and redemptive. For: *Deus incomprehensibilis*[EN132]. Christ cannot be understood, *quia est Deus*[EN133]. He cannot be mastered or conceived, because we live here (*W.A. Ti.* 2, 125, 4). No man, be he apostle or prophet, much less I or those like me, can know Christ fully in this life, can so know and understand truly who and what he should be. For He is true, eternal, almighty God and yet He hath taken on Himself mortal nature, and shown the highest obedience and humility even unto death; hence He Himself saith, "I am meek and lowly of heart." Now I cannot adequately express how it is with my own mind and heart when I am merry or sad; how can I then express the lofty affections and emotions of Christ? (*W.A. Ti.* 6, 65, 36). We must insist that on this retrospective side Calvin spoke rather less clearly and acutely than Luther. But he, too, sees that *hoc animo legendas esse scripturas ut illic inveniamus Christum. Quisquis ab hoc scopo deflectet, utcunque discendo se fatiget tota vita, nunquam ad*

[521]

[EN130] This is the principle which distinguishes our religion from all others: that we know that God has spoken to us, and we have been convinced with certainty that the prophets have not spoken with their own understanding but that they have merely gone forth as instruments of the Holy Spirit, which have been commanded from heaven. Therefore, whoever wants to advance in the Scriptures, let him take this on board first and foremost, that the Law and the Prophets are not teaching that has been passed down by the will of men, but have been dictated by the Holy Spirit

[EN131] For what else that is more to be revered can lie hidden in the Scriptures, after the seals have been broken, the stone has been rolled away from the sealed tomb, and the supreme mystery has been revealed: that Christ the Son of God has been made man; that God is three and one; that Christ has suffered for us and will reign eternally? Take Christ out of the Scriptures, and what else can you find in them

[EN132] God is incomprehensible

[EN133] since He is God

scientiam veritatis perveniet. Quid enim sapere absque Dei sapientia possumus[EN134] (*Comm. on Jn.* 539, *C.R.* 47, 125). According to Calvin it is also part of the equipment of the biblical writers in their speaking and writing of the Word of God that they had a prior *firma certitudo*[EN135] in their hearts regarding the divine nature of the experiences to which they then speak and write. *Semper enim Deus indubiam fecit verbo suo fidem*[EN136]. It is clear that our knowledge of their inspiration must in the first instance rest on the basis on which they themselves stand (*Instit.* I, 6, 2). Therefore for the Reformers the question as to the inspired Word was as such always the question of that which inspires and controls the Word. For them the literally inspired Bible was not at all a revealed book of oracles, but a witness to revelation, to be interpreted from the standpoint of and with a view to its theme, and in conformity with that theme.

3. The Reformers restored the context in which the inspiration of the Bible must be understood on the other side as well. As Luther insisted in innumerable passages the word of Scripture given by the Spirit can be recognised as God's Word only because the work of the Spirit which has taken place in it takes place again and goes a step further, i.e., becomes an event for its hearers or readers. How else will God be recognised except by God Himself? *Spiritus solus intelligit Scripturas recte et secundum Deum. Alias autem, etsi inielligunt non intelligunt*[EN137] (*Comm. on Rom.* 7¹, *Fi.* II, 165, 25). The nature of the heretic can be understood from this standpoint: *haereticus est, qui scripturas sanctas alio sensu quam Spiritus flagitat, exponit*[EN138] (*Ad librum ... Ambr. Catharini*, 1521, *W.A.* 7, 710, 16). And it was on the same point that Calvin expressed himself so vigorously. As he worked it out in *Instit.* I, 7, 4 and the *Commentary on 2 Tim.* 3¹⁶, *C.R.* 52, 383, his view was this. There exists an exact correspondence between the certainty with which the word of the apostles and prophets was the Word of God in itself, or for them, and the certainty with which it as such illumines us. In both cases only God can bear witness to God: *Deus solus de se idoneus est testis—in suo sermone*[EN139], first, and then *in hominum cordibus*[EN140]. And in both cases the God who attests Himself is the Spirit: no one else, but the same Spirit; *idem ergo Spiritus, qui per os prophetarum loquutus est, in corda nostra penetret necesse est*[EN141]. In the very same power in which the Word of God dwells in the human word of the biblical writers and goes out from it, it must come to us, i.e., must be known and received by us as the Word of God, so that we see that God has used the [522] prophets to teach us (*eorum se ministerio usum esse ad nos docendum*) and they faithfully transmitted what was commanded them (*fideliter protulisse quod divinitus erat mandatum*). That is how the concept of inspiration begins and ends on this side. We cannot speak of the inspiration of the Bible without that royal act of the original inspiration in which the risen Christ gave His own a part in His own divine Spirit. But no more can we speak of it without that other royal act—which is only a continuation of the first—in which the inspiration is imparted to us, in which here and now we are forced out of our position as spectators of the word and work of the biblical writers, in which the calling of the prophets and apostles

---

[EN134] The Scriptures must be read with the mind that seeks to find Christ there. Whoever misses this mark, though he may tire himself his whole life with learning, he will never arrive at the knowledge of the truth. For how can we be wise apart from the wisdom of God?

[EN135] firm certainty

[EN136] For God always creates assured faith in His Word

[EN137] The Spirit alone rightly understands the Scriptures and in God's terms. Otherwise (apart from Him) even if people understand it, they do not understand it

[EN138] he is a heretic who expounds the Holy Scriptures in a sense other than that which the Spirit demands

[EN139] God alone is the appropriate witness to Himself - in His own speech

[EN140] in the hearts of men

[EN141] Therefore, the same Spirit who has spoken through the mouths of the prophets must also penetrate our hearts

becomes an event to us by the ministry of their word and work. For ... *Mutuo quodam nexu Dominus Verbi Spiritusque sui certitudinem inter se copulavit, ut solida Verbi religio animis nostris insidat, ubi affulget Spiritus, qui nos illic Dei faciem contemplari faciat, ut vicissim nullo hallucinationis timore Spiritum amplexemur, ubi ilium in sua imagine, hoc est in Verbo, recognoscimus. Ita est sane .... Eundem Spiritum, cuius virtute Verbum administraverat, submisit, qui suum opus efficaci Verbi confirmafione absolveret*[EN142] (*Instit.* I, 9, 3).

If we take Luther and Calvin together, we can say that the way to that universal and moving view of inspiration which answers to the majesty of God, and as we find it in Scripture itself, was again opened up by the Reformation. The Reformers' doctrine of inspiration is an honouring of God, and of the free grace of God. The statement that the Bible is the Word of God is on this view no limitation, but an unfolding of the perception of the sovereignty in which the Word of God condescended to become flesh for us in Jesus Christ, and a human word in the witness of the prophets and apostles as witnesses to His incarnation. On their lips and understanding this is the true statement concerning the Bible which is always indispensable to the Church.

But the post-Reformation period first of all failed really to take the newly opened road to the meaning and understanding of the statement. And then it obviously took a different and mistaken way: mistaken, because it destroyed the mystery of this statement, because it necessarily resulted in a denial of the sovereignty of the Word of God and therefore of the Word of God itself. In this connexion we cannot pay too much attention to a remarkable parallelism: the development of the original Reformed Protestantism into the newer Protestantism which began in the so-called orthodoxy and became visible about 1700 was admittedly characterised by a gradual growth of uncertainty in the knowledge of the sin and justification of man and the judgment and grace of God. This uncertainty, as it concerned the question of revelation, was followed first by a quiet, then by an increasingly open and direct inflow of natural theology. To this development there corresponded, curiously enough, a stiffening in the understanding of the inspiration of the Bible which also began quietly but then developed no less definitely. The strictly supranaturalistic character of the statements which were the outcome of this stiffening tends to create an optical illusion. We first think that we are faced by a contradiction when we see orthodoxy becoming laxer and laxer in relation to natural theology and in secret to the doctrine of grace, but stricter and stricter in relation to the doctrine of the inspiration of the Bible. In reality the two belong intimately together. The gradually extending new understanding of biblical inspiration was simply one way, and in view of its highly supranaturalistic character perhaps the most important way, in which the great process of secularisation on which post-Reformation Protestantism entered was carried through. This new understanding of biblical inspiration meant simply that the statement that the Bible is the Word of God was now transformed (following the doubtful tendencies we have already met in the early Church) from a statement about the free grace of God into a statement about the nature of the Bible as exposed to human inquiry brought under human control. The Bible as the Word of God surreptitiously became a part of natural knowledge of God, i.e., of that knowledge of God which man can have without the free grace of God, by his own power, and with direct insight and assurance. That the highly supranaturalistic form in which this step was made was only a form used because no better was available is proved by the haste with which it was abandoned almost as soon as it was adopted.

[523]

[EN142] By a certain mutual bond, the Lord has joined the certainty of His Word and His Spirit together, so that a strong bond to the Word might reside in our hearts where the Spirit shines. There He makes us contemplate the face of God so that in turn we might embrace the Spirit without any fear that we are merely imagining, where we can see Him in His image, that is, in the Word. So it is in fact ... He who completed His work by the effective confirmation of the Word, sent the same Spirit in whose power He has directed the Word

2. Scripture as the Word of God

It was followed by the enlightenment and the ensuing "historical" investigation and treatment of the Bible, i.e., the character of the Bible as the Word of God was now transformed into that of a highly relevant historical record. And this merely revealed what high orthodoxy had really sought and attained under this apparently supranaturalistic form: the understanding and use of the Bible as an instrument separated from the free grace of God and put into the hands of man. If it should be our aim to-day to go back to the better understanding of the Bible which we find in the Reformers and above all in the Bible itself, then it is not a question of renewing the doctrine of inspiration of high orthodoxy in opposition to the Enlightenment and the development which followed it. Rather, we must carefully and consistently avoid the mistake of that orthodoxy—which is all the more dangerous because its supranaturalistic trend can make it appear advantageous. It is only at this root that the evil which broke out later can really be tackled.

Let us briefly review the historical facts. When we study the doctrine *De Scriptura sacra* in the 16th century confessional writings and in the works of the older Protestant teachers, at this point, i.e., in relation to the question why and how far the Bible is the Word of God, we almost always come across the general statements which we also find in the Reformers: that God or the Holy Ghost is its *autor primarius*[EN143]; that its content is "given" to the prophets and apostles (cf. *Conf. helv. prior*, 1536, Art. 1); that it is *mandata, inspirata. dictata*[EN144], etc., by divine "impulse." But an at best ambiguous mode of speech now begins to be the rule: in the composition of their writings the prophets and apostles acted as *amanuenses*[EN145] (W. Bucan, *Instit. theol.*, 1602, L IV, 2; *Conf. Bohem.*, 1609, I, 2) or as *librarii*[EN146] (A. Hyperins, *De theol.*, 1582, II, 10) or as *actuarii*[EN147] (*Syn. pur. Theol.*, Leiden, 1624, *Disp.* 2, 3). Can we still take this in the same sense as when Calvin (*Serm. on 1 Tim.* 4[1f.], *C.R.* 53, 338) described them as *ministres*[EN148]? Or is there already a return to the idea that they are mere flutes in the mouth of the Holy Spirit? What is certain is that the whole consideration of the doctrine has now obviously narrowed down again to the particular problem of biblical inspiration. The divinity of the Bible can again be referred to without those backward and forward relationships. Even the *testimonium Spiritus sancti internum*[EN149], by which we expect a decisive knowledge in this matter on both rides, is either remarkably separated from the living witness of the Spirit in Scripture itself—as though it were something different—or else brought into a no less remarkable relationship to all kinds of other convincing qualities of the Bible. Of course even at this period there were not wanting lights which blazed out like lightning shafts to show where the way could and should have been. For example, the *Leiden Synopsis* (*Disp.* 3, 7) could still maintain that the attitude of the biblical writers had been to some extent active, not passive: *commentatium et autorum rationem habuerunt*[EN150]. And in the same work we read (*Disp.* 2, 33): *Scriptura ... non nisi a Deo, qui eam dedit et a propria sua luce, quam ei indidit, pendere potest*[EN151]. A. Heidan (*Corp. Theol. christ.*, 1636, L I, 24 f.) finely distinguishes the *vis persuadendi verbi intrinseca et nativa a Dei verbo indita*[EN152] and the *testificatio et obsignatio*

[EN143] primary author
[EN144] commanded, inspired, dictated
[EN145] scribes
[EN146] librarians
[EN147] secretaries
[EN148] ministers
[EN149] inward witness of the Holy Spirit
[EN150] they had the mind of commentators and authors
[EN151] Scripture ... can only depend on God who gave it, and on His own light, which He has placed in it
[EN152] intrinsic and native power of the Word's persuasion placed in it by the Word of God

Spiritus in cordibus fidelium[EN153], going on to say of the latter that *hoc testimonium non est citra aut extra verbum quaerendum, in immediatis afflatibus et raptibus, sed in et cum scriptura est coniunctissimum, ita ut una numero sit actio Verbi et Spiritus sancti. Ut non sit aliud quam illuminatio intellectus, qua capax redditur ad intelligendum et persuadetur*[EN154]. The desire for certainty, which was rightly thought to be needed in the struggle with Rome and the sectaries, as well as in the dispute between Lutherans and Reformed, and above all in the positive proclamation of the Church, might well have been satisfied and better satisfied along these lines, and the lines of the Reformation concept of inspiration. But ever more clearly and definitely a certainty was sought and found quite different from the spiritual certainty which could satisfactorily have been reached on these lines, and which on these lines would have been recognised as the only certainty but also as real certainty. What was wanted was a tangible certainty, not one that is given and has constantly to be given again, a human certainty and not a divine, a certainty of work and not solely of faith. In token of this change there arose the doctrine of inspiration of the high orthodoxy of the 17th century. If previously the biblical writers had always been *amanuenses*[EN155], they now became mere *manus Dei*[EN156], indeed *calami viventes et scribentes*[EN157] (A. Calov, *Syst. Loc. theol.* I, 1655, 453, 551, 556). Even the flute-player of Athenagoras now recurs (H. Heidegger, *Corp. Theol.*, 1700, II, 34, quoted by A. Schweizer, *Glaubenslehre der ev.-ref. Kirche*, 1844 vol. 1, 202). Where it had been enough to say generally that God is the *auctor primarius* of Holy Scripture and to believe generally in "dictation," what was called the "extensive" authority of Holy Scripture was now formulated with legal preciseness (Gisbert Voetius, *Sel. Disp. theol.*, 1648, I, 29). *Tenendum est, Spiritum sanctum immediate et extraordinario dictasse omnia scribenda et scripta, tum res, tum verba, tum quae antea ignorabant out recordari non poterant scriptores, quam quae probe noverant, tum historica seu particularia, tum dogmatica universalia theoretica et practica, sive visu, sive auditu, sive lectione, sive meditatione ea didicissent*[EN158] (*ib.*, p. 32). And the Helvetic Formula of Consent of 1675 (*can.* 2) was preceded by Polan (*Synt. Theol. chr.*, 1609, 486) and G. Voetius (*ib.*, p. 33) in extending this definition expressly to the pointing—indeed, although this was rejected by most of the later men, Polan (p. 479 f.) actually extended it to the *keri* of the Hebrew text. According to G. Voetius (p. 44) the Scriptures of the New Testament were inspired to their authors, not in the Aramaic or Syrian which was their native language, but in Hellenistic Greek. Even things which the biblical authors knew also by their own experience, reflection and judgment they did not write down on the basis of this human knowledge but on the basis of divine inspiration (p. 46). In composing their writings they had no need of prior *studia, inquisitiones et praemeditationes*[EN159] (p. 47). Even the greeting of Tertius in Rom. 16[22] (p. 46) is inspired, and self-evidently a saying like that in which Paul speaks about the coat which he left behind in Troas, 2 Tim. 4[13] (Calov, 560). Since God puts His Word in a prophet's mouth,

---

[EN153] witness and sealing of the Spirit in the hearts of the faithful
[EN154] this testimony is not to be sought beyond or outside of the Word, in unmediated inspirations and raptures, but is most closely conjoined in and with Scripture, such that the action of the Word and the Spirit is singular in number. This is so that it might be nothing other than an illumination of the understanding, by which one is made able to understand and by which one is persuaded
[EN155] secretaries
[EN156] hands of God
[EN157] living and writing pens
[EN158] It must be held that the Holy Spirit dictated in unmediated and extraordinary fashion, everything which was, and was to be, written. Both things and words, matters which the authors previously did not know or could not remember, as well as things which they did truly know, both historical and particular details, and universal dogmas both theoretical and practical, they learned these things, whether by sight, by hearing, by reading, or by meditation
[EN159] studies, inquiries and considerations

2. Scripture as the Word of God

as Calov expressly declares (p. 565), it is not the prophet's but God's own Word, *in quibus nihil humani sit praeter organum oris*EN160. The sacred writers were not free to write down anything other—or in any other way than that dictated to them by the Holy Spirit (p. 565 and 570). That each obviously wrote in his own language and in that of his age is to be ascribed only to a special condescension of the Holy Spirit, and not to human co-operation (p. 575). If we ask why all this had to be stated with this almost terrifying pedantry and safeguarded against all possible defections, we always come up against the postulate that Holy Scripture must be for us a *divina et infallibilis historia*EN161. Truth is necessarily diffused over all Scripture and all parts of Scripture (*infallibilis et θεόπνευστος veritas per omnes et singulas eius partes diffusa est*EN162, Voetius, 31). Polan established the inspiration of the Hebrew, *quia si a Massoritis demum vera lectio et pronuntiatio prophetarum esset ostensa, essemus aedificati super fundamentum Massoritarum et non super fundamentum prophetarum* (p. 487). *Nullus error vel in leviculis, nullus memoriae lapsus, nedum mendacium ullum locum habere potest in universa sancta scriptura*EN163 (Calov, 551). Should there be found even the minutest error in the Bible, then it is no longer wholly the Word of God, and the inviolability of its authority is destroyed (p. 552). The same is true if even the tiniest fraction of it derives from human knowledge, reflection and perception (p. 555). "All Scripture is given by God ... " is what it says in 2 Tim. 3[16]. Therefore we cannot find in it even the smallest word which is not given by God and therefore infallible truth (p. 563). If it were otherwise, neither for theology nor for faith would there be any certainty, any certainty of grace and of the forgiveness of sins, any certainty of the existence and divine sonship of Jesus Christ. *Quid vero inde, nisi merus Pyrrhonismus, mera σκεπτική et academica dubitatio, immo merus atheismus?*EN164 And by not taking better care for His revelation God Himself would be the cause of human unbelief. *Principium debet esse certum, indubitatum, infallibile*EN165 (p. 579). *Si enim unicus scripturae versiculus, cessante immediato Spiritus sancti influxu, conscriptus est, promptum erit satanae, idem dt toto capite, de integro libro, de universo denique codice biblico excipere et per consequens omnem scripturae autoritatem elevare*EN166 (Quenstedt, *Theol. did. pol.*, 1685, I, c. 4, sect, 2, qu. 3, beb. 7). *Si verba singula non fuissent scriptoribus sacris suggesta per θεοπνευστίαν, scriptura sacra non proprie, non absolute et simpliciter ... esset dicique posset θεόπνευστος*EN167 (Hollaz, *Ex. Theol. accroam.*, 1707, Prol. 2, 27). H. Cremer (*PRE*² 9, 192) is right: "This doctrine of inspiration was absolutely new." But it was so, not in its content, which was merely a development and systematisation of statements which had been heard in the Church since the first centuries, but in the intention which underlay the development and systematisation. As we have seen, the earlier statements were not free from ambiguity. They did not escape the danger of a

[525]

EN160 in which there is nothing human except the instrument of the mouth
EN161 divine and infallible history
EN162 the infallible and divinely inspired truth is diffused through each and every part of it
EN163 since if the true reading and pronunciation of the prophets is finally shown by the Massoretic scribes, then we would have been built up upon the foundation of the Massoretic scribes, and not upon the foundation of the prophets. There is no error, even in minor matters, no lapse of memory, and there cannot be any place with falsehood in the entirety of Holy Scripture
EN164 But what then would follow, except pure Pyrrhonism, pure scepticism and the doubt of the academy, yes, even pure atheism?
EN165 The starting point must be certain, undoubted, and infallible
EN166 For if a single small verse of Scripture has been written with the unmediated flow of the Holy Spirit coming to a halt, then it would be easy for Satan to remove it (i.e. the inspiration of the Spirit) from a whole chapter, from a whole book, finally from the whole text of the Bible, and in consequence to take away the whole authority of Scripture
EN167 If the individual words had not been suggested to the sacred writers by divine inspiration, then Holy Scripture would not be and could not be described strictly, absolutely and simply as divinely inspired

71

docetic dissolving or of a mantico-mechanical materialising of the concept of the biblical witness to revelation. It is obvious that the "modern" 17th century doctrine of inspiration increased the danger with its development and systematisation of the statements. But there is no point in trying to attack it from this side. We have seen from the example of the Reformers that the statements as such, if only they stand in the right context backwards and forwards, can be made without giving rise to that danger; the mere "dangers" of a doctrine never entitle us to describe it as false doctrine. And again there is no point in joining the wolves of the 18th and 19th centuries and attacking the 17th century doctrine of inspiration because of its pointed supranaturalism. We must attack it rather because its supranaturalism is not radical enough. The intention behind it was ultimately only a single and in its own way very "naturalistic" postulate: that the Bible must offer us a *divina et infallibilis historia*; that it must not contain human error in any of its verses; that in all its parts and the totality of its words and letters as they are before us it must express divine truth in a form in which it can be established and understood; that under the human words it must speak to us the Word of God in such a way that we can at once hear and read it as such with the same obviousness and directness with which we can hear and read other human words; that it must be a codex of axioms which can be seen as such with the same formal dignity as those of philosophy and mathematics. The secular nature of this postulate showed itself plainly in the assumption that we may freely reproach the good God if it is not fulfilled, threatening Him with distrust, scepticism and atheism—a threat which was no less freely carried out in the following generations, when men became convinced that the postulate could not be fulfilled. This secularism was not merely a danger which threatened. It was openly present. Therefore we have to resist and reject the 17th century doctrine of inspiration as false doctrine. The development and systematisation of the traditional statements concerning the divine authority of the Bible meant an actualising of the Word of God by eliminating the perception that its actualisation can only be its own decision and act, that our part in it can consist only in the recollection and expectation of its eternal presence. This actualisation was arbitrary because it was obstinately postulated and maintained. In it the Word of God could no longer be the Word of God and therefore it was no longer recognised as such. The Bible was now grounded upon itself apart from the mystery of Christ and the Holy Ghost. It became a "paper Pope," and unlike the living Pope in Rome it was wholly given up into the hands of its interpreters. It was no longer a free and spiritual force, but an instrument of human power.

[526] And in this form the Bible became so like the holy books of other religions, for which something similar had always been claimed, that the superiority of its claim could not be asserted in relation to them or to the many achievements of the human spirit generally. What product of human inventiveness does not ultimately rest on the same claim to infallibility? What cannot be similarly invested with it? The intention in establishing the authority of the Bible along these lines was to avoid historical relativism, but it opened up the way to it, and theology and the Church did not hesitate for a moment to tread that way. In content the 17th century doctrine of inspiration asserted things which cannot be maintained in face of a serious reading and exposition of what the Bible itself says about itself, and in face of an honest appreciation of the facts of its origin and tradition. Therefore the postulate on which 17th century man staked everything proved incapable of fulfilment. But although this is important, in the long run it is only of secondary importance, because it is always debatable. What is more important is the fact of dogmatic history that once the doctrine arose it was believed for only a short time, but it remained for many ages, and still is to some extent at the present time, a kind of theological bogeyman, the logically necessary interpretation of the statement that the Bible is the Word of God, which has prevented whole generations and innumerable individual theologians and believers from seeing the true, spiritual biblical and Reformation meaning of the statement, causing them to go past Luther and Calvin and

even Paul in order to accompany Voetius and Calov. But the decisive fact is this. As a result of this doctrine of inspiration, the view of the Bible which in the Reformers, being genuinely and strictly a view of the Bible, was also a view of Christ here and the Holy Spirit there, and therefore of God's sovereignty and free grace, was now for long periods and for large sections of the Evangelical Churches restricted to the biblical documents as such and in their historico-literary givenness, about which this doctrine of inspiration had asserted such remarkable things. If the assertions themselves could not be accepted—and it was no evil but right and necessary that they should not—the restriction of outlook was accepted all the more intensively and obstinately. In no sense was it a fresh broadening of outlook when the Bible came to be interpreted as the document of a specific history and the so-called spirit of the Bible as the spirit of this history, as was variously attempted by the rationalists of the 18th century, by Herder, by Schleiermacher and by the conservative and liberal schools of the 19th century up to Ritschl and the religious historicists. All sorts of seemingly and actually more concrete views of the human form of the Bible were undoubtedly gained in these ways. But if we imagine that we shall find the Word of God in a history which can be studied on historico-literary lines, the sources of which we believe we have in the Bible, we escape the Docetism of our forefathers, who tried to close their eyes to the humanity of the Bible, only to fall the more heavily into a complementary Ebionitism. And a loftier manticism may even be advanced by the mystery of the newly instituted cultus of "God in history." What is certain is that the view of the connexion of the Word of God in the Bible with the work of Christ for us and that of the Holy Spirit to us, which was barred by the 17th century doctrine of inspiration, was hermetically closed off now that the latter could not be sustained on secondary grounds without breaking loose from its restriction of outlook. The knowledge of the free grace of God as the unity of Scripture and revelation had been lost. No wonder that the statement that the Bible is the Word of God was now dismissed as "untrue." Thanks to the happy inconsistency which has always been the best thing in Church history, this statement has survived and with it the Evangelical Church. Without its open or concealed truth, the latter could not have survived for a moment. But that is another story. Of the history of the doctrine of inspiration as such it must still be said that in the Evangelical Church it finally made the statement incomprehensible. After a promising start it was for the most part a chapter of accidents.

Instructed by our consideration of the ways to be taken and avoided, we will now try to state in the form of propositions what we can believe about the inspiration, the divine nature of the Bible and therefore about the statement that the Bible is the Word of God, more particularly in the light of the concept of Word. [527]

1. To say "the Word of God" is to say the Word of *God*. It is therefore to speak about a being and event which are not under human control and foresight. Our knowledge of this being and event does not justify us in thinking and speaking of them as though they were under our control and foresight. We know this divine nature which we cannot control or foresee when we know this Word, when we know, then, what we are saying when we say that the Bible is the Word of God. That we have the Bible as the Word of God does not justify us in transforming the statement that the Bible is the Word of God from a statement about the being and rule of God in and through the Bible into a statement about the Bible as such. When we have the Bible as the Word of God, and accept its witness, we are summoned to remember the Lord of the Bible and to

give Him the glory. It would not strictly be loyalty to the Bible, and certainly not thankfulness for the Word of God given and continually given again in it, if we did not let our ears be opened by it, not to what it says but to what He, God Himself, has to say to us as His Word in it and through it. With this recognition and adoration of the sovereignty of Him whose Word the Bible is, the knowledge of its inspiration, its character as the Word of God, will always have to begin.

2. To say "the Word of God" is to say the work of God. It is not to contemplate a state or fact but to watch an event, and an event which is relevant to us, an event which is an act of God, an act of God which rests on a free decision. That God's Word is from eternity to eternity does not allow us to evade it, as though for us who live in time it is not the event of its presence, its communion with us, its promise of our own eternal life. To its eternity there necessarily corresponds in its revelation the fact that for us and to us it is not present as that which is not the Word of God is present. But it happens, and happens as nothing else happens, as something new compared with all that we were or are or shall be, in fact with all that the whole world was or is or shall be. Even the fact that the Bible is present as the Word of God does not allow us to look at it in any other way. Indeed, it forces us to look at it in this way. It reminds us of the act of God achieved once and for all. If we have this recollection, if therefore the Bible is really present to us, we cannot possibly understand the Word of God which speaks of it except as the act of God which is now expected by us. Our knowledge of its character as the Word of God and therefore of its inspiration will thus consist in our willing approach to the Word of God promised in it; willing to let the new thing happen to us which, if we will hear it, will become event in our life and in the life of the whole world.

[528]

3. To say "the Word of God" is to say the miracle of God. It is not secretly to regard the new thing with which we now have to do in the Word of God as something old, i.e., bound by the presuppositions and laws, the customs and traditions of other happenings in our lives and in the life of our world. We reckon that the event of the Word of God is not a continuation, but the end of all other events that we know. We reckon that a new series of events has begun. Again, the in itself non-miraculous given-ness of the Bible as the Word of God, its existence amongst all the other facts of our cosmos, will not induce us to take any other view but rather to take this view. Yet in speaking of the act of God in Jesus Christ, it does itself speak of the grace of God as a reality which cannot be deduced or conceived in the context of the human existence which we know, a reality which posits the end of all other events and opens up a new series of events. That the Word of God is not under our control or foresight is proved by the fact that its content—and not only its content, but its reality as such—is the grace of God, which we have not deserved, the occurrence of which we cannot claim or bring about, which we can only accept because God is pleased to be gracious to us. If we allow the Bible to say this to us, and in so doing to speak the Word of God, how else can we think of the Word of God in

74

the Bible except as a miracle? How else or better can we describe the character of the Bible as the Word of God, how can we ascribe to it any higher value and authority than that in it we see the place where we must expect the miracle of the Word of God? No word can be too high for it if it is a description of this miracle and a confession of its truth. But however pious or well-meant the word which eliminates this miracle, which makes the Word of God in the Bible a part of our own higher nature, a remarkable property of a part of our former nature, which brings the Bible as the Word of God into the sphere of human competence, this word destroys its real dignity and authority, and denies the statement that it is the Word of God.

4. But if we are speaking of a miracle when we say that the Bible is the Word of God, we must not compromise either directly or indirectly the humanity of its form and the possibility of the offence which can be taken at it. An attempt to do so is tantamount to an attempt in our exegesis of the New Testament to understand the miracles recorded there by telling ourselves that the sick people who were healed according to these narratives were not really seriously sick or even that the Jesus who rose again on the third day did not really die on the cross. As truly as Jesus died on the cross, as Lazarus died in Jn. 11, as the lame were lame, as the blind were blind, as the hungry at the feeding of the five thousand were hungry, as the sea on which Jesus walked was a lake many fathoms deep: so, too, the prophets and apostles as such, even in their office, [529] even in their function as witnesses, even in the act of writing down their witness, were real, historical men as we are, and therefore sinful in their action, and capable and actually guilty of error in their spoken and written word. If the miracle happened to them that they were called to be witnesses of the resurrection and that they received the Holy Spirit, it was to them it happened, leaving them the full use of their human freedom and not removing the barriers which are therefore posited for them as for all of us. Their existence as witnesses, as it is a visible event in Holy Scripture, is therefore the existence of real men (and therefore not at all crowded out by the existence of God or hampered by any kind of magic in the fulfilment of their existence), men who as such, in the full use of their freedom and within the limits posited by it, have to speak to us the Word of God. That the lame walk, that the blind see, that the dead are raised, that sinful and erring men as such speak the Word of God: that is the miracle of which we speak when we say that the Bible is the Word of God. To the comprehension of this statement there belongs, therefore, the recognition that its truth consists in the removing of an offence which is always and everywhere present, and that this takes place by the power of the Word of God. This offence, like the offence of the cross of Christ, is based on the fact that the Word of God became flesh and therefore to this very day has built and called and gathered and illumined and sanctified His Church amongst flesh. This offence is therefore grounded like the overcoming of it in the mercy of God. For that reason it must not be denied and for that reason, too, it must not

be evaded. For that reason every time we turn the Word of God into an infallible biblical word of man or the biblical word of man into an infallible Word of God we resist that which we ought never to resist, i.e., the truth of the miracle that here fallible men speak the Word of God in fallible human words—and we therefore resist the sovereignty of grace, in which God Himself became man in Christ, to glorify Himself in His humanity. If we cannot make up our minds for this hard thinking, let us see to it that we are not shutting ourselves off from the real word of comfort spoken to us by the existence of the Bible as such. And if we want to assert a supposedly stricter concept of the value and authority of the Bible, let us see to it that we are not moving away from the strictness of its true value and authority. If the prophets and apostles are not real and therefore fallible men, even in their office, even when they speak and write of God's revelation, then it is not a miracle that they speak the Word of God. But if it is not a miracle, how can it be the Word of God that they speak, how can their speaking, and our hearing of their human words, possess as the Word of God the character of revelation? To the bold postulate, that if their word is to be the Word of God they must be inerrant in every word, we oppose the even bolder assertion, that according to the scriptural witness about man, which [530] applies to them too, they can be at fault in any word, and have been at fault in every word, and yet according to the same scriptural witness, being justified and sanctified by grace alone, they have still spoken the Word of God in their fallible and erring human word. It is the fact that in the Bible we can take part in this real miracle, the miracle of the grace of God to sinners, and not the idle miracle of human words which were not really human words at all, which is the foundation of the dignity and authority of the Bible.

5. If, therefore, we are serious about the fact that this miracle is an event, we cannot regard the presence of God's Word in the Bible as an attribute inhering once for all in this book as such and what we see before us of books and chapters and verses. Of the book as we have it, we can only say: We recollect that we have heard in this book the Word of God; we recollect, in and with the Church, that the Word of God has been heard in all this book and in all parts of it; therefore we expect that we shall hear the Word of God in this book again, and hear it even in those places where we ourselves have not heard it before. Yet the presence of the Word of God itself, the real and present speaking and hearing of it, is not identical with the existence of the book as such. But in this presence something takes place in and with the book, for which the book as such does indeed give the possibility, but the reality of which cannot be anticipated or replaced by the existence of the book. A free divine decision is made. It then comes about that the Bible, the Bible *in concreto*, this or that biblical context, i.e., the Bible as it comes to us in this or that specific measure, is taken and used as an instrument in the hand of God, i.e., it speaks to and is heard by us as the authentic witness to divine revelation and is therefore present as the Word of God. It is present in a way we cannot conceive: not as a third time between past and future, between recollection and expectation, but as

that point between the two which we cannot think of as time, which when it is considered immediately becomes once more either before or after. In this way it is the being present of the eternal Word, which is constitutive for its expectation and recollection, on which our time is based, just as the incarnation and resurrection of Jesus Christ as the centre of time is the basis of time in general. A genuine, fallible human word is at this centre the Word of God: not in virtue of its own superiority, of its replacement by a Word of God veiled as the word of man, still less of any kind of miraculous transformation, but, of course, in virtue of the privilege that here and now it is taken and used by God Himself, like the water in the Pool of Bethesda.

6. As to when, where and how the Bible shows itself to us in this event as the Word of God, we do not decide, but the Word of God Himself decides, at different times in the Church and with different men confirming and renewing the event of instituting and inspiring the prophets and apostles to be His witnesses and servants, so that in their written word they again live before us,   [531] not only as men who once spoke in Jerusalem and Samaria, to the Romans and Corinthians, but as men who in all the concreteness of their own situation and action speak to us here and now. We can know that in the life of the Church, and indeed in its life with the Bible, it is a matter of this decision and act of God or rather of the actualisation of the act of God which took place once and for all in Jesus Christ. In the whole Bible it is always a matter of this act. We can remember that the Bible has really already been for ourselves and others the place of this act. We can and should expect this act afresh. We can and should cling to the written word, as Jesus commanded the Jews, and as the people of Beroea did. We can and should search the Scriptures asking about this witness. We can and should therefore pray that this witness may be made to us. But it does not lie—and this is why prayer must have the last word—in our power but only in God's, that this event should take place and therefore this witness of Scripture be made to us. We are therefore absolved from trying to force this event to happen. This does not allow us to be unfaithful or indolent. It is the man who is faithful in seeking, asking and praying, who knows that the faithfulness of God and not his own faithfulness decides. But we are completely absolved from differentiating in the Bible between the divine and the human, the content and the form, the spirit and the letter, and then cautiously choosing the former and scornfully rejecting the latter. Always in the Bible as in all other human words we shall meet with both. And we may differentiate between them as we do in the understanding of a human word. But the event in which the word of man proves itself the Word of God is one which we cannot bring about by this differentiation. The Word of God is so powerful that it is not bound by what we think we can discover and value as the divine element, the content, the spirit of the Bible. Again, it is not so powerful that it will not bind itself to what we think we can value lightly as the human element, the form, the letter of the Bible. We are absolved from differentiating the Word of God in the Bible from other contents, infallible portions and expressions from

77

the erroneous ones, the infallible from the fallible, and from imagining that by means of such discoveries we can create for ourselves encounters with the genuine Word of God in the Bible. If God was not ashamed of the fallibility of all the human words of the Bible, of their historical and scientific inaccuracies, their theological contradictions, the uncertainty of their tradition, and, above all, their Judaism, but adopted and made use of these expressions in all their fallibility, we do not need to be ashamed when He wills to renew it to us in all its fallibility as witness, and it is mere self-will and disobedience to try to find some infallible elements in the Bible. But finally we are absolved from having to know and name as such the event or events, in which Scripture proves and confirms itself to us as the Word of God. We have seen that as the events of the eternal presence of the Word, as the hours of God, they cannot be grasped in time or can be grasped only in their before and after, in recollection and expectation. It is enough—and this is all that is required of us—that we should constantly approach these events and proceed from them. Similarly we cannot know our faith in its eternal form as our justification before God, but only as a movement ἐκ πίστεως εἰς πίστιν EN168 (Rom. 1 17), which as such is not justified. We can give to ourselves and to others an account of our faith; but we can only do so in thankfulness and hope, without showing the basis of our faith. And that is how we stand in relation to Holy Scripture. We can and must be summoned by it to thankfulness and hope. In obedience to this summons it will be seen in the reality and the judgment of God whether and to what extent we participate in the event of the presence of His Word. A consciousness of this presence as such, or an indication of this presence to others, does not lie in the sphere of human possibility and therefore cannot be demanded of us. "By their fruits ye shall know them." Therefore the presence of the Word of God is not an experience, precisely because and as it is the divine decision concerning us.

[532]

7. When we speak of the inspiration of the Bible or when we confess that the Bible is the Word of God, on the one side, in the sphere of time and sense, in the concrete life of the Church and of our own life as members of the Church, we have to think of a twofold reality. There is first the question of the text of the biblical witness: or rather of a definite portion of this text, which in a specific time and situation claims the attention of specific men or of a specific individual. If now it is true in time, as it is true in eternity, that the Bible is the Word of God, then according to what we have just said, God Himself now says what the text says. The work of God is done through this text. The miracle of God takes place in this text formed of human words. This text in all its humanity, including all the fallibility which belongs to it, is the object of this work and miracle. By the decision of God this text is now taken and used. And in the mystery of God it takes place that here and now this text acquires this determination. Yet it is still this text as such of which all this has to be said. It is as

---

EN168 from faith to faith

such that it will speak and attest, and be read and heard: and the Word of God in it and through it, not alongside or behind it, not in some place which we have first to attain to or even create beyond the text. If God speaks to man, He really speaks the language of this concrete human word of man. That is the right and necessary truth in the concept of verbal inspiration. If the word is not to be separated from the matter, if there is no such thing as verbal inspiredness, the matter is not to be separated from the word, and there is real inspiration, the hearing of the Word of God, only in the form of verbal inspiration, the hearing of the Word of God only in the concrete form of the biblical [533] word. Verbal inspiration does not mean the infallibility of the biblical word in its linguistic, historical and theological character as a human word. It means that the fallible and faulty human word is as such used by God and has to be received and heard in spite of its human fallibility. Whatever may be the value of the one who is commissioned and of his word, for us he now has the value of his commission. In this dignity he has to be respected, and his word respected. That we not only have him and his word, the biblical text, but in him and through him the Word of God, is something which we must leave to God. In this confidence, which will give us a proper freedom in relation to the human word as such, we do have to abide by the human word. For—and this is the second thing that has to be considered—in relation to the concrete text and no less concretely to ourselves, it is a matter of the event or the events of the presence of the Word of God in our own present: not the experience of its presence, but its actual presence—the presence upon which God decides, which we cannot create or anticipate, but the presence, which as the inconceivable, free presence of God Himself decides our past and future, defining our recollection as thankfulness and our expectation as hope. In face of the biblical text we are not bound to imagine that the Word of God is present. We are not called upon to use any devices to make it present. But in face of the biblical text we are clamped or pincered by thankfulness and hope and we must not try to escape from this clamp or pincer. Imprisoned in thankfulness and hope we must dare to face the humanity of the biblical texts and therefore their fallibility without the postulate that they must be infallible, but also without the superstitious belief in any infallible truth alongside or behind the text and revealed by ourselves—we must dare really to face it, i.e., to let the text speak to us as it stands, to let it say all that it has to say in its vocabulary and context, to allow the prophets and apostles to say again here and now to us what they said there and then. That is how it will always be when they do what we cannot force them to do and speak the Word of God in their human words. The door of the Bible texts can be opened only from within. It is another thing whether we wait at this door or leave it for other doors, whether we want to enter and knock or sit idly facing it. The existence of the biblical texts summons us to persistence in waiting and knocking. Their concrete form is a challenge to concrete effort. We can sum up all that must be said on this point in the statement that faith in the inspiration of the Bible stands or falls by whether the concrete life of the Church and of the members of the Church is a life really dominated by the exegesis of the Bible. If the biblical text in its literalness as a text does not force itself upon us, or if we have the freedom word by word to shake ourselves loose from it, what meaning is there in our protestation that the Bible is inspired and the Word of God? To say "Lord, Lord" is not enough. What matters is to do the will of God if we are to know His grace and truth—for that is the inspiration of the Bible.

[534]

8. But we must remember—and with this we can bring these considerations to a close—that the inspiration of the Bible cannot be reduced to our faith in it, even though we understand this faith as the gift and work of God in us. All that happens in the sphere of time and sense, in the concrete life of the Church and of our own life as its members, the eventuation of the presence of the Word of God in the human word of the prophets and apostles, can only be regarded as a repetition, a secondary prolongation and continuation of the once-for-all and primary eventuation of revelation itself. It was not for nothing, nor was it wrong, that the early Church wanted assurance of the dignity and authority of the Bible as the Word of God against the accident and self-will to which it is obviously exposed by its humanity in the reading and understanding and expounding of the Bible. We have thought of the divine inspiration of the Bible as an actual decision which takes place in the mystery of God as His work and miracle, and which has to be recollected and expected in faith and obedience and in faithful exegesis. But there is an obvious doubt whether this really does sufficient justice to the objectivity of the truth that the Bible is the Word of God, whether this description is not at least exposed to the danger and may be taken to imply that our faith makes the Bible into the Word of God, that its inspiration is ultimately a matter of our own estimation or mood or feeling. We must not blind ourselves to this danger. But we must ask ourselves how we are to meet it, how we can in fact do justice to the objectivity of the inspiration of the Bible. Yet obviously we can do justice to it only by refraining from even imagining that we can do so. We do justice to it by believing and resting on the fact that the action of God in the founding and maintaining of His Church, with which we have to do in the inspiration of the Bible, is objective enough to emerge victorious from all the inbreaks and outbreaks of man's subjectivity. To believe in the inspiration of the Bible means, because of and in accordance with its witness, to believe in the God whose witness it is. If we do not, how are we helped by even the strongest assurance of the divinity of its witness? And if we do, how can we ask for any special assurance of it? Is it not to believe without believing, if we want to make such an assurance indispensable? Certainly it is not our faith which makes the Bible the Word of God. But we cannot safeguard the objectivity of the truth that it is the Word of God better than by insisting that it does demand our faith, and underlie our faith, that it is the substance and life of our faith. For in so doing we maintain that it is the truth of the living God, beyond which there is none other, the power of which we are not allowed to doubt in face of the forces of human subjectivity, which

2. Scripture as the Word of God

we have therefore to know and recognise as such. But if this is true, then it stands that we have to understand the inspiration of the Bible as a divine decision continually made in the life of the Church and in the life of its members. That it took place once and for all in the resurrection of Jesus Christ and in the outpouring of the Holy Spirit, as the establishment of the Church, is not disputed. But this is known and acknowledged in its objectivity by the fact that we recollect and expect the same divine decision in the preservation of the Church, and our own fellowship with Jesus Christ and in the Holy Spirit. That the Bible is the Word of God is not left to accident or to the course of history and to our own self-will, but to the God of Abraham, Isaac and Jacob, the triune God as Him whose self-witness alone can and very definitely does see to it that this statement is true, that the biblical witnesses have not spoken in vain and will not be heard in vain. [535]

In view of what we have just said we will close with an admission of, if you like, a purely formal nature, the significance of which is that it points to the act of confession with which the doctrine of Holy Scripture is really concerned when its content is rightly understood. We have to admit to ourselves and to all who ask us about this question that the statement that the Bible is the Word of God is an analytical statement, a statement which is grounded only in its repetition, description and interpretation, and not in its derivation from any major propositions. It must either be understood as grounded in itself and preceding all other statements or it cannot be understood at all. The Bible must be known as the Word of *God* if it is to be *known* as the Word of God. The doctrine of Holy Scripture in the Evangelical Church is that this logical circle is the circle of self-asserting, self-attesting truth into which it is equally impossible to enter as it is to emerge from it: the circle of our freedom which as such is also the circle of our captivity.

When the Evangelical Churches of the Reformation and later were asked by their Roman adversaries how the divine authority of Scripture could be known and believed by men without being guaranteed by the authority of the Church, the Evangelical theologians gave the hard but only possible answer that the authority of Scripture was grounded only in itself and not in the judgment of men. *Credimus et confitemur, scripturas canonicas sanctorum proplutarum et apostolorum utriusque testamenti ipsum oerum esse Verbum Dei et autoritatem sufficientem ex semetipsis, non ex hominibus habere. Nam Deus ipse loquutus est patribus, prophetis et apostolis et loquitur adhue nobis per scripturas sanctas*[EN169] (*Conf., helv. post.*, 1562, Art. 1). We might just as well ask where we can base the distinction of light from darkness, of white from black, of sweet from sour (Calvin, *Instit.* I, 7, 2). *Quatstio. an scripturae sett sacra biblia sint Dei verbum? homine christiano indigna est. Ut enim in scholis contra negantem principia non disputatur, ita*

[EN169] We believe and we confess that the canonical Scriptures of the holy prophets and apostles of both testaments are truly the very Word of God and have sufficient authority from themselves, not from men. For God Himself has spoken to the patriarchs, to the prophets and to the apostles, and still does speak to us through the Holy Scriptures *indignum iudicare debemus, qui audiatur, si quis christianae religionis principium neget*[EN170] (J. Wolleb, *Chr. theol. comp.*, 1626, *praecog.* 7). This is not an embarrassed expediency but the wisdom of serpents and the harmlessness of doves. It is not an evasion of the actual point at issue, but its reference back to the only possible actuality. If only they had remained and gone further along these lines.

[536]   For the statement that the human word of the Bible is the Word of God we can obviously give only a single and incomparable basis. This is that it is true. This basis either exists of itself or not at all. It is either already known and acknowledged or it is not accepted.

Auctoritas scripturae quoad nos nihil aliud est quam manifestatio et cognitio unicae illius divinae et summae auctoritatis, quae scripturae est interna el insita[EN171] (J. Gerhard, *Loci theol.*, 1610 f., *L* I, *cap.* 3, 38).

As this one basis posited itself and was known and acknowledged, it became the basis of the Church. And as it posits itself again in the same self-glory and in that self-glory is again known and acknowledged, it alone is the power of its continuance. The Church does not have to accredit it, but again and again it has to be accredited by it. And all that we may adduce on other grounds for the authority of Scripture does not underlie this one ground and its divinity, but at best can be sustained only on the presupposition of this one ground and as pointing to it.

The 16th century was well acquainted with and even accepted—just as it accepted the authority of the Church under Holy Scripture—an apologetic which came down from the early Church and the Middle Ages, subordinate to but illustrating this one ground: *argumenta testimonia*[EN172], human considerations by which it was thought that the divinity of Scripture could later be more or less clearly brought out. Attention was usually drawn to the antiquity of the Bible, its miracles and prophecies, its decisive and victorious role in Church history. Calvin thought it necessary to devote a whole chapter of the *Institutes* to these considerations as they throw light on the existence of the Bible (I, 8: *Probationes, quatenus fert humana ratio satis firmas suppetere ad stabiliendam scripturae fidem*[EN173]). But he himself calls them *secundaria nostrae imbecillitatis adminicula*[EN174] and warns us in every possible way against thinking that we can regard and apply them as the grounds of faith: *inepte faciunt, qui probari volunt infidelibus, scripturam esse verbum Dei, quod nisi fide cognosci nequit*[EN175] (I, 8, 13). The verdict that Scripture is the Word of God is not a human but a divine judgment, and only as such can it be adopted and believed by us: *illius ergo virtute illuminati iam non aut nostro aut aliorum iudicio credimus a Deo esse scripturam .... Non arguments, non verisimilitudines*

[EN170] The question of whether the Scriptures or sacred books are the Word of God is unworthy of a Christian man. For just as it is impossible to dispute in school with someone who denies the principles, so also we ought to judge as unworthy to be heard anyone who denies the starting point of the Christian religion

[EN171] The authority of Scripture as it is to us is nothing other than the manifestation and the knowledge of that single divine and supreme authority, which is internal and intrinsic to Scripture

[EN172] testimonial arguments

[EN173] Proofs in as far as human reason can support

[EN174] secondary supports for our weakness

[EN175] They act stupidly, who want to prove to unbelievers that Scripture is the Word of God, because it cannot be known except by faith

quaerimus, quibus indicium nostrum incumbat; sed rei extra aestimandi aleam positae, indicium ingeniumque nostrum subiicimus ... quia inexpugnabilem nos veritatem tenere, probe nos conscii sumus ... quia non dubiam vim numinis illic sentimus videre ac spirare, qua ad parendum, scientes quidem ac volentes, vividius tamen et efficacius quam pro humana aut voluntate aut scientia trahimur et accendimur .... Talis ergo est persuasio quae rationes non requirat, talis notitia, cui optima ratio constet, nempe in qua securius constantiusque nuns quiescit, quam in ullis rationibus, talis denique sensus, qui nisi ex caelesti revelatione nasci nequeat. Non aliud loquor quam quod apud se experitur fidelium unusquisque, nisi quod longe infra iustam rei explicationem verba subsidunt[EN176] (I, 7, 5).
Unfortunately, Calvin found many later imitators in the enumeration and development of these secondary grounds, but not in his definitely expressed perception of the abysmal difference of these grounds from the one primary and real ground, not in his awareness of the superiority and self-sufficiency of that one ground. The *testimonium Spiritus sancti internum*[EN177], on which alone he and the Reformation as a whole based faith in the Bible as the Word of God, at a later date gradually but irresistibly became one ground with others, and the other grounds gained an interest and acquired an importance as though they were, after all, autonomous. The unarmed power of the one ground, that in the Bible God has attested Himself to be God and still does so, came more and more to be regarded, as it was never meant to be regarded in the 16th century, as the power of a particular spiritual experience, which at some point we have to have of the Bible. But on this understanding, it could not have the force of a real ground. Calvin had seen in it only the power of an objective proof. But it was now suspected to be only subjective and in the strict sense not a proof at all. Therefore the witness of the Holy Spirit necessarily retired and finally disappeared behind the rational proofs which Calvin had treated only as luxuries. This was the state of things at the end of the 17th century. In S. Werensfels (*De triplici teste, Opusc.* I, 179 f.) we find the witness of the Holy Spirit transformed into the human conviction which as readers of Scripture we ourselves can form of the meaning and credibility of what we read according to our own knowledge and conscience. And a little later in J. D. Michaelis (*Comp. theol. dogm.*, 1760, § 8) we find the blatant assertion that never in all his life has he experienced this testimony of the Holy Spirit, and that he does not envy those who think they have and believe that they must maintain *illa quae in codice sacro insunt divinitatis et argumenta*[EN178]. At this point the battle was lost. More recently there has been no lack of voices advising us that at least a historical appreciation of the original position has not been forfeited. We can summon A. Ritschl as a witness. He could once write of the *testimonium Spiritus sancti*[EN179]: "Even if this concept does comprise all that is meant by religious experience, it is formally quite differently constructed from the concept of experience; in fact it is quite opposed to it. By experience we mean a movement, the subject of which is the human Ego; but in the *testimonium*

[537]

[EN176] Therefore, we believe that Scripture is from God because we have been enlightened by His power and not by our own or anyone else's judgment ... We do not seek arguments or analogies upon which our judgment can rest; rather, we subject our judgment and our minds to the object which is located outside the risk of guess-work, since we are rightly convinced that we hold the indestructible truth ... since we sense that we see and breathe the indubitable power of the Spirit, by Whom we are drawn and fired to obey, indeed knowing and willing, yet more vividly and powerfully than by any human will or knowledge ... Therefore such is the persuasion which does not require reasons, such is the knowledge which agrees with the best reason, namely in which the mind can rest more securely and constantly than in any reasons; finally, such is the sense which cannot be born except by heavenly revelation. I am saying nothing other than what any believer experiences in himself, except that words fall far short of any right description of the matter

[EN177] internal witness of the Holy Spirit

[EN178] those points of divinity and arguments which are contained in the sacred book

[EN179] witness of the Holy Spirit

Spiritus sancti[EN180] the Ego is thought of as an object, and its experience of salvation and conviction of the truth as the operation of another power" (*Rechtf. und. Versöhnung*⁴ 2 Bd., 6). But even when it is rightly understood, Ritschl declared the concept to be "unusable."

Scripture is recognised as the Word of God by the fact that it *is* the Word of God. This is what we are told by the doctrine of the witness of the Holy Spirit. According to His humanity Jesus was conceived of the Holy Spirit, to be born of the Virgin Mary for us. Again, according to His humanity, Jesus is redemptively present by the Holy Spirit in the Lord's Supper. And by the Holy Spirit the witnesses of His humanity became and are also the witnesses of His eternal Godhead, His revelation was apprehended by them and through them it is apprehended by us. When we say "by the Holy Spirit" we mean, by God in the free and gracious act of His turning to us. When we say "by the Holy Spirit" we say that in the doctrine of Holy Scripture we are content to give the glory to God and not to ourselves.

H. Alstedt (*Theol. schol.*, 1618, 27, cited H. Heppe, *Dogm. d. ev. ref. Kirche*, 1861, new edn., 1935, 24) wrote these words: *Auctoritas et certitudo scripturae pendet a testimonio Spiritus sancti et haec est demonstratio demonstrationum maxima. Auctoritas namque dicti vel scripti cuiuscumque pendet ab ipso eius auctore. Multum situm est in hac regula, quippe basi totius theologiae*[EN181]. D. F. Strauss was right to criticise this rule: "Who can now attest the divinity of this witness? Either itself again, which is nobody: or a something, perhaps a feeling or thought in the human spirit—this is the Achilles' heel of the Protestant system (*Die chr. Glaubenslehre*, vol. 1, 1840, 136). Indeed, who does attest the divinity of this witness? What Strauss failed to see is that there is no Protestant "system," but that the Protestant Church and Protestant doctrine has necessarily and gladly to leave his question unanswered, because there at its weakest point, where it can only acknowledge and confess, it has all its indestructible strength.

[EN180] witness of the Holy Spirit

[EN181] The authority and certainty of Scripture depends upon the witness of the Holy Spirit and this is the greatest proof of proofs. For the authority of any spoken or written word at all depends upon the one who is its author. Much rests on this rule, which in fact is the foundation of all theology

AUTHORITY IN THE CHURCH

The Church does not claim direct and absolute and material authority for itself but for Holy Scripture as the Word of God. But actual obedience to the authoritative Word of God in Holy Scripture is objectively determined by the fact that those who in the Church mutually confess an acceptance of the witness of Holy Scripture will be ready and willing to listen to one another in expounding and applying it. By the authority of Holy Scripture on which it is founded, authority in the Church is restricted to an indirect and relative and formal authority.

1. THE AUTHORITY OF THE WORD

Holy Scripture attests to the Church (and through the Church to the world) the revelation of God, Jesus Christ, the Word of God. The power in which it does so is the power of the object to which it bears witness and which has also made and fashioned it as that witness. The witness of Holy Scripture is therefore the witness of the Holy Spirit. He is indeed the power of the matter of Holy Scripture. By Him it became Holy Scripture; by Him and only by Him it speaks as such. In doing so it mediates revelation; it presents Jesus Christ; in the servant form of a human word it speaks the Word of God. Those who hear it, hear Him. Those who wish to hear Him must hear it. This is the Evangelical principle of Scripture as such: the universal, fundamental and self-sufficient thing which has to be said about the attestation and mediation of revelation. And on this perception and confession there depends the answer to the question, how it comes about for us, for the Church (and through the Church for the world), that the witness of Holy Scripture is apprehended and accepted in virtue of the witness of the Holy Spirit. How does obedience to the Word of God in Holy Scripture arise? The question is analogous to the basic question: how is the revelation of the triune God effected? And if in the latter case a closer explanation of this very revelation compels us to reply: objectively by the incarnation of the divine Word in Jesus Christ and subjectively by the outpouring of the Holy Spirit of God, so too in relation to obedience to the attestation and mediation of this revelation, in relation to the Word of God in Holy Scripture, we have to distinguish between an objective and a subjective element, i.e., an outer and an inner determination of this obedience. In both cases we are [539] dealing with determinations whose subject is God. The reality of the attestation and mediation of His revelation is in the same sense and just as strictly

85

His work as is revelation itself and as such. But our present concern is to understand the reality of this attestation and mediation to us. Now to understand the reality of revelation itself and as such, the doctrine of the triune God had to divide into the doctrine of the incarnation of the Word and that of the outpouring of the Holy Spirit. The same division will be necessary to understand the reality of its certification and transmission by Holy Scripture. The truth and force of Holy Scripture in its self-attesting credibility is itself—and this is something we must never lose sight of—a single and simultaneous act of lordship by the triune God, who in His revelation is the object and as such the source of Holy Scripture. But if we ask how this truth confirms itself to us, how this power is effective in us—if we ask how the self-witness of Holy Scripture as the Word of God can enlighten the Church (and through the Church the world), then without denying the unity of the divine Word we have to distinguish between that which enlightens and those who are enlightened, between something objective and something subjective, between the external aspect and the internal, or, to put it concretely, between the possibility of God for man and the possibility of man for God. Only by making this distinction can we see them together as is needed, and therefore understand the reality of the witness to revelation in Holy Scripture, i.e., grasp it in the possibilities actualised in it. By attempting to grasp these possibilities as such, we repeat, as it were, on a lower level the division into the doctrine of the incarnation of the Word and that of the outpouring of the Holy Spirit. The possibilities are—objectively the authority of Holy Scripture instituted in the Church, by which the definite authority of the Church itself is established and limited; and subjectively the overruling freedom of Holy Scripture in the Church, which is again the basis and limit of the definite freedom of the Church and its members. We have to consider both the authority and the freedom if we want to reply to the question, how we arrive at obedience to God in Holy Scripture. Authority is the external determination under which this becomes possible for man from God—freedom is the internal determination, the determination under which it is possible for God from man. Either way it is primarily and strictly a matter of the authority and freedom which belongs to Holy Scripture itself in the Church. But either way it is secondly a matter of the authority and freedom of the Church as such, subject to Holy Scripture. Holy Scripture is the ground and limit of the Church, but for that very reason it constitutes it. Having authority and freedom in the Church, it lends that authority and freedom to the Church. We have to take this into account. For only as this takes place does it actually come about that Holy Scripture is obeyed as the Word of God [540] in the Church, and through the Church in the world. We are not asking now why this happens. We have already answered that question. It happens because Scripture is the Word of God and makes itself known as such. We are now asking genetically how it happens—just as in the doctrine of the incarnation of the Word and the outpouring of the Holy Spirit we could not discuss the "Why?" of revelation, but, against the background of the doctrine of the Trinity, only its "How?" To the same question of the method, this time of the mediation and attestation of revelation, we will now reply in this and the following section with the doctrine of authority and freedom in the Church.

When we speak of "authority" in the Church we mean first and generally that there is in the Church an authority which in relation to similar authorities stands in a closer relationship to the basis and nature of the Church, which has a greater part in its historical and material origin, which has therefore a claim to be more closely heard and regarded as more normative than other authorities. Fundamentally and in general, authority in the Church is an authority which has precedence because of its more primitive nature. Holy Scripture itself is such an authority in the Church. It is so in this general sense because it is a record, indeed historically it is the oldest extant record, of the origin and therefore of the basis and nature of the Church. That there are other authorities in the Church, which stand in a definite relationship to its basis and nature, which have a part historically and materially in its origin, and which have therefore in their own sphere a claim to be heard and respected and so in their own way to rank as authorities, is not radically denied by the existence of Holy Scripture. But not all these other authorities possess the character of records and none of them has the character of the oldest record. Therefore Holy Scripture has always in the Church a unique and in its way singular authority. But in its character as authority in this general sense, the authoritative significance of Holy Scripture cannot be exhaustive for the Church.

The appeal to the "written nature" and the age of the Bible never played a decisive part in the Reformation either on the Lutheran or the Reformed side. We find incidental mention of it in the *Conf. Helv. prior*, 1536, *Art.* 1 and in Calvin, *Instit.* I, 8, 3 f. On the lips of the Reformers the *Ad fontes!*[EN1] of the Humanists had another meaning, even in the case of those who like Zwingli were not so far from Erasmus.

In this general sense, Holy Scripture may have a singular authority in the Church, but that authority is still mediate, relative and formal. Mediate means temporal, historical and human. Consequently it is authority in the way in which there is earthly authority in other spheres as well, *iure humano*[EN2], authority which is subject to better instruction, to correction, to interpretation by other well-known authorities of a similar nature, to contradiction by an authority which perhaps reaches the same level and is then rated higher, and above all to a *ius divinum*[EN3] from which it derives its validity. Relative: this [541] means that like all other authoritative powers in the Church it can only represent the divine authority. And if this is the case it is not merely possible but necessary to appeal from Scripture (always recognising its unique value) to a true and original Word of God which we have to conceive of quite differently. The Church can and should go beyond the representative and preliminary

---

[EN1] To the sources!
[EN2] by human law
[EN3] divine law

judgment of Scripture to the supreme and real Judge and Lord. Formal: this means that at bottom and practically Holy Scripture is on a level with other witnesses to divine revelation, simply as witness, as pure form. It is not therefore the ground on which we know the promise that the revelation of God will and can be present in its attestation. The promise, by which in fact all witness lives, is known on quite a different ground, for which we should have to seek according to our own choice and in our own strength if we did not have it in Scripture.

Therefore on this view we have to say with Schleiermacher that faith in Christ "must be presupposed, if a special place is to be made for Holy Scripture" (*Der chr. Glaube*, § 128).

Now it is true that even in this general sense, i.e., as a very old record, Holy Scripture is authority.

Therefore, like Schleiermacher, who emphasised something on which the Reformers laid no stress at all (*Der chr. Glaube*, § 129, *Kurze Darstellung*, § 105), we can find the authority of Holy Scripture, or at any rate the New Testament, in the fact that it contains what are historically the first records of the Church's life.

Holy Scripture is also, in fact, a human historical record. Therefore in its relation to divine revelation it can also be compared to witness. It is also a mediate, relative, formal quantity. It asks and always has to be also evaluated as such. But to the extent that this has to be the case, the question how we come to obey it can never be answered. The real obedience of the Church is to an authority which has to be distinguished from Holy Scripture, to something immediate, absolute and material, which has to be sought or has already been found side by side with or even beyond Holy Scripture.

Therefore according to Schleiermacher the obedience of the Church is not to this thing as such which is historically the oldest and most primitive, but to it only as it has a "normal dignity," whose presence in Holy Scripture is decided by knowledge from quite a different source.

We then have to ask to what extent this different knowledge can claim to be knowledge of divine revelation, to what extent therefore that direct and absolute and material thing side by side with or above Holy Scripture is rightly equated with God or with Christ or with the Holy Spirit and therefore made the object of the real obedience of the Church. What is certain is that, in this determination of its obedience, in the last resort the Church will necessarily [542] have to rely on its own judgment. It will be itself which necessarily ascribes to that direct and absolute and material authority side by side with or above Holy Scripture, from which Scripture receives its mediate, relative and formal authority, its character as divine revelation. It must seek out Scripture for itself and itself give to it this supreme dignity. To be able to do this it must already be mistress of divine revelation, already know and participate in it. Divine revelation must be an original possession of the Church enabling it to declare with certainty where and what revelation is and therefore where and what the witness of revelation is.

Schleiermacher, the authoritative theologian of Neo-Protestantism, could actually ascribe this original possession of revelation to the Church in his doctrine of Holy Scripture. So, too, could and can Roman Catholicism.

If this were the case, the Church would itself actually be a direct, absolute, material authority. It would always, in fact, be the Church which instituted this authority and necessarily recognised itself in it. Its obedience to this authority would, in fact, be the fulfilment of its own striving and volition. It would then be quite impossible to find in it obedience and not self-regulation, to see in the authority accepted in the Church an authority over the Church and for the Church.

In opposition to this possibility we first have to lay down that where the Church really is the Church, then as the Church of Jesus Christ it finds itself in a known and therefore real relationship of obedience to what constitutes its basis and nature and therefore to Jesus Christ the Word of God. A relationship of obedience, however, is a relationship in an antithesis, an antithesis in which there is an obvious and genuine above and below. To a relationship of obedience two partners are necessary. They have a definite unity but they are no less definitely distinct in this unity. They stand in a definite and irreversible order, united, but distinct. One of them, and only one commands. The other has to submit to this command—just to submit. Now it is in such a relationship of obedience to Jesus Christ that we find the Church in the original act of revelation attested by Holy Scripture, in the confrontation of the apostles with the Crucified and Risen One, which has its Old Testament prototype in the confrontation of the prophets of Israel with Yahweh. Neither in Old Testament nor in New Testament do we find even only a trace of the possibility that this relationship of obedience, in which the biblical witnesses became what they were, recipients of revelation, was later dissolved and transformed into one in which these men could confront Yahweh or Jesus Christ as those who had a control of their own over that which was revealed to them, in which the Church could even partially rule itself. In Holy Scripture there is no sequel of an assured possession of revelation which from the standpoint of these men would be prior to revelation, a view of revelation side by side with or even [543] above revelation. They are never recipients of revelation in the sense that they appropriate revelation and can then recognise and evaluate it for themselves. They are recipients of revelation in the sense that revelation meets them as the master and they become obedient to it. It is because they are obedient that they are prophets and apostles. It is because they are obedient that they have the Holy Spirit. It is because they are obedient that they are appointed and commissioned to be Christ's witnesses to others, to the nascent Church and to the world. The Church of Jesus can exist only when it repeats this relationship of obedience. A revelation which the Church can recognise and evaluate on the basis of its own possession of revelation and from an independent view of revelation, even if it is called the revelation of God or Christ or the Holy Spirit, is not as such the revelation on which the Church of Jesus Christ is founded.

89

And the Church which in such a relationship to revelation ascribes to itself that direct and absolute and material authority is not as such the Church of Jesus Christ, even if it does quite seriously wish to call itself the Christian Church. The existence of the Church of Jesus Christ stands or falls with the fact that it obeys as the apostles and prophets obeyed their Lord. It stands or falls with the known and actual antithesis of man and revelation, which cannot be reversed, in which man receives, learns, submits and is controlled, in which he has a Lord and belongs to Him wholly and utterly.

But the relationship of obedience between the prophets and apostles and their Lord is a unique relationship as such. It is as unique as the incarnation of the divine Word, as the outpouring of the Holy Spirit, as the reconciliation of man with God in Christ's death and the revelation of it in His resurrection, as the forty days after Easter between the times. This between the times is a self-enclosed time, which does not return, or rather returns only in and with the return of Jesus Christ Himself. The Church's time, our time, is a different time. And this time is not simply a prolongation and continuation of that time. Therefore the existence of the Church does not mean the existence of new prophets and apostles who will receive God's revelation in the same direct way, and will be commissioned and empowered as its witnesses. If the Church of Jesus Christ exists only when there is a repetition of this relationship of obedience, then we must say: *Either,* outside that between-the-times there is no Church of Jesus Christ at all. The Church of Jesus Christ existed only once, in the prophets and apostles themselves, or strictly: in the forty days after Easter, in which the apostles saw the promise of the prophets visibly fulfilled before them. Since the appearance of that light the world has returned to its original darkness, and the memory of that light has become only an empty expectation. *Or,* the promise of the forty days is truly and visibly fulfilled before us as [544] was Old Testament prophecy in the forty days themselves: Ye shall be my witnesses. and: Lo, I am with you always. The unique revelation did not take place in vain, nor did that unique relationship of obedience take place in vain. Both of them, the revelation and the obedience of the prophets and apostles, continue to exist: indirectly, but in full, unbroken reality, a copy of the revelation in which this is always truly and validly present, and a model of the obedience, which even though there are no more prophets and apostles, can and should be seriously repeated in every age. This authentic copy of revelation and this authentic model of obedience to it is therefore the content of the witness of the prophets and apostles in Holy Scripture. It is therefore true that Holy Scripture is the Word of God for the Church, that it is Jesus Christ for us, as He Himself was for the prophets and apostles during the forty days. The result is that in their witness the Church itself has to do personally with its Lord. Therefore in the *per se* mediate, relative and formal quantity of Scripture, in which their witness is presented to us, it has to do with the self-subsistent and self-maintaining direct and absolute and material authority, with its own existence, nature and basis. Consequently the Church cannot evade Scripture. It cannot try to appeal past it directly to God, to Christ or to the Holy Spirit. It cannot assess and adjudge Scripture from a view of revelation gained apart from Scripture and not related to it. It cannot know any "normal dignity," which has to sanctify Scripture as the earliest record of its own life and make it its norm. It cannot establish from any possession of revelation the fact and extent that Scripture too is a source of revelation. Scripture confronts it commandingly as Holy Scripture, and it receives revelation from it in an encounter which is just as concrete and concretely ordered as that which according to Scripture originally took place between the Lord and His witnesses. It obeys Holy Scripture. Not as though it were obeying some long deceased men and their humanity and theology. But it obeys the One whom it has pleased to give certain long-deceased men, in and with and in spite of their humanity and piety and theology, a commission and authority. Therefore it serves the Word of God in the sign and guise of the word of these men. As it hears *them*, it hears it. And as it hears them, it *hears* it. The incarnation of the Word of God and the outpouring of the Holy Spirit has happened, is happening and will happen for the Church (and through the Church for the world) in every age, because in face of the uniqueness of revelation the Church is ready to receive its authentic witness and to accept and transmit it as authentic.

It will be as well to scrutinise sharply this either–or. If the promise "Ye shall be my witnesses" and "Lo, I am with you always" is not fulfilled, and therefore if Scripture is not the Word of God for the Church, then the revelation of God is only a memory, and there is no Church of Jesus Christ. There may well be a human community which is puffed up with the illusion that in it the life and influence of the prophets and apostles are perpetuated and [545] that therefore it stands with them in an immediate relationship to the direct, absolute and material authority of God, Christ and the Holy Spirit. This illusion, this forgetting of the uniqueness of revelation and with it of the prophetic-apostolic situation, works its own revenge: by raving about what does not pertain to it, the Church shows itself at once to be incapable of the relationship of obedience in which the prophets and apostles stand to revelation. It will pervert this relationship of obedience into one in which it thinks that by virtue of possession and knowledge and power it can evade God, Christ and the Holy Spirit, in which it has not merely to obey but to control. And inevitably it will more and more be the one who really controls. Inevitably it will more and more approximate to that direct, absolute and material authority, and finally proclaim itself more or less directly identical with it. Inevitably it will become a Church which rules itself under the pretext of obedience to revelation. And it can easily happen that when the illusion as such is more or less clearly felt and discerned, another human fellowship will arise, which, tired of this presumption, will make it its purpose to cherish that lovely recollection. There will then be possible a cultus and theology of the revelation which, according to the sacred books, once took place long ago, a revelation which at bottom does not affect us because it cannot be revelation to us, but which always surprises and claims and solemnises us from afar, not without a certain devotion and enjoyment. If Holy Scripture is not the Word of God, if it has only a mediate, relative and formal authority, it is possible to have a Church of ineffective although quite impeccable orthodoxy. It is possible, therefore, to have the Catholic Church, and the various Neo-Protestant applications and variations of the Catholic concept of the Church: all of which presuppose the great illusion regarding the uniqueness of revelation; all of which are on the way to a pantheistic identification of Church and revelation. And on the other hand it is also possible either in the Catholic or the Protestant form to have a reflection of the true original: a dead Church, a Church which is assembled around revelation as around a lifeless idol, a Church which sees the uniqueness of revelation and, for that very reason, despairs of itself. But the two Churches are not at bottom two Churches. They are only the two poles between which the life of the one Church would have to swing in a highly unnecessary and dangerous tension, were it not that Holy Scripture is the Word of God. They are the two poles between which the life of the one Church, whether it calls itself Catholic or Protestant, will necessarily swing, if it has not the faith that in Holy Scripture God Himself speaks to it. For without that faith it will alternately be swollen with arrogance and sink in self-despair. In its own eyes and those of the world it will now be great and arrogant, now small and hateful, not in the glory and poverty of Christ, but either way as a representative, like all other worldly constructs, of the darkness in which the world will necessarily lie if God has not revealed Himself, or if He has curiously done so only once, and therefore in vain as far as other ages are concerned.

If this Church in the one form or the other is not the Church of Jesus Christ, if there is a real Church of Jesus Christ distinct from this Church—although perhaps only as the mystery of God which is constantly declared in this Church, then it is because the saying is literally true and fulfilled: Ye shall be my witnesses and, Lo, I am with you alway. If this is true, if it is believed because it is true, then the revelation is determined far above the Church in the word of the prophets and apostles to whom it is said: the word of revelation, not the Church's own word, but the outside word which is spoken to it, so that it cannot seize or possess or control that revelation. And if this is so it will always bow before it. It will learn of it. In genuine obedience it will participate in it. At this level it will not be far from it, but in its garb as a human word, with which we can deal to-day and every day in human form, it will be

[546] near. Then, if the attested God is present to it in human testimony, if Scripture is the Word of God, it will live by the revelation of God, avoiding both arrogance and despair, experiencing and declaring His presence in our present, being the companion of His age in our age, not in an arbitrarily selected garment of pomp or poverty, but in the genuine humiliation and also the genuine glory of Christ.

In this either–or the Church will again and again have to choose. Will and can the Church decide to receive revelation by accepting the authentic witness of it? Is it therefore resolved to ascribe direct absolute and material authority only to Holy Scripture and not to anything else, not even to itself? At this point we stand before one of the severest conflicts in its history. Although not felt in all its severity, it was present from the very first. It broke out openly in the Reformation and counter-Reformation of the 16th century. Since then, together with other well-known antitheses, it has constituted the frontier which separates the Roman Catholic Church and the true, Evangelical Church, and which will inexorably separate them, so long as both continue to be what they are. Yet the nearest and most pressing opponent and disputant of the Evangelical Church is not open Catholicism as such, but the heresy of Neo-Protestantism which has broken out within it, and which in this matter has shown itself at the crucial point to be simply the extended arm of the errant Papist Church. The Evangelical, and with it the true Church, stands or falls by the fact that (apart, of course, from the revealed and proclaimed Word of God which is identical with Scripture) it understands exclusively the statement that the Bible is the Word of God, claiming direct, absolute and material authority neither for a third authority nor for itself, and therefore taking in full and, if the objection is made, "narrow" seriousness the confession of the newness, uniqueness and divinity of the revelation attested in Scripture and the acknowledgment that the Church owes this concrete obedience. On the other hand, it is no less essential and important for the Roman Catholic system that it should reject this alleged narrowing down of revelation to its biblical attestation, putting a definite element in Church life which is given the name of divine revelation, the so-called tradition, side by side with Holy Scripture, then broadening this element more and more until the whole of Church life seems to be included in it, then subordinating and co-ordinating Holy Scripture under and with this whole, and finally declaring this whole and therefore itself to be identical with the revelation of God. The same relativising of Holy Scripture first of all in relation to certain elements, then to the totality of Christian history, the same inclusion of Holy Scripture in this history, and finally the same equation of this history as such with divine revelation is also the very essence and characteristic of the Neo-Protestant doctrine of Scripture. The distinction between the two consists in the fact that the reality of the Church equated with revelation has in Catholicism, in the form of the Roman hierarchy, a theoretical and practical definiteness and mobility which the Neo-Protestant "history" of Christianity, lacking any visible form, can never have. Yet the two are one in the fact that behind both there stands the possibility to extend the long line of equations by another line, i.e., by identifying not only Christian history but the history of religion, indeed in the long run all history or human reality generally, with revelation. Therefore we have to say that in this conflict a decision of final magnitude is involved. A historical consideration on the relationship between Scripture and tradition is indispensable at this point. (Cf. for what follows: H. J. Holtzmann, *Kanon und Tradition*, 1859; Josef Ranft, *Der Ursprung des katholischen Traditionsprinzips*, 1931).

Even to-day the prejudice still exists that the concrete, polemical sharpness of the Reformed Scripture principle, the unconditional rejection of a Church tradition rivalling Holy Scripture as a source of revelation, is a peculiarity of the Reformed Church. And the same holds of the opinion based on this prejudice that from the standpoint of Lutheranism it is not impossible that an understanding might be reached with Catholicism in this matter. [547] This historical prejudice has support in the well-known fact that the Scripture principle is in fact expressed more or less sharply and explicitly at the head of all the more important confessional writings of the Reformed Church with more or less acuteness and explicitness, whereas in the basic Confession of the Lutherans, in the Augsburg Confession and Luther's catechisms generally, it does not receive specific mention. Let us take as an example the *Conf. Gallic.*, 1559, *Art.* 5 and see what the Reformed Church accepts and rejects in this matter: *Nous croyons que la parole de Dieu qui est contenue en ces livres est procedee at Dieu, duquel elle seule prend son authorité et non des hommes. Et d'autant qu'elle est reigle de toute vérité contenant tout ce qui est necessaire pour le service de Dieu et nostre salut, il n'est loysible aux hommes, ne mesmes aux Anges d'y adiouster, diminuer ou changer. Dont il s'ensuit que ne l'antiquité, ne les coustumes, ne la multitude ne la sagesse humaine, ne les iugements, ne les arrestz, ne les edicts, ne les decrets, ne les conciles, ne les visions, ne les miraclez, ne doivent estre opposez à icelle Escripture saincte, ains au contraire toutes choses doivent estre examinees, reiglees, et reformees selon icelle*[EN4]. But in view of this and similar passages we must not forget that there are some Reformed confessional writings, like the Berne Synod of 1532, the Basel Confession of 1534 and especially the *Heidelberg Catechism*, in which we need a microscope to find the Scripture principle, as we do in the older Lutheran documents. Consequently the fact that on the Reformed side the matter is made more explicit than on the Lutheran rests solidly upon the fact that in this as in other matters the Reformed Confession represents the common substance of the Evangelical

---

[EN4] We believe that the Word of God which is contained in these books has proceeded from God, from whom alone it takes its authority, and not from men. And since it is the rule of truth containing that which is necessary for the worship of God and for our salvation, it is not lawful for men, nor even for angels, to adjust, diminish, or change it. From this it follows that neither antiquity, nor customs, nor the view of the majority, nor human wisdom, nor judgments, nor prohibitions, nor edicts, nor decrees, nor councils, nor visions, nor miracles must be opposed to this Holy Scripture; on the contrary, these things must be examined, regulated, and reformed according to it

teaching at a later stage, at the stage at which it was already achieving, provisionally, a final form, and therefore with a clarity which had everywhere existed in practice right from the outset, but which was hardly ripe for theoretical expression in the third decade of the century—the great period of the Lutheran reformation. That at the end of the Reformation period the Lutheran Church understood itself to hold the same doctrine and to make the same confession as the Reformed is brought out quite unequivocally in the two parts of the preface to the Formula of Concord, where Holy Scripture, "the prophetic and apostolic writings of the Old and New Testaments " are mentioned as "the one judge, rule and guide," as "the clean, pure spring of Israel," by which as "the only touchstone all teachers should and must be known and judged, whether they are good or bad, right or wrong." "Should an angel from heaven come and preach otherwise, let him be accursed," is quoted from Gal. 1⁸. "But other writings of the old and new teachers, as they are called, should not be equated with Holy Scripture, but all subjected to it and accepted only as witnesses ...." And these statements were far from being a later correction and amplification on the part of the Lutheran Church. They simply made explicit what Luther himself at any rate had not only practised, but a hundred times implicitly and explicitly asserted. Do we not have it in his own words in the Schmalkaldic Articles, which were given the status of a public confession, that: "We must not make the work or words of the holy Fathers into articles of faith .... We are told that the Word of God must constitute articles of faith, and no one else, not even an angel" (*Bek. Schr. d. ev.-luth. Kirche*, 1930, 421, 18)? It is hard to see how far the decision taken here is in any way less radical and irrevocable than that of the Reformed confessions. With a good conscience a Lutheran can no more make even slight concessions in this matter to the Catholic position than a Reformed Protestant.

We will compare this Evangelical decision directly with the Roman Catholic one, as determined and made in its basic form on 8th April 1546 at the fourth session of the Council of Trent: the *puritas ipsa evangelii*[EN5], the truth and order (*veritas et disciplina*) which was promised by the prophets, expressed by Christ Himself, and proclaimed by the apostles at His behest, is contained in *libris scriptis et sine scripto traditionibus, quae ab ipsius Christi ore ab apostolis accepta aut ab ipsis apostolis Spiritu sancto dictante quasi per manus traditae ad nos usque pervenerunt.* And then the Council declares that the books of the Old Testament and New Testament it *nec non traditiones ipsas, tum ad fidem, tum ad mores pertinentes, tanquam vel oretenus a Christo, vel a Spiritu sancto dictatas et continua successione in ecclesia catholica conservatas, pari pietatis affectu ac reverentia suscipit et veneratur*[EN6] (*Denz.* No. 783). Hence Holy Scripture is one, but not the only source of our knowledge of revelation. Apart from what we know from Holy Scripture, Christ, or even the Holy Ghost, have told the apostles other things which we have to hear and reverence as "truth and order." These other things are the tradition which has come down to us from them transmitted from hand to hand. Its bearer and guardian has been the Catholic Church in its historical continuity. And to this second visible source of knowledge we have to ascribe the same authority as to the first. At the Council of Trent this decision was not made without difficulties and disputes. Three bishops in particular, of Fiesole, Astorga and Chioggia, according to a Catholic interpretation, "repeatedly evoked the displeasure of the leaders of the Council and other fathers, partly by their tactlessness, partly by their opposition to the obvious standpoint of the majority, especially in relation to the *pari pietatis affectu*[EN7]," and it was only by threats that they could be reduced to silence (Ranft, 7).

[548]

[EN5] very purity of the Gospel

[EN6] venerates and receives with reverence and equally pious affection these traditions which pertain both to faith and to ethics, whether from the mouth of Christ, or dictated by the Holy Spirit and preserved in continuous succession in the Catholic Church

[EN7] equal affection piety

1. The Authority of the Word

The logic of the preceding developments was against them and their doubts, and milder suggestions were necessarily opposed by a council which had made it its appointed task to fight the Reformation. If the Reformed decision was no novelty in the Church, neither was the Tridentine, and we have to concede that the scales had long come down on the latter side. Had it been otherwise, the Reformation would not have had to be carried through in the painful but unavoidable form of a disruption.

Already in Irenaeus we find "true gnosis" defined as ἡ τῶν ἀποστόλων διδαχὴ καὶ τὸ ἀρχαῖον τῆς ἐκκλησίας σύστημα κατὰ παντὸς τοῦ κόσμου EN8 (C. o. h. IV, 33, 8). And in Origen the *credenda veritas*EN9 is that, *quae in nullo ab ecclesiastica et apostolica traditione discordat*EN10 (Περὶ ἀρχῶν I praef. 2). Basil distinguished among the Church doctrines: τὰ μὲν ἐκ τῆς ἐγγράφου διδασκαλίας—τὰ δὲ ἐκ τῆς τῶν ἀποστόλων διαδοθέντα ἡμῖν ἐν μυστηρίῳ EN11. By oral tradition Basil had in mind a secret tradition. And if it were neglected we would be thoughtlessly ignoring the most important part of the Gospel (*De Spiritu sancto* 27, 66). In Basil, and later in Epiphanius, we find that the need for παράδοσις EN12 side by side with Scripture is grounded on the complaint that the apostolic tradition contained in Scripture is incomplete: οὐ γὰρ πάντα ἀπὸ τῆς θείας γραφῆς δύναται λαμβάνεσθαι EN13 (*Adv. Haer.* 61, 6). Tertullian had already expressed himself even more plainly on the ambiguity of Scripture: *Non ergo ad scripturas provocandum, nec* in his *constituendum certamen, in quibus aut nulla aut incerta est victoria*EN14 (*De praescr.* 19). And Chrysostom could turn to good account the passage 2 Thess. 2[15] which was so gladly used in later Catholic polemics. From it we learn that the apostles transmitted many things that were not put in writing: ὥστε καὶ τὴν παράδοσιν τῆς ἐκκλησίας ἀξιόπιστον ἡγώμεθα. παράδοσίς ἐστιν, μηδὲν πλέον ζήτει EN15 (*In. ep. II Ad. Thess. hom.* 4, 2). And at the second Council of Nicea in 787 the stage had been reached when those who reject the παράδοσις ἐκκλησιαστικὴ ἔγγραφος ἢ ἄγραφος EN16 can be expressly anathematised (*Denz.* No. 308). But what is this apostolic tradition which is accepted and has to be heard side by side with Scripture? Even in the 16th century the charge could be brought against the decree of the Council of Trent that it speaks of apostolic traditions without stating what concretely it wants to be understood as such. The charge is well founded only to the extent that the Council was content to repeat the answer already given with increasing definiteness in the Early church, pointing to the historical continuity of the Catholic Church. In effect this answer simply means that the recognition and indeed the universal recognition of the Church shows a definite tradition to be apostolic, and therefore authentic, and therefore revelation. We have seen this answer already in the words of Irenaeus. Similarly we find in Jerome that there are [549] many things which are accepted in the Church only on the basis of tradition but which have still gained for themselves (*usurpaverunt*) the *auctoritas scriptae legis*EN17. Who decides where

---

EN 8 the teaching of the apostles and the ancient orders of the church throughout the whole world
EN 9 truth to be believed
EN10 which is in disagreement with no ecclesiastical and apostolic tradition
EN11 those which derive from written teaching, and those which were given to us through the teaching of the apostles by the mystery
EN12 tradition
EN13 for not all things can be grasped from the divine Scripture
EN14 Therefore a challenge must not be laid down to the Scriptures, nor is a dispute to be resolved by them, in which there is either no success, or uncertain success
EN15 such that we also consider the tradition of the church to be worthy of faith. There is tradition: seek nothing more
EN16 ecclesiastical tradition, written or unwritten
EN17 the authority of the written law

this should be the case? The *consensus totius orbis*[EN18] (*Dial. c. Luciferianos* 8). *Quod universa tenet ecclesia nec conciliis institutum, sed semper retentum est, non nisi auctoritate apostolica traditum rectissime creditur*[EN19] (Augustine, *De bapt.* IV, 24, 31, cf. II, 7, 12 and V, 23, 33). Universality as the mark of what is apostolical and therefore ecclesiastical could just as well be regarded temporally (i.e., with respect to the age of a particular tradition) as spatially (with respect to its geographical dissemination). It was in the first sense that Tertullian understood and used the proof of prescription: *id esse dominicum et verum, quod sit prius traditum, id autem extraneum et falsum, quod sit posterius immissum*[EN20] (*De praescr.* 31). But in the utterances especially of Augustine the emphasis seems to fall rather on spatial universality. Comprehensively the answer to the question would have to be formulated as follows: apostolic and therefore authentic tradition is what the Church which is general and universal in these two dimensions recognises to be such. By the turn of the 4th and 5th centuries what the Church as such has to say side by side with Holy Scripture, even if only in amplification and confirmation of it, already has a particular weight of its own, so that the saying which we have already quoted from Augustine—which the Reformers attempted in vain to interpret it *in meliorem partem*[EN21]—now became possible: in answer to the question what we are to tell those who still do not believe in the Gospel, Augustine has to confess, obviously on the basis of his personal experience: *Ego vero evangelio non crederem, nisi me catholicae ecclesiae commoveret auctoritas*[EN22] (*C. ep. Man.* 5, 6). That I have the Gospel and can believe in it is obviously, as Augustine sees it and as he was rightly understood in later Catholic polemics, itself a gift of Church tradition. Therefore the saying foreshadows that inclusion of Scripture itself into the tradition which was expressly accomplished at a much later date.

In spite of all the evidence to this effect, the attitude of the Church fathers on this matter was not unequivocal. The Reformers, too, could appeal to the early Church. The statement: *quia non possit ex his* (*sc. Scripturis*) *inveniri veritas ab his qui nesciant traditionem; non enim per literas traditam iuam, sed per vivam vocem*[EN23] is cited by Irenaeus (*C. o. h.* III, 2, 1) as gnostic and heretical. Against the idea that age as such legitimates a tradition, Cyprian especially objects in many of his letters (63, 14; 71, 3; 73, 13, 23), and supremely in the saying: *consuetudo sine veritate vetustas erroris est*[EN24] (74, 9). Similarly and even more pregnantly Tertullian, the father of the proof of prescription, could write boldly enough: *Dominus noster Christus veritatem se, non consuetudinem cognominavit*[EN25] (*De virg. vel.* 1). In Athanasius we find a clear distinction between the "holy and inspired writings," which are self-sufficient (αὐτάρκεις) in the declaration of truth, and other writings which may be used as a commentary on them (*Adv. gentes* 1). Similarly, Augustine could declare that *in iis, quae aperte in scripturis posita sunt, inveniuntur illa omnia, quae continent fidem moresque vivendi, spem scilicet et caritatem*[EN26] (*De doctr. chr.* II, 9). But we must note that these statements, although they

---

[EN18] agreement of the whole world

[EN19] What the universal church holds, even if it has not been established by councils, but has always been believed, is most rightly to be believed if it has been passed down on apostolic authority

[EN20] that which has been passed down of old is dominical and true, but that which has more recently been added is foreign and false

[EN21] in a more charitable sense

[EN22] But I would not have believed the Gospel, had the authority of the Catholic Church not compelled me

[EN23] since the truth cannot be discovered from them (i.e. the Scriptures) by those who are ignorant of the tradition; for it has not been passed down in written form, but by the living voice

[EN24] custom without truth means that the error is old

[EN25] our Lord Christ described himself as 'the truth', not as 'a custom'

[EN26] in those books which are publicly numbered among the Scriptures, all those things are found which maintain faith, and the morals for living, namely, hope and love

contradict the others, never attain to that clear and critical confrontation of Scripture and tradition which we have in the Reformation decision. The introduction of that "heretical" statement by Irenaeus has only a dialectical significance. Elsewhere Irenaeus (cf. *C. o. h.* II, 4, 1–2; IV, 24, 3) is one of the first of many who co-ordinated and subordinated Scripture to tradition. What corresponds to *consuetudo*EN27 in Cyprian is the ambiguous concept of Church *ratio*. And, of course, in Tertullian the *veritas*EN28 which is so impressively opposed to *consuetudo*EN29 is not the *veritas scripturae*EN30 of the Reformers, but a substance of truth imparted to the Church and developing in history with inward consistency from its original seed, so that its true and normative manifestation could just as easily be its developed rather than its earlier form. Even in Tertullian the proof has a form which is related to the future. Hence he can occasionally say, in what must be understood as a purely dialectical contradic-   [550] tion he can occasionally tell himself: *In omnibus posterior a concludunt et sequentia antecedentibus praevalent*EN31 (*De bapt.* 13). From the statements of the fathers which point in this other direction I would not venture to deduce more than that in the development of the Catholic system there was always a recollection of its opposite and therefore a retarding element.

The classical and in pre-Reformation and counter-Reformation times the standard representation of the Catholic conception is to be found in a writing which we may think it significant was composed by a professed semi-pelagian and, in the first instance, obliquely directed against the Augustinian doctrines of predestination and grace: the *Commonitorium of* Vincent of Lerins, A.D. 434. In this work we are told that the way to the knowledge of the *veritas catholicae fidei*EN32 is twofold: *Prima scilicet divinae legis auctoritate, tum deinde ecclesiae catholicae traditione*EN33. Why must there be the second as well as the first? Because, says Vincent, although in itself Holy Scripture is a sufficient authority, in view of its exalted nature (*altitudo*) it cannot be understood in the same sense by everybody, because the same passages in the Bible are continually being interpreted by different people in different ways. But it is necessary, and care must be taken, that the exposition of the prophets and apostles should be an ecclesiastical and therefore a universal or catholic one: *ut id teneamus, quod ubique, quod semper, quod ab omnibus creditum est*EN34. For this purpose we have to ask concerning it, taking as our criteria universality, antiquity, consent. *Universitas*EN35 belongs to a definite position which can claim to be ecclesiastical when spatially and geographically it is everywhere that of the Church: *antiquitas*EN36, when it has been that of those who have gone before and the fathers; and *consensio*EN37, when it is held by all or almost all those who at any time bear the teaching office (the *sacerdotes et magistri*EN38). In the *ubique*EN39 and *semper*EN40 Vincent was obviously only repeating and summarising what preceding centuries had worked out concerning the nature of tradition as it has to be distinguished from Scripture.

EN27 custom
EN28 truth
EN29 custom
EN30 truth of Scripture
EN31 In all matters, the latter statements are conclusive, and subsequent statements prevail over what precedes
EN32 truth of the Catholic faith
EN33 The first is evidently by the authority of the divine law, then secondly by the tradition of the Catholic Church
EN34 so that we may hold what has been believed in all places, at all times, by all
EN35 Universality
EN36 antiquity
EN37 consent
EN38 priests and teachers
EN39 in all places
EN40 at all times

But at the same time, and it is here that we see the independent significance of his state-ments, there is added a third criterion, the *ab omnibus*[EN41], which is not merely a repetition of the *ubique*[EN42], which does at least indicate the problem which obviously has to be answered even when the *universitas*[EN43] and *antiquitas*[EN44] have been established as the signs of what is catholic and therefore apostolic. For with the addition he puts the question: Who does *in concreto*[EN45] decide the presence of what is universal in time and space? Theoretically this question was left open by the Council of Trent in its declaration on the principle of tradition, though in practice there can be no doubt what was intended. But even in this instrument of the counter-Reformation it appears that the retarding element was still at work. In Vincent, however, it had already been overcome in principle. Vincent gives the theoretical answer to the question, and although from the standpoint of more recent devel-opment we cay say that even in him it lacks final precision, it is clear enough in its own way. Beyond the constitutive *ubique*[EN46] and *semper*[EN47] there is a regulative *ab omnibus*[EN48]. That is, the interpretation of tradition and—because tradition on its part is the authentic inter-pretation of Holy Scripture—the interpretation of Holy Scripture is the concern of the exist-ing teaching office in its *consensio*[EN49]. The darkness in which Tertullian had once put the earlier above the later, and also the later above the earlier, is now illuminated. The *veritas catholicae fidei*[EN50], that of the truly catholic exposition of Scripture which corresponds to its object and is therefore carried out within the framework of tradition, is on the one hand according to 1 Tim. 6^{20} a *depositum: quod tibi creditum est, non quod a te inventum, quod accepisti, non quod excogitasti, rem non ingenii sed doctrinae, non usurpationis privatae, sed publicae traditionis, rem ad te perductam, non a te prolatam, in qua non auctor debes esse, sed custos, non institutor sed sectator, non ducens sed sequens.*[EN51] Therefore *Timotheus*, the *sacerdos, magister, tractator*[EN52], *doctor* of that time, is summoned to guard, preserve and maintain: *quae didicisti doce, ut cum dicas nove non dicas nova*[EN53]. But in this *nove*[EN54] we already meet the second thing which faces not only backwards but forwards: *preciosas divi dogmatis gemmas exculpa, fideliter coapta adorna sapienter, adice splendorem, gratiam, venustatem, intelligatur te exponente illustrius quod ante obscurius credebatur. Per te posteritas intellectum gratuletur quod ante vetustas non intellectum venerabatur*[EN55]. Its activity is not merely to conserve but in conserving to produce. There is, Vincent declares, progress in the Church. Of course there is no *permutatio: ut*

[551]

[EN41] by all
[EN42] in all places
[EN43] universality
[EN44] antiquity
[EN45] in practice
[EN46] in all places
[EN47] at all times
[EN48] by all
[EN49] consent
[EN50] truth of the Catholic faith
[EN51] deposit, that which has been entrusted to you, not that which has been invented by you; which you have received, not which you have thought up; a matter not of the mind, but of doctrine, not of private possession, but of public tradition; a thing brought to you, not revealed by you, of which you ought not be the author but the guardian; not the originator, but the follower; not the leader but the disciple
[EN52] priest, teacher, handler, instructor
[EN53] what you have learned, teach – so that when you speak anew, you do not say new things
[EN54] 'anew'
[EN55] polish the precious gems of divine doctrine, fit them faithfully, and adorn wisely, add splen-dour, grace, loveliness, and may what was previously believed dimly be understood more clearly as you expound it. Through you, posterity will rejoice in the understanding that which previous generations had revered without understanding

1. *The Authority of the Word*

aliquid ex alio in aliud transvertatur[EN56], but there is a *profectus religionis: ut in semetipsum res amplificetur. Crescat igitur oportet el multum vehementerque proficiat tam singulorum quam omnium, tam unius hominis quam totius ecclesiae, aetatum ac saeculorum gradibus, intelligentia, scientia, sapientia, sed in suo dumtaxat genere, in eodem scilicet dogmatae eodem sensu, eademque sententia. Imitetur animarum religio rationem corporum, quae, licet annorum processu numeros suos evolvant et explicent, eadem tamen quae erant permanent*[EN57] (22–23). Therefore the tradition does not change, but it grows, just as a natural organism remains the same in nature and kind and yet grows, and to that extent is always the same yet always made new. But the conserving and producing use of tradition is in one hand and under one guidance and responsibility, and this hand and guidance and responsibility is that of the Timothy addressed by Vincent, i.e., those who at any time bear the teaching office of the Church in their mutual *consensio*[EN58]. This *consensio*[EN59] must obviously guarantee that both the conserving, i.e., the care for *ubique*[EN60] and *semper*[EN61], and also the production should be kept free from accident and self-will in the service of this genuine tradition as directed to the future. We cannot assess too highly the contribution made by Vincent of Lerins in his theoretical elucidation of this matter, even when we remember that he was only formulating what had already been put into practical effect in the Church of his time, and continued to be so throughout the Middle Ages, but what even the Council of Trent obviously did not dare to formulate and proclaim as dogma with the same precision. Vincent drew the cords tighter than those who preceded him. He derived the one *corpus*[EN62] of the *depositum*[EN63] from the unexplained combination of Scripture on the one hand, with its need of exposition and development, and tradition on the other, which does expound and develop Scripture. He understood this *corpus*[EN64] as a whole as a living thing, which even as it remains the same, can and must also grow. Above all, he put both the maintenance and development into the hands of the teaching office of the Church, thus making the latter the visible subject of tradition. In all this he shows plainly which way things were moving and had to move once the first steps had been taken. When we remember Vincent, we cannot say of the counter-Reformation decision of the Tridentinum that it was hurried and exaggerated. Rather, the fathers of Trent, with perhaps too much sobriety and moderation, raised to the dignity of a confession a perception which had had a long life in the Popish Church and which it might have confessed much earlier, if it had not been restrained by what is (in the light of more recent developments) a puzzling timidity. But even though we cannot say why it should be the case, it was in fact restrained for a long time from openly making a dogma of the doctrine of the two sources, which is itself only a preliminary word. The proclamation of the truth by the Reformation was needed for the lie to come to fruition even in the measure in which it did so at Trent.

[EN56] transformation, such that anything be changed into something else

[EN57] progress of religion, such that the thing in itself is amplified. Therefore it is right that understanding, knowledge and wisdom increase and progress much more forcefully, both at individual points and in their entirety, both among individuals and in the whole church, in the course of generations; but exactly in its own way, that is, in its own doctrine, in its own sense, and in its own meaning. The religion of souls should imitate the reason of bodies, which can develop and extend their limbs in the course of the years, yet they remain the same things which they were before.

[EN58] consent

[EN59] consent

[EN60] in all places

[EN61] at all times

[EN62] body

[EN63] deposit

[EN64] body

§ 20. *Authority in the Church*

What was really intended was the identification of Scripture, Church and revelation. This lay behind the decree about tradition, and might well have been stated in it in accordance with the meaning of the developments which had preceded it. Indeed we can find a compromising hint of this identification in the Tridentinum itself to the extent that in the utterances on the translation and elucidation of the Bible, which were regarded more as practical injunctions, a statement was adopted which was later incorporated into the *Professio fidei Tridentina*, formulated in 1564, and which forbids the exposition of Holy Scripture even *privatim, contra eum sensum, quem tenuit et tenet sancta mater ecelesia, cuius est iudicare de vero sensu et interpretatione Scripturarum sanctarum, aut etiam contra unanimem consensum patrum*[EN65] (*Denz.* No. 786).

[552]

The Catholic thesis, as laid down in the Tridentinum, was maintained and defended in the 16th century, and from then on right up to the present day, on the following individual grounds. It was pointed out that Christ Himself spoke, but neither wrote nor gave any commission to write, that Scripture is also younger than the Church with its oral tradition, and not only younger but actually based on the latter, a work of the primitive Church and dependent on the Church's decision for its canonical validity. It was said again, as it had been so often in the early Church, that the Bible is dogmatically insufficient. There are also many decisions and directions of the Church recognised even by Protestants: for example, the doctrine of the Trinity, the baptism of infants and the observance of Sunday, all of which are based only on the tradition of the Church, not on Scripture. It was emphasised—and in view of the internal dissensions of the Protestants the argument had a new and telling force—how difficult it is to interpret the Bible, how great is the danger of an arbitrary subjectivism in its readings and how pressing the resultant need for a secondary authority to regulate the understanding of Scripture. Further, a series of passages was adduced from Scripture itself which seemed to justify the presence and validity of such a secondary authority. By way of example, I will cite those which the greatest Catholic champion of the 16th century, Cardinal Bellarmine, regarded as particularly cogent (acc. to Ranft, 29): Jn. 16^{12}: "I have yet many things to say unto you, but ye cannot bear them now"; Jn. 21^{25}: "There are also many other things which Jesus did, the which if they should be written every one, I suppose that even the world itself could not contain the books that should be written"; Ac. 1^3: "To whom also he shewed himself alive after His passion by many infallible proofs"; 1 Cor. 11^2: "I praise you that ye remember me in all things, and keep the traditions, as I delivered them to you"; 1 Cor. 11^{23}: "I have received of the Lord that which also I delivered unto you"; 1 Cor. 11^{34}: "The rest will I set in order when I come"; 2 Thess. 2^{15}: "Therefore, brethren, stand fast, and hold the traditions which ye have been taught, whether by word or our epistle"; 2 Tim. 1^{13}: "Hold fast the form of sound words, which thou hast heard of me"; 2 Tim. 2^2: "The things that thou hast heard of me among many witnesses, the same commit thou to faithful men, who shall be able to teach others also." And last but not least for the validity of tradition, the voice of tradition itself was adduced in the form of well-known testimonies from the early Church.

Reformed Protestantism did not need to be embarrassed by these arguments. The argument that Christ spoke but did not write anything reveals the basic confusion between the revelation of God and its attestation, and therefore the fatal lack of clarity in relation to the divine ruling of the Church and human ministry within it. It is, of course, obvious that there is a tradition which is older than Holy Scripture and on which Holy Scripture as such is founded: it is the way from revelation as such to its scriptural attestation. This way was the

---

[EN65] in private, against that sense which the holy mother church has held and does hold, the church whose purpose it is to make judgment on the sense and the interpretation of the Holy Scriptures; or also, against the unanimous consent of the fathers

way of the prophets and apostles distinguished by that direct encounter with Jesus Christ Himself. But it certainly was not the way of the Church founded and founding itself on their witness. To the later Church this way was closed when their witness took on written form. When that happened, the Church entered on a new way in so far as it is now the bearer of revelation only as the bearer and proclaimer of that witness—of that witness in the concrete and visible state in which it possesses it and not—as we need to note of all the New Testament passages quoted—in a state which can be manifested only by the perpetuation of prophets and apostles, i.e., the continuance of direct revelation. It is not the Church which has produced the witness, but the witness which has produced the Church: certainly before it was laid down in Scripture; but in this first form of its operation, on the original way before it became Scripture, it is invisible to the Church. It does not know it except as Scripture. Or by virtue of what insight and authority can it go behind its written form? If it knows and recog-   [553] nises its canonicity as the Word of God, this is grounded in itself, or in the revelation attested in it, in the manifestation of Jesus Christ and the institution of the prophets and apostles, and not in the judgment of the Church which later acknowledges the fact. Is the Church really taking its own judgment seriously, is it really recognising Scripture as canonical, as the Word of God, if it deduces from it the right to be and act as the bearer of a special Word of God apart from its function in the service of Scripture? If it does take it seriously, or rather, if it takes seriously what it acknowledges by this verdict, then no tradition however old and universal can prove that tradition has to be heard side by side with Scripture as an authority in the same sense. The equation of these authorities, and concealed behind it that of the Church itself with revelation, was an error and falsehood which we find already in Irenaeus and Augustine. Of course the Church has to preach, to teach, to judge, to decide. It has to do it with authority, and not merely in a repetition of biblical texts, but in the freedom commanded it, i.e., in the exposition and application of these texts, and necessarily going beyond them. But for the proclamation of the Church to try to be more than the exposition and application of Scripture, for it to make an autonomous claim to revelation, appealing to and basing itself on a direct and uncontrollable secret apostolic tradition, for it to be free itself from the discipline and criticism of Holy Scripture, from the possibility of appealing from its own mediate to this immediate authority, for it to ascribe to itself another position than that of a secondary ministry of attestation—that is quite impossible if the Church knows what is meant by its own judgment concerning the canonicity of Scripture. And in view of this we must say of the much deplored difficulty of explaining the Bible and of the fact of the many variations and contradictions in the explanations found, that what has always so widely divided the minds of men in the exposition and application of Holy Scripture has not been too great, but too small, a faithfulness in the perception that the Church must hear in Scripture and only in Scripture the Word of God. What Catholicism has for the most part done is classically typical of all heresies. In the exposition and application of Scripture it thinks that outside of Christ and the Holy Spirit as self-attested in Scripture it can also claim a Christ who may be known directly and a Holy Spirit who can be received and works directly—He may sometimes go by other more secular names. He may even be identical with human reason or vitality or nature or historical consciousness. And where this happens, then Scripture, which is clear in itself and in subject-matter, becomes obscure, the demanded freedom in exposition and application becomes self-will, and a divergence of the various expositions and applications becomes inevitable. There is no more dangerous subjectivism than that which is based on the arrogance of a false objectivity. Not the fact that Holy Scripture as the Word of God is obscure and ambiguous, but the fact that it is the Word of God for the Church on earth, and therefore a teacher of pupils who are lost sinners, is what makes the much deplored divergence in its understanding possible, and, unless the miracle of revelation and faith intervenes, quite inevitable. But this divergence can be avoided only by this miracle and certainly not by denying it in advance. It will not be avoided if, instead of accepting in faith the grace which meets them in Scripture, the pupils give way to their own sin, renouncing the relationship as pupils in which all their hope should be set, and each trying to be the teacher of Scripture or at least an equal partner in discussion. But even if in so doing they appeal to Christ and the Holy Spirit, even if ever so many of them should enjoy the finest *consensio*^{EN66} among themselves—on this path they can only increase the fragmentation and make it incurable.

[554]

Not too little but much too much traditionalism, i.e., enthusiastic belief in a direct access to revelation granted to the Church, was always true of the older Protestants as well. We have only to think of the fanatics and enthusiasts and mystics of the 16th century, who sowed the harvest of Protestant sectarianism which is so often derided in Roman polemics. But not only of them. Even in the two great official Evangelical Confessional Churches the Scripture principle was not taken too seriously but too little seriously. Too many direct certainties and self-evident truths were presupposed, some of them taken over from the Middle Ages, some of them dictated by the Renaissance, some of them newly developed, but all regarded as an inalienable possession of the Church, with the expressed or unexpressed character of a second source of revelation side by side with Holy Scripture. We have only to think of the alleged natural law, of Aristotle who, in spite of Luther's protest, quickly entered his own again as "the" philosopher (and to whose place and function other philosophers could equally well be appointed later), of the idea of the *corpus christianum*^{EN67} which was so critically important for the status of the Reformation Churches in state and society, but above all of the reality of the Confessional Churches as such, which was posited absolutely or almost absolutely. We have only to think of the magic and the practical influence of the magic exercised by the name of Luther and to some extent of Calvin. We have only to think of the almost magical authority which the Confession of Augsburg, laid before emperor and empire, acquired for Lutheranism. Are not all these non-scriptural authorities no less than the supposed apostolic traditions of the Tridentinum? On what ground and with what right did they all come—even in the 16th century—to be openly treated with the same seriousness as Scripture? And it was these authorities which brought about the same disastrous result even in Protestantism. The Protestant exposition and application of Scripture did not become so subjective and self-contradictory in the school of Holy Scripture itself, in which Protestantism ought to have been according to its own programme, but in the school of these other authorities, which were unconsciously accepted and described as *pari pietatis affectu et reverentia*^{EN68} and of equal value with Holy Scripture, not in the school of Luther and Calvin, but secretly very much in the school of Vincent of Lerins and in the spirit of the supposedly disputed Tridentinum. For that reason the 16th and 17th centuries were right when they tried to ensure that the cheap gibes of their opponents at this subjectivism and contradiction did not affect in the slightest the *perspicuitas scripturae sanctae*^{EN69}, when they were fundamentally agreed that the way out of this obvious dilemma did not lie backwards, in concessions to the Catholic principle of tradition, but only forwards, in a more energetic acceptance and application of the Evangelical Scripture principle. If they had only sought and taken that way more seriously ! The real weakness of the older Protestant position is that it did not do so much more definitely. Here, as elsewhere, the weakness was that from the very first it included in itself too much of Neo-Protestantism to be able to confront Catholicism not only with words but more effectively with deeds.

EN66 consent
EN67 'Christendom'
EN68 (treated) with equal pious affection and reverence
EN69 perspicuity of Holy Scripture

1. The Authority of the Word

The weakness is betrayed in the fact that in the 17th century attempts were already being made to find the way out not only in practical but in radical contradiction to the Reformation decision and with more or less open concessions to the Tridentine dogma—in other words, backwards.

It was not the first and best who led the way in this direction. The great Dutch jurist and historian, Hugo Grotius, is the one of whom we have to think (cf. Holtzmann, 41 f.). That he was an Arminian is in this context just as characteristic as was once the semi-Pelagianism of Vincent of Lerins: the battle against the freedom of grace is the root of Neo-Protestantism as well as of Roman Catholicism. Deeply impressed by the well-known arguments of Catholic polemics, Grotius made the radical concession: *stat omne verbum in duobus testibus, in scriptura et traditione, quae mutuo facem sibi alluent*[EN70]. Of course when he said this Grotius did not intend to say the same as the Tridentinum. What he had in mind was two sources of revelation, of equal seriousness and mutually self-declaratory. And by tradition he meant the *antiquus et universalis consensus veteris ecclesiae*[EN71] distorted by the Scholastics, as he thought   [555] he could see it in the essential and unanimous testimonies of the Church fathers and at the heart of the official Romish tradition. We shall have to ask how this "old" Church can be delimited from the mediaeval. But let us suppose that this question can be answered. We then have to ask how the decision of this early Church can have equal dignity with that of Holy Scripture? And in seeing and acknowledging in its own past a second source side by side with the first, does not the Church *eo ipso*[EN72] appoint itself the judge over both and therefore over Holy Scripture? And by what right does it do so? If Grotius faced the last two questions even less directly than the fathers of Trent did, there can be no doubt that his historical conjoining of the Bible and the earliest tradition, no less than the Tridentine dogma which extends the concept of tradition right up to the present time, necessarily demanded the idea of a possession of revelation under the control of the contemporary Church, an idea which would necessarily involve an open repudiation of the Reformation decision.

Grotius' counterpart in Lutheran Germany was the much discussed Georg Calixt of Helmstedt (cf. Holtzmann, 43 f.; W. Gass, *Geschichte der protostantischen Dogmatik*, vol. 2, 1857, 68–216). He is even more interesting than Grotius, because on the one hand the origins of the thesis are clearer in his case, and on the other the thesis is worked out more carefully and yet more definitely. Calixt could regard himself as a good Lutheran in that he did undoubtedly value the doctrine of justification by faith as the one and important insight and confession of his Church, and stated it fairly correctly as understood by the Reformation. But at the same time he belongs to that increasing number of Evangelical theologians who from the 17th century onwards did not give full weight and content to the concept of faith in this doctrine, but with a strange lack of certainty conceded that faith might unfortunately mean even an inactive and ineffective intellectual belief, and that therefore if the way of salvation is to be fully expounded it is necessary that without altering the doctrine of justification there should be added to it some conclusion on the necessary fruits of faith, on the minimum of moral righteousness in the believer indispensable to eternal bliss. In other words the idea arises, or recurs, that grace must be enlarged by man. The moral disposition and sentiment acquire an independence quite alien to the Reformers. It is of a piece with this that in Calixt the significance of the doctrine of justification has faded compared with that of the common dogma of the ancient Church, against the background and as the result of

---

[EN70] every word stands on two witnesses, on Scripture and tradition, which mutually illuminate each other
[EN71] ancient and universal consent of the old church
[EN72] by the same token

which he rightly enough understands it. The affection of Calixt is definitely not for the doctrine of justification, but for the general doctrine of the Trinity and the incarnation, and to that extent not for the Lutheran but for the ancient Christian-Catholic Church, out of which the Lutheran proceeded with its doctrine of justification. Calixt could also regard himself as a good Protestant to the extent that he could most sharply differentiate himself from the latest Jesuistic-curial Catholicism now being erected on the foundation of Trent. But again he did it in favour of that Christian Catholicism which he thought could be discovered behind the disruption of the 16th century and the corruption of the Middle Ages, and by which he now measured and criticised and compared the Lutheran and Reformed Churches, trying to indicate their true unity. According to Calixt there is a *consensus quinquesaecularis*^{EN73}, an essential agreement of the teachers, confessions of faith and conciliar resolutions of the first five centuries both among themselves and with Holy Scripture, which itself must be understood as part of this original *corpus*^{EN74}. For in this period the Church received from the Word of God the doctrinal substance indispensable to it, and in receiving it, it gave and appropriated it to itself (Gass, 110). Holy Scripture attests the legitimacy and therefore the normativity of the consent of the Church of this period. And conversely the Church of this period attested by its consent the perspicuity and sufficiency of Holy Scripture (Gass, 126). Therefore and to that extent the Church of this period is the criterion for the Church and Churches of all later periods, when the emergence of specific and alien doctrines partly destroyed that consent. It is the judgment on the more recent Popish Church, but also the higher, judicial and unifying authority in face of the Popish Church on the one hand and Protestantism on the other, and also in face of the inner dissensions within Protestantism. It constitutes, so to speak, the sound, natural stem of all historical Christianity, the core of truth, which has been maintained and can be recognised in all its excrescences and extuberances, and the rediscovery and universal acceptance of which would restore health and unity to the Church. Now there can be no doubt about the richness and consistency and also the good, i.e., humanly speaking most enlightening, intention of this conception. But for all this we cannot fail to see that it marks a definite and open reaction from the Reformation insight concerning Holy Scripture. With Calixt as with Grotius, we have first to ask whether the doctrine of the *consensus quinquesaecularis*^{EN75} in antithesis to the later Church does not rest on a great illusion? Whether, in fact, that earlier Church did not very definitely contradict itself? Whether in many of its agreements it was not very definitely opposed to Holy Scripture? Whether Roman Catholicism and all sorts of other views later seen to be heresies were not present in the post-apostolic age and especially the succeeding centuries? Whether from the standpoint of Holy Scripture the Church of that period, as of all periods, was not in need of reformation and therefore not at all in agreement with or one with Scripture, but confronted by and subjected to it to its humiliation and redemption. But even if it were as Calixt presupposed: can we really say in the one breath that the Church has received the Word of God from Holy Scripture and also given and appropriated it to itself, even if the latter takes place in the most perfect way? Must we not give to the primary witnesses the first word, a word which is radically and qualitatively first, even as compared with the most perfect of secondary witnesses? Can we bind the Church in the same way to the latter as to the former? Again, even if the Church did genuinely find itself in agreement with Holy Scripture and pursued a real reciprocity in its relation to it, it must not be overlooked that both the agreement and the ensuing dignity of the Church are radically lost again, or to what extent a full and open restoration of the two is

[556]

---

^{EN73} consent of five hundred years
^{EN74} body
^{EN75} consent of five hundred years

radically impossible. Calixt maintained a latent continuance of that sound stem even in the later Church, and he demanded and prophesied a universal reformation of the Church to restore, i.e., to make visible again its continuity with that normative Church which still had a latent existence. But in this Church, which is secretly present and will again become visibly and actively normative, the Church is not placed under Scripture but side by side with it, receiving the Word of God from it as it gives it to itself. The historical premiss on which Calixt maintains and proclaims the normativity of that early Church, i.e., that Church as the norm, is actually the premiss of an independent possession of revelation by the Church. Calixt definitely rejects an infallible Pope as the official representative and controller of this possession of revelation. This is to the credit of his desire for Protestantism. But what is the real difference if the Pope is replaced by an expert on early Church history, or a well-meaning architect of unity, who can now pass judgment? Behind the fallible professors and ecclesiastical politicians and other representatives of the present-day Church there still stands an infallibility of the Church as such. If the *consensus quinquesaecularis*[EN76] is really the norm of the Church and can be known as such, somewhere in the present-day Church we can know about revelation *a priori*[EN77] just as well as by being taught out of Holy Scripture. We are somehow in that original agreement with Holy Scripture which makes possible a reciprocity of receiving and giving. We started from the obvious uncertainty in Calixt in relation to the doctrine of justification. It was inevitable: those who think that it must be enlarged by a special doctrine of the fruits of faith necessary to salvation have not understood its presuppositions and therefore its meaning, even though they may state it correctly. [557] When he asserted the unity of the Lutheran Church with that of the Middle Ages and antiquity, Calixt could do so sincerely and boldly not least because he accepted the doctrine of justification only with this need for expansion and this expansion, not least because he thought he should correct the Reformed doctrine of original sin by teaching that the result of original sin involves only a severe weakness, but not a positive corruption of human nature (Gass, 133), not least because he obviously wanted to understand the activity of the regenerate as a co-operation of natural and supernatural acts based on the indwelling of the Holy Ghost (Gass, 101). And inevitably, too, Calixt adopted a mediating position even in the question of knowledge, even in the relationship of reason and revelation which had not been thoroughly elucidated by the Reformers: "Revelation does not need violently to enter into its rights, for in the sphere of spiritual activity as a whole there is a position which it has to occupy, there are points of contact which it has to grasp, there are tokens by which the consciousness of its truth is strengthened ... both kinds of intellectual appropriation (reason and revelation) exist side by side by divine arrangement" (Gass, 88). In face of these positions we can only say that the Neo-Protestant parallel to the Catholic principle of tradition which achieved definite shape in Calixt was not only possible but inwardly necessary. In all its shoots the theology which says "and" derives from one root. If you say "faith and works," "nature and grace," "reason and revelation," at the appropriate place you logically and necessarily have to say "Scripture and tradition." The "and" by which the authority of Holy Scripture is relativised in both Roman Catholicism and Neo-Protestantism is only the expression, one expression, of the fact that already the majesty of God has been relativised in His fellowship with man. And in this primary relativising both are equally remote from the Reformation decision.

Because of its weakness in carrying out the principle of Scripture, Protestantism entered on a great crisis. In the course of it, at least in its Neo-Protestant form, it developed into a pseudo-Church only too similar to that of Catholicism. That is, it became a Church which in

---

[EN76] consent of five hundred years
[EN77] independently

its history and presence is itself revelation. This development was, of course, always hampered by the recollection of the Reformation decision. But Catholicism had only to express itself more definitely and clearly in the direction which had become unequivocally plain at the very latest in Vincent of Lerins, but which had been immanent in it from the very first and to which—as distinct from the uncertainty of Protestantism in relation to its principle—it maintained a cautious but tenacious loyalty throughout the centuries. Here, too, the children of this world were wiser than the children of light. We saw how in addition to the parallelism of Scripture and tradition the Tridentinum decreed the subordination of all biblical exposition to the teaching office of the Church. But as often asserted for polemical purposes, was not the canonising and transmission of the Bible the work of the Church, and did not this, too, mean the superiority of the Church? The fact is that even before the Tridentinum Johann Eck (*Enchir.*, 1529, *de eccles. resp.* 3) could write: *Scriptura non est authentica sine autoritate ecclesiae. Scriptores enim canonici sunt membra ecclesiae*[EN78], and he called this argument the *Achilles pro catholicis*[EN79]. Indeed, as early as 1517 Sylvester Prierias had penned a statement which at that time even Catholics felt to be daring: *Quicumque non innititur doctrinae romanae ecclesiae ac romani pontificis tamquam regulae fidei infallibili, a qua etiam sacra scriptura robur trahit et auctoritatem, haereticus est*[EN80] (*Dial.* 15). It corresponds only too well that in the *Professio fidei Tridentinae* (1564, *Denz.* No. 995) tradition—now expressly defined as *apostolicae et ecclesiasticae traditiones*[EN81]—is mentioned before Holy Scripture. And so, after the Tridentinum, the *Cat. Rom.* (1556, I, *c.* 10, *qu.* 14) developed the doctrine that the apostolicity of the Church consists in the fact that its proclamation is true as that which did not arise yesterday or to-day, but was already represented by the apostles. To resist the doctrine of the Church is to resist the doctrine of the apostles themselves, to sever oneself from the faith, to resist the Holy Spirit. *Qui Spiritus primum quidem apostolis tributus est, deinde vero summa Dei benignitate semper in ecclesia mansit*[EN82]. It is not surprising, therefore, that in the next century (cf. Holtzmann, 55f.), on the one hand the concept of tradition was more and more definitely expanded to cover all the Church's historical development (including Holy Scripture at the outset, and the explicit and implicit decisions of the present-day Church at the close), and on the other the present teaching office of the Church comprised in the Papacy was more and more definitely referred to as the mouthpiece of this tradition. That in the service of the apostolic tradition the Church has not only a conserving function (as the Tridentinum has it) but also a producing one (as we find already in Vincent) is something which is expressed with increasing clarity. Occasionally now (especially in Jesuit literature) there is an openly derogatory mention even of the antiquity of the Church so highly valued in opposition to the Protestants. The ecclesiastical practice of any century can now, it is claimed, be ascribed directly to the Holy Spirit without reference to antiquity. Indeed, that side of Tertullian's proof of prescription which looked to the future now took on new life in the saying of the Jesuit Salmeron: *quo iuniores eo perspicatiores esse doctores*[EN83]. It is now recognised and openly declared that there are many conciliar findings and episcopal constitutions, many solemn announcements of the early Church, which now have no prac-

[558]

[EN78] Scripture is not authentic without the authority of the church, for the canonical writers are members of the church

[EN79] Catholic Achilles (i.e. the argument which, like Achilles, could defeat all opposition)

[EN80] Whoever does not stand upon the doctrine of the Roman church and of the Roman pontiff as the infallible rule of faith, from which even Holy Scripture draws its strength and authority, is a heretic

[EN81] apostolic and ecclesiastical traditions

[EN82] Indeed, this Spirit was first sent to the apostles, but then has remained in the church constantly by the supreme kindness of God

[EN83] The younger the teachers, the more perceptive

tical significance or authority, indeed that the Church fathers were guilty of not a few hetero-doxies and errors. In Baroque Jesuitism Augustine especially was fearlessly renounced. Mention is made of the obscurity of this father who was not without importance in the early Church, just as Catholic polemics used to speak of the obscurity of Holy Scripture: his real views are so recondite and confused that we can only assume either that he does not want to be understood, or that he had not sufficient command of language for the purpose ; and in addition he is of a passionate nature and inclined to extremes, ebbing and flowing like the ocean. In the Jansenist disputes it could be definitely stated that the reputation of Augustine had been more harmful to the Church than useful. And Brisacier (in the struggle against Jansenism) could even go so far as to say that the early Fathers and Councils are dead rules, which have no relevance to the burning questions of the time, but only serve to impress with the show of antiquity: they are strings to which we do not tie men but beasts! Statements like this were exaggerations for which later Catholic theology was not responsible and which self-evidently were never the officially stated opinion of the Church. But it is still instructive that, in the century in which we find the Protestants Grotius and Calixt relativising the authority of Scripture by an over-serious proclamation of the authority of the early Church, the Roman representatives of the same undertaking, the best-known exponents of progressive modern Catholicism, were questioning the authority of that Church. Both could, in fact, take place for the sake of the same alleged possession of revelation by the present-day Church. Yet it was no extravagance, but it had become the common habit of the Church, and still is even in contemporary Catholic dogmatics, not to speak as Trent did of two, but quite expressly of three sources of Christian knowledge. Scripture, tradition and the Church. Actually, of course—and this is an exaggeration, but a very characteristic one—nine co-ordinated sources of knowledge could be mentioned: Scripture, tradition, the Church, the Councils, *Sedes Apostolicae*[EN84], the fathers, orthodox theologians, reason, philosophy and history. There is no doubt that Catholic dogmatics and proclamation does even to this day listen to all these authorities *pari pietatis affectu*[EN85], just as in its own way Neo-Protestant proclamation and dogmatics also does. Tradition as a second source had in fact included all the eight authorities apart from Holy Scripture. The emphasis on the Church, especially the present-day Church, in what became the more customary triad shows the actual mouth to which we have to listen if we are to know *in concreto*[EN86] what tradition is in this comprehensive sense, to which we have to listen if we are to know *in concreto*[EN87] what Holy Scripture is and what is the meaning and content of Holy Scripture. To close the circle, all that was needed was an express decision as to where the mouth of the present-day Church must be sought and heard. And that decision did not remain untaken. [559]

In conclusion, we may also mention it as an interesting fact from this same century that it was not a Protestant but the French Oratorian, Richard Simon, who was the pioneer of a historico-critical science of biblical introduction. Only in the 18th century was he followed on the Protestant side by Johann Salomon Sender and others. For Simon himself the matter stood consciously and expressly in direct relationship to the Tridentine principle of trad-ition. "Catholics who are convinced that their religion does not depend wholly on the text of Holy Scripture, but equally on the tradition of the Church, cannot be shocked if they find that the unfavourableness of the times and the negligence of the copyists has introduced the same alterations into sacred writings as profane. Only prejudiced or ignorant Protestants can be shocked by it" (*Histoire critique du vieux test.*, 1678, 1, 1). Even without any Scripture,

---

EN84 Apostolic Seats
EN85 with equally pious affection
EN86 concretely
EN87 concretely

the Christian religion could have maintained itself by tradition alone according to Simon (1, 4). The freedom to investigate the human form of the Bible, which Simon derived from this genuinely Catholic perception, seemed at that time, at any rate to Catholics like Bossuet, novel and dangerous. Quite wrongly! The historico-critical investigation of the Bible could only have been dangerous to the Catholic system if it had taken the form of a free investigation of truth and therefore a free inquiry into the original form of the biblical witness of revelation. In its artlessly expressed humanity it would then be self-revealed in its exaltation over the Church both past and present, over every alleged possession of revelation. But that was certainly not the opinion of Simon, just as it was not the opinion of Semler and the Neo-Protestant biblical criticism that followed him. It was the freedom of biblical criticism which Simon so radically claimed—Bossuet did not really need to work so zealously for the suppression of his books—and not the freedom of faith based on the freedom of revelation. It was Simon who openly and unreservedly spoke "the final word in the whole Jesuit development of the principle of tradition" (Holtzmann, 60): *l'écriture, soit qu'elle ait été corrompue, ou qu'elle ne l'ait point été, peut être citée comme un acte authentique, lorsqu'elle est renfermée dans les bornes, que nous avons marquées ci-dessus; c'est à dire, lorsqu'elle se trouve conforme à la doctrine de l'église*[EN88] (3, 22). It is not therefore critical investigation, but the doctrine of the Church, which finally decides the authenticity of the Bible. Critical investigation is good enough to make way for the doctrine of the Church by proving that the Bible cannot have authenticity of its own. A a critical investigation it can also do otherwise—because it is not bound and therefore not really liberated by the question of revelation. The biblical tradition may or may not be "corrupted." In any case, if it comes into conflict with the doctrine of the Church, criticism can be honourably suppressed. That is how it was with the Roman Catholic origin of modern biblical criticism. Neo-Protestantism has no *doctrine d'église*[EN89] or papal Biblical-Commission visibly to direct and control its criticism of the Bible. But beyond all the alleged critical liberty of investigation it has all the better knowledge of the mighty tradition of the human consciousness of self and of history, by which it is decided with no less certainty than by a visible Rome within what limits the Bible is and is not an authority, whose command investigation as such loyally accepts and to whose judgment it is subordinated in the same honourable way as the "free" investigation of an externally known "Catholicism." In this connexion, too, we have to see that there is an underlying unity in the struggle against the authority of the Word, which is really the struggle against the freedom of grace.

[560]   We will conclude our historical survey with a glance at the two events in the history of Catholicism in the 19th century which give to the problem a final acuteness.

The first of these events is one to which not enough attention has been paid, the existence of the Catholic so-called Tübingen School. We can summarise the significance of this school as follows. Catholic theology now takes notice of the idealist-romanticist philosophy and theology of the turn of the 18th and 19th centuries, which was a continuation and renewal of the humanistic, enthusiastic and mystical side-movements of the 16th century, and in which Neo-Protestantism reached and passed its peak. It sees that there is an inward relationship between Catholicism and this a-Catholic system, and it makes its aspirations its own. Enriched in this way, it finds that it can gather together theoretically the results of previous Catholic development and represent them with a new power to modern man. (Cf. for what follows, Ranft, 46 f.) Already in the course of that 17th century development of the principle of tradition, especially at the hands of the Jesuits, the expression had been incidentally

---

[EN88] Scripture, whether it has been corrupted or whether it has not, can be cited as an authentic source, as long as it is kept within the parameters which we have demarcated below, that is, when it is in conformity with the doctrine of the church

[EN89] doctrine of the church

108

1. The Authority of the Word

coined: *Traditio successione continua vivit in animis fidelium semper*[EN90] (Holtzmann, 89). And now, after a century in which there had been no visible advances, at the end of the Enlightment and in relation to its real or supposed overthrow by the "Storm and Stress," idealism and romanticism, in the circle of J. M. Sailer (whom Clement Brentano styled "the wisest, truest, most sincere and consecrated Bavarian") the idea of a "living" tradition again became powerful. What was meant was the tradition of Christendom in continuity with the inwardness of the God-guided heart in which it has its true being, while its objective form in history and the Church, although we must honour it, has to be understood more as a condescension to man as he now is. This position has a clear affinity to the philosophy of religion of Leasing and Kant. It is naturally only a first attempt in this direction. To assimilate itself to Neo-Protestantism in this form, the form of the older Enlightenment, was too difficult a task for Catholic theology. With an even more open attachment to Neo-Protestantism, this time the Neo-Protestantism of Hegel and Schleiermacher, and better able to safeguard the specific interests of the Catholic Church, the Tübinger J. S. Drey has to take up again the thesis of Sailer and try to overcome its weakness by his view of the Church, i.e., of revelation as a living organism, which has developed and still develops out of the life-principle within it under the guidance of the divine Spirit, so that in its life the static principle, i.e., that which is originally given by God, is continually moved and kept in progress by the dynamically living principle—which is tradition. Drey avoids a conception in which Scripture itself is a fixed system and not a part of life which has its own movement revealed in clear advances (e.g., from the Gospels to the Epistles). For on this view tradition is only an enlargement, a supplementing or adding to Scripture by oral tradition, and Christianity and theology are the stereotyped impress of the *corpus* of Scripture and tradition as now immovably written and mechanically passed down. No, Scripture, tradition and theology are the living movement and development of the Christian spirit in the Church. We have to listen to them because this movement and development takes place in them. We have to listen to them first and decisively in what is the last stage of the development of that spirit: in the objectivity of the living faith of the present and in the subjectivity of the conceptual expression this faith creates for itself in its temporal and historical antithesis. In the distinction made by Drey between the static and dynamic principle of revelation on the one hand, and the subjectively-outward and the subjectively-inward element in theology on the other, we can see an after-effect of the Enlightenment which by the logic of Catholic thinking had to be and was actually carried a step further. But does not Catholicism have within itself these distinctions of the Enlightenment? Can they not equally well be used by it in its attempt to understand and explain itself? The Tübingen school from the very first could never quite rid itself of these distinctions. But it understood better how to restore and maintain the balance [561] between the two elements disturbed by Sailer and even Drey, the real dialectic between the static and the dynamic, the objective and the subjective. And it always concluded with the thesis so much emphasised by Drey, that we have to listen to the Church, the present-day Church, if we want to hear revelation. To the extent that it did this it was essentially a genuinely Catholic school. Its idealistic interpretations of revelation (like the Catholic biblical criticism inaugurated by Richard Simon, although in another way) were admirably calculated to repeat the Tridentine relativising of the authority of the Bible in a manner illuminating to the modern consciousness, but without at the decisive point leading or wanting to lead—and how could it?—to any other conclusion than that of the authority of the Church demanding obedience to-day. The classical exponent of this theology, who gathered the finest fruits of Neo-Protestantism into the Catholic barns, was after Drey the man who is rightly honoured as the father of modern German Catholicism, J. Adam Möhler (*Die Einheit*

[EN90] Tradition lives always in unbroken continuity in the souls of the faithful

109

der Kirche, 1825; *Symbolik*, 1832). Möhler, too, who knew Schleiermacher particularly well, started from the distinction between, faith and doctrine, spirit and letter, hidden root and visible shoot, pious self-consciousness and outward ecclesiasticism in the life of the Church, i.e., of revelation. But more clearly than in Drey and in a definite Catholic improvement on Schleiennacher, the two elements are now shown to be originally co-ordinated with each other, so that the Catholic conclusion that we must listen to the Church can now be understood *a priori*[EN91] from within. According to Möhler's first great book, there corresponds to the unity of the spirit of the Church the unity of its body, to the mystico-spiritual and doctrinal inner unity, in which the individuality of the believer has its place, the outer unit, increasingly represented in the bishop as the unity of the congregation, in the unity of the episcopate (seen in the metropolitan Synods and the General Council) and finally in the unity of the Roman *cathedra*[EN92]. This correspondence which transcends and organically comprehends the antithesis of idea and history, doctrine and action, inward and outward truth, inward and outward witness, this higher unity of both unities rests on the fact that, as the human spirit is everywhere the same, so too Christ is one and His work one (*Symbolik³*, 342). But the unity of Christ is transferred to the Church, because it is the community founded by Him, "in which the activities developed by Him during His earthly life are continued under the leading of His Spirit to the end of the world by means of an apostolate ordered by Him and persisting without a break" (p. 334). Further: "The Church is the Son of God continuing to appear among men in human form, always renewing Himself, always becoming young, His continual becoming-flesh" (p. 335). "It is His visible form, His continuing and eternally self-rejuvenating humanity, His eternal revelation" (p. 360). What took place between Christ and the apostles can be described as follows: "To the action of the Saviour in proclaiming His Word there corresponded that of the apostles: the Word in their mouth at once became faith, the possession of man, and after His ascension it was no longer present except in this faith of the disciples of the Lord." The divine Word became human faith and in that way, without ceasing to be the divine Word, it passed over into the realm of human comprehension, analysis, reflection and judgment (p. 374). The same thing happens when as the apostolic word it becomes the faith of the first post-apostolic generation: the doctrine of Scripture now becomes the doctrine of the Church, again without any break; on the contrary, always being understood more fully, always attaining to greater clarity in controversy with heresies (p. 375 f.). That, then, is how it lives and grows and works, always the same, and yet always new. Just as the world is maintained in the reality once and for all posited by God and by virtue of the living power imparted to it by God in and with creation, i.e., as it is renewed in such a way that there is a continual impartation from that which lives now to that which will live in the future—so tradition is the extended self-impartation of the original, divinely spiritual life-force once and for all posited with the founding of the Church (*Einheit der Kirche*, 11 f.). "The essential content of Holy Scripture is eternally present to the Church, because it is its heart's blood, its breath, its soul, its all" (*Symbolik²*, 383). The Church is therefore "the Christian religion become objective." "As the Word spoken by Christ ... entered with His Spirit into a circle of men, and was adopted by them, it took form, it assumed flesh and blood, and this form is the Church ... As the Redeemer by His Word and His Spirit founded a community, in which He allowed His Word to be living. He entrusted His Word to that community to be preserved and transmitted. He deposited it in it, in order that it might go out from it and grow and reach out always the same but eternally new and with ever new power. His Word can never be separated from the Church and His Church from the Word" (p. 336 f.). The revelation in Jesus Christ would either have failed

[562]

[EN91] independently
[EN92] bishop's chair

altogether or succeeded only in part if it had been only a momentary incorporation of the truth, "if the personal manifestation of the Word had not been sufficiently strong to give its sound the highest degree of most intensive movement and to create the most complete imaginable activity, i.e., to breathe in the breath of life and creatively to produce a union, which would again show forth the truth in a living way and be the example of sufficient authority for every age: or represent Christ Himself" (p. 343 f.). "The authority of the Church mediates everything that rests on authority and is authority in the Christian religion, i.e., the Christian religion itself, so that for us Christ Himself remains our authority only to the extent that the Church is our authority" (p. 345). From this it follow that "it must be inerrant" (p. 339). "If the divine element is the living Christ and His Spirit in it is that which is inerrant, and eternally infallible, then the human element is also infallible and inerrant, because the divine does not exist for us apart from the human; it is not the human in itself, but the instrument and manifestation of the divine" (p. 336). "The divine Spirit, to whom the leading and quickening of the Church is entrusted, in its unity with the human becomes a specifically Christian sensibility, a deep and sure feeling, which, standing in the truth, leads to all truth ... a profoundly inward mind, which is particularly adapted to grasp and accept the written Word, because it is in harmony with that in which the Holy Scriptures themselves were composed" (p. 359). "What then is tradition? It is the specifically Christian mind as it is present in the Church and continues to develop under the Church's nurture, a mind which is unthinkable without its content, which is rather formed on and by its content, so that we have to call it a filled mind. Tradition is the Word, living continuously in the hearts of believers. The exposition of Holy Scripture is entrusted to this mind as the common mind; the explanation which it gives ... is the judgment of the Church, and the Church is therefore the judge in matters of faith" (361 f.). And: "all dogmatic and moral developments which can be regarded as results of formal universal activities (of the Church) must be respected as utterances of Christ Himself" (p. 364). "The Church expounds Holy Scripture" (p. 360). Therefore its life is always one: on the vertical plane of temporal succession as well as on the horizontal of temporal conjunctivity, whereas heresies are betrayed and judged as such by the fact that they are and set up innovations and peculiarities outside its unity. "Nothing sweeter hovers before the imagination of the Catholic, and nothing speaks to his feelings more beneficially, than the idea of the harmonic involution of countless spirits, which, scattered over all the surface of the earth, freely empowered of themselves to enter into every deviation on the right side and the left, nevertheless, even as they preserve their various peculiarities, constitute a great band of brothers for mutual development of their life, representing one idea, that of the reconciliation of man to God, and being therefore reconciled and made one amongst themselves" (p. 339 f.). Möhler thought it important—and this insight has recently been given an express historical basis in the book by J. Ranft—that what [563] he represented as the law of the organic unity of revelation and Church, Scripture and tradition, is identical with that law which covers all the ordinances of human life. Just as Christ lives in His Church, so there lives in the history of every people—as long as the people itself lives, Pan is not dead—preserving what is proper to it, rejecting what is alien, self-consistent in the most varied expressions, a national spirit, that is, the particular character of this people, impressed on its deepest, most secret existence, and differentiating it from all other peoples: and so too the history even of heathen religions shows how an original religious view is logically carried through and organically built up and expanded in its later development. It is the law to which Christian heresies too are subject: did not the congregation which the reformer of Wittenberg built up and all Lutheranism develop according to his spirit? Did it not show itself to be the infallible expositor of his Word? "The infallibility of the Church in its exposition of the divine Word is formed and has to be judged by this pattern" (p. 362 f.). A Catholic review of Möhler's achievement runs as follows: "The nature

of the Church in the union of its eternal divine basis and temporal human development undergoes a radical reinterpretation. The appeal to the principle of tradition which seemed outwardly to be a hampering and retrospective outlook suddenly became an appreciation of the continually living attesting mystery of Christ Himself. At a particularly important point Möhler thus succeeded in throwing light on the darkened picture of ecclesiastical teaching. What the Tridentinum had stated only in simple formulae ... what the post-Tridentine theologians had saved in a bitter theological contest, he was able to grasp fully with the help of the idealistic understanding of spiritual movements" (Ranft, 60). We can set against this the morose verdict of D. F. Strauss: "So Möhler could derive the sole-redemptive Popish Church with no greater difficulty from the Christian consciousness than Schleiennacher could his Redeemer. He could give the Christian consciousness a form, in which it seemed interchangeable with the modern principle of progress" (*Ges. Schriften* II, 222). How was it possible—we must ask—for Catholic theology to achieve such results as Möhler did with the help of Hegel and Schleiermacher, or (as Strauss thought) so badly to misuse their achievements? Prudently but foolishly Strauss had nothing to say on this question. But the Catholic author joyfully and confidently let out the secret: "Möhler was able to make use of the finest insights of idealistic philosophy just because they were in some sense an interpretation of the most vital phenomenon of the history of Christian dogma, the progress of the development of Christian doctrine" (Ranft, 52). It was really a waste of time for Protestant critics of Möhler's system to accuse him of "Schleiermacherising" and to charge him with transmuting Catholic doctrine. Möhler himself had already given the answer: Why should we not speak rather of a catholicising of Schleiermacher? (Ranft, 52); which means that we have to weigh the possibility that in availing himself of his ideas and formulations, Möhler did represent Catholic doctrine, and in doing so understood Schleiermacher at the deepest possible level and rightly applied him in this way? And do we not have to admit that he is right? The Catholic and the idealistic interpretation of Christian history both do go back to the same conception. They are at one in what ultimately emerges and is expressed in Möhler: in the identity of the Church and its faith and its Word with the revelation which is its basis. The only point is that the Catholic is the original and proper form of this understanding, and the idealistic a derivative form, which (in a preliminary self-misunderstanding) at first contradicted the former. Aware of its identity with Christ, the Catholic Church can in the last resort, if at all, only be interpreted idealistically. And the finest insights of idealistic philosophy are, in fact, only "in some sense an interpretation" of the phenomenon of the movement of Christian history seen through Catholic, i.e., crypto-Catholic eyes. Möhler as a good
[564]   Catholic was able to see in the secondary idealistic form of that conception its primary and Catholic one, and therefore instead of rejecting it to adopt it into Catholic thinking. At the same time, as a good idealist, he was able to dissolve the idealistic self-misunderstanding, to help the modern consciousness to fulfil its deepest intention, i.e., to help it on the way back to Rome. And that he was able to do this is his really remarkable historical achievement in this matter. By this personal union he represented the best interests of both partners, while giving to the authority of the Church the final word which was also the first. And he did well not to let himself be led astray either by the doubts of anxious Catholics or by the ill-founded scoffing of his Protestant opponents. It was along the lines and with different variations on the ideas of Drey and Möhler that their successors, J. Kuhn and Franz Anton Staudenmaier taught in Tübingen. The decisive positions of this school have become the common possession of Catholic theology, although more strongly in the second half of the 19th century than in the first that theology was to enter into a new relation to the "earlier theology," meaning especially Thomas Aquinas: a development which outwardly forced the elements taken over from German idealism more and more into the background because of their alien form. But what took place or was brought out with the existence of that school could

not be and was not reversed or concealed again. We must not be surprised if among the later Catholic dogmaticians we again hear Scripture and tradition spoken of in the more abstract and old-fashioned manner of sub-Tridentine theology as two separate sources of revelation, and elsewhere of Christ and His revelation as opposed to both. At a first glance we miss the boldness and energy with which Möhler related and ultimately united these things. But we are much mistaken if we imagine that there has been a real withdrawal, if we overlook the fact that these insertions (which were not really the invention of Möhler) had everywhere become the common possession of the Catholic theological consciousness, that the ideal-istic construction with which the Tübingers had defended and justified them could be scrapped or relegated to the museum once it had fulfilled its purpose—occasionally being brought out, of course, and directly applied right up to our own time (e.g., by Karl Adam, and also by Erich Przywara). Once the synthesis had been achieved which is indispensable for a German Catholic theology, and with this synthesis behind one, it was possible again to think and proceed analytically without revealing at every point the identifications made by Möhler, but with the decisive content of his views, quite independently of idealism, as the starting-point and goal. In this sense the second, modern German Catholic theologian of any size, Matthias Joseph Scheeben, who is representative of the new repristination of Thomas, of a Catholic theology of the older and strict style, stands entirely on the shoulders of Möhler.

In the German-speaking area at least, Scheeben was *the* theologian of the pontificate of Pius IX, and especially at the time of the Vatican Council at which—and here we come to the second event which is decisive for our present problem—the final term was put to the whole development as concerns the teaching office of the Church. When Catholic theology related Scripture and tradition as sources of revelation and then represented them more or less clearly as a single context of tradition, from the days of Irenaeus their considerations and assertions had almost always led to a more or less clear indication of a third authority side by side with Scripture and tradition, or rather as the elected mouth, or the authentic exponent of both: of the Church itself, i.e., the Church of the present day, visible and represented in the authoritative pronouncements of its teaching office. Therefore the real importance of Möhler's thinking did not consist in his identifying of what ultimately became the complex of Scripture and tradition with revelation, with the incarnation of the Word, with Jesus Christ, but in his attempting to understand the whole divine dignity and authority ascribed to this complex only as a predicate of the Church, the present-day Church, as the living bearer of the apostolate, the representative of Jesus Christ. The Church it is into whose faith [565] the Word of God has come and in whose faith it has actually gone forth. The Church has the Word; expounds it; is revelation *in concreto*[EN93], not a new revelation, but the old revelation, self-enclosed and for that very reason perfect and complete. The Church is Jesus Christ, speaking, ruling, acting, deciding to-day. Once again, the identification was old, very old. Even in the 2nd century the Roman Catholic Church as such has already its basis in this identification, and it is along these lines, which since then cannot again be new, that all Roman Catholic progress has been made. As a Catholic Möhler had only systematised what all informed and progressive Catholics had always meant and said on this matter. And as an idealist Möhler had only made explicit the relationship between Roman Catholic progress and progress in the sense of the Neo-Protestantism which resisted the Reformation on its other flank. It now needed only a final clarification not yet explicitly made in Möhler but prepared and announced in all Roman Catholic development—and always clearly and logic-ally announced and prepared. The consummation now reached cannot possibly be regarded as an innovation, as was partly the case within the Catholic Church. And on the

---

[EN93] concretely

Neo-Protestant side, it is only as a result of that persistent self-misunderstanding, only because the way home has not yet been found, that it can be received with the horror with which it was partly received when it came. Again, in Möhler the question had not yet been finally made clear, where that Church which is identical with revelation, i.e., where that mouth which declares revelation, where that authority of the Church which is identical with the authority of the Word of God, has to be sought and heard *in concreto*[EN94]. To this question Möhler still gave the traditional answer, which was correct but incomplete, that it has to be heard in the voice of the whole episcopate united to its popish centre, as the legal successor and bearer of the apostolate proved by unbroken succession, as the visible representative of Jesus Christ. Thus Möhler left unresolved the problem involved in this answer. He set side by side Conciliarism and Curialism, the system of Episcopacy and that of Papacy, "of which the latter, without failing to recognise the divine institution of bishops, specially stresses the strength of the centre, while the former, without denying the divine institution of the primate, tries to find the main strength in the periphery. In so far as each recognises the divine nature of the other, they constitute most useful opposites for the life of the Church, so that by their efforts the individual free development of parts is safeguarded and their conjunction to an inseparable and living whole is also maintained" (*Symbolik³*, 399). Many loyal Catholics would have been glad to maintain the concept of the Church's authority in this dialectical form. But had these loyal Catholics rightly understood the meaning of previous Catholic development and therefore its starting-point and origin? Had not Möhler himself written some time before: "The whole view which the Catholic Church has of itself, as a visible institution taking the place of Christ, would be lost, or rather, would not have arisen at all, without a visible head. With a visible Church a visible head is necessarily posited." Could or should the description of this indispensable head, of this concrete culmination of the authority of the Church, be content with this dialectical parallelism of Council and Pope? That the Council as representative of the "periphery" of the Church cannot speak or decide as the voice of the Church to-day and therefore as the living Jesus Christ without the Pope, the representative of its "centre," was something which had not only been claimed by the Popes from early in the first Christian millennium, but had actually been acknowledged and even theoretically maintained by the overwhelming majority of standard theologians. In this unique position of supreme teacher and judge, the Pope was what not only Möhler, but also the representatives of certain centrifugal tendencies, like the Gallicanism of the 17th and 18th centuries, had always been prepared to concede: the "centre" of the Church's life as opposed to its episcopal "periphery." But would not the very opposite be maintained, that the Pope cannot speak and decide authoritatively without the actual and express co-operation, but only with the explicit sanction of the bishops? To the word and decision of the Pope should there not be ascribed the infallibility which belongs to the divine authority of the visible Church and therefore to its visible head, only if and to the extent that he speaks out of the total consciousness of the Church represented in the episcopate, i.e., as supported by the vote of the bishops united in Council? Could it be concluded that what Möhler called those "most useful opposites" would never in fact work out otherwise than beneficially ? As long as the equipoise between Pope and Council was maintained, was not there always the possibility of a disunity within that "visible head"? And was it indeed a head? Had the Church a mouth by which it could speak with authority, infallible, ultimate, absolute authority, and possessing which it could preserve its identity with the living Jesus Christ? Is the first word, that the visible Roman Catholic Church stands and speaks in the place of Jesus Christ, because it itself is the continually-living Jesus Christ Himself—is that first word a final word, is it really spoken in a way in which it can be received and believed, unless it is unreservedly

---

[EN94] concretely

transferred and applied to the official status and utterance which admittedly constitutes its organising centre, the centre of its teaching office, the episcopate? Was not the whole transformation of the authority of Scripture into that of the Church, which had been the meaning of the development from Irenaeus to Möhler, quite futile, because that meaning was still equivocal and finally obscure, so long as there had not emerged as the last and concrete culmination of the incarnation of the Word one man, who as the living bearer of the tradition identical with revelation, and therefore himself revelation as it has to be heard to-day, represents the Church, or the Christian humanity which has attained possession of revelation, and executes its self-government? Could the insight which had been ripe for expression so long be suppressed any longer, that this is in fact the nature and function of the Romish Pope? Could it be suppressed that the official decision of the Pope is quite unreserved and needs no confirmation; that as such and in itself it is the decision of the whole episcopate and therefore the decision of the infallible Church, the infallible decision of Scripture and tradition, the infallible declaration of revelation and therefore itself infallible revelation for the present age; that by virtue of his supreme authority and apostolic power according to the Lord's promise, and under the guidance of divine providence, the Pope will never speak except out of the common consciousness of the infallible Church, and in his official speaking utterances will never say anything but infallible revelation for the present age? Could this be suppressed any longer when it had been true from the beginning and had for so long, although only partially at first, been known to be true? That was the question with which the Catholic Church was consciously faced under the pontificate of Pius IX (the same Pope who in 1854 had defined the dogma of the Immaculate Conception of Mary, and who, at the same Council at which the infallibility was decided, gave dogmatic authority to the Thomist doctrine of reason and revelation). The answer given by the Catholic Church through the mouth of the Vatican Council, and the latter through the mouth of the Pope himself, is to be found in the *Constitutio dogmatica I de ecclesia Christi* of the 18th July 1870. The decisive passage is at the end of Ch. 4 (*Denz.* No. 1839) and it reads as follows: *Itaque Nos traditioni a fidei christianae exordio perceptae fideliter inhaerendo, ad Dei Salvatoris nostri gloriam, religionis catholicae exaltationem et christianorum populorum salutem, sacro approbante Concilio, docemus et divinitus revelatum dogma esse definimus: Romanum Pontificem, cum ex cathedra loquitur, id est, cum omnium Christianorum pastoris et doctoris munere fungens pro suprema sua Apostolica auctoritate doctrinam de fide vel moribus ab universa Ecclesia tenendam definit, per assistentiam divinam ipsi in beato Petro promissam, ea infallibilitate pollere, qua divinus Redemptor Ecclesiam suam in definienda doctrina de fide vel moribus instructam sese voluit; ideoque eiusmodi Romani Pontificis* [567] *definitiones ex esse, non autem ex consensu Ecclesiae, irreformabiles esse.—Si quis autem huic Nostrae definitioni contradicere, quod Deus avertat, praesumpserit: anathema sit*[EN95]. Note well that it is not with the consciousness of innovation, but with the consciousness of loyalty to its tradition and development from the very first, that the Church makes this declaration. It is the Pope himself who makes it: with the consent of the Council, which according to its content he did

---

EN95 Thus, we, in adhering faithfully to the tradition received since the beginning of the Christian faith, for the glory of God our Saviour, the exaltation of catholic religion and the salvation of Christian peoples, with the approval of the Holy Council, we teach and define that the doctrine of divinity has been revealed: that the Roman Pontiff when he speaks from his seat, that is, when in the office of the pastor and teacher of all Christians he acts on his supreme apostolic authority and defines the teaching on faith or ethics to be held by the whole church. This takes place by the divine help promised to him in blessed Peter, to be strong in the infallibility by which the divine redeemer wills his church to be instructed in the definition of teaching on faith or ethics. Therefore the definitions which come from such a Roman Pontiff, even if from himself but not from the consensus of the church, are unchangeable. But if anyone presumes what God excludes, namely to contradict this definition of ours, let him be anathema

115

not need, but which he is glad to have stated, not as a violation of his own authority, but rather as a confirmation of its fulness. The declaration states an ecclesiastical or papal doctrine and at the same time describes this doctrine as divinely revealed dogma, i.e., as an interpretation of revelation with the authority of revelation itself. Therefore it already assumes in form what it asserts in content. That is, in the doctrine as fashioned in this way it states that the Romish Pope is in possession of the infallibility with which Christ clothed the doctrinal decisions of His Church. It is not the man himself elected to be Pope who as such possesses this infallibility. It is this man to the extent that in his office as shepherd and teacher of the Church, and as such using his apostolic authority, he pronounces and decides in matters of faith and morals. Yet it is the Pope himself who in the last resort has to decide when these three conditions obtain. He does not possess infallibility of himself, but on the basis of the divine aid promised him in the person of Peter. The Pope does not only possess it, but it is proper to him in his particular office, and that directly and quite independently of any other teaching office. Within these limits, which are not reservations but elucidations, he possesses infallibility and therefore his decisions are authoritative and therefore final decisions in themselves and not on the basis of the consent of the Church. Refusal to accept this doctrine means separation from the Church. This declaration of the *Vaticanum* has a special preliminary history in the history of the doctrine of the primacy of Peter and the primacy of the Roman see. But it has also behind it the history of the doctrine of Scripture and tradition, and properly and definitively it can be understood only from this standpoint. It is the closing of that circle, the opening of which is marked by the dualistic formula of Irenaeus (repeated in the Tridentinum), the continuation by the triad of Vincent of Lerins, and the culmination by the synthetics of Möhler. Since the *Vaticanum* we can know what was not previously known, viz., where and what the Church is *in concreto* which teaches revelation. It is interesting that it requires the primacy of Peter and the Popes to make it possible for the Church as it is identical with revelation to have this concrete point. But more interesting is the fact which had for a long time been obvious but was only now admitted: that the Church as it is identical with revelation possesses such a point; that to this day there can be seen from every place and by every man a place and man where heaven and earth meet, where God and man, the Word taught by Christ and proclaimed in faith in Him are directly one, "a living authority resting on divine operation in all the contentions of the world" (Leopold v. Ranke, *Die röm. Püpste, Meisterwerke*, vol. 8, 299); that this one place and this one man in their particularity only make manifest the glory which is actually imparted to the whole Church as such and as its own. That there is this man and place, that there is this living authority, that is what the *Vaticanum* has stated—not with the impossible intention of giving something to the Pope or the Church which they did not previously possess, but defining and proclaiming as a dogma essential to salvation something which it had always had in all its fulness, *quod ubique, quod semper, quod ab omnibus creditum est*[EN96]. It had always been the case everywhere, and as revealed truth, that the Church speaking by the mouth of the Pope was the revelation of truth. On the authority which the Church has, it now confirms—and this is the singular significance of this declaration of the Vatican even from the formal standpoint—to itself and to the world the fact that it has this authority; that is. that it has it in the supreme concreteness of the fact of the office which now delivers this declaration about it and therefore about itself, of the office which—in the greatest formal similarity to the Johannine Christ—is at once the subject and the object of this declaration. The circle is now actually closed. We can now know where and what is the authority of the Church as it is identical with the authority of the Word of God. The Vatican declaration was not made without strong opposition even within the Catholic Church, indeed even within the episcopate which had assembled for the

---

[EN96] that which has been believed in all places, at all times, and by all

1. *The Authority of the Word*

Council. A group of mainly German, but also French and Oriental bishops, made themselves at the Council the representatives of this opposition. Their weakness consisted *a priori*[EN97] in the fact that it was not fundamental, i.e., that its representatives were always having to explain that in the real point at issue, i.e., the recognition of the revealed truth of this declaration, they were at one with the Pope and the majority of the Council, but that on serious grounds they could not agree that the time was opportune, as they called it, for its proclamation as a dogma. It was argued that this proclamation was not necessary, because the corresponding belief had already been expressed generally, and directly as well as indirectly by the Councils of Florence and Trent. The declaration might be open to misunderstanding as regards the infallibility which still had to be maintained, afterwards as well as before, of the whole episcopate as such. It would make more difficult both reunion with the Eastern Church and the return of the Protestants. It might cause dissension among the bishops and in the Catholic world as a whole. It would threaten the local authority of bishops. It was calculated to centralise the life of the Catholic Church in an unhealthy way. Behind these arguments there was an inarticulate but, in the 19th century, very timely concern—and warning notes could be heard throughout Europe and even in America—that the declaration might stimulate opposition to the Church, that it might bring it into fresh conflicts with the sponsors of modern culture and especially with the more or less liberal powers of state. We can understand all this from the human standpoint, but we cannot be surprised that an effective opposition was quite impossible on this basis. The supporters of the new dogma could reply with every appearance of truth and soberness that the declaration must follow, just because its content, although it had been accepted for a long time, yet in spite of the statements of earlier Councils had always been doubted and disputed in various circles simply because it had not been clearly defined and proclaimed as dogma. The infallibility which we certainly have to assert of the episcopate as a whole cannot be compromised by that of the Pope, but is merely confirmed by it, since the Pope is the head of the episcopate. Union with the Eastern Church and the return of the Protestants cannot be furthered by lowering conditions to a minimum as in a business transaction, but only by making it known as clearly as possible that in the Roman Catholic Church they are dealing with the infallible Church. The declaration cuts away the ground from any possible dissension among the bishops or Catholics generally. "Where the Church has spoken, the faithful are not open to temptation. While the Church is silent, the spirits of error rage" (Archbishop Manning, in *The Ecumenical Council,* 1869, vol. 2, 37). Silence on a revealed truth because of fear of the opposition it might cause is equivalent to the tacit admission that it is not revealed truth at all. The declaration will not lessen but enhance the authority of the bishops in their local spheres. And since its content relates only to the last and supreme stage of the Church's authority, it cannot exercise a disruptive, centralising effect upon the life of the Church, but lends to the decisions of all episcopal courts certitude and stability. We may add that in face of the tacit concern about the opposition to be expected from modern society and the state, Pius IX and the majority of the Council were of the opinion that in this very declaration the Church would by this reaffirmation of the earlier presuppositions of the Papacy strengthen itself as the Church against all the external and internal forces of hostility or indifference, defending itself most effectively by attack. In this attitude L. v. Ranke could not but see [569] "something grand" (*op. cit.,* p. 267 f.). "What is true," the friends of the new dogma argue, "must also be defined as true in the Church. What Jesus Christ thought worth revealing, must also be worth declaring." "In the Church of God and in the truth of revelation it is always opportune to declare what God will have revealed to men" (Manning, 39), and especially when it is denied, as it had often been since the Council of Trent. Even as Protestants

---

[EN97] of necessity

117

we cannot avoid the impression that the trend which carried the day at the Council was inwardly stronger, to the extent that, in developing—as we have to see it—the error and falsehood to its supreme point, it had in its favour the logic of all Catholic development within which—if with the Reformed perception we are not to reject it at its source and therefore as a whole—any arrest is impossible, especially on purely opportunist grounds. We cannot deny to the supporters of the new dogma the witness that—always within the anti-Christian sphere which they occupied in common—they did think and act more spiritually than their opponents. Above all, we must understand that it was not due to any lack of conviction or character if the bishops of the defeated minority—and especially the Germans—emerged after the Council as adherents and defenders of its declaration. Their opportunist arguments could not bind them and—once the Church had spoken—it was not right that they should do so. Once we see the inner necessity of the Vatican dogma we shall not be so much surprised by certain outward peculiarities of that Council, as many were at the time both inside the Catholic Church and without. This Council, as distinct from most of the early ones, was summoned without any direct co-operation on the part of even Catholic governments, although the France of Napoleon III especially would have been willing to sponsor it. But was not the former co-operation of the political arm based on the reality or apparent reality of the *Corpus christianum*^{EN98}, which had long since disintegrated? Were not all modern States now established on religious neutrality? From this standpoint, was it not right for the Church to take charge of its own affairs? Moreover, the convening of this Council was only by the Pope, and not by the College of Cardinals, which in earlier councils had always acted with him. Again—and this had given rise to complaints as early as Trent—the order of business given the Council by the Pope laid down that the proposing of subjects for discussion is basically a matter for the Pope, that bishops must first submit their motions to the Pope, or to a papal Congregation, who have full power either to pass or not to pass them on to the Council. Again the presiding power seems to have been used with doubtful good faith, or at least not always as many would have desired it in the sense of a freedom of action and speech after the parliamentary manner. But after all a Council is not a Parliament. We shall have to say of these arrangements that ultimately they only anticipated the result of the Council, since they gave to it a form in which it became itself a witness to what it declared. If this declaration was a circle by which the authority of the Pope was proclaimed on the authority of the Pope—how could it be otherwise than that the Council itself should declare that authority by accepting these arrangements? If apart from the parliamentary form, for which there was rightly no place in the Church, we recall the possibility of fraternal discussion and a general decision, which can be reached according to the "order of business" of an Evangelical Synod, all that we can say is that the Catholic Church, which includes the so-called "suppressed" minority, had long since renounced this possibility. It would have been a μετάβασις εἰς ἄλλο γένος ^{EN99} if the Council had not formally taken, or been given, the actual form which it did. In any other form, that which it intended to and did say concerning the infallibility of the Pope would have been disavowed from the very outset. The minority bishop was quite right who later wrote: *Concilium Vaticanum apertissima principis petitione et circuli vitiosi errore illud tandem definivit, quod ab omni initio definitum stabilitumque pratsupposuit. Pontifex semet personaliter infallibilem ab initio usque ad finem gessit, ut semet personaliter infallibilem tandem definiat*^{EN100} (acc. to *PRE*² 20, 472). He was wrong only in that

[570]

---

^{EN98} Christendom

^{EN 99} confusion of categories

^{EN100} The Vatican Council eventually defined, by the most blatant special pleading and the error of vicious circularity, that which it presupposed from the very beginning as definite and established. The Pope treated himself as personally infallible from beginning to end, such that he eventually defined himself as personally infallible

as a Roman Catholic bishop he thought he had a right to deplore what he described in this way.

As is well known, the internal Catholic resistance to the Vaticanum, so far as it was maintained, stiffened into the so-called Old-Catholic movement and Church. From the outset it had no great prospects, for it did not and could not live by anything essentially different from those opportunist grounds alleged against the declaration, and this only to the extent that it received help from powerful forces outside the Church. Old Catholicism as such means a maintaining of the dualism which we still find in Möhler. In practice, it means either the return to an episcopal-conciliar system, which could only be an exclusive, limiting possibility in earlier Catholic development, which puts the authority of the Church fundamentally above that of Scripture, as in the papal system, but as distinct from it cannot give to the question, where and what is this authority of the Church, any concrete answer. Or, it means a transition to the Parliamentarianism of modern religious societies, which is now so common in the Protestant Churches, and which cannot basically be improved in opposition to the papal system. In recent years Old Catholicism has become inwardly strong where it has fundamentally tried and succeeded in linking itself to the Evangelical Scripture principle. But in this it is greatly hampered by the fact that it can only do this in principle, while in practice it has to recognise and carry with it a rather arbitrarily composed complex of Church traditions alien to Scripture, and at the same time by this very link it ceases to be Catholicism and therefore Old Catholicism. Old Catholicism means a state of indecision between two decisions, which can be made only with a fundamental and practical Yes, or a fundamental and practical No.

But the opposition to the Vatican dogma aroused in the modern non-Catholic world of culture, including the Neo-Protestant Church, was and is absolutely impossible. In the year 1870 and later only one authority could enable a valid protest to be made against the fully closed circle of the Roman Catholic doctrine of revelation, that is, an Evangelical Church with a good conscience in respect of its own faithfulness to the Reformation Scripture principle, a Church whose authority stood under and not over the Word, whose doctrine and preaching was directed at all points not according to the self-consciousness or historical consciousness of modern man, but only according to the witness of the prophets and apostles. We can quietly assume that at that time and since the right answer to the Vaticanum has been secretly given in many Protestant pulpits in the name of this Church, an answer certainly involving a confession of repentance in the name of the whole of modern Protestantism. But there was then no instrument to gather together these voices and to give expression to and make known the Evangelical verdict on the crime of the Vatican in proper proportion to its flagrant nature. There was no Protestant Church with a unanimous confession. The loudest Protestant voices at that time, and in the years of the *Kulturkampf*, were, for all their loudness, broken voices. And those who used them lacked the one thing which they needed to be able to say No to the Vaticanum with authority. Without that, the Roman stroke—and Pius IX had timed it rightly—caught the modern world of culture at that stage of complete inward dissolution on which it had entered in the second half of the century, when it tired of classical idealism. From what standpoint could the Popish Church be attacked when it equated itself with revelation? From the conception which had been taken over from the 18th century of a universal human reason identical with the highest truth? Compared with the new or rather the age-old doctrine of identity of the Popish Church such a conception, which had in any case paled, could never be more than a weaker and less vital partner, however illuminating it might be to sound commonsense. Or from the standpoint of the still prevalent romantic individualism? This, too, was emulated in depth and perspicuity by the [571] Vatican dogma, or the older Catholic idea of the representative individual incorporating the Church in the fulness of his competence and authority. From the standpoint of the modern positivistic concept of knowledge? Certainly the empiricism of the recent natural and historical science seemed specially formed as an iron wall against the mystery of newly revived ecclesiasticism. And who amongst those who were educated after this manner did not then believe that they were separated from Pius IX and his Council by unbridgeable antitheses in principle? But did not this science leave too much open, not actually if involuntarily to affirm that mystery in spite of and even in its agnosticism and atheism? And again, in relation to its own principles, did it not make too evident a use of a doctrine of infallibility which for all its contradiction of Rome was bound to act indirectly as a confirmation of the papal claim to infallibility? From the thought of the modern national, legal and welfare state? In the 19th century, both before 1870 and after, the Church was in fact severely attacked along these lines and suffered a considerable weakening in authority. How much it had to concede to Napoleon I and later to the new Italy in the varying stages of its growth and finally to Bismarck's Germany and even to the radical cantonal governments of Switzerland! If only the modern states, with all the jealousy with which they sought to maintain their prestige against the Vatican, had not at the same time felt so deep a need to prop up their never very stable authority against the forces of revolution by leaning on the authority of the Church. And if only in their nationalistic and socialistic developments they had not secretly been on the way to a politico-cultural totalitarianism, which when it emerged openly was bound to confront the absolutism of the Roman system of revelation with a similarity of structure far too close for any serious objections to be made to it, in spite of occasional misunderstandings here and there. Or finally from the freedom of the Protestant conscience? "Luther at Worms" was a favourite figure in the second half of that century, and the motif of a religiously flavoured defiance of the hierarchical claim of Rome was gladly accepted as the deepest note in the universal chorus of protest even outside the circle of the Protestant Church. What was not seen was that Luther's freedom and defiance had been related to the concrete Word of Scripture, whereas the freedom and defiance which were now worked up were just freedom and defiance as such, the "it seems to me" of an autonomous conscience, in virtue of which man was still lord of Scripture, as had always been the case in Catholicism, and was now with a conclusive and demonstrative clarity. That the walls of Jericho would fall down at the sound of the trumpets of the "Evangelical Covenant" was something which the inhabitants had no reason to fear. For centuries the Jesuits had had an incomparably better understanding of the use of this sort of freedom of conscience. The opposition of the modern non-Catholic world to the closed circle of the Catholic system could not be anything more than a blind panic. The Council of Freethinkers which met at Naples at the same time as the Vatican Council was for good reason bound to end as a pitiable farce. It would have been different if the Vatican dogma had come up in the time of Kant and Goethe, Schleiermacher and Hegel, but the world of 1870 was one which was highly disunited in itself, and its arguments were bound endlessly to oppose and cancel out each other. In the ultimate thing in which it was at one by virtue of its origin in the Renaissance and its recent highwater period, it was far too closely related to the now consolidated Catholicism to be in a position to offer it any consistent or dangerous opposition. Had not Möhler shown long ago that it was quite possible, and with comparatively little trouble, not merely to translate its most intimate intentions into Catholic terms, but to make them vital and effective in their Catholic centre? Therefore it was certainly more than diplomatic optimism, and more than contempt, when the German *Kulturkampf*[EN101] ended by Bismarck, for many years the apparent embodiment of modern non-Catholic opposition, being made a Knight of the Papal Order of Christ. One of the great moments of the Vatican Council was when a representative of the minority ventured to argue from Church tradition against the opportuneness of the new

[572]

[EN101] cultural struggle

1. The Authority of the Word

dogma. In reply Pius IX uttered his now famous saying: "I am tradition!", which is only a variant of the equally famous saying of Louis XIV, to the effect that he, as king, was the state. The latter word is, of course, a genuinely "modern" one. It is unthinkable except against the background of the Renaissance. The same is also true of its Popish variant. Again, that saying of Louis XIV contains within itself the whole French Revolution, just as conversely the sayings of political liberalism with their peculiar emphasising of the individual are notoriously open to the sudden change into an absolutism, in which the individual can again be the state in the sense of Louis XIV. Similarly, the dictum of Pius IX contains in itself all theological and ecclesiastical liberalism—as its opposite, but only the dialectical opposite, which can be changed into it. And conversely, it is not basically impossible that theological liberalism should lead to a recognition that all Christian tradition and authority is comprised in a single individual. The following words were written by a Viennese professor of theology, E. Commer (in an address on the 25th Jubilee of Leo XIII, *PRE.²* 20, 474): *Affirmamus, ecclesiae esse unum caput in duabus personis distinctis, Christo scilicet et Petro. Sicut humanitas Christi est quasi instrumentum animatum coniunctumque divinitatis, quae propria filii est, simili quoque modo pontifex maximus dici potest primarum instrumentum humanum animatumque ipsius verbi incarnati ac divinitatis, quacum coniunctus est auctoritate vicarii universa. Recte igitur papa ... alter Christus appettabatur*[EN102]. And before we rightly steel ourselves against such blasphemy we should read what, e.g., A. E. Biedermann (*Chr. Dogm.*, 1869, 792 f.) worked out concerning the general principle of divine sonship as the true meaning of the biblical and ecclesiastical doctrine of the divinity and humanity of Christ. If in the Roman Pope acting in his office we recognise the *alter Christus*[EN103], the human instrument of the divinity bound up with him, it is impossible to see why in the individual definitions of the God-man in the Bible and the Church we should not recognise generally the definitions of the relationship between God and man, between the absolute and the finite spirit. And if the latter is possible, why should the former be fundamentally impossible? Between the mythologically singular and the speculatively universal identification of man with divine revelation there can be no final and serious contradiction. If the one is possible, then basically the other is also possible. If the one is false, then basically the other is also false. Those who affirm the one cannot basically reject the other. The rejection of the one is possible only if it is bound up with the basic rejection of the other. The place from which both can be discerned as false and therefore rejected, the place from which Jesus Christ can be seen in His incomparable glory as the Lord of man—that place had been abandoned no less by the Roman Catholic Church than by the modern non-Catholic world which rejected its dogma, and no less by that world than by the Roman Catholic Church. To this we can only add that in the family quarrel between the two the Roman Catholic Church will always enjoy the relative advantage, which it did in the period of the *Kulturkampf* after the Vatican decree. It will do so because its heathenism has a much more comprehensive Christian covering. It will do so because it has a much more pronounced anti-Christian character. It will do so because it consists much more definitely in a perversion of the truth. It will do so because it has a much stronger share of living force of the Word of God falsified by it. Its familiar and opposite has some fragments of Christian knowledge, but for the most part it has to nourish itself on naked heathendom. Its anti-Christian character has still to develop before it can meet the Roman Church with the

---

[EN102] We affirm that there is one head of the Church in two distinct persons, that is, Christ, and Peter. Just as the humanity of Christ is, as it were, an instrument directed by and joined to the divinity which is proper to the Son, in like manner also the Pope can be described as the primary human instrument, directed by the incarnate Word Himself, and by the divinity with whom he is joined by the universal authority of the Vicar. Therefore the Pope is rightly named a second Christ

[EN103] another Christ

same weapons and even on the same level. But however that may be, the real decision is not taken in this family quarrel, but on that front where Catholicism and the modern world were encountered—and will be—by an Evangelical Church which stands under Holy Scripture.

[573]   All that now remains for us is to describe positively and negatively the nature and the meaning of the Evangelical decision on this matter as it was made at the Reformation, and as it must be made again and again wherever the Evangelical Church is true to its name.

The Word of God in the revelation of it attested in Holy Scripture is not limited to its own time, the time of Jesus Christ and its Old and New Testament witnesses. In the sphere of the Church of Jesus Christ it is present at all times, and by its mouth it wills to be and will be present at all times. This is the Evangelical confession of faith. In this confession of the vitality and therefore of the presence of the Word of God as already actualised and to be actualised again and again there is included the Church's confession of itself, i.e., of its institution and preservation by the Word of God for the authority entrusted to it and the mission enjoined upon it.

The confession includes first a confession of the reality of a fellowship of the Church in space as well as time, i.e., of a unity based upon the Word, which the Church has within itself in past, present and future: a unity in faith and proclamation, a unity of that which it receives in the gift which constitutes it and of that which it does in fulfilling what is enjoined upon it. The confession includes therefore a confession that where the Church is there are also brethren in faith and proclamation. The present-day witnesses of the Word of God can and should look back to the witnesses of the same Word who preceded them and away to those contemporary with them. In this matter it is impossible to speak without having first heard. All speaking is a response to these fathers and brethren. Therefore these fathers and brethren have a definite authority, the authority of prior witnesses of the Word of God, who have to be respected as such. Just because the Evangelical confession is a confession of the vitality and the presence of God's Word actualised again and again, it is also a confession of the communion of saints and therefore of what is, in a sense, an authoritative tradition of the Word of God, that is, of a human form in which that Word comes to all those who are summoned by it to faith and witness in the sphere of the Church and by its mouth—of a human form which is proper to it in the witness of these fathers and brethren, before they themselves come to faith and witness, and which is to that extent prior to their faith and witness—of a human form with which they have always to reckon, and, in virtue of that priority, with a definite respect proportionate to the witness of the Church as such.

Second, this confession includes a confession that the witness of the presence of the Church has a definite authority to the extent that it is the witness of the living and present Word of God, and takes place in that response to its transmission and in recognition of its definite authority. Where men speak in the Church according to the manner of the Church, i.e., in fulfilment of that witness, and where to that extent the Church itself speaks, it means that that [574] priority is again set up and established, that that hearing, which is respectful in the true sense, is presupposed and demanded, that for the hearers there is again created that responsibility, without which, of course, the Church itself could not speak, but which is a matter for the hearers now that it does speak responsibly. But again, in so far as the Church speaks, there arises a human form of the Word of God, which as such always precedes the faith and witness of the hearers, and with which the latter have to reckon in the same way as in the fellowship of saints in faith in the vitality and presence of the Word of God we have to reckon with that prior witness of the fathers and brethren. Once again, therefore, we have a tradition of the Word of God which is authoritative in a definite sense.

In this twofold form, then, the Evangelical confession of the Word of God includes a confession of the authority of the Church. We shall return to the meaning and content of this confession in the second part of the section. But before we say a single word about the authority of the Church—and this is the parting of the ways where the Evangelical decision is ineluctably and irrevocably made—we have to insist that there is an authority *in* the Church which is also an authority *over* the Church. This authority is itself the basis of all authority in the Church, from which it has its definite value and validity and without which it would not possess it, without which it never has and never will really exercise it. But this authority limits the authority of the Church, that is, it does not destroy but defines it. By it the authority of the Church is not only instituted but directed, so that whenever the authority of the Church is heard this authority has also to be heard with it as the first and final and decisive word. There is an authority in the Church which at the risk of the complete destruction of the authority of the Church itself cannot be transformed and dissolved into the authority of the Church, or at any cost be identified with it. How, then, can we speak of an authority of the Church in this twofold sense? How does it arise that in the communion of saints there is a tradition of the Word of God, resting on responsibility and demanding and evoking responsibility? The Evangelical confession which has to be set against Catholicism and Neo-Protestantism is as follows. It arises in so far as the existence of the Church, which possesses and exercises this authority, is a unitary act of obedience, an act of subjection to a higher authority. It is in this act of obedience that it is what it is, the Church, ἐκκλησία EN104, *evocatio* EN105. It is not the Church apart from this act. It is not so if and when it repudiates this obedience. But it repudiates it when the authority to which it subjects itself is not really a higher authority distinct from and superior to its own. It repudiates it when it subjects itself to an authority not vested in but instituted by itself and therefore immanent in

---

EN104 'calling-out' (church)
EN105 'calling-out'

123

[575]   it. It repudiates it when it subjects itself to its own authority. Even when its own authority has and is the plenitude of authority (and the more so the more it is), obedience to it is the very antithesis of obedience. It is self-government. But self-government is a—indeed it is the great prerogative of God. Self-government in the creaturely sphere can only mean the usurping of this divine prerogative of God and therefore the open disobedience of the creature. But the self-government of the Church is the admitted essence of both Catholicism and also Neo-Protestantism. In the one case the final decision rests with the teaching office of the Church which comprises both Scripture and tradition and expounds them with unchallenged authority, identifying itself with revelation. In the other it rests with the less tangible but no less infallible authority of the self-consciousness and historical consciousness of man. But either way it rests with the Church which then has to obey it. And to the extent that this is the case, the Church knows no higher authority than its own. It invests its own authority with all the marks of a higher authority, an authority which transcends itself as the Church. It is all the more careful to expunge any transcendent authority not identical with its own. It lays its anathema and contempt upon the possibility of obedience to any authority not identical with but transcendent to its own, describing it as separation from the Church. And in doing all this it refuses to obey. It makes itself like God. And it therefore ceases to be the Church. And in addition, it loses its own authority no matter how highly it values and extols it, no matter with what fulness it apparently possesses it. A higher authority which is transformed and dissolved into its own authority, which has been adopted and assimilated into it and has therefore disappeared, is not really a higher authority and obedience to it is not real obedience—even when the authority of the Church into which it has been assimilated arrays itself in all the predicates of divine revealedness, and obedience to the authority of the Church arrayed in this way bears all the marks of the most profound and sincere piety. The Church is no longer the Church where it does not know a higher authority than its own, or an obedience other than that of self-government. And from a Church which does not have an authority different from its own authority there is necessarily taken even the authority which it has. In a state of disobedience it cannot be the recipient and the subject of an authoritative tradition of the Word of God resting on and demanding and evoking responsibility. It cannot be the communion of saints. Bound to no prior human form of the Word of God, it will be unable itself to remain a prior human form of the Word and therefore to bind itself. It will not be able to evoke that respectful hearing of its witness.

    The decision in favour of a Church of obedience as opposed to a Church that is self-governed is necessarily and unavoidably imposed upon us by the
[576]   fact that the Christian Church cannot reflect on its own being, or live by it, without seeing itself confronted by the Lord, who is present to it but as its real Lord, with a real authority which transcends its own authority. Its Lord is Jesus Christ. He has called it into life and He maintains it in life. In Him it believes.

Him it proclaims. To Him it prays. It is related to Him as the human nature which He assumed is related to His divinity. It looks up to Him, as He is present to it, and it partakes of His Holy Spirit, as the earthly body looks up to its heavenly Head. He and He alone, with the Father and the Holy Spirit, can have divine glory and authority in the Church. But He does have it. The Church would not exist without Him, just as the creature would not exist without the Creator. It is the same relation as that of the Creator and creature which exists between Him and His Church. In His distinctness from it He is one with it; and in its distinctness from Him it is one with Him. The relation between Jesus Christ and His Church is, therefore, an irreversible relation. Whatever the glory and authority of the Church may be, the glory and authority of Jesus Christ are always His own. And as the glory and authority of the Church are based on the glory and authority of Jesus Christ, as they are established in the Church and are the very nature of the Church, so they are also limited by them. The glory and authority of Jesus Christ cannot, therefore, be assumed or subsumed, but will always be fulfilled and maintained in a contradistinction between the disciples and the Master, the body and its members and their mutual Head. The basis of the Church, its commission and authorisation, even the personal presence of Jesus Christ in His Church, does not remove the possibility and necessity of this differentiation between its authority and His. It is in this very contradistinction and only in it that there exists and consists the unity of Christ with His Church and His Church with Him. If it lives as His Church and has as such its own authority, it lives in obedience to Him, in an obedience which neither openly nor tacitly can ever be self-government.

But we must give a less equivocal form to all these statements if they are to present a clear picture of the Evangelical decision in matters of the authority of the Word. It may be that many of the cleverer, and to that extent better, representatives of Catholic and Neo-Protestant theology believe that they can follow and agree with us so far in spite of their very different position. Certainly, they may say, above the authority of the Church as its basis and limit there stands the direct and absolute and material authority of God Himself, the authority of Jesus Christ as the Lord of the Church whom it must obey. Certainly this relationship is in itself irreversible. Certainly there is in it an irremovable distinction between the higher and the lower, the glory and authority of God and that of the Church. Certainly, the latter must always be preserved by the former and therefore distinguished from it. But supposing, they then go on to ask, there is this preservation even in distinction, supposing [577] the Church is really obedient, supposing the Word of God is really living and present in it? Can we and must we not reckon with this possibility? Is it impossible *a priori* for the teaching office of the Church actually to speak pure, divine and infallible truth by its papal mouthpiece, in virtue of the divine grace promised to the Church—and self-evidently in subordination to the authority of God and in the service of Jesus Christ? May not something of the same be the case when in Neo-Protestantism the modern consciousness of self and history lays hold of the Word? But if we may and must reckon with this possibility, then have we not obviously to reckon also with the fact that, without being in itself more than the Church, the Church is itself the tradition of the Word of God and therefore present revelation and therefore Jesus Christ? But if we have to reckon with this possibility—by whom or what can its claim to actuality be resisted? We at once reply to this question that the claim is resisted by the very fact that it is made at all. The Church, whose authority is preserved in the differentiation from the divine authority, the Church which is *obedient* to its Lord and in which the Word of God is living and present, will definitely *not* make that claim. Of course, it will be the tradition of the Word of God and therefore present revelation and therefore actually—as the earthly body of the heavenly Head—Jesus Christ Himself. But this will be true as the act and truth of Jesus Christ in the power and mystery of the Holy Ghost. The glory and authority of the Church will then be a predicate of His divine glory and authority, as once in the incarnation of the Word human nature was a predicate of His eternal Deity and therefore Deity could be beheld in the flesh according to Jn. 1^{14}. But the glory and authority of God are not then a predicate of the Church—as little as once the eternal Word was a predicate of the flesh. There can, therefore, be no question of the Church claiming to be as such the tradition of the Word, revelation. Jesus Christ Himself. The grace directed to the Church cannot be transformed into a possession and a glory of the Church. When and where the grace of God is directed in all its fulness to the Church in this differentiation, it cannot and will not try to say of itself what the Catholic and Neo-Protestant Church thinks that it should say of itself. It will receive what is actually given it of divine glory and authority. It will be thankful for it. It will accept it and let it be effective. It will shine in this borrowed light. But it will not boast about it as though it were its own possession. It will not attire itself and act as though it had any claim or control in the matter. Out of the fact that Jesus Christ does actually acknowledge it it will not derive any personal glory, or self-commendation, and it will certainly not make a dogma of it. It will remain in the place, it will always return to the place in which the grace of God has come to it, i.e., the place of obedience, the differ-

[578]   entiation between its own authority and that of Jesus Christ Himself. Not in denial of the fact that it is adopted by the living and present Word into unity with Him, but in recognition of and gratitude for this exaltation, it will remain in this place, it will always return to it, it will not leave it with the claim that it itself has and is direct and absolute and material authority. In the knowledge of the eternal Jesus Christ and in fellowship with Him it will be modest, knowing that He is in it and it in Him in the distinction of the Creator from the creature, of the heavenly Head from His earthly body. In this place it recollects and expects His blessing. This humility, which in the fulness of what it receives and has constantly turns to the origin and object of faith, is the very essence of the Evangelical as distinct from the Catholic and Neo-Protestant decision.

1. The Authority of the Word

But we have still to give to our description of this Evangelical decision its final point and sharpness. Where is it that a Church which derives from the presence and grace of Jesus Christ a claim to direct and absolute and material authority divides from a Church which remains in and constantly returns to the differentiation in which Jesus Christ is present and gracious to it? The dialectic by which in the former case the change is made from thankful reception to an arbitrary attempt to possess, from recognition of the divine authority of God to the claiming of divine authority, from obedience to self-government—this dialectic seems always to be so strangely irresistible. If in the antithesis between God and man there is fellowship created by God, if there is the self-giving of God to man, if the revelation of God is made actual to man—is not the antithesis necessarily overcome, does not the giving of God necessarily mean a possessing by man, no matter how radically impossible this possessing may be to man in the first instance? Is it not imparted miraculously by that divine giving? Who knows, if we follow out this dialectic, we might even accuse the Evangelical decision—and the accusation has been made—of resting on an unchildlike, unthankful defiance of grace, on an arbitrary persistence in revolt from Jesus Christ, in the human estrangement from God, which has been overcome by Jesus Christ. It might be argued against it—and it will be argued against it—that the true humility of faith consists in the very fact that the Church does assume the divine glory and authority lent it by Jesus Christ and to that extent claims and exercises it. What is it, therefore, that concretely prevents this change and makes it impossible? What is the necessity concretely imposed upon the Church, according to the Evangelical view, to remain in that differentiation and therefore in the distinction between its authority and the authority of Christ and therefore in the subordination of the former to the latter, to resist as a temptation the *Eritis sicut Deus*EN106 even in this form—even if it comes in the garment of the promise and grace of Jesus Christ Himself? The answer can only be the simple one that this concrete necessity is the fact of Holy Scripture. It is not self-will that the Evangelical Church persists in that [579] differentiation, that it claims to be the school in which Jesus Christ is the Master, and the flock in which He and He alone is the Shepherd, the kingdom of which He and He alone is the King, that it takes care not to reverse this order in its own interest. The Church is not in a position to have an opinion on this question. It cannot choose between this possibility and the opposite one in which it itself is Master, Shepherd, King. The latter possibility is in fact closed to it. It is closed to it because Jesus Christ is gracious and present in His Word. This is, of course, by the power and life of His Holy Spirit. Yet this Spirit of His is simply the Spirit of His Word. And His Word, in which He Himself is present and gracious to His Church—and which must not be replaced by or confused with the word which the Church itself has and has to speak—is the word of the biblical witnesses, the Word which He Himself has put in the mouth of His

---

EN106 'You will be like God'

127

prophets and apostles. Therefore His Word always confronts the word of man in the Church in the form of a human word, i.e., the prophetic-apostolic word. His Word (and therefore His presence and grace) is not an idea which, once it has enlightened the Church, once the Church has made it its own, becomes the idea of the Church itself. And the authority of His Word cannot be assimilated by the Church, to reappear as the divine authority of the Church. His Word—the same Word by which He imparts Himself to the Church, in which He lives in the Church, in which He Himself sets up His authority in the Church—is given to the Church in such a way that it is always His Word as against its word: the Word which it has to hear and proclaim and serve and by which it lives, but which in order that this may happen is prevented from being assumed or subsumed into the Church's word, which asserts itself over against it as an independent Word, as one which is always new to the Church in every age and has to be newly encountered by it. Its form as the word of the prophets and apostles is the safeguard of its independence and newness. It vests it with the healthy strangeness which it needs if it is to be said to the Church of every age as the Word of its Lord. It creates and maintains the healthy distance from the Church of every age which is needed if the Church is to hear it before and as it itself speaks, if it is to serve it before and as it takes its authority and promises on its own lips, if it is to live by it, before and as it lives its life as its own. Its form as the word of the prophets and apostles strengthens the differentiation in which alone the Church of every age can receive revelation and be the bearer of revelation. Because He has entrusted and commissioned His Word to His prophets and apostles, because He has made them the rock on which He builds His Church, the authority of Jesus Christ is a concrete authority. It stands over against the authority of the Church. It cannot be assumed

[580] and assimilated by it. Neither gradually nor suddenly, neither with an appearance of arrogance nor with one of humility, can it be transformed into the authority of the Church. It is always autonomous, just as the men of the Old and New Testaments and their human word are always autonomous, over against the mass of churchmen who have adopted and reproduced, declared and proclaimed their witness. Beyond anything that the Church itself has said and can say, rightly or wrongly, loyally or disloyally, there stand these witnesses saying always to the Church what they have already said. They are not in any sense the first of a long series with whom those who come later in the same series can be compared with a like dignity and claim. They do, of course, initiate this long series, but they do so as those who were instituted by Jesus Christ Himself in all the uniqueness of His own reality. They are, of course, a human sign, but the sign which calls to every other sign and by which every other sign is set up. They are the first, who not only initiated the series as a whole, but who must initiate afresh each individual link in it if it is properly to belong to the series. It is really the Word of Jesus Christ Himself which as called and instituted witnesses they have to speak to the Church. They have to speak it, therefore, in a way in which the Church could never speak it to itself. It can speak it

to itself and the world only as a repetition of their word. According to Eph. 2^{20}, 3^5 it can be built up only on their foundation, the foundation of the apostles and prophets, not alongside this foundation. There is, therefore, no direct connexion of the Church with Jesus Christ and no direct life by His Spirit—or rather the direct connexion of the Church with Jesus Christ and its direct life by His Spirit is that it should build on the foundation which He Himself laid by the institution and calling of His witnesses, i.e., that it should hold to their word as His Word. They and they alone in the Church can have direct and absolute and material authority, the authority of the sign which is given with the revelation itself. And they do not need to claim it. It does not need to be ascribed to them. They have it. For without them there would be no Church. Their existence is the concrete form of the existence of Jesus Christ Himself in which the Church has the foundation of its being. In the Church the tradition of the Word of God, obedience towards Jesus Christ and subjection to His authority are not an open question but are ordered and regulated from the very first and for all time by the existence of the apostles and prophets. The life of the Church has always to fulfil itself in the form of a new subordination to the prophetic-apostolic word, in the form of a new erection of that first and basic sign: a subordination and erection which cannot be considered in relation to any other authority in the Church, because all other authorities in the Church are themselves conditioned by the fact that they are subordinated to that word as the concrete form of the Word of Christ and only to that extent are they authorities in the Church.

It is at this point, then, that the Evangelical Church on the one hand divides [581] from the Catholic and Neo-Protestant Churches on the other. In the 16th century—not as an innovation, but in re-discovery and restoration of an order disturbed in the very earliest days—the Evangelical decision was taken that the Church has not to seek and find the Word and authority of Jesus Christ except where He Himself has established it, that it and its word and authority can derive only from the word and authority of the biblical witnesses, that its word and authority are always confronted by those of the biblical witnesses, and are measured and must be judged by them. This is what the Reformation was trying to say and did say in its affirmation that Holy Scripture alone has divine authority in the Church. It was not ascribing a godlike value to the book as a book and the letter as a letter—in some sinister antithesis to spirit, and power and life. But it wanted Jesus Christ to be known and acknowledged as the Lord of the Church, whose revelation would not have been revelation if it had not created apostles and prophets, and even in the present-day Church can only be revelation in this its primary sign. But this primary sign of revelation, the reality of the apostles and prophets—and we need not blush to say this, it is not contrary to spirit and power and life but is the strait gate which we will not bypass if we do not want to miss the reality of the spirit and power and life of God—has the form of book and letter in which the apostles and prophets continue to live for the Church and in which with the Word of Jesus Christ

Himself they too—to the Church's salvation—are prevented from being assumed and subsumed into the spirit and power and life of the Church, in which form they can always confront the Church as a concrete authority, and therefore as the source of its authority.

The fact that the primary sign of revelation, the existence of the prophets and apostles, is for the Church book and letter, does not rob it of its force as witness. If the book rises and the letter speaks, if the book is read and the letter understood, then with them the prophets and apostles and He of whom they testify rise up and meet the Church in a living way. It is not the book and letter, but the voice of the men apprehended through the book and letter, and in the voice of these men the voice of Him who called them to speak, which is authority in the Church. Why should it be a dead authority because it stands in the book and letter—as though for that reason it could not speak, as though it could not maintain and exercise its authority in the most vital and varied and effective way, as though it had not done so throughout the centuries? The written nature of this primary sign cannot prevent it from being in the Church of every age a real sign, a sign just as powerful and definite as was once the personal existence of the living prophets and apostles to the growing Church of their day. But it is its written nature that is also its protection against the [582] chance and self-will to which it would be exposed without it. Its written nature makes it a sign which, however differently it may be seen and understood and, of course, overlooked and misunderstood, is still unalterably there over against all misunderstandings and misinterpretations of it, is still unalterably the same, can always speak for itself, can always be examined and questioned as it is, to control and correct every interpretation. Its written nature guarantees its freedom over against the Church and therefore creates for the Church freedom over against itself. If there is still the possibility of misunderstanding and error as regards this sign in virtue of its written nature, there is also the possibility of being recalled by it to the truth, the possibility of the reformation of a Church which has perhaps been led into misunderstanding and error. How and along what way could the Church rethink its existence as the Church and reorientate itself accordingly if it could hear the voice of the first witnesses, and in them the voice of Jesus Christ Himself, only through the medium of an unwritten tradition, or, even if written, it silenced the autonomous speaking of Christ Himself through His witnesses by an irrevocable interpretation bound to a definite authority? Would it not then be left to its own devices without any possibility of a reformation in the light of its origin and object? But if behind every alleged or genuine oral tradition, over and above every authority in the Church, there is a Holy Scripture, and if this Holy Scripture is as such recognised as the judge by which from the very outset all ecclesiastical tradition has to be judged and to which all ecclesiastical judges have always to listen, then that means that the Church is not left to its own devices, that the source of its renewal is open, and therefore that it itself is open to be renewed and reformed in the light of its origin and object. In the 16th century this source of renewal was found again in the witness of the prophets and apostles. The Church again became open to renewal by this witness. We can therefore understand that the written nature of this witness was regarded as a gift which had to be received with particular thankfulness from the providence which rules over the Church. Therefore not what was really meant, *De prophetrum et apostolorum testimonio*[EN107], or ultimately *De verbo Domini*[EN108], but *De sacra scriptura*[EN109] became the theme and title of the fundamental declarations in which the Evangelical decision for the authority of Jesus Christ against an equivalent authority of the Church found expression. It was in the written nature of the prophetic-apostolic witness that the cogency was found to prove again this witness against the whole weight of the Church and its tradition and teaching office. It was as written that this witness could directly enter the arena side by side with its ecclesiastical interpretations and be directly appealed to as witness and judge. It was as written that it could be the criterion above all warring opinions, no matter how interpretations might differ and continue to differ. It was as written that it then rose up in face of the whole Church from its concealment in a mass of tradition and in the chorus of voices [583] past and present. It was as written that it maintained against the Church the newness and strangeness and superiority of a higher authority.

But this is only one example. Not merely for the 16th century but for the Church of every age Holy Scripture as such is the final point and sharpness of the fact which the Evangelical decision makes unavoidably necessary. In every age, therefore, the Evangelical decision will have to be a decision for Holy Scripture as such. As such, of course, it is only a sign. Indeed, it is the sign of a sign, i.e., of the prophetic-apostolic witness of revelation as the primary sign of Jesus Christ. Of course, the Church can only read Scripture to hear the prophets and apostles, just as it can only hear the latter to see Jesus Christ with them, and to find in Him—and properly, ultimately and decisively only in Him, the prior direct and material and absolute authority on which its authority depends, on which it is founded and by which it is everywhere and always measured. But again, it can distinguish between seeing Jesus Christ, hearing His prophets and apostles and reading their Scriptures, and yet it cannot separate these things, it cannot try to have the one without the other. It cannot see without hearing and it cannot hear without reading. Therefore if it would see Jesus Christ, it is directed and bound to His primary sign and therefore to the sign of this sign—if it would see Jesus Christ, it is directed and bound to Holy Scripture. In it His authority acquires and has that concreteness as an authority higher than the Church which arrests the apparently irresistible revulsion of obedience to self-government. We can appropriate God and Jesus and the Holy Ghost and even the prophetic-apostolic witness in general, and then

---

[EN107] On the testimony of the prophets and apostles
[EN108] On the Word of the Lord
[EN109] On Sacred Scripture

exalt the authority of the Church under the name and in the guise of their divine authority. But in the form of Holy Scripture God and Jesus Christ and the Holy Ghost and the prophets and apostles resist this change. In this form their divine authority resists the attack which the Church and its authority is always making upon it. Whenever this attack is made and seems to have succeeded, it again escapes it. Rightly or wrongly, in loyalty or disloyalty, the Church may say a thousand things expounding and applying Scripture. But Scripture is always autonomous and independent of all that is said. It can always find new and from its own standpoint better readers, and obedience in these readers, even in a Church which has perhaps to a large extent become self-governing, and by these readers a point of entry to reform and renew the whole Church and to bring it back from self-government to obedience. If the Reformation of the 16th century means the decision for Holy Scripture, conversely we must also say that for every age of the Church the decision for Holy Scripture means the decision for the reformation of the Church: for its reformation by its Lord Himself through the prophetic-apostolic witness

[584] which He established and the force of which is revealed and effective because it is written. Let the Church go away from Scripture as such. Let it replace it by its traditions, its own indefinite consciousness of its origins and nature, its own pretended direct faith in Jesus Christ and the Holy Ghost, its own exposition and application of the word of the prophets and apostles. In the proportion in which it does this, it will prevent that entry upon which its whole life and salvation rests, and therefore at bottom refuse to be reformed. All kinds of "life," evolutions and revolutions will be possible in the Church. It can include conservative and progressive thinking in their constant action and reaction. There can be undeniable tensions and party conflicts like those between Catholicism and Neo-Protestantism, or like the internal Catholic battles between Realists and Nominalists, Episcopalians and Curialists, Benedictines and Jesuits, or the internal Neo-Protestant between Orthodox and Pietists, "Positives" and "Liberals." And these may give the deceptive appearance that the Church is really alive. But it does not live in the inner movement of these tensions. In them we see rather the process of decay to which the Church is at once subject when it ceases to live by the Word of God, which means by Holy Scripture. What is ultimately at issue in these tensions is the very secular antithesis of various human principles which can all be reduced easily to the denominator of this or that philosophical dialectic, and which ultimately reflect only the deep disunity of man with himself. And in these tensions the Church is obviously only disputing with itself. And in this debate properly both partners are right and both wrong. According to the circumstance of the age the debate may end with a victory for this side or that, but neither party, not even the victor, can say Amen with an ultimate certainty and responsibility, because neither way is it or can it be a matter of confession, i.e., of responsibility to a higher tribunal confronting both partners with concrete authority. These debates in the Church are conducted in the absence of the Lord of the Church. But are they then

really conducted in the Church? Has the Church not ceased to be the Church the moment it wants to be alone with itself? And does it not want to be alone with itself, if it will not stand with its authority under the Word in the concrete sense of the concept, and therefore under Holy Scripture?

It is here that we come to the final positive meaning of the Evangelical decision: it is taken in the thankful recognition that the Church is not alone, that it is not left to its own discussions and especially that it is not left to itself. It would be, the moment its authority ceased to be confronted by that divine authority. For then clothed with divine dignity the Church would have to stand and live by itself like God. And however grand it might seem to be in its godlikeness, for the creature which is distinct from God that means only misery, the misery of sin and death. From this misery of the solitariness of the creature fallen in sin and death the Church is snatched away by the fact that God in Jesus Christ is [585] present and gracious to it in concrete authority, which means in an authority which is different from and superior to its own. It is the Word of God as Holy Scripture which puts an end to this misery. Because Holy Scripture is the authority of Jesus Christ in His Church, the Church does not need to smooth out its own anxieties and needs and questions, it does not need to burden itself with the impossible task of wanting to govern itself, it can obey without having to bear the responsibility for the goal and the result. Because Holy Scripture is the higher authority established within it, the Church has a higher task than that which is at issue in those party conflicts, namely, the task of confession, which itself can only be again a thankful confirmation of the fact that its Lord is among it in His witness. Under the Word, which means Holy Scripture, the Church must and can live, whereas beyond or beside the Word it can only die. It is this its salvation from death which it attests when it makes, not the Catholic or Neo-Protestant, but the Evangelical decision.

2. AUTHORITY UNDER THE WORD

All that we have still to say about the authority of the Church itself can be understood in the light of the commandment in Ex. 20^{12}: "Honour thy father and thy mother." Obviously there can be no conflict between this commandment and the first: "I am the Lord thy God, which have brought thee out of the land of Egypt, out of the house of bondage. Thou shalt have none other gods before me." What it demands is self-evidently limited by the first commandment. But the dignity of what it demands is not reduced and lessened by the demand of the first commandment. On the contrary, because the first commandment is valid, in its own sphere the commandment to honour father and mother is also valid. It is in the people which has none other God but the One who brought them out of Egypt that father and mother are honoured by the children as the visible bearers and representatives of their own adherence to this people. The connexion of this commandment with the basic command-ment which as such constitutes the people Israel, and the comprehensive sense in which the latter has to be understood, are clearly brought out in the saying in Lev. 19^{32}: "Thou shalt rise up before a hoary head and honour the face of the old man, and fear thy God: for I am the Lord." We can see the same order in what the Old Testament says about the blessing which fathers can and should pronounce on their children and the priests on the whole people: the fact that men bless is not the denial but a confirmation of the real truth that Yahweh blesses and keeps, Yahweh makes His face shine and is gracious, Yah-weh lifts up His countenance upon those who are blessed and gives them peace (Num. 6$^{22f.}$). Again, the fact that Yahweh blesses and keeps and is gra-cious is not a denial but an institution and confirmation of the human bless-ing, the fatherly and priestly blessing pronounced on His people. At this point, too, we can and must recall the prophetic saying in Jer. 6^{16}: "Thus saith the Lord: Stand ye in the ways, and see, and ask for the old paths, where is the good way, and walk therein, and ye shall find rest for your souls." And the saying of Bildad in Job 8^8 points in the same direction: "For inquire, I pray thee, of the former age, and prepare thyself to that which their fathers have

[586]   searched out." The new and strange word of the witness of revelation in the name of Yahweh points here to an earthly-historical way along which the people has always been led thanks to the revelation within it: "I have con-sidered the days of old, the years of ancient times" (Ps. 77^5)—and which as such has something to say to the people in which it will again recognise the "good way." The former way is not, of course, to be regarded as an autonomous word, distinct from the present revelation of Yahweh, another authority side by side with that of the prophetic word. But the revelation too, the prophetic word, cannot and should not be spoken and heard without remembering the former way of Yahweh with His people. From this standpoint we have to admit basically and generally that Cyprian was right when he said: *disciplinam Dei in ecclesiasticis praeceptis observandam esse*^{EN110} (*Ad Quir.* III 66). We understand it in this way: that there is an authority of the Church which does not involve any contradiction or revolt against the authority of Jesus Christ, which can only confirm the *disciplina Dei*^{EN111}, and which for its part is not negated by the authority of Jesus Christ, by the *disciplina Dei*^{EN112}, but is established, con-firmed and yet also defined and delimited by it. *Ut sacrilega esset partitio, si fides vel in minimo articulo separatim ab homine penderet, sic ludibrio Deum palam habent, qui praeteritis ministris, per quos loquitur, illum se magistrum recipere simulant*^{EN113}

---

^{EN110} the discipline of God is to be observed in the commands of the Church
^{EN111} discipline of God
^{EN112} discipline of God
^{EN113} Just as, if the faith depended even in the smallest article on man, such a share would be sacrilege, so also those who ignore ministers and claim that they welcome God as their teacher make open sport of the God who speaks through those ministers

(Calvin, *Comm. on Act* 15²⁸, *C.R.* 48, 362). The Church has a genuine authority.

Under the Word and therefore under Holy Scripture the Church does have and exercise genuine authority. It has and exercises it by being obedient, concretely obedient, by claiming for itself not a direct, but only a mediate authority, not a material but a formal, not an absolute but a relative. It has and exercises it by refraining from any direct appeal to Jesus Christ and the Holy Spirit in support of its words and attitudes and decisions, by not trying to speak out as though it were infallible and final, but by subordinating itself to Jesus Christ and the Holy Spirit in the form in which Jesus Christ and the Holy Spirit is actually present and gracious to it, that is, in His attestation by the prophets and apostles, in the differentiation from its own witness conditioned by its written nature. Therefore, it has and exercises it in the concrete humility which consists in the recognition that in Holy Scripture it has over it everywhere and always and in every respect its Lord and Judge: in the incompleteness of its own knowing and acting and speaking which that involves, in the openness to reformation through the Word of God which constantly confronts it in Holy Scripture. It is in this way, in this concrete subordination to the Word of God, that it has and exercises genuine authority. What is meant is genuine, human authority, i.e., a genuine capacity to attain and demonstrate it by its words and attitudes and decisions, by its whole existence: not with the superiority of heaven over earth, of eternity over time, of God over man, but with that of earthly elders over earthly children; not only with the meaning and force of a natural ordering, but, as in the Old Testament commandment, in the sense of the sign to which the natural order is consecrated and exalted in the sphere of God's people; in such a way, then, that the human superiority attained and demonstrated reflects the superiority of heaven over earth, of eternity over time, of God over man; in such a way, then, that the latter super- [587] iority is reflected in that which it attains and demonstrates like the light of the sun in water. How can the water try to pretend that it is the sun? How can it try even to make out that the reflecting of the sun is a property immanent to it? And when and where is water a pure and infallible and final reflector of the sun? Yet it cannot be denied that when the sun shines it does reflect its light. And in this sense the Church has and exercises a genuine, human authority. It is genuine, therefore, not only in the sense that it is there and has its place in the same way as amongst men it is there and has a place in the relationship between elders and children, or rulers and subjects. But—and here it escapes all creaturely analogies—it is genuine in the sense that within this creaturely subordination and to that extent in the analogy it is also a sign (only a sign but a chosen and appointed sign) of that subordination to the Word of God in which the Church itself lives and to attest which it is commissioned and empowered in virtue of this ordering. In respect of this genuine human authority of the Church we have to go further and say that far from being only a remarkable and doubtful instance of human authority in general, far from there being a human authority in general, in the idea of authority or the reality of natural or historical laws, ecclesiastical authority is a reflection of the authority of God in His revelation in relation to all other authorities in the human sphere. It is true, original, primal authority, the type of all other authority. This is just as certain as that fatherhood is found first not on earth but in heaven, not among men but in God Himself. Similarly, the authority of the Church is the reflection of the heavenly divine fatherhood revealed in Jesus Christ and not of any creaturely fatherhood. Because there is revelation and the Church, there is also the family and the state, not *vice versa*. If the order of the family or the state wants to be and have genuine authority, it can do so only as an imitation of the authority of the Church. It can live only by the fact that there is first of all the authority of the Church. The authority of the Church is not open to question, like all other authority. Yet we must not forget that all this depends on the authority of the Church being genuine. And this depends on the Church itself being obedient, concretely obedient, and therefore standing not above or alongside, but under the Word of God. The authority of the Church disintegrates and ceases to have this typical primal significance in relation to all other authorities if the Church tries to renounce that obedience, if it tries to be and exercise the essential authority of God instead of the human authority which is a sign.

"They alone are spiritual fathers, who rule and direct us by the Word of God"(Luther, *Gr. Kat., Bek. Schr. d. ev.-luth. K.*, 1930, 601, 29). *Certe nemo erit in ecclesia idoneus doctor, qui non filii Dei ante fuerit discipulus ac rite institutus in eius schola: quando sola eius autoritas valere debet*[EN114] (Calvin, *Comm. on 1 Jn.* 1¹, *C.R.* 55, 300).

[588]   Our first question is how this genuine authority, the authority of the Church under the Word, comes into being. Our starting-point in replying is that the Church is constituted as the Church by a common hearing and receiving of the Word of God. The common action of hearing and receiving is partly contemporary: it takes place among those who belong to the same age and period of the Church. But to a much greater extent it is non-contemporary: it takes place among those who belonged to an earlier and those who belonged to a later age in the Church, between the present age and those which preceded it. A common hearing and receiving is necessarily involved either way where the Church is the Church. The life of the Church is the life of the members of a body. Where there is any attempt to break loose from the community of hearing and receiving necessarily involved, any attempt to hear and receive the Word of God in isolation—even the Word of God in the form of Holy Scripture—there is no Church, and no real hearing and receiving of the Word of God; for the Word of God is not spoken to individuals, but to the Church of God and to individuals only in the Church. The Word of God itself, therefore,

---

[EN114] certainly, no-one will be a suitable teacher in the Church who has not previously been a student of the Son of God and properly enrolled in His school, since His authority alone should avail

demands this community of hearing and receiving. Those who really hear and receive it do so in this community. They would not hear and receive it if they tried to withdraw from this community.

But this common action is made concrete in the Church's confession. We will take the concept first in its most general sense. Confession in the most general sense is the accounting and responding which in the Church we owe one another and have to receive from one another in relation to the hearing and receiving of the Word of God. Confessing is the confirmation of that common action. I have not heard and received alone and for myself, but as a member of the one body of the Church. In confessing, I make known in the Church the faith I have received by and from the Word of God. I declare that my faith cannot be kept to myself as though it were a private matter. I acknowledge the general and public character of my faith by laying it before the generality, the public of the Church. I do not do this to force it on the Church in the peculiar form in which I necessarily hold it, as though I were presuming either to want or to be able to rule in the Church with my faith as it is mine. On the contrary, I do it to submit it to the verdict of the Church, to enter into debate with the rest of the Church about the common faith of the Church, a debate in which I may have to be guided, or even opposed and certainly corrected, i.e., an open debate in which I do not set my word on the same footing as the Word of God, but regard it as a question for general consideration according to the Word of God commonly given to the Church. But because my confession is limited in this way, I cannot refrain from confessing, I cannot bury my talent. Irrespective of what may come of it or whether it may be shown that I have received ten talents or only one—I owe it to the Church not to withhold from it my faith, [589] which can be a true faith only in community with its own, just as conversely it cannot be too small a thing for the Church, in order to assure itself afresh of a true faith in the community of faith, in order not to miss anything in its encounter with the Word of God, to take account even of my confession of faith and to enter into a debate which is open on its side as well.

But it is obvious that before I myself make a confession I must myself have heard the confession of the Church, i.e., the confession of the rest of the Church. In my hearing and receiving of the Word of God I cannot separate myself from the Church to which it is addressed. I cannot thrust myself into the debate about a right faith which goes on in the Church without first having listened. Of course, we must presuppose that I do also myself directly hear and receive the Word of God, but not in such a way that I can be content and satisfied with this direct hearing and receiving. If I do not also hear indirectly, if as a member of the Church I have not heard and received its confession of faith which is prior to mine—heard and received it as is proper to the witness of men who are not themselves Jesus Christ but are members of His earthly body before me—how can I hear and receive the Word of God? What right have I to confess and therefore to take part and be heard in that debate? If my confession is to have weight in the Church, it must be weighted with the fact that I have heard the Church. If I have not heard the Church, I cannot speak to it. I have from the very outset excluded myself from the fellowship of the Church's confession, which is the aim of the debate which goes on in the Church. If I am to confess my faith generally with the whole Church and in that confession be certain that my faith is the right faith, then I must begin with the community of faith and therefore hear the Church's confession of faith as it comes to me from other members of the Church. And for that very reason I recognise an authority, a superiority in the Church: namely, that the confession of others who were before me in the Church and are beside me in the Church is superior to my confession if this really is an accounting and responding in relation to my hearing and receiving of the Word of God, if it really is my confession as that of a member of the body of Christ. This is not a direct but an indirect superiority; not a material but a formal; not an absolute but only a relative. In the sign of this superiority, in the confession which is superior to my confession, of those who before and with me are members of the body of the Lord, I see a reflection of the superiority of the Lord Himself—only a reflection, but the reflection of His superiority. And in honouring and loving the Church in this sign—under the sign but none the less truly—I honour and love the Lord of the Church. His Word and kingdom is the Church in which I have to confess my faith. By His Word it lives and with His Word He rules it to this day. I have to remember, of course, that this rule of His in the Church was and still is a rule among sinners. Therefore, in what I hear as the confession of the Church, I will certainly have to reckon with the possibility of falsehood and error. I cannot safely hear the voice of the Church without also hearing the infallible Word of God Himself. Yet this thought will not be my first thought about the Church and its confession, but a necessarily inserted corrective. My first thought in this respect can and must be a thought of trust and respect which I cannot perhaps have for the men as such who constitute the Church, but which I cannot refuse to the Word of God by which it lives and Jesus Christ rules it. How can I know Jesus Christ as the Lord who has called me by His Word if in relation to the rest of the Church I do not start from the thought that despite and in all the sin of the men who constitute it it too has been called and ruled by the same Word? Because my sins are forgiven me, I am bold to believe and, in spite of the sin of which I am conscious, to confess my faith as created in me by the Word of Christ. And if this is the case then in relation to the rest of the Church and its confession I cannot possibly begin with mistrust and rejection, just as in relation to our parents, no matter who they are or what they are like, we do not begin with mistrust and rejection or with the assertion that we must obey God rather than man, but with trust and respect and therefore, in the limits appointed to them as men, with obedience. As in and with the confession of the Church I hear the infallible Word of God, I have to reckon first and above all with the lordship of Jesus Christ in His Church and the forgiveness of sins, which is operative in the Church; not with sin and therefore with the possibility of falsehood and error which it involves.

[590]

138

And this means that I have not primarily to criticise the confession of the Church as it confronts me as the confession of those who were before me in the Church and are with me in the Church. There will always be time and occasion for criticism. My first duty is to love and respect it as the witness of my fathers and brethren. And it is in the superiority posited by this fact that I shall hear it. And as I do so, as I recognise the superiority of the Church before and beside me, it is to me an authority. This is how the authority of the Church arises. It always arises in this way, that in the community of hearing and receiving the Word of God which constitutes the Church, there is this superiority of the confession of some before others, this honour and love, this hearing of the confession of some by others, before the latter go on to make their own confession. Before both and therefore above both is the Lord of the Church with His Word. Only under His Word can some confess and others hear their confession before they confess themselves. But under His Word there does arise this priority and superiority of some over others, the necessity that in the Church we should listen to other men before we go on to speak. Under His Word there is, therefore, a genuine authority of the Church.

Our next question is: In what does the authority of the Church consist which [591] arises in this way? In accordance with what we have just said we will obviously have to put the question rather more precisely: In what consists or what is the confession of the Church in the narrower sense of the concept which we have now reached, the confession of the Church which I have to receive with trust and respect, the confession of the some to whom others have to listen before they can confess? First, we might mean the totality of voices which together make up the chorus or choruses of the fathers and brethren, who as such witness to others how the Word of God has previously been and is heard and received in the Church. But there must obviously be a chorus or choruses, not a confusion of many independent voices, if we are to hear not a cacophonous chaos, but wholeness and therefore the confession of the Church. A single voice may perhaps reach us and make itself understood as such, but in it we cannot possibly hear the confession of the Church. We can hear the Church only where it is spoken out of a community of hearing and receiving the Word of God and therefore in fellowship. There must be two or three according to the saying of Jesus if, subjected with them to His Word, we are to hear from their lips the confession of the Church. An individual as such cannot in isolation be to us a father and brother in the Church. But if there is a chorus or choruses self-expressed in the higher confession of the Church, so that their word can be heard and heard as a word of the Church, then we have obviously to put our question even more precisely: How do these choruses arise, i.e., how does there arise this common speaking out of the community of hearing and receiving the Word of God? We have already described the life of the Church under the Word as a debate which comes into being because the members of the Church owe and pay one another and must receive from one another a mutual accounting, responding and witness of their faith. If this debate is not idle talk, if it really takes place on the basis and at the instance of the Word of God commonly heard and received, it has a common end. And what can this end be if not the common proclamation of the Word of God heard and received which is the task laid upon the Church with this gift? For the sake of this task questions have to be asked and answered in the Church about faith, about the hearing and receiving of the Word of God. There has constantly to be a common enquiry concerning a true faith and to that extent concerning the Word of God as truly heard and received. This task is the compelling practical ground why the faith of the individual cannot be, as it appears to be, a private matter, why the individual with his faith is responsible, why he is forced to come before the public of the Church, why he has to make his faith known to others and submit to their judgment, if he is legitimately to play an active part in that general search after a true faith. The meaning and purpose of the debate conducted in the Church is obviously not the debate as such, the encounter, the contact, the stimulating and instructive exchange on the task of the Church's proclamation. Otherwise it would degenerate into mere talk, or at any rate to the level of preparatory academic discussion such as we might find in a poor theological seminar. But the Church is not a poor theological seminar. Much less is it a religious debating club. Its debate stands under a binding purpose and this purpose is that of union or unions in relation to a true faith. The immediate goal cannot be that of remaining apart, but of coming together and standing together in view of the actual coming together in proclamation. The immediate goal and necessary result of a debate on true faith conducted in the Church is that those who take part in it should make a common confession of their faith.

[592]

So far all the ecumenical Church conferences, even that of the summer of 1937, have shared with the conferences of ministers customary in all Protestant Churches the peculiarity (emphasised in this case by the solemnity and publicity of the occasion) that for all the honest protestation that they were acting as a Church the majority of those taking part, and even the leaders, did not appear to see that this is the immediate goal and necessary result of a debate conducted in the Church. What are we to make of attempts at discussion and reunion in which a confession is not at least proposed, in which indeed it is basically not even intended? (Cf. on this Eduard Thurneysen, "*Oxford 1937*" *Kirchenbl. f. d. ref. Schweitz*, 1937, No. 19.)

As a work of man this confession is, of course, subject to more than one reservation. The agreement on which it rests can never be more than a partial agreement, an agreement at definite points, points in the knowledge of the Word of God which are particularly important or controversial in the Church of the time. Other points have to be left open for later or similar discussions. Basically this kind of agreement can never lay claim to more than a preliminary significance. In joy and thankfulness at such agreements the Church cannot escape the possibility that in such further discussions as become necessary they may be again questioned, transcended and corrected by the Word of God as newly read and understood. Indeed, the possibility of mistaken agreement

140

and the necessity of rejecting their authority at a later stage cannot fundamentally be denied. Therefore this agreement cannot claim to be more than a partial and temporary agreement, which takes place in faith and in calling upon the Holy Spirit, a human agreement as seen from the standpoint of the Word of God. On the basis of such an agreement we can speak a common word, but a common human word, not commonly the Word of God. In such a uniting we cannot, therefore, speak from heaven, we cannot speak revelation.

In such agreements in the Church it is better not to claim the prophetic "Thus saith the Lord" and the apostolic "It pleased the Holy Ghost and us" (Ac. 15^{28}). The prophets and apostles could and had to speak in that way, but not the Church, which only applies and expounds their witness to revelation.

All these reservations do not alter the fact that wherever there is this agreement, and therefore a Church, debate about true faith has reached its goal, [593] and a Church confession has come into being: human, partial, preliminary, but of the Church, audible, and therefore audible as the expression of a common hearing and receiving of the Word of God—they do not alter the fact that this confession has authority, i.e., the claim to be heard by others before they confess themselves. Where two or three, gathered in the name of the Lord, "after there has been much disputing" (Ac. 15^{7}), confess their faith in concert, there I as a member of the Church have reason always to consider this before I intervene in the Church's discussion. That these two or three were really gathered together in the name of the Lord, i.e., really in a common hearing and accepting of the Word of God, I will not deny to them in advance—for I believe in a forgiveness of sins and therefore I also see and understand the Church under the forgiveness of sins. On a closer hearing I may not be able, or may be only partially able, to ascribe to them the presence of this basic presupposition of Church confession. I may have to declare the result of their agreement to be more or less false and therefore their authority wholly or partly unfounded. But this is something which I cannot know in advance. What I can and should and must concede in advance—and the fact of their agreement confirms this prior judgment—is that this presupposition has been fulfilled, that what they say in common they say with the authority of the Church, and that therefore I have always to listen to it. If I wanted to have it otherwise, if I wanted not to give them this honour and love, where would be the love and honour which I owe to their Lord and mine, where would be the seriousness of my hearing and receiving and myself believing and confessing the Word of God in the Church and therefore in community with others?

To sum up: The authority of the Church is the confession of the Church in the narrower meaning of the concept, i.e., the voice of others in the Church reaching me in specific agreements and common declarations and as such preceding my own faith and the confession of it. Church authority always consists in the documented presence of such agreements. If there are definite limitations in the nature of such agreements and their results, this does not hinder the fact that in this limitation they are and have authority, that they have to be heard by others, and indeed heard before these others speak—that is, especially before they question these agreements and their results and their authority either in part or in whole. It is enough for the moment that they are radically questioned by the Word of God. But this is true of others, too, and of the whole Church. Within this common questioning there does exist this precedence—human, partial, preliminary, but set up as a sign of the basic questioning of the whole Church within the Church—of the confession of the Church over the faith and the confessions of faith of others.

[594] We come now, and at this point we must turn to the concrete historical life of the Church, to the question of the form in which the authority of the Church has this existence. According to what we have just said, there can be no question of the form of ecclesiastical life in history and at the present day—in its totality as a confused and varied juxtaposition of many different and neutralising factors and constructs, traditions and customs, personal or general developments and influences, outwardly or inwardly conditioned determinations—embracing as such the confession and therefore the authority of the Church. As such, history, even ecclesiastical history, has neither divine nor even ecclesiastical authority. The form of a Church confession and therefore the form of Church authority is always that of a decision. The movement of Church affairs, the reality of Christian faith, so far as it knows no questions and therefore no need of answers and therefore agreements, even the emergence of all sorts of questions and answers and the genesis of controversies, even the unrestricted debating of the Church, for all their importance and significance in other directions, cannot as such be the form of the life of the Church in which it becomes the authority of the Church. In their indecision they cannot be heard and respected as the confession of the Church. Ecclesiastical history can be heard and respected as ecclesiastical authority only when there is discussion on the basis of a common hearing and receiving of the Word of God, and in that discussion one of those agreements, and in the documenting of that agreement a common confession, in matters of faith—hence, only when answers are given to the question of a true faith by way of speech and counter-speech, agreement and a common declaration in the face of Holy Scripture. It is not at all the case that this kind of happening cannot be distinguished from others and therefore is swallowed up again in the series of other happenings. But can we not see in any happening we like this answer, agreement and decision? We can, of course, if we are either God Himself or an impartial spectator and student of ecclesiastical history, impartial, that is, as regards the faith of the Church. What all-seeing God perceives in Church history is always and at every moment—in the good and the bad, to salvation and perdition—an answer, agreement and decision in the face of His own Word entrusted to the Church in Holy Scripture. Because He is the Lord and Judge of all, there is no ecclesiastical authority for Him. And for the impartial spectator and student

too, although in a different way, the differences in ecclesiastical life are all smoothed out. Everywhere he sees the same thing, the same attempts to state the essence of Christianity, the same two or three arriving at certain agreements, the same preliminary decisions. He finds everything equally important because everything appears equally unimportant. For the unbiassed historian of churches and heresies in his godlikeness there is ultimately only Church history as a whole, and no Church authority. Church authority only exists for the Church, and the Church only exists where there is faith in the Church's sense, i.e., in obedience to the Word of God. Where there is faith we do not [595] stand above Church history, like God and in his own way the impartial historian. We stand in Church history. Church history is lived. We are concretely claimed for the task of the common hearing and receiving of the Word of God, for the task of its common proclamation and therefore for discussion concerning true faith. We are claimed because we ourselves are always summoned to confess. We will always be open to projected agreements and Church confessions. In fact we will be on the lookout for them. And from the infinite variety of ecclesiastical happenings, certain events will stand out of themselves in virtue of their content, i.e., in virtue of what they have to say to us in our position in the Church, in our confessional situation, in the face of our encounter with the Word of God and the task which evolves out of it. Whatever may be the case with others in another position and another situation, in this event, and not in the many others, we ourselves encounter the confession and therefore the authority of the Church. Others may be responsible for overlooking this event, not hearing in it the confession of the Church, not acknowledging the authority which we think we perceive in it. And we ourselves will be responsible for overlooking events in which others think they hear the confession of the Church and see its authority. But where in our position and our situation face to face with Holy Scripture we receive an answer, an answer given in the light of Holy Scripture to the question of our faith, there we must hear the confession of the Church and affirm its authority and there, and only there, we can do so. Decision therefore is not merely the Church's confession as such, as laid down in the Church. It is also its recognition in the rest of the Church and its validity as Church authority accorded in that recognition. Decision is, therefore, the institution and existence of the authority of the Church in the entire range of this event: a common decision of those who speak—perhaps centuries ago— and of those who hear to-day. It is in these common decisions, in which a word is spoken here and there it is taken as a word to be respected, it is in the existence of these agreements that we live out the Church's history, and that both in the one case and the other, then and now, in them and in us, there lives the one Church of Jesus Christ. It may be that in both cases, then and now, as their decisions and as our own human decisions in which there is no freedom from sin, these decisions are mistaken, sick and under judgment—when was it otherwise? But in both cases, then and now, they are made in the light of Holy Scripture and therefore for all their sin they are not without grace, because not

143

without the ruling of the Lord of the Church, not without His pardon. If we believe this—and how can we believe at all, if we do not believe it?—then caught up in these common decisions, as the hearing Church here face to face with the teaching Church there, and together with it as the confessing Church [596] in these decisions, we will know and love and honour the life of the Church of Jesus Christ and His government and His justification and sanctification of sinful man; which means concretely, we will accept the Church there as an authority to the Church here, we will concede it that precedence, that right to be heard first, we will make our own confession only in response to its confession.

And now in and because of this common decision, the confession of the Church there, which is prior to the Church here, has a specific historical form: the form of the event which answers the question of the Church here in its own position and situation. This confession has therefore a historical meaning and content; it has form and contour. It consists in letters, words and statements. It is distinguished from so many other authorities, which might in themselves be an authority for the Church but in actual fact are not, by the fact that according to the will of the Lord of the Church it is this confession which speaks to it, and that according to the will of the same Lord it has heard this confession. If over against God it is and has in itself no more authority than any other human answer, agreement and decision reached in the sphere of His Church, it is now by God Himself as the power that rules the Church, through His Word in face of which it has taken place and been recognised, that within the limits appointed by it, it is exalted to be an authority, a word which has precedence and must be respected. And this exaltation is something which even the godlike historian, who does not think that there can be any such exaltation, has grudgingly to acknowledge as a fact. If he does not stand apart but has his place in the Church and accepts his situation and task in the Church, then he will not merely have to accept the fact as such. In principle, and perhaps also in practice, he will have to see the necessity that he in the Church here should confess the confession of the Church there in its specific historical form, because as the exposition and application of Holy Scripture it has spoken to the Church here in such a way that it must always hear and respect it.

To sum up: on both sides, on the side of those who wield it and also on that of those who recognise it, the form of the Church's authority is determined by a decision in virtue of which the one side speaks in the light of Holy Scripture and the other hears what is spoken in the light of the same Holy Scripture. What is spoken and heard, as distinct from much else that is spoken and heard but not in this unity, constitutes, determines and conditions the form of Church authority.

From this it follows that it is not theologically possible to denote and enumerate the authorities which are and have Church authority in this sense. Church authority is spiritual authority: in all its forms it rests on the fact that there and here, then and now, two decisions meet in obedience to the Word of

God and constitute one of these unities of common confession. The unities can, of course, be historically established and morphologically described. By custom, agreement and decision they may become Church law. But because of the spiritual character of these unities it is not possible theologically to say that such and such are Church authority, even though they are clearly established historically, or as Church law. It is not possible as it were to list them in a catalogue of Church authorities. Theologically, the mystery of the twofold decision, the mystery of obedience to the Word of God in which an authority becomes a Church authority and is recognised as such, must always be respected as a decision. Theologically, the contingent aspect of this decision, that it does happen in relation to this or that authority, cannot be made a principle. If that were to happen this authority would be equated with Holy Scripture or the Word of God. And that is what must not happen. Theologically, we can, properly speaking, only point out: (1) that wherever the Church exists and lives there will and must also be Church authority, and in a specific historical form; and (2) that granted the existence of this authority in a specific historical form, it has as such to be respected. We must now address ourselves to the second of these tasks. In doing so we will try to think through what we have said already with the help of some examples. [597]

1. We assume that between the Church now and here and the Church then and elsewhere there exists a unity of confession in respect of the compass of Holy Scripture, the so-called biblical Canon. We have already touched this question in an earlier context, but we must take it up again, because the fixing of the Canon is the basic act of Church confession and therefore the basic establishment of Church authority. The fact that there exists a Canon of Holy Scripture, i.e., a prophetic-apostolic witness of the revelation of God in Jesus Christ which in principle is prior to all the proclamation, teaching and decision of the Church, is posited in and with revelation itself. What this Canon is, of course, is also decided with revelation by God Himself and therefore in heaven, but not in such a way that the Church on earth is spared from having to decide it itself, that is, to know and confess what is *in concreto*EN115 the compass of that witness posited with revelation by God Himself. As a human document, this witness waits for human faith in its character as witness, and therefore for the counter-witness of this human faith. It is marked off by God and therefore in itself, but it waits to be taken and understood as marked off in this way and therefore to become the divine-human basis and law of the Church. It is only by becoming this, only in this decision, that it can be. It is only by being taken and understood and attested that it is marked off for us and exercises its function as a first and dominant sign of divine revelation. If the Canon has divine authority from God and in itself, its establishment as the Canon, its designation and delimitation as such, is an act of the Church, an act of its faith, its knowledge, its confession. Does that mean that the divine

---

EN115 concretely

[598] authority of the Canon is surrendered to human self-will? We could say that only if we were not confident that the prophetic and apostolic witness has the power to speak for itself with divine authority, and therefore to awaken a corresponding counter-witness to its authenticity in the Church, if in spite of the fact that that witness has been given it, we regarded the Church as a playground of human self-will instead of the sphere of the lordship of Jesus Christ. If we believe that the Lord is mightier than the sin which indisputably reigns in the Church, if we believe that He is the victor in the struggle against grace which is undoubtedly widespread even in the Church, then we can count on it that a genuine knowledge and confession in respect of the Canon, and therefore a knowledge and confession of the genuine Canon, is not at least impossible in the Church, not because we have to believe in men, but because if we are not to give up our faith we have to believe in the miracle of grace. But if we can count on this, then in what has been believed and known and confessed in the Church regarding the compass and text of the Canon, we cannot basically and exclusively see a work of human self-will. If the decisions made in this respect by the early and earlier Church are not made in heaven but on earth, to the extent that we do not have to oppose to them another witness in the strength of our own faith, knowledge and confession, to the extent that we do not have to contradict them, when we ourselves hear and receive the Word of God, they come to us and concern us and guide us as earthly pointers to the decision made in heaven. They bind us with the power of Church authority. Even our contradiction, even our different witness, can only be a later one, a liberation from a bondage accepted in the first instance but then shown to be wrong. We have still to hear first, to hear the Church, i.e., the others, the elders in the Church, before we can speak lawfully. I have first to be told by the Church which Scripture is Holy Scripture. The Church has had more than one discussion on the subject. Expressly or tacitly it has later repeated and reaffirmed its agreement to meet certain doubts. Upon each new generation, baptised and instructed in it, and hearing its preaching and called to the preaching office, it lays the confession that this or that belongs or does not belong to the Canon of Holy Scripture. It is only with human, not with divine authority, that this can be said to the younger Church by the older. Similarly, it is only with human, not with divine authority, that in this matter a protest can be made by the Evangelical Church against the different Roman Catholic contribution, against its inclusion of the so-called Old Testament Apocrypha in the Canon. But this confession and this protest is the confession and protest of the Church, in whose fellowship the Word of God must have reached us if we ourselves are to believe and confess it. If the Church can only serve the Word of God and if this service is only a human and, as such, a fallible service, we cannot escape this service, what it says to us in this service has authority, we have to accept it as at first normative for us, and therefore until we are better

[599] informed we have to approach the Holy Scripture laid before us by the Church—not otherwise, and in its full compass as presented to us, and there-

146

fore without addition or subtraction—the collection of those documents in which we too have to seek the witness of divine revelation. The Church with its existing and already attested faith promises us that we shall not seek this witness in it in vain. Except in its ministerial function, in a human way, by its preaching and instruction on the basis of this Canon, the Church cannot ensure that we shall find this witness in this Canon. We shall find this witness only in virtue of its self-witness, that is, in virtue of the authority of the Holy Ghost. The Church can point us to the decision made in heaven in respect of the genuine Canon. But it can do so only on earth and in earthly fashion, which means in the power and framework of its faith and perception. Therefore, if we are to be able to affirm and repeat it (in the power and framework of our own faith and perception), if there is to be that unity of confession between it and us, its indication or decision requires that direct confirmation by the self-witness of what is attested by it, which can take place only in our own encounter with the Word of God in Holy Scripture. But we have already received this direct confirmation in part when we began to believe as members of the Church. For in what but the Word of God in the Scripture which the Church calls holy have we put our faith? And to receive more of this direct confirmation, we will first have to hold to the indication given us by the Church in its confession of this or that form of the Canon if we do not want to deny and abandon again our own membership of the earthly body of the heavenly Lord. Nor will we ever with our own perhaps different confession be able to break this connexion, or renounce the honour and love which we owe our elders and others in the Church. But first and before we on our part can confess at all in the Church, either to agree or disagree, we always have to believe in the Church and therefore upon the basis proposed to us by the confession of these elders and others in the Church.

In practice, then, the course of things for us as individuals, as newcomers coming to the Church to-day, will be roughly as follows. Our starting-point will be a definite agreement with the proposal made us by the earlier and rest of the Church, in which we already find ourselves when we believe in the Word of God in Holy Scripture. But we shall then find that the content of this proposal can be used by us only in part, and very much in part, i.e., we shall find the further witness of revelation which the Church promises us only in definite parts of the Canon indicated to us, but in others we shall not find it. It may and probably will be the case that we are not able to find it in the greater part of the Canon indicated to us. But assuming that this is so, it is much more important to establish the positive side: that we have actually found it in one, even if only a small, part of what is proposed. If this is really the case, if we think we have received a direct confirmation in respect of at any rate a smaller part of what is proposed (let us say in respect of certain psalms, or gospels, or epistles, or even specific passages in these books), this may incline us to judge favourably in respect of the rest of what is proposed. And this pre-judgment will at once acquire a practical significance if it is [600] not just a matter of our opinion, if in these few parts of the Church's Canon or even these few passages we have found not merely the probable echo of our own feeling and judgment, but objectively the witness of divine revelation and therefore the Word of God as the Word of our Lord and of the Lord of His Church, if in hearing them we have really come to the

147

obedience of faith. Placed in this obedience and *ipso facto*[EN116] brought into agreement, even if only partial, with the witness of the Church, we shall definitely be ready to hear further this witness in relation to the Canon, and therefore not to cease but to continue searching the witness of the Word of God in those parts of the proposed Canon so far closed to us. On the basis of our limited but real consent to the confession of the Church, we shall be basically ready to reckon with the fact that if a much bigger section of the proposed Canon is silent for us, the fault may not be in what is proposed, but in some small degree in ourselves. Of course, it may be in what is proposed if it is a human and fallible proposal. But why should it not just as easily be in ourselves? And if we have to agree with it at one point by virtue of our own faith and perception, if the Lord of the Church has made known to us at one point the human and fallible service of His Church, why should it not be more natural to seek the fault in future in ourselves, and therefore to remain open to the confession of the Church and therefore to continue our investigation of the witness of divine revelation in the rest of the proposed Canon in the light of this confession and its authority? Again, it will be the case in practice that no individual completes this inquiry in such a way that on the basis of his own faith and perception, his confession always coincides with the then confession of the Church. Rather, we all have to reckon with the fact that for us definite and perhaps very large parts of the Church's Canon will be closed to our life's end, that it will be difficult or impossible for us really to hear the witness of revelation promised in respect of these parts too by virtue of our own faith and perception. But equally definitely we can reckon with the fact that the impulse to seek the blame for this certainly abnormal condition in what is proposed to us rather than in ourselves will have been at any rate diminished. And if we believe that in all honesty we are not conscious of any fault of our own in this matter—why should we not ultimately form our own negative private opinion respecting this or that part of the Canon closed to us in this way? But why should we want to see more than a private opinion in this negative restriction? Are we so certain that it is right and is it so important that for the sake of it we must challenge the confession of the Church? Can we not accept the latter, even if we ourselves cannot wholly agree with it on the basis of our own faith and perception? Are we so convinced of the rightness and importance of our in part negative restriction—which it is presupposed that we ourselves cannot alter again—that even in relation to the rest of the Church and the later Church we are sure that here, in respect of these parts of the Church's Canon which we have rejected, there can be no fulfilment of the promise, as there was for us in respect of the other parts? With our rejection of these parts can we presume to oppose the Church or its existing confession in the name of the Church itself? If we are not sure of this, if at bottom we are only putting questions to the Church's confession, on what grounds can we properly contest its churchly authority? We can make a serious protest against the Church's Canon only when we are so sure of it in content that we are bold to submit it to the judgment of the Church, not merely as our private opinion, but with the responsible intention of replacing, renewing and correcting the Church's confession in relation to the Canon by a new one. This possibility is not excluded. But how serious and difficult it is may be seen from the fact that Luther did not use it in respect of his well-known doubts on the Epistle of James, nor did the 16th century opponents of the Eusebian *Antilegomena*, but they were satisfied to state their doubts merely as private opinions and not

[601]
to press them. Again, Luther did not try to have raised to an ecclesiastical confession his opinion that the *Loci* of Melanchthon was a *libellum non solum immortalitate, sed canone quoque ecclesiastico dignum*[EN117] (*De servo arb.*, 1525, W.A. 18, 601, 5). And it is also worth noting that out of modern biblical criticism which has been so radical in the sphere of private opinions

---

[EN116] thereby

[EN117] book worthy not only of immortality, but also of the status of ecclesiastical canon

148

and discussions the desire for a new confession in relation to the Canon has not emerged and confronted the Church in such a way that it has seriously had to take up the question of a new definition of the Canon.

The question of the genuine Canon is not basically closed by the existence of the Church's Canon. Even in the light of the Church's Canon individuals have every right to raise it. Indeed, it is in practice the rule that it is an open question for the individual. But this does not affect in the least the existence and validity of this Canon. So long as it is not abolished or replaced, its proposal remains, and with it its authority and dignity and validity and the need to take it seriously, to have confidence in its promise, i.e., always to return to it. Future instruction is always reserved. The fault may not actually be in us but in the proposal. But this future instruction, like the past, will have to demonstrate itself as an instruction of the Church by the Church and not merely a private indoctrination of individuals. These individuals, however numerous, have not merely to know what they want, but also to want what they know, i.e., they must be bold to test the churchly legitimacy of their intention, which in the first instance can only be a private intention on the basis of a private opinion, by confronting the Church with the clear and responsible demand for a new confession; a confession which will mean a narrowing or broadening of the Church's Canon or its replacement by a quite different Canon. They must be bold to appeal to the Holy Spirit of Scripture as the Word of God in proof of the necessity of this intention. And they must be bold to expect that this Holy Spirit will witness to the rest of the Church in this way. So long as they are not bold to do this, so long as they will not accept this responsibility, so long as they perhaps do not have the serious desire for it, so long, therefore, as their new confession has not really established itself as the confession of the Church in place of the old one, their objection to the old confession—however remarkable or deserving of consideration it may in fact be—can never have any greater significance than that of a murmuring compared with the authority of the old one. This murmuring can and must remind the Church that its authority is circumscribed and preliminary, a human authority, against which there may be not only murmuring but even serious protest. It can and must bring before the Church the question whether its existing confession in relation to the Canon is still its confession and can and must continue to be so. It can and must summon it to examine itself in respect of its existing confession, and then either to reaffirm in research and doctrine, preaching and instruction, that this is still its confession, or to make a new and better one. But as long as the old proposal is in force, as long as a new proposal is not responsibly made and [602] adopted and proclaimed as the new decision of the Church on the basis of new discussion and agreement, the objection to it is only a murmuring to which we cannot give anything like the same hearing as we give to the voice of the Church. The voice of the Church and therefore the existing Canon of the Church must always be heard first, its content investigated and its possibilities exhausted.

We may ask how the matter stands in relation to the text of the Bible. Is it possible and necessary to count on a unity of confession in this respect too, and therefore on a basic text or perhaps even a translation of Holy Scripture which is ecclesiastically authoritative and has to be respected in the same sense as the Canon marked off by the Church? The Roman Catholic Church gives an affirmative answer, although strangely and characteristically not in respect of a normative form of the basic Hebrew and Greek text, but only of a normative Latin translation. It is as such that the Council of Trent defines (*Sess.* IV, 1546, *Denz.* No. 785) the *vetus et vulgata editio, quae longo tot saeculorum usu in ipsa ecclesia probata est*[EN118], and therefore demands: *ut ... in publicis lectionibus, disputationibus, praedicationibus et expositionibus pro authentica habeatur et quod nemo illam reicere quovis praetextu audeat vel praesumat*[EN119]. We see in this edict once again the utter self-glorification with which in Catholicism the Church controls the witness of divine revelation, subjugating the voice of this witness to its own Latin voice. The procedure is not calculated to invite imitation, and it has not been imitated on the Evangelical side in relation either to a translation or even to the basic text, so that we do not have to reckon with a unity of confession in this matter. Of course the legend of the origin of the Septuagint (Irenaeus, *C. o. h.* III, 21, 2) has a significance that is not altered by the fact that it is a legend: it raises the legitimate question of a single and authentic text of Holy Scripture. And we certainly cannot say that this question, whether in relation to the basic text or translations, is clearly and exclusively a question of historical philology. The decision on this matter—especially as regards translations, but also incidentally the basic text—is also a question of faith, i.e., of theological insight. It is, therefore, right and necessary that the Church should be interested in the biblical text from both standpoints. It should not entrust and abandon itself to the decisions necessary in new editions of the Bible without considering the judgment of all kinds of historical and linguistic experts, a judgment which may be very limited because of its theological or non-theological background. But at the same time—and at this point I no longer accept my exposition in the 1927 *Prolegomena*, p. 371 f.—it corresponds to the facts of the case if the Church is certainly summoned to a constantly recurring task by the problem of the text, but does not go on to lay down certain confessional results as in the fixing of the Canon. The fluidity of the basic text, the fact that it is known to us only in different traditions, but not in a primal form which can be clearly fixed as such, the obvious openness of the question of the genuine text—all this belongs to the human and therefore the divinely authoritative being and character of Holy Scripture, to the freedom of the Word of God in relation to its readers and expositors, a freedom which we would clearly transgress with a confessional decision. This is particularly true of translations. Every translation is obviously an explanation. And by its very nature of course—unlike a confession of faith—it is an explanation for which an individual must usually take the main responsibility. Even if a translation can actually acquire a certain tacit authority in the Church, as Luther's did, it is inadvisable to underline this factual authority by a formal decision and declaration on the part of the Church, to tie the Church expressly to the private work of an individual, and in this way to paralyse all further work in the task of translation. Of translations we can only desire that as many as possible will arise and be disseminated in the Church in order that those who are not linguistic experts may have a share in the task of translation by a mutual comparison and completion. And of the basic text we can only desire that it may always be made known to the Church with the fullest possible addition of variants, i.e., the contribution of tradition in all its variety, and that there

[603]

[EN118] The Old Vulgate edition which has been tested by the long use of so many centuries in the same church

[EN119] in public readings, disputations, sermons and expositions, to be considered as authentic, such that no-one should dare or presume to reject it for any reason

may then be and continue to be—from the historical and philological and also from the theological standpoint—the critical consideration of this contribution which this makes possible. A *textus receptus*[EN120] is not offered by Church confession, or any court to which we can ascribe authority. There are good reasons for this. And if we are not to reckon with new facts, that is, facts which are still unknown, with the future discovery of a primal form which forces itself upon us as the norm, it is impossible to see how the present-day Church can ever reach the point of confession in this matter, i.e., of setting up and proclaiming a *textus receptus*[EN121] to the Church of the future.

2. We assume that between the Church now and here and the Church then and elsewhere there exists a unity of confession in respect of the authority of the word of specific ecclesiastical teachers, i.e., specific expositors and preachers of the Bible, whose word has in fact emerged from all the words of other expositors and preachers and spoken to the Church of their day and of a later day, and still speaks to the present-day Church, in a way which cannot be said of other teachers of their own or other periods. Because the Church then and since has heard these teachers especially, because it has received their word with particular attention and gratitude, it has made confession of the point. And as the present-day Church we ourselves are summoned to give our assent to this confession of the particular attention which ought to be paid to these teachers. It is a fact which we cannot prove to be theologically necessary, which we cannot postulate, which theologically we cannot prove to be real, but which we can only explain on the assumption of its actuality: that there are "Church fathers" and that these fathers have a definite ecclesiastical authority.

Ecce quo te introduxi: conventus sanctorum istorum non est multitudo popularis; non solum filii sed et patres ecclesiae sunt[EN122] (Augustine, *C. Jul.* I, 7, 31). *Talibus post apostolos sancta ecclesia plantatoribus, rigatoribus, aedificatoribus, pastoribus, nutritoribus crevit*[EN123] (*ib.*, II, 10, 37). According to this estimate of one who was himself a father, fathers are members of the Church who have actively taken part in the life of the Church in a way which is so distinctive and so obviously different from what the best of others do that they stand out as a particular "convent of saints." Later generations were able to state with greater precision what are the characteristics of a father. Ecclesiastical fathers (*patres ecclesiastici*), according to Roman Catholic doctrine, are "those writers of the Church's past, who distinguished themselves by age, sanctity of life, purity of doctrine and the Church's recognition" (B. Bartmann, *Lehrb. d. Dogm.*[7], 1928, vol. 1, 30). They must be distinguished from mere "ecclesiastical writers" (*scriptores eccl.*), to whom these predicates do not belong or belong only in part, among whom we have to reckon an Origen and Lactantius. And distinguished in this way they constitute one of the sources of Church tradition. Among them, and also among the theologians of later times, the papal proclamation then distinguishes "ecclesiastical teachers" (*doctores ecclesiae*), of whom it is thought to be known that with the holy martyrs and virgins they will wear an aureole in Heaven. Amongst those who qualify as such are Ambrose, Augustine, Jerome, Gregory the Great, Athanasius, Basil, Gregory Nazianzus, Chrysostom, Anselm of

[604]

EN120 received text
EN121 received text
EN122 Behold, I have introduced you to this point: the convent of those saints is not a popular multitude: there are not only sons, but also fathers of the Church
EN123 After the apostles, by such planters, waterers, builders, pastors and feeders, does the holy Church grow

Canterbury (from 1720), Thomas Aquinas (from 1567), Bonaventure (from 1588), Bernard of Clairvaux (from 1830) and others.

The Reformation obviously did not recognise this theological hierarchy and its importance as a second source of revelation. Of an uncritical subjection to the so-called *consensus patrum*[EN124], which according to Catholic doctrine constitutes the criterion of a completely valid proof from the fathers, let alone to the the authority of any one of even the older teachers, there could be no question on the basis of the Evangelical Church and its Scripture principle. Still, the Reformation did regard certain fathers of the Church as *testes veritatis*[EN125], accepting that they have to be regarded as in some sense normative, although always under the norm of Holy Scripture. This can easily be shown from Luther as well as Calvin, especially in relation to Augustine. "Where the holy fathers and ancient teachers, who explained and expounded Scripture, do not fall by this plumbline, we will recognise and accept them not alone as expositors of Scripture, but as elect instruments by which God hath spoken and wrought" (*Conf. helv. prior.* of 1536, Art. 3). *Quia enim Ecclesia est Catholica, Deus semper excitavit in diversis locis aliquos, qui consentientem confessionem de sano verae doctrinae intellectu ad confirmationem posteritatis ediderunt. Et bonae mentes valde confirmantur, quando vident, eandem vocem doctrinae omnibus temporibus in Ecclesia sonuisse*[EN126] (M. Chemnitz, *Loci*, 1591, *Hypomn.* 6). It was not in accordance with the practice of Protestant theology in the age of orthodoxy if occasionally (as in G. Voetius, *Disput.* I, 1648, 74 ff.) the distinction between Church fathers and Church writers was in theory completely obliterated, and it was maintained that there can be no question of anything but an impartial hearing of all the voices of the past, that there can be no special authority of particular fathers in the Evangelical Church and its theology.

This theoretical purity was quite out of place, for in the Evangelical Church and its theology the confession had long since found a place for new fathers and "elect instruments," i.e., the Reformers themselves. It is not unnecessary to recall the excesses of this kind of confession as they occurred even in the century of the Reformation. It is a matter for astonishment when only ten years after Luther's death N. Amsdorf declares: *neminem tanta praeditum sapientia, fide, constantia post apostolos fuisse aut deinceps futurum esse, quantum in reverendo viro D. M. Luthero non sine ingenti administratione donorum Dei conspeximus*[EN127] (Introduction to the Jena edition of Luther's Works, *E. A. Op. lat.* v.a. I, 12); or when we are told by Michael Neander (1576), quoted by W. Gass, *Gesch. d. prot. Dogm.* vol. 1, 1854, 228: *Non itaque fervet zelo pietatis, qui huius viri (sc. Lutheri) historiam, labores, pericula, certamina ac plane coelestia dona non saepe cogitat, admiratur ac pro hoc viro Deo agit saepius gratias et qui post Biblia sacra Lutheri libris non primum locum tribuit et magnificat ut coelestem divinum ac preciosum thesaurum … Lutherus suam theologiam a priori habuit i.d. ex coelesti quadam revelatione*[EN128]; or

---

[EN124] consensus of the fathers

[EN125] truthful witnesses

[EN126] For since the Church is catholic, God always raises up in different places some who have published a harmonious confession of the sound understanding of true doctrine for the strengthening of generations to come. And good minds are greatly strengthened, when they see that the same voice of doctrine has rung out at all times in the Church

[EN127] We have seen that no-one since the apostles has been – or ever will be – endowed with such great wisdom, faith, and constancy as that in Dr Martin Luther, with his huge grant of the gifts of God

[EN128] Thus, he does not burn with piety who does not often contemplate the life, the labours, the dangers, the struggles and the obviously heavenly gifts of this man (i.e. of Luther), and who does not marvel and, more often, give thanks to God for this man, and who does not attribute prime place to the books of Luther after the Holy Bible, and who does not praise them as heavenly divinity and precious treasure. Luther possessed his theology independently, that is, by a certain heavenly revelation

when Andreas Fabricius (1581, *ib.*, 228) extols him as *theander, megalander,* φωσφόρος θεολόγων, φωστήρ τε καὶ μέγα θαῦμα οἰκουμένης EN129, the prophet and Elijah of Germany, no less unique than Paul and John the Baptist; or when J. Gerhard (*Loci.*, 1610 f., *L* XIV, 32) seriously found in Luther a fulfilment of Rev. 14⁶: the prophecy of the *angelus volens per medium coeli habens aeternum evangelium* EN130; or when it could be seen written on a Wittenberg stove: "The Word of God and the teaching of Luther will never fail." But the Reformed, too, sometimes spoke in the same way and it was sung of Calvin's *Institutio*:

> *Praeter apostolicas, post Christi tempore, chartas*
> *Huic peperere libro saecula nulla parem.* EN131
> (P. Thurius)

Now behind all these and similar excesses there is the serious fact that in and with its reform- [605] ation by the Word of God and in the service of this divine reformation the Church of that period also heard the human word of Luther and Calvin in such a way that it could no longer consider its earthly historical existence as a Church without not only the Word of God but also this human word, without the teaching and instruction of these Reformers. As the Church reformed by the Word of God it became *eo ipso* EN132 the Church of Luther, the Church of Calvin. Both men, and many of their companions with them, actually possessed and exercised in their life-times (as "doctors of Holy Scripture"—and therefore as spiritual, but because spiritual, not only spiritual leaders of their Churches) an authority which far exceeded that which they enjoyed in their local ecclesiastical and academic offices. And in their own spheres they undoubtedly possessed and exercised this authority right up to the beginning of the 18th century. If it could have been forgotten in their respective Churches, the polemics of Catholic opponents would have seen to it that it was always revived. Against these polemics, and especially the accusation that the Reformation and its Churches were illegitimate, Lutheran orthodoxy introduced into its dogmatics a proper article *De vocatione beati Lutheri* (cf. J. Gerhard, *Loci*, 1610 f. *L* XXIII, 118 f.; A. Calov, *Systema loc. theol.*, 1677, VIII, *art.* 3, *c.* 2, *qu.* 2; A. Quenstedt, *Theol. did. pol.*, 1685, IV, *c.* 12, *sect.* 2, *qu.* 3; D. Hollaz, *Ex. theol. acr.*, 1707, IV, *c.* 2, *qu.* 10). Two points are demonstrated: (1) the regularity of Luther's calling as priest and doctor and (2) the fact of his extraordinary calling. Everywhere in Scripture there are found *vaticinia de opere reformationis, quae licet disertam et specialem nominis Lutheri mentionem non faciant, implicite tamen organi, per quod opus illud perficiendum erat, denotationem continent* EN133 (J. Gerhard, XXIII, 124). Not rhetorically, but by way of argument, attention is drawn to Luther's profound and powerful exegesis of Scripture, his *animus heroicus et in periculis etiam maximis imperterritus* EN134, his fulfilled prophecies, his position and successes as a preacher of the Word in the fight against Antichrist. The first subject of the doctrine of the Lutheran Church is clearly about to become its object. Now it is no accident that the Reformed dogmatics of the same period, faced with the same external situation, never gave rise to an article *De ministerio Calvini* or the like, and that there could not—and if the Reformed want to be true to Calvin, there never can be—a Calvinism and a

---

EN129 a divine man, a great man, the light-bringer among the theologians, both a shining light and a great wonder of the world
EN130 angel flying through the middle of the sky with the eternal gospel
EN131 Except for the writings of the apostles, after the time of Christ, no age has produced an equal to this book.
EN132 by the same token
EN133 Oracles concerning the work of the Reformation which, granted, do not make explicit and special mention of the name of Luther, but which implicitly contain reference to the instrument through which that work was to be accomplished
EN134 heroic mind, which was not afraid even in the greatest dangers

Calvinistic Church in the sense in which there is still a Lutheranism and a Lutheran Church. This is not explained merely by a theological abnegation of human glory, but more decisively by the fact that Calvin's authority—which in its own sphere was no less powerful than that of Luther—was of a radically different kind in that it rested far less than Luther's on the impression of his personality and life and far more on his ecclesiastical teaching as such. It cannot be ignored that the Lutheran confession of Luther both then and now comes far too dangerously near to the proclaiming of the basic ecclesiastical authority and therefore of the divine authority of this man, and thus to a real endangering of the Scripture principle. The same phenomenon will meet us again when we consider the problem of the Church confession. Calvin was a teacher of the Church in a purer sense in that to him more than Luther it was given to lead the Church by his doctrine, in spite of and in its Calvinian distinctness, to Holy Scripture itself, binding it to its substance and only in the concern for the substance to himself. But within these limits he undoubtedly exercised in the Reformed Church and its theology the same function as that of Luther on the Lutheran side. A voice from the 17th century which is also instructive in content will perhaps attest this in place of many others: that of Abraham Heidan, who in the prolegomena of his *Corpus Theol. chr.* 1676, in the context of a review of the most important dogmatic literature which he could recommend to his students makes honourable mention of Melanchthon and then goes on

[606]

to say: *Sed sublimitatis characterem et verum ὕψος in Calvino miror, qui ita me quandoque attollit et sublimen rapit, ut non sim amplius apud me. Si ab ullo a Calvino me θεολογεῖν didicisse gloriari possum … Hie aliquid dicam, iuvenes. quod velim vos memori mente recondere: non ab alio autore melius disci, quomodo et in explicationibus et in disputationibus utendum sit verbo Dei: hic solus concionari docet*[EN135].

With the authority of the Reformation confession (and also with it the acceptance of the Evangelical Scripture principle, i.e., with the divine authority of the biblical witness of revelation), the ecclesiastical authority of the Reformers began to fade in the Evangelical Church from the beginning of the 18th century and was finally eclipsed. One of Luther's "prophecies" was definitely fulfilled: *Tum enim multi volentes esse magistri surgent, qui praetextu pietatis perversa docebunt et brevi subvertent omnia, quae nos longo tempore et maximo labore aedificavimus. Manebit tamen Christus regnans usque ad finem mundi, sed mirabiliter, ut sub papatu*[EN136] (*Comm. on Gal.* 4⁹ *W.A.* 40, I, 611, 17). Certainly the firm popularity which has been retained by the figure of Luther even in modern developments, and in particular the estimation as an apostle of freedom of conscience or a religious personality or a German which he has been accorded more recently on every possible or impossible count, is no substitute for a recognition of his ecclesiastical signification as a Reformer and Church teacher. The same is naturally true of the different strains of "historical Calvinism." The Reformers enjoyed ecclesiastical authority, and will recover it, only where the Reformation confession has authority. But this, too, stands or falls with the acceptance of the Evangelical Scripture principle, or materially with the divine authority of Holy Scripture. Where this is recognised, the recognition of the ecclesiastical authority of the Reformers as expositors and preachers of

---

EN135 But I marvel at the character of sublimity and true majesty in Calvin who so lifts me on high and raises me upward that I am no longer in myself. If I can boast that I have learnt to be a theologian from anyone, it is from Calvin … Now let me say, young men, something which I want you to lodge in the memory of your mind: Not from any other author can one learn better how to use the Word of God in expositions and disputations. He alone can teach to speak publicly

EN136 For then, many will rise up wishing to be teachers, who will teach on the twisted pretext of piety, and will overturn in a short time everything which we have built up in this long time and with very great labour. But Christ will still reign until the end of the world, yet amazingly it will be as though He is under the pope

Holy Scripture will be automatically ensured. So, too, will assent to the former confession of the Church.

What is certain is that the authority of the Reformers in the Evangelical Church is analogous to that of the "Church fathers," i.e., "Church teachers," in Roman Catholicism. This means that although in the latter case the matter is wrongly related to the doctrine of tradition as a second source of revelation, we cannot ignore the problem actually raised, and act as though there were for us no "elect instruments" but only an equally significant or insignificant collection of "ecclesiastical writers." Already in the sphere of a true and Evangelical knowledge of the Word of God there are outstanding teachers of Holy Scripture who as such have to be regarded as outstanding teachers of the Church. The question is, how and in what limits they have to be regarded in this way. But it has also to be considered whether in these limits they have not to be regarded in a much stricter sense as what they are than the fathers of Catholicism.

To get to the root of this matter we have to be clear especially about this point. Holy Scripture in its divine authority speaks to each generation in the Church in the form of a definitely defined Canon. To that extent it speaks with human authority, the authority of the preceding Church. But similarly, it never speaks to any generation or individual in the Church alone, as the naked, written word which has come down to us. It speaks to us as to those who belong to the fellowship of the Church and have a place in its history. Most frequently, perhaps, it speaks externally not as the word written and read but as the word preached. But even as direct readers we cannot withdraw from our particular place in the Church which has baptised and instructed us, or from its witness with regard to the understanding of what we now undertake to read and understand. If Holy Scripture alone is the divine teacher in the school in which we find ourselves when we find ourselves in the Church, we will not want [607] to find ourselves in this school of the Church without fellow-pupils, without co-operation with them, without the readiness to be instructed by older and more experienced fellow-pupils: as fellow-pupils, but to be instructed. And basically the older and more experienced fellow-pupil is simply the Church teacher. He is, in fact, older and more experienced in a qualified sense of the words. He is not only a son but a father in the Church. We have to be instructed by him. But the fact that he is so is something which can only happen. We have to treat it as a presupposition. Therefore if we are asked how we came to accept the existence of these teachers, we can only reply with a counter-question: how can we be members of the Church and obedient to the Word of God and not do so? What is sure is that the Church hears—and it is only as its members and not as spaceless and timeless monads that we hear the Word of God in Scripture. But if we hear it as members of the Church, then we also hear the Church, and therefore we do not hear the echo of the Word of God only or first of all in our own voice, but in the voice of others, those who were before us in the Church. All others, and all who were before us? No, not all, but those who according to the confession of the Church have spoken and still speak in such a way that others had and still have to listen to them. Those, then, in whose voice, according to the confession of the rest of the Church, we have to hear the Church's voice, whom we have to hear therefore with the authority of the Church. Can we deny in principle the existence of these older and more experienced fellow-pupils, and therefore the ecclesiastical authority of particular teachers? Surely not in principle. And even in practice we could not do so without the danger and suspicion that the real concern of the self-glorifying which we enjoy as those who hear only the Word of God is a secret emancipation from a genuine hearing of the Word of God rather than the assertion of that Evangelical Scripture principle of which we perhaps make such ostentatious parade.

An interesting peripheral phenomenon of Neo-Protcstantism is the peculiar behaviour of the so-called Biblicism whose existence and character are strikingly presented in Gottfried Menken (1768–1831) of Bremen, a writer who has never received sufficient notice in dogmatic history. Even in his youth the characteristic complaint was made against Menken that it was "his obsession to try to construct his Christianity out of the Bible alone" (Gildemeister, *Leben und Werke des Dr. G. Menken*, 1861, II, 7). That is the more or less explicit programme of this modern Biblicism. "My reading is very limited yet very extended; it begins with Moses and ends with John. The Bible and the Bible alone I read and study" (*ib.*, I, 21). He is not concerned with "what is old or new, with defending or attacking, with assent to the doctrine of any ecclesiastical party, with orthodoxy or heterodoxy, but only with the pure and genuine teaching of the Bible" (*Schriften*, 1858 f., VII, 256). And the Church? Menken prefers to avoid the word. For him and for all modern Biblicists it is a question of "Christianity," "reality" the "truth," the "kingdom of God." The Church is "the eternally pure possessor and [608] preserver of the divine." Yet only too often its doctrine has "come under the influence of a passing philosophy or the superstitiously venerated theology of the fathers" (*Schriften* VII, 264). "In any case, where is the Church? Is it in the East or the West? Does it gather under the staff of the ecumenical Patriarch in Constantinople or under the threefold crown of the Pope at Rome? Finding no rest or portion in the world, did it long ago retire with the ancient Syrian Christians into the heart of Southern India or with the Waldenses into the valleys of Piedmont? In the fellowship of the Holy Ghost did it infallibly and irrevocably express itself at the Diet of Augsburg or at the Council of Trent or at the National Synod of Dort? Or finally is the true and perfect idea of Christian truth and doctrine to be found in the *Idea fidei Fratrum?* These few questions point to many things and embrace a large part of Christianity; but many different events, and systems and confessions and millions of Christians are outside their scope: Nestorians, Monophysites, Mennonites, Arminians, Jansenists, Mystics and Quakers; and many others, who all make claim to the name of the Christian Church and the treasure of Christian orthodoxy. These few questions are enough to show that, if we are not ignorant, or if after the customary manner and usage of sectarianism which becomes almost second nature, when we use the word Church we do not regard the confession of the Fathers and the sum total of those who agree with it as the only Christian fellowship in which true doctrine is to be found and to which alone, therefore, or primarily the name of Church belongs, it is not easy even to know what the Church believes and teaches. At an informative glance at so many different periods, countries, languages, systems, costumes and customs, at the confusion and tumult of so many different and contradictory and warring sects, at the medley of so many different confessions and catechisms, it seems difficult and almost impossible to find a standpoint where with insight and material truth we can say: I believe and teach what the Church believes and teaches" (*Schriften* VII, 238). In these circumstances how can the Church have authority? "What is offered me as old is honoured by you as such only because it is found in a 16th century catechism from the Palatinate or Saxony, or because an

11th century Archbishop of Canterbury or a 5th century Bishop of Hippo thought in this way and formulated and determined the matter accordingly. But if you could add to these human authorities a greater one in the utterances of a 2nd century Bishop of Lyons, which you cannot, it would not make any material difference. For it does not matter to me to learn how Ursin or Luther or Anselm or Augustine or Irenaeus thought about the matter and formulated and determined it—they and their decisions are too new. I want that which is old, original and solely authentic: Holy Scripture itself" (*Schriften* VII, 263 f.). If these statements and arguments had been handed down without name or context, we might suppose that their author was of the Enlightenment instead of the passionate opponent of the Enlightenment which Menken actually was. And we find a similar agreement with Neo-Protestant anti-confessionalism in the later writer J. T. Beck, and partly too in Hofmann of Erlangen, and occasionally even in A. Schlatter. What does this agreement mean? We obviously have to ask whether here the Bible individually read and autonomously understood and expounded is not set up with the same sovereignty as others have exalted reason or feeling or experience or history as the one principle of theology? In this context does not the special treatment of the Bible—to the extent that it does not come under the relativism with which the Church is considered—take on something of self-glorification? Are we not dealing with a pious, but in its audacity no less explicitly modern leap into direct immediacy, with a laying hold of revelation, which, involving as it does a jettisoning of the fathers, although it purports to be a laying hold of the Bible, is perhaps something very different from the obedience of faith which only occurs when revelation lays hold of us by the word of the Bible? By nature is this absolutism of the Bible any different from that other absolutism which constituted the decisive characteristic of the spirit and system of the 18th century as it [609] culminated in the Enlightenment? And can it be very different in its consequences? Will those who will have the Bible alone as their master, as though Church history began again with them, really refrain from mastering the Bible? In the vacuum of their own seeking which this involves, will they perhaps hear Scripture better than in the sphere of the Church? In actual fact, there has never been a Biblicist who for all his grandiloquent appeal directly to Scripture against the fathers and tradition has proved himself so independent of the spirit and philosophy of his age and especially of his favourite religious ideas that in his teaching he has really allowed the Bible and the Bible alone to speak reliably by means or in spite of his anti-traditionalism. On the contrary, in the very Neo-Protestant peculiarities which we find at crucial points especially in Menken but also in J. T. Beck, we are instructed that it is not advisable for serious students of Scripture so blithely to ignore the 16th century catechisms of the Palatinate and Saxony, or that 5th century Bishop of Hippo, or to refuse the guidance and correction afforded by the existence of Church fathers, as that Biblicist programme involves. Otherwise there may be too easy and close an approximation to all kinds of other modern Titanisms. The Biblicism of the Reformers, as distinct from modern Biblicism, did not make this approximation because not in spite but in application of the Evangelical Scripture principle it kept itself free from this anti-traditionalism. J. A. Bengel, whose name is often mentioned in this context, showed at this point much greater wisdom than his more recent followers. Of course, we must not ignore but properly respect the fact that this modern Biblicism did find itself in a relative opposition to Neo-Protestantism generally. It did give a necessary reminder of the Evangelical Scripture principle and in its own way it made an effective modern application of it at a crucial period. By way of it some important and true exegetical discoveries were made, and its outstanding representatives had a great personal dignity. But again that cannot prevent us from definitely rejecting its procedure in relation to the fathers as a basically liberal undertaking, just as we reject the thoughtlessness and lack of respect shown by all Neo-Protestantism in this regard.

Neither in principle nor in practice, therefore, can we deny the existence of the ecclesiastical authority of specific teachers in the Church. But if this is the case, then it is of itself understandable theologically—assuming that it is a fact—that in the Evangelical Churches it was the Reformers who acquired this authority. If our Churches confessed that they were reformed by the Word of God and not simply by Luther and Calvin, their reformation did take place by the witness borne to them by Luther and Calvin. Therefore the witness of Luther and Calvin is decisive and essential for their existence as this Church, as the Churches reformed in this way, and therefore for the whole contingency of their existence as the Church of Jesus Christ. This may not be true as a constitutive, but it is certainly true as a regulative principle. If they free themselves from this witness they are no longer these Churches and therefore no longer contingently the Church of Jesus Christ. But supposing that by a new contingent fact they were brought beyond the Reformation and therefore loosed from the authority of the Reformers, and that they recognised the fact just as consciously and definitely as they formerly recognised the Reformation and therefore the authority of the Reformers? Why should such a development be impossible?

[610] That it has taken place has been asserted more than once in the last 400 years. The first time was in the 16th century itself and in the lifetime of the Reformers, when various sectarian groups tried to explain the work of Luther and Calvin as merely preparatory, an introductory stage already passed, to that third kingdom of the Spirit initiated by their own insights. The same process, the replacement of the conviction by a new one which made the Reformation and the authority of the Reformers out of date, was repeated in the 17th century when the English Independents attempted their radical reconstruction of the life of the Church, at the beginning of the 18th century when Pietism enjoyed its first period of expansion, again when Schleiermacher, with his characteristic genius, summed up and gave form to the whole theological contribution of the century, and again at the beginning of the 19th century when the great awakening swept Evangelical Europe. It was repeated again in certain religio-ecclesiastical phenomena which accompanied the recent political revolution in Germany. The remarkable thing is that although in these centuries the Evangelical Churches were widely and deeply separated from their Reformation origin, so far there has never been any actual and decisive severance of these Churches from the authority of their origin. That authority was often more misunderstood than understood, but it was always reasserted and exercised. More than once—at any rate in Pietism and the awakening—the best and most effective feature in these supposed innovations, quite contrary to their original impulse, consisted in a partial rediscovery and renewal of the Reformation inheritance. Constructive power was displayed by only one of the 16th-century communities which separated themselves from Rome and were now moving away from the Reformers. This was the Church of England, which from the very first had been not so much an Evangelical Church as a final achievement of the great reforming attempt of the late Middle Ages carried through with the help of Lutheran and Calvinistic influences. Every other product of this movement sooner or later had to choose between condemning itself to a precarious isolation like the Unitarians in Poland and Siebenbürgen or reversing the movement as far as it had gone, and in some sense and to some degree, perhaps with all kinds of evasions and diminutions, continuing to recognise the authority of the Reformers. Of course, pure Neo-Protestantism means a break with the Reformation. But in these four centuries there was

very little pure Neo-Protestantism. If in the 19th century the Evangelical Church and its theology had built on the foundation of Schleiermacher's *Reden über die Religion* and *Glaubenslehre*, it would have become purely Neo-Protestant, and fulfilled the intentions of the humanists and enthusiasts of the 16th century by breaking with the Reformation. But although the Neo-Protestant infection went deep, wisely the Church did not build on Schleiermacher and was not therefore reconstructed. It was a purely literary fancy if about 1900 anyone dared coolly describe Schleiermacher as the "Church father of the 19th century." In spite of the greatness of his achievement and the intensity of his influence, the theology of Schleiermacher became only the starting-point and centre of an esoteric tradition in the Evangelical Church, but not the contingent fact which separated the Evangelical Churches from their Reformation origin and forced them into new paths. In his deepest intentions, as he finally revealed them in his letters—destroying any illusions about his connexion with the Reformation—Schleiermacher did not find any successor among the leading theologians of the 19th century. But his relatively most loyal personal disciples. August Twesten and Alexander Schweizer, made it their life's task to interpret him, the one in the Lutheran, the other in the Reformed sense, as the true fulfilment and continuation of the work of the Reformers. That they did not and could not succeed in this is another matter. But by trying to do so they at least admitted that Schleiermacher's theology was not a factor by which the Church could be refashioned, thus reverting—with all kinds of misunderstandings into a recognition of the supreme authority of the Reformers. And had not Schleiermacher himself finally prepared the way for this return by his participation in the Reformation celebrations of 1817 and 1830—in spite of his deepest intentions? In this form the recognition of the Reformers in the 19th century was increasingly reaccepted. Even those who in fact went quite different paths did not want to admit that they were not covered and justified on these paths by their shadow. If it was necessary skilfully to adapt them for this purpose, as was done especially by A. Ritschl and his disciples, there was no longer any desire to cease appealing to them at every opportunity, and wherever possible pretending to be their most loyal followers. Paul de Lagarde, whom we can place alongside Schleiermacher as one of the few pure Neo-Protestants, was completely alone in his fierce aversion to Luther. And even his disciples, the so-called religio-historical school, accepted his verdict only in the weakened form that we find in the historical construction of E. Troeltsch. For the rest they hastened—this time under cover of the hero-worship of Carlyle—to join in the general praise of the Reformers. At root the attitude of more recent Evangelical theology to the Reformers gives rise to many questions. And the same is true of the relation of more recent Evangelical Churches, of the part played in modern proclamation by references and appeals to the Reformers, by the awakening and honouring of their memory, by the utilisation of their writings and individual thoughts. There is no doubt that in doing this there are many who are either the victims of serious illusions regarding their own agreement with the Reformers, or else combine their honouring and celebrating of the persons of the Reformers with variations from their teaching which put in a strange light the loyalty professed to them. There is no doubt that the construction usually brought in to help—an affirmation of the Reformers and a simultaneous and vigorous denial of the "orthodoxy of the 17th century," which is decked out with all the characteristics of a bogey—is historically and in content quite impossible. But the remarkable fact remains that there was a sense of obligation to this loyalty to the Reformers, that there was a hesitation to confess a really new Protestantism, that the most outspoken Neo-Protestants were often the most eager to emphasise their Lutheranism, and even their Calvinism (e.g., at the Calvin celebrations of 1909). How much easier it would have been if they could have freed themselves from this historical burden and left Luther and Calvin as well as orthodoxy quite resolutely behind. But actually to make this break was not so simple, and in view of the difficulties in the way there is no point in bringing

[611]

against these generations the charge that they were dishonest and illogical. The law which initiated the Evangelical Church in the 16th century was in fact stronger than all the aberrations of which members have been guilty in recent centuries. In spite of Neo-Protestantism there had been no obvious emergence of a new law to reinitiate the Church. Whether it wanted or not, it was still the Church of Luther and Calvin. This is the secret of the strange picture which it presented at this period in its relation to the Reformers. Is it not almost touching to see with what tenderness even the latest form of Neo-Protestantism, the conception of the so-called "German Christians," still thinks that it can and should maintain the relationship at any rate to Luther and in part to Calvin, even though it is also felt necessary to appeal with a greater emphasis than ever before to new revelations sandwiched between? Would a really emergent "German National Church" actually dare to renounce the claim to stand in this continuity, and the claim which that would mean for it? And if it won that freedom could it be more than a new sect? So far the ecclesiastical authority of the Reformers has been stronger than all kinds of attempts at liberation. And now in face of all this unusual development we must not overlook one thing especially: and that is that the remarkable concern of the newer Protestantism for its relationship to the Reformers had as its necessary concomitant a new and active interest in them from the historical standpoint. The

[612] same 19th century which, carrying Schleiermacher's secret tradition, brought Neo-Protestantism to full flower was also so constantly occupied with the memory of the Reformers that by comprehensive new editions of their writings and a ceaseless historical investigation of their life and work it was bound to contribute signally to the living maintenance and in part emergence of their original form, and in this way it involuntarily but necessarily introduced the Reformers themselves to check its own interpretations and misinterpretations, as was not the case in much of the age of orthodoxy. The work of these generations saw to it that the ecclesiastical authority of the Reformers—they could now speak and be heard again in a new way—was not merely the shadow of a remote past, but could again acquire the most up-to-date significance. If that was not the intention, e.g., of the Strassburg editor of Calvin's works, that is how it turned out apart from and in spite of his intention. In the light of the last fifteen years, we can now speak of a Luther renaissance in the Evangelical Churches and their theology, and also of a corresponding Calvin renaissance. Even to-day the two phenomena are equivocal. But we cannot deny them. And if we see and understand them in a proper connexion with preceding developments, we can at any rate see in them a final symptom that so far there is no question of having to reckon with any turning away from the authority of the Reformers to the authority of a new fact on which the Church can be grounded.

If such a development is not fundamentally impossible, we are taught by our consideration of history so far that much greater things are necessary for it to take place. Neo-Protestantism has certainly not been capable of it. One thing after another may arise in the Church. There may be all kinds of ecclesiastical movements. Strong reactions may be produced. But these things cannot of themselves give rise to a fact which will found a Church like the witness of Luther and Calvin. They cannot compel the Church to a new confession. But unless this happens and a corresponding new confession emerges, unless someone feels competent even seriously to demand the replacement of the authority of the Reformers by another authority, not to speak of the Church as such taking note of this replacement and pronouncing upon it, unless this is the case, then involuntarily perhaps but in fact the Church returns to this authority, and there is good reason—exactly as in the problem of the Canon—

to accept the previous confession of the Church at any rate as a hypothesis, that is, as the basis on which we have to stand: in other words, not to play truant from the school of Luther and Calvin until we are better instructed, but to learn in it what there is to be learned. It is a matter of instruction in understanding Holy Scripture, when and to the extent that the Reformers are genuine teachers of the Church. This instruction must never be neglected because of the consideration that there might ultimately be others who can give us this instruction better. So long as these other teachers are not to hand, we have reason to stick to those who are. Indeed it is not impossible that these teachers—who have not so far been replaced—may with the confirmation of Holy Scripture itself continue to remain as they have remained till now.

But now we must ask whether and in what sense alongside the authority of the Reformers there can be any serious question of an authority of later teach- [613] ers within the Evangelical Church itself, and also perhaps of certain pre-Reformation witnesses. Neither can be dismissed in principle; but in practice, i.e., in answering the question where and in whom the Church has to recognise these further teachers, we cannot be too careful. Not every Church witness who at some point and period is an example and stimulus to certain members of the Church is for that reason a father, to whom the Church can and must trust itself, in the sense that the line held by him is the right one for it. This real guidance of the Church, as it was exercised by Luther and Calvin, is a rare thing. We must examine closely what we are demanding of ourselves and especially the Church when under some strong impression we believe that here or there we have found this paternal authority. As individuals we can learn from many. We can learn from those who have no significance or only a limited significance. We can learn even from those who are weak and misguided. But that does not make it right to regard all those to whom we are indebted for something as teachers of the Church and, where possible, to try to force them upon the rest of the Church. We shall destroy the confidence of the Church and create confusion if we rush on to make announcements of this kind, which by their nature can only be a matter for the experience and confession of the whole Church, and not for individual preference. The questions which we have to ask are as follows.

(*a*) Has the one proposed been an expositor of Scripture who, like the Reformers, has helped and can still help the Church to understand the Word of God rightly? There are many of whom that definitely cannot be said, even though we cannot deny to their Christian thinking, speaking and writing, depth, seriousness and force, even though they perhaps led a most godly and charitable life. We have to remember that both these appearances, the intellectual and the religious and moral, are of themselves equivocal: they are to be found even in notorious heretics. The question and only question which has to be asked—in the light of Scripture itself—is whether the teacher in question has expounded Scripture and proclaimed the Word of God, and done it correctly. It is not the acuity and depth, nor even the holiness of the Christian which builds the Church, but only the Word of God. Therefore when we ask whether and to what extent anyone can have authority in the Church, the question which is ultimately decisive is whether he has served the Word of God.

(b) If it is true that we have to recognise this authority first in the Reformers—because they rightly expounded the Word of God, then a second question which we have to put to all teachers before and after them is how their teaching stands in relation to the confession of the Reformation? The primitive and mediaeval Catholic Church which had not yet been reformed by the Word of God, but as distinct from the post-Tridentine Church had also not denied the Reformation, is for us the one Church of Jesus Christ, whose witness we must therefore be ready to hear in principle. And we also cannot refrain from believing that there may be a real if secret fellowship of saints and therefore the Church of Jesus Christ in post-Tridentine Catholicism and the Neo-Protestant aberration. We have therefore no *a priori*[EN137] cause to stop our ears in any direction when we ask concerning the fathers of the Church.

[614]

An Athanasius and an Augustine were for the Reformers themselves so obviously fathers in this special sense, and their struggles and achievements were so plainly the presuppositions of the Reformation confession, that it would be good for us to hear them as they were heard in the 16th century and in the later Evangelical Church. In their case, as in all the others, even the oldest, we. must also not hear them in so far, that is, as they could and did become not so much the fathers of the Reformation as of post-Tridentine Catholicism. The Reformation and the authority of the Reformers does undoubtedly involve retrospective selection and decision, and of such a kind that we cannot count unreservedly with the authority of any one of the older fathers.

The Roman Catholic criterion of the *consensus patrum*[EN138] must be interpreted by us in this sense, that the doctors of the early Church are an authority for us to the extent that their doctrine did not need to be reformed, but as a correct exposition of Holy Scripture bore prior witness to the Reformation. Within these limits the Evangelical Church and its theology, if it really is to be a Church of Jesus Christ, can never listen too much to the witness of the primitive and mediaeval Church. There are elements in this witness which can only be rightly seen and assessed in the light of the Reformation, which were only really brought out at the Reformation. Conversely, there are certain decisive elements in the witness of the Reformers which can only be understood in their positive relationship to the witness of the primitive and mediaeval Church. Even in the 17th century the real or supposed awareness of this relationship was so strong that a comprehensive work could appear in Strassburg under the title *Thomas Aquinas veritatis evangelicae confessor*[EN139]. Optimistically, the most important factor was overlooked, which makes Thomas—of whom neither the Reformers nor their contemporary opponents had any exact knowledge—the typical father of post-Tridentine Catholicism with his doctrine of the *Principia*. Yet it is the case that on a careful reading we do find even in Thomas lines of thought which, if they do not point us to the Reformation,

---

[EN137] prior
[EN138] agreement of the Fathers
[EN139] Thomas Aquinas, confessor of the Gospel truth

certainly do not point us to Jesuit Rome. And there is a lot that the Evangelical theologian can learn in Thomas as a well-chosen compendium of all preceding tradition. The same is even more true of an Anselm of Canterbury and in another way of a Bonaventura. There can be no question, of course, of an unreserved attachment to these pre-Reformation authorities unless we are to be hopelessly launched on the way of Roman Catholicism.

The same question has to be put even more sharply to post-Tridentine Catholic and Neo-Protestant theologians. Modern Catholic or Neo-Protestant teaching may voluntarily or involuntarily state and accentuate Evangelical truth. If it does us this service, why should we not gratefully acknowledge it, and there, too, hear the voice of the fathers? There is a right exposition of [615] Holy Scripture and therefore an attestation of the confession of the Reformation even in the Church which resists the Reformation and in that which later repudiates it. As correct exposition it must be heard, no matter where it comes from. But within the Evangelical Church which holds the Reformation presupposition we can never put this question too sharply.

It is justifiable and meaningful to regard as Church fathers in this special sense the in their own way and to some extent great men of the age of orthodoxy in so far as according to its own conscious intention the theology of that period did try to be ecclesiastical scholarship, a comprehensive exposition of Holy Scripture and a comprehensive development of the Reformation confession. We must be careful in our estimate of the authority of these orthodox theologians, because the beginnings of later arbitrariness do in fact appear in their dogmatic systems. Among the later ones, although there is no question of Neo-Protestantism in the narrower sense of the concept, we have to note that they frequently find themselves in a mutual opposition and reaction which were as such historically necessary and beneficial, but which had their limitations in the incidental and one-sided character of the antitheses and often in the concessions which were made at the very outset to the opposition. We surely do most honour to these later writers when we accept their authority only to the extent that they repeated and renewed for their own age the witness of the Reformers.

(*c*) A real teacher of the Church who can be seriously accepted as such can be definitely recognised by the responsibility to the Church which is peculiar to his witness. There has always been a right exposition of Scripture, in the sense of the Reformers, which has lacked this characteristic because it has, so to speak, been done in its own strength and at its own risk. Neither as hearers and learners nor speakers and teachers have its authors had before them the whole Church, the universality of its needs and hopes, errors and genuine experiences, knowledge and confession, but only a specific part, the problems of their own life and their more immediate temporal, geographical or spiritual environment. This need not be a lack in every respect. In some respects it may be an advantage. Exposition and teaching of this kind has often had most important results. But only that expositor is qualified to be a teacher of the Church who is not essentially or strictly an improviser and individualist but who sees clearly that he must state his case and bear his witness to the whole Church before and after him, who has not merely been alone with God and the Bible and the writings of the Reformers, but who has stood before the whole Church with God and the Bible and the writings of the Reformers, and is therefore confident and competent to speak not only to himself or to an incidental or selected circle, but intelligibly, responsibly and authoritatively to the whole Church.

This forward and backward universality was a particular feature of the witness of the Reformers themselves, but also of that of the orthodox fathers, whereas it is completely lacking in the newer theology, which had far too much the stamp of occasional literature. Yet we have to allow that, measured by this criterion, Schleiermacher's *Glaubenslehre* would stand, and also the works of many of his nearest successors like A. Schweizer, J. A. Dorner, A. E. Biedermann, F. H. R. Frank and, in its own way, that of H. Lüdemann and from the Ritschlian school the dogmatics of Julius Kaftan. Indeed, to some extent they have won a kind of ecclesiastical authority in their own definite circles. If genius often prefers other ways, it must be noted that no one can be a teacher of the Church by virtue of genius alone. It must also be noted that a preference for other ways as such does not prove any one to be a genius.

[616]

(*d*) It has to be asked further whether as an expositor of Scripture, in agreement with the witness of the Reformers and in responsibility to the Church, the proposed father has spoken and still speaks a word which means actual decision for the later Church. Both in the past and more recently many things have been said which are true and important and also responsible and of universal relevance but which do not have this significance later, and perhaps can never have it again, or may perhaps some day recapture it. Some words which have been spoken in the Church and for the Church come home to us, and others do not come home to us for a variety of reasons. A teacher of the Church is the one who in exposition of Holy Scripture has something to say which comes home to us. But that means that we must always reckon with the existence of latent teachers of the Church. Many of those whom we no longer hear to-day will never be heard again. But there are also others who, although they are not heard to-day, will one day be heard again. What remains of their authority is in the first instance only a memory: the neutral memory of a great name, bound up with facts and relationships and his reactions to them which are also neutral. Their authority is then suspended, as it were. It would be a very arbitrary undertaking to try artificially to assert them again. If they come to life again in the power of the Holy Scripture which they are concerned to expound, Scripture itself will see to their authority. We have to reckon with this possibility. We cannot, therefore, ignore such recollections of former authority which have now become neutral. Their hour might suddenly come. Those who are now silent might speak again, as according to the confession of the Church they once spoke to their age. The facts and circumstances in relation to which their names and reactions and word were once significant may suddenly return—for there is nothing new under the sun—and the decision which they demand may again be a relevant one. We have perhaps overlooked something if this has not already happened. In the modern period the Reformers themselves were for a long time only latent teachers of the Church. And it is to the Church's good that it has not ceased to give them its attention. We have to see to it that we are open and ready on every side. Already the past history of the Church has become its up-to-date story in the most unexpected places. Something which we thought to be a thing of the past perhaps becomes suddenly alive. And as in the case of the Canon it is perhaps our fault if many who can and ought to be fathers to us are simply dead and have nothing to say.

What can be the practical reach and significance of the authority of such a [617] teacher of the Church? It is quite certain that his figure cannot in any way be equated with those of the prophets and apostles, nor can his writings even remotely try to crowd out and replace their writings or his witness their witness. Again, it is not a matter of the Church being not only directed and bound to Holy Scripture but also committed to give particular honour and loyalty to the ἐξουσία[EN140] of "Lutheranism" or the ἐξουσία[EN141] of "Calvinism." A Church perhaps thinks it right and important to value its history and historical form as such, and therefore the memory of its teaching as that of the heroes and leading figures in this history. But it may do this in the purely secular sphere and be commended for doing so on purely human grounds. And this has nothing whatever to do with the recognition of the ecclesiastical authority of its teachers. "Lutheranism" and "Calvinism" are hypostases for which there are many secular parallels. An enthusiasm for them is not in itself blameworthy. But like many similar enthusiasms it stands under the question whether it is not like the angel worship which was so strictly forbidden in Gal. 4[8f.], Col. 2[8 20f.], i.e., something which may crowd out that worship of God in spirit and in truth which makes the Church the Church. In point of fact the teacher of the Church and his personality and definite influence and his conception of Christianity and of the Church's past and future and his positive and negative historical relationships all add up to a law which can be comprehended by human reason and fulfilled as an ideal, and as such they are an excellent source of natural theology. Once this law has been set up, once the Church has decided that apart from being a Christian and Evangelical Church, it must also be Lutheran or Calvinist, then we have to reckon with the possibility that the inevitable will happen, that when we give natural theology an inch it will want a yard, it will want everything: the Church will become more and more Lutheran or Calvinist and proportionately less and less Christian and Evangelical. This deflection always threatens when the disciples of a Church teacher acquire even very slightly the character of an independent group. The authority of such a teacher can only be indirect, formal and relative, i.e., it can only be what the concept prescribes: the authority of a human doctor of Holy Scripture whose task it is to acquaint his pupils not so much with himself as with the object which is his and their concern, to point and bind them not so much to himself as to this object. But if something different

---

[EN140] authority
[EN141] authority

takes place between a Church teacher and his pupils, if the teacher forces himself—the fault may be his or that of the pupils—into a position side by side with the object which he has to make known and binding, that is not merely an encroachment, but it means that the very thing which cannot and should not intentionally take place in this relationship has taken place. For this object will not tolerate anything side by side with it. We cannot be pupils of Holy Scripture and also pupils of the person and system of a second master. That is to destroy the Church and the school of the Church. The pupils have no longer to learn from this teacher, they have to beware of him. When this happens there are no real masters, or we do not honour the real masters. The real masters who are honoured as they ought to be are those by whose person and system the pupils are educated and fashioned to be only scholars of Holy Scripture. The honour which we ought to pay these real masters is to let them carry out their service, to be willingly educated and fashioned in this way. We only dishonour them if we make the honouring of their person and system an independent interest. But we also have to remember that where it is a matter of the authority of a Church teacher it is a matter of the confession of the Church as in the Canon and the confessions. A real teacher of the Church has not spoken to and for himself but to and for the Church of his time. Therefore it is not his individual voice as such but in that voice the voice of the Church of the time which gives him the authority of a teacher for us. Again, it may not be wrong to value him as a private person, or his doctrine as a private doctrine, to honour, e.g., in Luther the hero, doctor, poet, theological genius and the like. But it is still the case that this estimation, however great and well grounded, does not contribute in any way to his recognition as a teacher of the Church. Indeed, it might be a hindrance to his recognition as a teacher of the Church. Infatuated with his private figure, we might not love him in his mission and function. If we love him as a teacher of the Church, then we listen to the Church when we listen to him. Again, that means above all that we accept his instruction in Holy Scripture as such—the early Church witnesses to him as a servant of the Word of God. But it must also mean that we have to measure him not only by the Scripture which he expounds but also by the confession of the Church whose voice he is: which means concretely by the confession of the Church of his day. Therefore in cases of doubt we do not have to understand and assess Scripture and the confession by the standard of this or that teacher, but we have to understand and assess every teacher by the standard of Scripture and the confession; we have not to put Socrates above the truth, but the truth above Socrates—and that in order to give Socrates the honour due to him. The real teacher of the Church never can and never will be accepted and treated by us in any other way.

It is the case, then, that the recognition of the ecclesiastical authority of a teacher not only does not exclude but strictly demands a critical, and even a very critical, attitude to him. When we hear him, that means that we have to pay attention to the lines of his exposition and make them our own. But when we do that, we cannot simply repeat what he has drawn.

We have to copy it in responsibility to the Scripture and confession which have spoken to us through him. And that means that we have to draw it out and and develop it. And that means also that we have also not to listen to him: at those points, that is, where everything considered we do not find that his voice agrees with the voice of Scripture and the voice of the [619] Church speaking independently in the confession. There can be as little question of a repristination of the teaching of Lather and Calvin as of the orthodoxy of the 17th century in the present rediscovery and reacknowledgment of the authority of the Reformers. If there were, we would not be giving them the honour due to them, but refusing it. Not those who repeat the doctrine most faithfully, but those who reflect upon it most faithfully so that they can then expound it as their own doctrine, are their most faithful pupils. But to reflect on their doctrine means to draw out the line indicated by them as it needs to be drawn in accordance with a new investigation of Scripture and the confession in reply to modern questions. As witnesses accredited by the confession of the Church of their day, they have ecclesiastical authority for the Church of to-day. Therefore the Church of to-day, with all the experience which it has since acquired and the responsibility in which it itself stands, has to listen to them. This may mean deviation and contradiction as regards the historical form of their doctrine. The Church of to-day would not be accepting them if it were simply accepting or reproducing them in their historical form. It would be accepting them not as the Church of to-day, not obedient to its own calling along the lines of the Reformation, but as an institute of antiquities—the worst dishonour of which it could be guilty for all its well-meant veneration.

Therefore the positive significance of the ecclesiastical authority of a teacher consists in this: that in its existence the Church has a "form of doctrine," which with its human limitations can, of course, only be a token and copy of what is called this in Rom. 6^{17}, but which as a token and copy still has a right and necessary function. The existence of prominent teachers of the Church creates a concrete inequality in the Church. If there are many teachers in the Church, not every one is called to be a teacher of the Church. Within the same office some are of higher rank, some of lower, some have to sketch out the Church's line, others to copy it. Does that mean that an ecclesiastico-theological hierarchy is set up? From this standpoint would it perhaps be possible to justify the special office of the bishop or even the Papacy? Certainly not, if the teacher of the Church is rightly understood in his character as a copy and token of the form of the doctrine given to us, which can only be Jesus Christ, i.e., Holy Scripture itself. The small inequality in the Church posited, of course, with its own existence cannot then actualise the great inequality between its Head and members—which is the usual intention when a special episcopate is instituted—but only denote it. But it will denote it—and this is the special dynamic of the existence of an ecclesiastical teacher—on the basis of an event which really took place in the life of the Church and of the corresponding confession of the Church itself. Compared with this, of what significance is the existence of an episcopate furnished with even the most exalted prerogatives? In the existence of a real teacher of the Church the human direction of the Church has become a fact, while the demand for a special episcopate is always based on and leads to the postulate that while this direction is a

[620] good thing, and a necessary thing, in effect its existence is always bound up with the charismatic endowment of those who exercise it. As that direction which is event and fact, and recognised and acknowledged as such by the Church, it is the task of the existence of a teacher of the Church, in so far as it is understood as a mission and charge of Jesus Christ, quite independently of the question of charismatic endowment which is unavoidable in relation to a bishop, to denote and display and emphasise the power and the true and in the last resort only direction of the Church by Jesus Christ or by Holy Scripture itself. And the Church always needs this denoting, displaying and emphasising. It is not a matter of indifference whether the Church and especially those who hold teaching office in the Church in their mode of thought and teaching are always looking to the human pattern of the attitude and direction of Luther and Calvin, and also of the fathers of the early Church, or whether alone with God and the Bible they are looking to create and fulfil individual ideals of prophecy, priesthood and pastorate, or may even be looking to constitute and realise the fortuitous pattern laid down by the then representatives of a superior episcopate. Obviously the authority of a Reformer cannot be replaced either by our own authority on the basis of individual Bible study or by that of the changing representatives of such an office. It is as a spiritual authority, and in its restricted character as a copy and token of the real "form of doctrine," that the authority of an ecclesiastical teacher will be a real and effective and not a fictitious authority, able to exercise with the Canon and confession of the Church that concrete discipline, especially within the teaching Church, for the sake of which authority is necessary.

3. We assume that between the Church to-day and here and the Church then and elsewhere there must be a unity of confession in respect of specific declarations of the common faith, i.e., of confession in the strictest sense of the concept: the confession of the Church. A Church confession is a formulation and proclamation of the insight which the Church has been given in certain directions into the revelation attested by Scripture, reached on the basis of common deliberation and decision. It will be our first task to explain the decisive elements in this definition.

(*a*) The confession of the Church involves the formulation and proclamation of a definite ecclesiastical understanding of the revelation attested in Holy Scripture. Therefore from the outset the confession and its authority does not stand above or alongside, but as a Church confession under Holy Scripture. Therefore it does not speak by direct revelation, and what it says cannot be a source of revelation for the Church which listens to it.

Even believing in the presence and help of the Holy Spirit a council has "no power to make new articles of faith" (Luther, *Von den Konziliis und Kirchen*, 1539, W.A. 50, 607, 7). "For articles of faith must not grow on earth through concilia as by new and secret inspiration. But they must be openly given and revealed from heaven by the Holy Ghost. Otherwise they are not articles of faith" (*ib.*, 551, 28). Councils "ought to confess and maintain the old faith [621] against new articles" (*ib.*, 618, 11). Similarly, e.g., the Nicene Council "did not newly discover or set up the article of the divinity of Christ, as though it had never previously existed in the Church" (*ib.*, 551, 15). The truth which had been revealed from the start was rather upheld and confirmed and declared by that Council in relation to the demands of the period, that is, against the Arian heresy.

Self-evidently the confession of the Church cannot speak on the basis of a supposed and immediate revelation which is different from that attested in Holy Scripture. It does not confess God in history or God in nature, as individuals, and it may be many individuals, in the Church think they see Him. It does not confess this or that element of Church tradition and custom. It confesses Jesus Christ, and Jesus Christ as attested by the prophets and apostles. It confesses the one Word of God, beside whom there is no other. This does not prevent it confessing in definite historical situations, in answer to definite questions, contradicting and explaining in a definite antithesis. But it does prevent it speaking on any other ground than Holy Scripture or any other truth than that attested in Holy Scripture.

Non alibi quaeramus Deum quam in eius verbo, nihil de ipso cogitemus nisi cum eius verbo, de ipso nihil loquamur nisi per eius verbum[EN142]. This general rule has to be observed with particular care when it is a matter of a *publica confessio*[EN143]. We must see to it, *ut nihil in ea deprehendatur, quam ipsissima scripturae veritas … ut non ex variis hominum placitis consarcinata, sed ad rectam scripturae normam diligenter exacta sit*[EN144]. That it is a *conceptae intus fidei testificatio*[EN145] does not prevent *ut solida sit et sincera*[EN146], and for that reason it must be drawn *e puris scripturae fontibus*[EN147] (Calvin, *Adv. P. Caroli calumnias*, 1545, *C.R.* 7, 311 f.). *Si hodie suos consessus haberent sancti patres, uno ore clamarent, nihil sibi minus licuisse, vel etiam fuisse in animo, quam tradere quidquam, nisi Christo praeeunte, qui illis unicus, sicut et nobis, magister fuit*[EN148] (*Comm. Ac.* 15² *C.R.* 38, 341).

The confession of the Church explains Scripture, it expounds and applies it. It is, therefore, a commentary. It is not enough for it to repeat biblical texts. It can point to them in order to make clear in what connexion it wishes to explain Scripture. But at bottom it must speak in its own words, in the words and therefore in the speech of its age.

[EN142] Let us not seek God elsewhere than in His Word; let us say nothing about Him except through His Word

[EN143] public confession

[EN144] that nothing can be perceived in it (i.e. in the confession) except the very essence of the truth of Scripture … so that it is not stitched together by various decisions of men, but has been completed diligently according to the correct norm of Scripture

[EN145] testimony of faith received within

[EN146] that it be solid and sincere

[EN147] from the pure sources of Scripture

[EN148] If the holy fathers could hold their councils today, they would cry with one voice that they were permitted nothing less than, nor had anything else in mind but to pass on anything except what Christ had already passed on: for He was their only teacher, just as He is for us

Neque vero confessionem duntaxat eam recipimus, quae ex solis scripturae verbis superstitiose contexta sit et consuta, sed iis verbis conscribendam esse contendimus, quae et sensum habeant intra scripturae veritatem limitatum et quam minimum habeant asperitatis[EN149] (Calvin, *C.R.* 7, 312).

But because it is the Church itself which speaks, listening to Scripture and bearing its witness to its truth, the confession cannot be anything more than a commentary, or try to stand on the same level as Scripture.

[622] The other symbols and adduced writings are not judges like Holy Scripture, but only the witness and declaration of faith how in disputed articles Holy Scripture has always been understood and expounded in the Church of God by those living at the time, and contrary doctrines rejected and condemned (*Form. Conc. Epit., De summ. Concept,* 8). *Interpretationis autem humanae seu Ecclesiasticae autoritas est Ecclesiastica tantum, non divina et Canonica: quia non immediate ab ipso Deo dictata est, sed hominum deliberatione et consilio tradita, quorum alii plus, alii minus habent lucis, alii maiora, alii minora dona intelligendi et explicandi res divinas. Proinde interpretatio Scripturae Ecclesiastica atque ita et Ecclesiastica Confessio seu expositio fidei quaecunque, item et Catechesis et quaecunque piorum hominum scriptio seu tractatio … non est simpliciter probanda, admittenda atque acceptanda, sed cum hac exceptione et conditione, quatenus cum Scriptura Sacra, tanquam cum unico fonte veritatis caelestis et salvificae, fundamento immoto et regula fidei et bonorum operum nunquam fallente, consentit*[EN150] (Polanus, *Synt. Theol. chr.,* 1600, 711).

(*b*) The confession of the Church involves the expression of an insight given to the Church. Holy Scripture has been given to the Church as the source of its knowledge of divine revelation. It is not individuals, or any group of individuals, but the Church itself, represented by those who can and must speak in its name, which has to give an account of its faith to itself and the world in the confession of the Church. The confession speaks for and to the one universal Church. Obviously we cannot and must not understand this in any legal or statistical sense. We can only understand it spiritually. From the legalistic and statistical standpoint, no confession (not even those of the so-named "general" councils) ever arose and was proclaimed as the confession of the whole Church for the whole Church. From the legal and statistical standpoint every confession has only been a confession in the Church, proceeding from one part and directed to the other parts of the Church. Its calling to speak in the name of the one universal Church to the one universal Church is grounded only on the Holy Scripture which is given to the one universal Church as the

---

[EN149] Indeed, we do not accept merely that confession which is superstitiously woven and sown together with the words alone of Scripture, but we contend that it must be composed of those words which both have their meaning limited by the truth of Scripture, and have as little severity as possible

[EN150] The authority of a human or ecclesiastical interpretation is only ecclesiastical, not divine or canonical. This is because it has not been dictated directly from God himself, but passed on by the deliberation and counsel of men, of whom some have more light and some less; some have greater, and some lesser gifts of understanding and explaining divine matters. Therefore, an ecclesiastical interpretation of Scripture and thus also an ecclesiastical confession or any exposition of the faith, likewise also a catechism and any writing or treatment from pious men, must not be wholly approved, admitted or accepted except on condition that, and in so far as it agree with Sacred Scripture, with that single source of heavenly and saving truth, the unmoved basis and rule of faith and good works which never errs

witness of the one revelation given to all. Therefore no ultimately decisive justification can be adduced for the summoning and meeting and special authorisation of individual members of the Church as "authors" of a confession
except once again Holy Scripture itself. Those who find themselves assembled
to draw up and impose a confession (even though in virtue of their office as
the representatives of many communities they are a more or less legitimate
"synod" or "council") dare only adduce to others as their authorisation and
authority that they have come together in obedience to the Word of God and
have to confess this or that. It is quite clear that when they do this they put
themselves under the judgment of the Word of God, accepting the risk that
they may be publicly disavowed and given the lie by the Word of God to which
they appeal and think and declare that they are obedient. There is no confession without this risk and danger. And obviously for those who venture to come
before the Church with a confession, there is also the danger that they will
have the witness of Holy Scripture in their favour, but that in the rest of the
Church they will speak to deaf ears and therefore, isolated with the Word of
God, they will necessarily be in their Church heretics and oddities, unauthor-   [623]
ised innovators or even invincible reactionaries. But this does not alter the fact
that if the claim of their confession to be Church confession is to be heard or
even discussed they must dare to speak to the whole Church in the name of the
whole Church. How can it be otherwise if they are really trying to speak from
Holy Scripture and to attest the Word of God? The courage to accept the risk
involved is at least one test of the genuineness of their enterprise and action. A
confession is not a Church confession which seeks only to represent the
importance of one group in the Church or to declare and prove the equal
justification of particular interests which may perhaps represent only the local
or national peculiarity of one part of the Church which is supposed to be the
will of God. However limited and oppressed the authors of a confession may
be in the Church, if they really have to confess, i.e., to confess the Word of
God, they cannot possibly dare to speak of themselves and from their own
small comer, or in order to secure recognition for themselves and this corner.
Not fearing to make the unheard-of claim which this involves, they must be
confident to speak from and to the one universal Church. They must accept
responsibility for expressing the voice of the *una sancta catholica*[EN151]. Otherwise they must be silent or at any rate not regard their speaking as the confession of the Church. To confess involves a mission within (and also without) the
Church. If we are not conscious of any such mission, if we only want to be
heard and suffered on specific points, we cannot make any important, i.e.,
ecclesiastical, confession.

But in a spiritual and not a legal and statistical sense some of the resolutions of early
Church Councils were genuine confession, made with that certainty which can be achieved
and proved only in the venture of obedience to Scripture, but with that certainty made with a

---

[EN151] one holy catholic (Church)

definite claim to speak in the name of the whole Church to the whole Church. And although outwardly at first it might plainly happen in the name of a fragment of the then Church, that is how the Reformed confessions have also spoken. That is why they were so careful to prove their connexion and agreement with the confession of the early Church. Their intention was not really to expound a faith which only arose in 1517 and which is only the faith of the adherents of certain territories or spiritual communities. What they were trying to confess again was the one old faith of the Church and therefore in their confession they challenged the whole Church, not merely to tolerate this faith, but as they heard it re-confessed to accept it. And from our own days we can add that the confession of the Evangelical Church in Germany, which is so necessary for the present age, although its legal and statistical basis is open to question, cannot remain only the declaration of a party or school, or the theological justification of the standpoint of those who still wish to maintain a biblical-reformed Christianity. Without considering the external and internal risks we must dare to speak in the name of the German Evangelical Church and "to the public of all Evangelical Churches in Germany," aggressively and with the consciousness of a mission. For that reason the Barmen declaration of May 1934 closes with the words: "The Confessional Synod of the German Evangelical Church declares that in the recognition of these truths and the rejection of these errors they find the indispensable theological basis of the German Evangelical Church

[624]

.... It asks all whom it concerns to return to the unity of faith, love and hope. *Verbum Dei manet in aeternum*[EN152]." Declarations which do not take this line, whatever significance they may have, do not have the significance of Church confessions or the right to be heard as such. *Confessio fidei traditur in symbolo quasi ex persona totius ecclesiae, quae per fidem unitur*[EN153] (Thomas Aquinas, *S. theol.* II 2, *qu.* 1, *art.* 9, *ad.* 3).

(*c*) The confession of the Church involves an insight which is given or gifted to the Church. This is bound up with the fact that it has not invented its content, but discovered it only in Holy Scripture and as a gift of the Holy Spirit. But this discovery has to be distinguished from the kind of discovery which might at any time be the result of the searching of the Scriptures enjoined upon us. A confession is distinguished from a summarising of the results of theological work by the fact that its authors did not set out to comment on the Bible or to understand the nature of Christianity or practically to preach again, except that this time this preaching was to everyone. All that can and should take place at any time. But not every time in which it can and should take place is also a time of Church confession.

Both in modern times and from the very first it has been done most lavishly and certainly not without the gift of the Holy Spirit without necessarily involving a new confession. The need of the latter may have been felt and tentative attempts made to supply it. But such attempts could not and cannot succeed if set only against this background. We cannot confess because we would like to confess in the belief that confession is a good thing. We can confess only if we must confess. Theological work of a theoretical or practical kind is not the instrument of this compulsion. Theological work as such is quite unable to produce a Church confession, although it is indispensable to its formation when a confession arises, and if it is serious its final goal must always be the Church's confession.

[EN152] The Word of the Lord endures forever
[EN153] A confession of faith is passed on as if, symbolically, from the body of the whole Church, which is united by faith

Church confession is a Church event. It is the result of an encounter of the Church with Holy Scripture, which in its contingency cannot be brought about by even the most serious theological work. When in a special situation in the Church Holy Scripture speaks to the Church, when in view of definite and urgent questions nothing remains but what Scripture has to say, when in the avoidance of definite errors we can take refuge in the scriptural truth which opposes them, when in the Church we cannot lay hold of scriptural truth, but only receive it, when therefore the Church has not found this truth but this truth has found the Church—then and then alone can there be Church confession. The genuine Credo is born out of a need of the Church, out of a compulsion which in this need is imposed on the Church by the Word of God, out of the perception of faith which answers to this compulsion. Credo in the sense of Church confession the Church can say only when all its other possibilities are exhausted, when reduced to silence it can say nothing else but Credo. But then it can and will say it with certainty and power. If the Church's confession involves an insight given to the Church, then the confession cannot understand itself or rightly let itself be understood as an exposition of favourite human ideas, or convictions, or the so-called reflections of faith. It [625] certainly rests on exegesis, but it is more than biblical inquiry. It certainly arises only with a dogmatic consciousness, but it will proclaim more than theologoumena. It is certainly proclamation, but its power will not be only that of edification. The faith of its authors will certainly be heard in it, but it will not be because of this subjective faith that it has a right to be heard. Because and to the extent that it rests on an insight given to the Church, a genuine Church confession can and must speak authoritatively: it cannot simply publish its findings as a subject for discussion and free choice. What the confession formulates and proclaims claims to be Church dogma. In saying Credo it has characterised its pronouncements as those whose content it cannot and will not force on anyone, but with which it challenges everyone to take up a position, to decision whether he can reject them as contrary to the Word of God or must accept them as in agreement with the Word of God. Here again it is Holy Scripture which is the basis of the certainty of the confession and the judge over it. It is Scripture which—in this twofold sense—stands behind dogma.

If this office of Scripture as judge is either forgotten or denied, the confession is unauthentic and unauthoritative inasmuch as it claims to be itself revelation, like Roman Catholic dogma. It is Scripture which—in this twofold sense—makes a confession authentic and therefore authoritative. If the certainty based on it is dented, the confession is unauthentic and unauthoritative inasmuch as it then falls to the level of a non-challenging exposition of human conceptions, as in the far too anthropocentric understanding of confession in both older and more recent congregationalism.

(*d*) The confession of the Church always involves the statement and expression of the insight given to the Church in definite limits. This limitation does not contradict either the intended universality of the confession or the certainty proper to it as Church dogma. On the contrary, it is in this very limitation that it is universal and Church dogma, and therefore has ecclesiastical authority. The dignity and validity of Church confession cannot rival that divine authority. It would rather be destroyed if it wished to do so. It is based on the fact that it is limited by it. Indeed, ultimate and decisive legitimacy is from Holy Scripture to whose witness the Church replies in confession with its own witness. To be limited by its origin and object does not weaken but establishes and confirms its authority as a Church authority. The impulse and courage to make a confession, to accept responsibility for the claim which it raises and to go through with this claim, the capacity for a strictly theological attitude which is not afraid of any consequences, the joy which is the secret of the power of a Church confession—all these are rooted in the fact it is the statement and expression of the insight which is given to the Church in definite limits. No more than this, but—in this negation of any imaginary and therefore impotent infinitude—this all the more really and concretely in the finite sphere of the Church. In a confession we always have to do with a definite limit of insight. This emerges first in the legal and statistical uncertainty which we have already mentioned. Obviously it is never more than a part of the Church which stands behind a Church confession. One part of the Church has in a definite need and in a definite faith in that need accepted something definite as the witness of Holy Scripture, and with its own witness it makes a definite reply to it in the face of other parts of the Church. Because and to the extent that Holy Scripture is the determining factor, there is a limitation in all this, and yet by it the authority of the Church's confession is also established and confirmed.

[626]

In the first instance, the limit of Church confession coincides remarkably with geographical limits.

In the primal forms of a general Christian confession finally brought together and formulated in the so-called *Apostolicum*[EN154] we undoubtedly have first the voice of the European West grouped around the Church of Rome, although with the constant influence of the East as well. On the other hand, in the Nicene and Niceno-Constantinopolitan confessions of trinitarian faith in God, and in the christological definitions of Ephesus and Chalcedon, we have to do for the most part with the decision of the East—although it was not made without the strong co-operation of the West. Again, in the important *Arausicanum* II (529), in which the Church dealt with the suggestions of Augustine, we have a typically Western confession. The Reformed confessions can and must be understood as a statement of the faith of the European North—which was again split territorially—and the *Tridentinum*[EN155] (and the *Vaticanum*, too, with its essentially Italian majority) as the corresponding answer of the European South. And now that there are African and Asiatic mission Churches with an ever increasing consciousness of independence, and American Christianity and Church life, in spite of all its connexions with the European mother-Church, is beginning to develop more and more into an entity *sui generis*[EN156], the confessional inheritance of the early Church and

---

[EN154] Apostolic Council
[EN155] Council of Trent
[EN156] in a category of its own

the Reformation has automatically become *in globo*[EN157] a European matter, i.e., it is felt to be so across the seas. It cannot be denied that the definite limits which can be seen in all confessions stand in a constantly shifting relationship to political, cultural and economic groupings and movements. An exhaustive understanding of these limits obviously cannot be gained from this standpoint or from the geographical aspect generally. But there is no doubt that the problem has to be considered from this standpoint. It may give peculiar strength, or weakness, to a confession that it is the confession of this group here or that group there.

But the definite limit of Church confession may also have a temporal character.

We speak of old and new confessions and both may mean either an underlining or a questioning of their authority. The temporal limitation of Church confession is very correctly and clearly expressed in the Latin text of the passage which we have already quoted from the Formula of Concord: *explicant et ostendunt, quomodo singulis temporibus sacrae literae in articulis controversis in ecclesia Dei a doctoribus, qui tum vixerunt, intellectae et explicatae fuerint*[EN158]. But in this temporal limitation they are, according to the Formula of Concord, genuine *testes veritatis*[EN159]. For example (according to the introduction to the Book of Concord, *Bekenntnisschr. der ev.-luth. Kirche*, 1930, 761, 16) it can be said of the Augsburg Confession that *ne latum quidem unguem vel a rebus ipsis vel a phrasibus quae in illa habentur, discedere, sed iuvante nos Domini spiritu summa concordia constanter in pio hoc consensu perseveraturos esse decrevimus*[EN160]. If the present of such a confession has become past, the antiquity which it acquires can guarantee its value. The Church of a later date can then regard it as particularly important to subscribe to this confession, because in so doing it confesses the one unchangeable faith of all ages. It can then indignantly refuse to try to make or receive any individual or new confession of faith "with any confession which it lays alongside the old one" (Formula of Concord, *ib.*, 833, 25). But originally, as we see from the contemporary correspondence of Melanchthon, Luther and others, the *Confessio Augustana*[EN161] was not called a *confessio*[EN162] at all but only an *apologia*[EN163]. It is first called a *symbolum*[EN164] in the preface to the Formula of Concord (*Bekenntnisschr. d. ev.-luth. K.*, 1930, 741, 13). With the same delicacy, in its formal and open confession the German Church to-day has refrained from applying the title "confession" to such newly formulated and circulated statements as the Barmen decision, but has been content to call them a "theological declaration" or, in the case of the first free Reformed Synod of January 1934. a "declaration on the right understanding of the Reformation understanding in the modern German Evangelical Church." Yet there can be no doubt that the *Augustana*[EN165] and the Formula of Concord and also these modern documents do in themselves have many of the characteristics of confessions and therefore of new confessions as compared with the older ones. The *Augustana*[EN166] and the other Reformed

[627]

[EN157] in worldwide terms
[EN158] They explain and demonstrate how at individual times, the sacred letters have been understood and explained in debated points in the church of God, by the teachers who lived at the time
[EN159] witnesses of the truth
[EN160] We are resolved not to depart from the things themselves nor from the phrases contained in it even by a finger's breadth, but with the Spirit of the Lord helping us we will persevere in constancy with utmost agreement in this holy confession
[EN161] Augsburg Confession
[EN162] confession
[EN163] defence
[EN164] symbol
[EN165] Augsburg Confession
[EN166] Augsburg Confession

confessions did not want to be confessions in so far as they had no new faith to confess—but they were confessions in so far as they did confess the old faith anew. The necessity and legitimacy of a new statement and expression of the old faith, the need which in certain circumstances cannot be denied to make new decisions in the face of new questions and the equivocal nature of the old confession in respect of this new situation, the lawfulness and duty of saying clearly to-day in what sense we see ourselves compelled to confess with the old confession the Word of God—that is the peculiar value of a new confession, quite irrespective of whether it accepts the name or not. That is how the Nicene Creed came to stand alongside the Apostles', the Niceno-Constantinopolitan alongside the Nicene, the Ephesian and Chalcedonian alongside the Niceno-Constantinopolitan. That is how the Reformation Churches confessed, looking back to and repeating the confession of the early Church. That is how confession has been made in our days, looking back to and explaining and confirming the Reformation confessions and under declaration and confirmation of the same. In every case a new confession was needed which could not be a new one but only a new and preciser version of the old. In every case the old confession was still valid, but it could not really be valid except in a preciser form and therefore as enlarged by a new confession. More clearly than the geographical, the temporal limitations of Church confessions are mutually conditioned, and the old and the new can and must mutually create and confirm their authority. But it is obvious and cannot be denied that there is a definite limit of insight, that the old confession is enclosed by the new, to the extent that it must be interpreted by it, and the new by the old, to the extent that it can only be an interpretation of it.

But the definiteness of the limit of Church confession has a wider and above all a material character. A confession does not arise as a free and comprehensive exposition of the faith of the Christian Church in such a way that the various confessions confront each other as different expositions of one and the same theme.

[628]   If a Church or ecclesiastical fellowship wants to declare its faith as such, perhaps at the head of its constitution, to make clear its nature in relation to the world around it, it can, of course, do so. But it ought not to do more than name the name of Jesus Christ as the object and Holy Scripture as the source of its faith, and then relate itself to a real confession. A Church confession with Church authority will never arise on the basis of so harmless an intention.

A Church confession with Church authority has always arisen in a definite antithesis and conflict. It always has a pre-history, which does not consist in the discussion of an academic or even an ecclesiastico-political desire to re-confess the common faith, or in the discussion of the fulfilment of this desire. It consists rather in controversies in which the existing confession of the common faith and therefore the existing exposition and application of Holy Scripture is called in question because the unity of the faith is differently conceived, and there is such different teaching on the basis of the existing unity that the unity is obscured and has to be rediscovered. The expression which is valid and which was once really the expression of unity no longer suffices. If the Church wants to preserve its unity, it must give it a more accurate expression: an expression in which a judgment is pronounced and a decision made in matters of doctrinal difference, an expression which recognises the one doctrine or the other or perhaps a third which mediates between them as the doctrine of the Church, and is therefore confirmed and confessed by the Church. On the basis of such a pre-history every confession acquires and possesses its own particular aspect. It is certainly not that of a truncated *summa theologiae*. Neither is it—not even if it has the form of a catechism—that of a popular biblical theology or dogmatics. It is rather the aspect of the Church declaring itself in the act of that definite decision, the necessity of which makes the confession necessary. When the Church confesses or when confession is made in the Church, then the Church or those who confess in the Church stand face to face with what is claimed to be a definite exegesis of Scripture, perhaps a new one, perhaps one that has disturbed the Church for some time: or it may be with a doctrine which claims to be taken from Scripture or related to it. This confronting doctrine is the occasion of the confession in that it claims to be the expression of a possible expression no less justifiable than others of the existing unity of the Church in faith.

We must be clear that, e.g., Arianism and semi-Arianism, which in this way constituted the occasion of the 4th century confessions, did not arise only with a claim to be tolerated but with a claim to be the only legitimate expression of the existing unity in faith. Similarly the Reformation confession has to do with an opponent which understands and represents its doctrine exclusively. Again, the dogma of the "German Christians," at any rate at the outset, was not intended to be that of a trend in the Church, but the new dogma of the German Evangelical Church. At a first glance the case was rather different with the liberalism of the 18th and 19th centuries, which made an explicit and provisional claim to be no less justifiable than other movements, and, as a rule, would even go so far as formally to postulate the existence of a conservative counter-movement as the dialectical complement of its own existence, something which, e.g., in Switzerland, has partially attained to the dignity of dogma in the form of a doctrine of the necessity and value of two or even three ecclesiastical trends. In face of opposition to this—in itself, of course, very liberal—view liberal toleration has, of [629] course, usually reverted very quickly to a fairly extreme intolerance. How can it be otherwise than that behind the proclamation of the equal justification of a doctrine there should stand the declaration of its sole justification? How can it be otherwise than that heresy, even if only in the attenuated form of a general doctrine of toleration, should want to be not merely one opinion, but the doctrine of truth, the expression of Church unity, and that therefore it is bound to be intolerant whether it will or no? Even where there is apparently only a claim for sufferance, we have to reckon with the fact that counter-doctrine of this kind is seeking not merely to expand the existing unity of faith, but to destroy it, replacing it by another. The battle of confession must be waged, therefore, as a battle for the very substance, a battle for the life and death of the Church.

In the face of the counter-doctrine the confession turns away again from the existing and now equivocal expression of the unity of faith as it is perhaps presented in an older confession to Holy Scripture as the judge of the controversy which has arisen. Or rather the authors of the confession see that they are bound by Holy Scripture in a different way and direction from their opponents. Therefore they have to understand differently the existing expression of the unity of faith which the emergence of the counter-doctrine has now made equivocal. But they cannot prevent their opponents from appealing to this existing expression. In the form of a decision a new expression of the old unity of faith must now be sought and found: an expression which brings out the other way and direction, in which (unlike the representatives of the counter-doctrine) we find ourselves bound by Holy Scripture, an expression which makes manifest the judgment of Holy Scripture in the current controversy as the confessors claim to have heard it.

In the 4th century the Arians appealed to the *Apostolicum*[EN167] as well as the Athanasians. Similarly the Antiochenes in the 5th century appealed to the Niceno-Constantinopolitan Creed as well as the Alexandrians. Again in the 16th century the Catholics as well as the Evangelicals appealed to the great Councils of antiquity, and in 1933 the German Christians appealed to the Reformation confessions as well as their opponents. In every case the confession was an attempt to clarify a situation which had become obscure. The opening words of the Formula of Concord: *Credimus, confitemur, docemus*[EN168] indicate the seriousness and responsibility of these attempts at clarification. *Credimus*[EN169]: What is at stake and has to be affirmed is the Christian faith demanded by Holy Scripture, the unity of the Church. Therefore no one should think that the conflict and its issue are incidental, a matter which might be settled in some other and less serious way. *Confitemur*[EN170]: It is not a matter of a free heart-faith of individuals, which may perhaps be possible or actual *in abstracto*[EN171], but of the faith of the Church which has to be attested and made known in the Church and through the Church to the world, if the Church is not to abandon its obedience to its Lord. *Docemus*[EN172]: It is not a matter of an academic or an individual decision but before and behind the confession stands the actual life of the Church. Preaching and instruction will correspond to the confession. It is, therefore, a part of the recurrent worship and congregational life of the Church which is voiced in the confession.

[630] But it is the meaning and intention of a doctrinal decision which in this way has become the content of Church confession that with the Yes expressed in it, i.e., with the scriptural exegesis and doctrine positively stated in it, a definite No is also said to the counter-doctrine which is its cause, the latter being rejected as an expression of the Church's unity and its churchly status denied. If this was not its intention, what intention could it have? Without the No the Yes would obviously not be a Yes, but a Yes and No; perhaps Yes, perhaps No, but certainly not the Yes of a *credere, confiteri, docere*[EN173], not the Yes of a responsibility bound by Holy Scripture and accepted before God and the Church and the world. It is obviously by the No that the clarification of an obscure situation is accomplished in a confession, the completed decision being characterised as decision by a mention and rejection of the counter-decision.

This clarification is made in the language of the Roman Catholic symbols by the usual formula: *Si quis dixerit … anathema sit.*[EN174] *Anathema sit* does not mean (not at any rate with

---

EN167 Apostles' Creed
EN168 we believe, we confess, we teach
EN169 we believe
EN170 we confess
EN171 in the abstract
EN172 We teach
EN173 believing, confessing, teaching
EN174 If anyone says … let him be anathema

the accent of modern usage): let him be accursed, but: in accordance with reality let him find himself in the eyes of the whole Church outside the unity of the Church, with his counter-doctrine. Let him no longer claim to represent with this doctrine the doctrine of the Christian Church. Let him be quite clear that he can defend his counter-doctrine only as one which is alien to the Christian faith. The same is said by the formulae which we find in the Reformation confessions: *Reprobamus, reiicimus, exsecramus, damnamus ... secus docentes*[EN175]. The declaration of the first free Reformed Synod of 1934 put it in this way: "Therewith (with the positive statement) is rejected the view ... " and the Barmen declaration of 1934: "We reject the false doctrine ..." It is natural that such formulae are not pleasant reading for those who defend the doctrines concerned. It has to be remembered that they have not to be applied rashly. It is also understandable historically that Neo-Protestantism regards them as radically hierarchical, uncharitable and abhorrent. But against all possible objections on this score we have to make it clear that the confession has to state something definite, but cannot do so without making it clear that it is not stating something equally definite. In a confession the opponent, and with him the whole Church, have not to hear the No only, but they certainly have to hear it as well. And it is not the case that this No can and will disturb and destroy an existing unity and has therefore to be condemned as a sin against love. It is rather the case that this No makes clear once more that unity of the Church which had been obscured, that it can and will restore that threatened unity, and that it has therefore to be regarded as a particular work of love. It is, of course, self-evident that the confession, with its exposition of the doctrine which is agreeable to Scripture, is to the whole Church a call to the renewal of unity and to the representative of the counter-doctrine in particular an invitation to return to that unity of faith which has now been expressed in a new and more accurate way. For the sake of this invitation he must be told clearly that he needs it, because he is outside this unity, because in defending his counter-doctrine he is *anathema*[EN176]. In order that a sick man may be treated by a physician, he has to know and accept the fact that he is ill. Confession helps him to do this with its *anathema*[EN177] or *damnamus*[EN178]. Now there is no doubt that the whole venture of a confession emerges in this *damnamus*[EN179]. It is all to the good that when we think we can and should go on to confess, we should accept it as the acid test: If we have not the confidence (or the explicit confidence) to say *damnamus*[EN180], then we might as well omit the *credimus, confitemur*[EN181] and *docemus*[EN182] and return to the study of theology as before. The time is not ripe for confession. Fear of the *damnamus*[EN183] is a sure sign: we are not at all certain that the doctrine confessed is really agreeable to Scripture and the expression of the unity of the [631] Church, which we would be confident to maintain and defend as such against its opposite with all the seriousness and responsibility of the *credimus, confitemur, docemus*[EN184], simply because we had to. We are wanting to express only an opinion and conviction or even a mere emotion against the opponents of which it would be highly inconsiderate and unreasonable to pronounce a *damnamus*[EN185]. There is a danger—it necessarily hangs like a sword over

---

EN175 we reprove, we reject, we abominate, we condemn ... those who teach otherwise
EN176 anathema
EN177 anathema
EN178 we condemn
EN179 we condemn
EN180 we condemn
EN181 we believe, we confess
EN182 we teach
EN183 we condemn
EN184 we believe, we confess, we teach
EN185 we condemn

every confession—either that we shall sin against an existing unity of faith if we say *damnamus*[EN186] in what is only a strife of opinions and emotions, or else that basing ourselves on mere opinions and emotions with our *damnamus*[EN187] we shall separate ourselves from the real unity of the faith now actually represented by the opponents upon whom we have laid our *anathema*. The actuality of this danger of the *damnamus*—with which we can easily pass judgment on ourselves one way or the other—can never emphasise too strongly the seriousness and responsibility with which alone we can legitimately pronounce the *credimus, confitemur, docemus*[EN188]. But again the danger is no reason why we should not pronounce the No which is inseparably bound up with the confession made in obedience to the Word of God. That doctrinal decision and its expression is already serious, responsible and dangerous in itself and in its positive content. The representatives of the opposite already regard as arrogant, uncharitable and intolerant the *credimus, confitemur, docemus*[EN189] as such. We have only harmlessly and positively to repeat, e.g., the clauses from the *Apostolicum: conceptus de Spiritu sancto, natus ex Maria virgine ... tertia die resurrexit a mortuis*[EN190], and at once those who deny these clauses all feel that they are attacked and insulted, even though there is no mention of *anathema*. In the measure that an opponent understands the confessing Yes, he will hear the claim which stands behind it, and with the Yes he will hear the perhaps concealed No to his counter-doctrine. If the Yes does not in some way contain the No, it will not be the Yes of a confession. And if—as clever confessors have sometimes attempted, who were not really confessors at all—we try to express the Yes in such a way that the No concealed in it is concealed to as many as possible, that as many as possible can rally under the banner of a very general Yes, this can only take place as intended at the price of the Yes. If we want to boast of the love which lies in this procedure we forget that in wanting to confess our aim was to be precise for the truth's sake and not to generalise, and that the present renunciation of truth certainly cannot take place in the service of love.

It is the No and therefore the differentiation from another supposed insight which gives to a confession its definite characteristics, displaying it in its material distinction from and opposition to other confessions; in its material distinction from confessions which precede it and are clarified and made more precise by it, or which will follow it and clarify and make it more precise; in its material opposition to confessions, against whose content it makes a protest or in which a protest is made against its own content. But the aspect which each confession has in distinction from and opposition to others shows us that we have to do with only a limited part of the insight given to the Church. More clearly than the geographical and temporal, the material limitation of Church confessions shows them to be in a mutual parallelism and contradiction which as such compromises all of them in respect of the compass of the insight expressed in them. This parallelism and contradiction is, of course, that of a mutually asserted exclusiveness. By their utterly opposed contradictory definitions of the unity of faith, by their different exposition of Scripture, by their

---

[EN186] we condemn
[EN187] we condemn
[EN188] we believe, we confess, we teach
[EN189] we believe, we confess, we teach
[EN190] Apostles' Creed: received by the Holy Ghost, born of the Virgin Mary ... on the third day he rose again from the dead

mutual *damnamus*[EN191], the confessions reveal the divided nature of the   [632]
Church itself. Although there is always a feeling for the relation to Jesus Christ
and an appeal to Holy Scripture and to certain documents of an earlier existing unity of faith, the relation and appeal have become so widely ineffective
that in the decisions which are now necessary there is no unity in faith in Jesus
Christ, in the exposition of Holy Scripture and in the understanding of those
documents of an earlier unity. There is so little unity that although we can
recognise the common confession of the Christian faith in the fact of that
appeal, and of the proclaiming the name of Jesus Christ, in the use of His
sacraments and perhaps in the confessions of individual Christians, or in individual utterances of the Church, we cannot do so in the confession made concerning these points. And there is no supra-confessional and supposed
ecumenical standpoint from which we can look beyond the dialectic of this
controversy, wherever possible understanding it as the organic development of
a whole in its separate parts and therefore removing the contradictions of the
confessions. We should have to take up a place outside the Church and therefore avoid the need to judge concerning the content of the decisions made
one way or the other in the Church, we should have to be without a confession,
if we were to be able to think and judge supra-confessionally. And in thinking
and judging in that way we should have all the confessions against us. For
(including Neo-Protestantism) they all want it to be understood that their Yes
and No is not a dialectical link which will be absorbed in a higher unity, but the
true and indeed the only true expression of the Church's unity.

It does not make any difference to this self-witness of all the confessions—which is inevitable if we presuppose the seriousness and responsibility of real confession—that in the
Lutheranism of the 19th century there was a popular theory which expounded the Lutheran confession as the organic centre between the relative aberrations of the Roman Catholic and the Reformed Churches, or that again the Church of England claims to be the
organic centre between Catholicism and Protestantism. We can speak of a removal of confessional antitheses, of an approximation to an ecumenical standpoint, only—and necessarily—when the opposition of the earlier confessions of two Churches has been made obsolete
by a new and common confession and has become a mere difference in theological thinking, when therefore the earlier *damnamus*[EN192] has been retracted in the fight of mutual
understanding of the two confessions. But where new facts like this do not arise, we have to
face up to the other fact, that the confessions do to a large extent mutually oppose and limit
one another.

If we are conscious of the seriousness and responsibility of our own exposition and doctrine and therefore confession, if we can be confident in faith
that with our Yes and No we are obedient to the Word of God, we have to
accept this fact and accept it willingly in all its force. But how can this happen
from any standpoint without our confession being seriously understood and
handled as an invitation to all existing opposites? But in this case when do we

---

[EN191] we condemn
[EN192] we condemn

[633]   not face the further fact of the absolute impotence of this invitation? When is there no occasion to pray that the Lord of the Church Himself should restore the unity in His Church which we cannot restore without disloyalty to Him? When do we not face the broader fact of the incapacity, the obvious limitation of the insight expressed in our own confession? Does not that which can obviously gain only a very limited hearing and assent suffer from the limitation of the perception expressed in it, no matter how honestly its confessors think that in relation to it they are obedient to God, and how little for loyalty's sake—for they have no other understanding of Scripture than their own—they are able of themselves to break through its limitation? This limitation of all the confessions is not merely seen in their actual parallelism and contradiction. Is it not a depressing if necessary fact that although all confessions have, or claim to have, their basis in Holy Scripture, their occasion is always the arising of an error, i.e., a confusion in the faith and knowledge of the Church? But that means that the confession is not the exposition of a genuinely comprehensive insight. If it were, it would triumphantly precede the error and confusion, not allowing it to arise and develop, but nipping it in the bud. But unfortunately the confession usually comes too late. It is only an attempt to cover the well when some children at least have been drowned and the great wasting of the Church has already taken place.

> How broadly the majority of great heresies have had to develop, how long it has almost always been left to individuals to oppose them and their solitary voices were not recognised as the voice of the Church and the one-sidedness with which perhaps they raised their opposition was corrected by the common witness of the communion of the saints—until finally things reached such a pass that these forerunners were vindicated, and general understanding and decision became possible, and a word of the Church, or a word spoken in the name of the Church, opposed the error and confusion in the Church in the form of a confession!

Better late than never. But the fact that it is "late" marks the confession clearly as a document of human and therefore limited insight. There is also a further point. Because a confession is occasioned by error and confusion in the Church, in content it is an answer to them, and therefore, although it is based on Holy Scripture, in the choice of its themes it is determined by a question which is put in what is admittedly a highly incompetent way. And not only in its choice of themes. To confess is to react. But where there is a reaction, there is not merely the danger, but it is inevitable, that our thesis should be directed at the antithesis which we have to reject and that by our Yes and No we should keep it alive—even if only as a reflection. At some point in our thesis of confession—if only in the form of the questioning which it has to allow— there still lurks the rejected antithesis. And does not that limit the insight expressed in it—not to speak of the human fallibility of its authors, the temporal limitation of their exegetical and dialectical methods, their restricted

[634]   power of self-expression? When we consider all these points together, the spatial, temporal and material limitations of all confessions, we may well ask how

in these circumstances there can ever be any authority at all in any confession.

But, on the other hand, we have maintained that the authority of a confession rests decisively on its limitation. We must now explain this. It is true that the limitation of every confession is the unmistakable sign of its humanity. But so far we have spoken only of the appearance, the visible form of this limitation. We had to speak of it, for if we wanted to see it at all, we had to see it in its visible form. But it is another question whether we have to understand it in the light of its visible form as such: in other words, whether the fact that there always has been and still is confession, confession with all the dangers which this undertaking involves, confession with all the burden of responsibility which it demands, confession with the courage to accept this responsibility and to defy those dangers, although the men in the Church who made the confession could never be ignorant of the spatial and temporal and material limitation of what they were doing—whether this fact can be explained by saying that in a kind of intoxication these men strangely overlooked and forgot the limitation of what they were doing, so that when all the illusions and phantasies have been deducted the only reality which remains is a matter of geography and politics, certain determinative factors in time, and finally a series of dialectical situations in the evolutionary process of Christian thought and utterance as determined by its environment. That would mean that the limiting of the confession was to be understood in the light of its visible form as such. Now it is clear that the confession whose limitation is understood only in this way will in certain circumstances always be regarded as interesting and worthy of historical notice, but that it cannot be Church authority in a serious, theological sense. But that raises the question whether the limitation of a Church confession in these ways, which we cannot deny but have to emphasise, can in fact be understood only from this standpoint. It means that we have not yet understood this limitation as a mark of the particular humanity of the confession, and it is important that it should be understood in that way. The particular humanity of the Church's confession consists in the freedom, the joy of responsibility, the certainty and the love, in which it has always taken place in spite of the limits of those who make it. But do we explain this particular feature by saying that it is only a forgetting of these limits, an enthusiastic accompaniment which we cannot consider when we try to establish the reality involved? This particular feature may have a quite different meaning which cannot be understood from the general fact that they were men from the West and the East, of this period or that, and in this or that controversy, nor from any enthusiastic overlooking and ignoring of this general fact. It may well be [635] that they confessed what and how they did in a particular obedience, and the human limitation of their confession was the concrete form of their obedience. Their confession cannot then be explained in terms of their geographical or temporal or material limitation. It can be explained in that way too. There can be no question of ruling out the "historical" interpretation. Even that enthusiasm has played a definite role in every confession. But the very opposite may also be true. The geographical and temporal and material limitation can be explained in terms of the confession, in so far as the confession itself (with or without enthusiasm) was obedience to the Word of God, in so far as it corresponded in this or that definite form to the will of God. What objection can we make to the possibility of this second interpretation, if we are not to eliminate from the list of important considerations the Word and will of God as the power which rules the Church, and with them the possibility of the Church's obedience to them, if we are to agree that that Word and will are the real subject of what happens in Church history? If we do agree on this, then we will certainly not deny the varied limitation of all Church confessions, but we will also reckon with the fact that they have a meaning not only from below, but also from above, in the fact that it is the Word and will of God and not creaturely powers and forces which have imposed upon these confessions their different limits. It was Holy Scripture speaking to the Church which at this or that time and place imparted to different people their definite measure of the Spirit and of faith, blessing but also judging, spreading light but also darkness according to the free and right and perfect will of God. That is why there are necessarily so many confessions in the Church. That is why these confessions are so different and even contradictory. That is why there is an ecclesiastical East and West. That is why there is a primitive Church and a modern Church mutually confirming one another. That is why one confession is so painfully but undeniably at odds with another. What has to be said from below, in the light of the visible form as such, can and must be said. But it is from above, in the light of the overruling of the Word and will of God, that the last and decisive thing has to be said. In the visible form we see only the creaturely material, and in this creaturely material we see the guiding hand of the Lord of the Church who determines and disposes in this way or that. If we reckon also with this second interpretation—and we clearly believe in the Word and will of God, in the Lord of the Church, if we do reckon with this second interpretation—then at least it is no longer inconceivable that the Church's confession may have Church authority and that it always does have it in the very thing which seems to compromise it, i.e., in the limitation which betrays its humanity. In this limitation and therefore this humanity, the confession of the Church, once made, is a palpable and authentic historical document, which

[636] can oppose and confront the rest of the Church and the later Church as a concrete disputant, as flesh of its flesh. When discussion does arise, will the geographical and temporal and material limitation of the confession speak for or against its authority? Either may very well happen. Its origin at this point or that, its early or modern nature, its concrete attitude: all these may tell for or against its value and validity. A final decision cannot be reached in the light of its limitation as such. This decision is reached when we see the basis of this limitation, the ways and judgments of God. In other words, it is reached when confessions are seen in the light of the lordship of the Word of God over and in

the Church by means of Holy Scripture and when they are heard and tested in this light. Seen and tested in this light the Church confession acquires a character which does not belong to it in virtue of its limitation: perhaps the character of a document of the wrath and judgment and rejection of God, and therefore that of a negative authority, of a document which warns the Church away because it is a codification of heresy and falsehood; but perhaps the character of a document, in whose human limitation we do not only see, as we do see, the traces of the wrath and judgment and rejection of God, not only the general disobedience of man to His Word, the general blindness of all human thinking about Him, the general helplessness to speak rightly of Him, but over and above these things His sin-forgiving grace, the power of His Word to assemble and give a new basis to His Church, and therefore even in the sphere of human error and falsehood a definite perception of the truth. With this character the Church confession acquires and is Church authority in its very limitation, as a document which, as we know and cannot conceal, is either Eastern or Western, old or new, corresponding only too well to this or that theological situation in the Church, with all the traces of space-time creatureliness and scars of historical controversy which it bears in itself. And although in this light we can still see that which we may call the enthusiasm necessarily associated with the genesis of every confession, the hazardous human venture of the Yes and No pronounced in the confession, even this particular humanity now stands under another sign. It is still an accompaniment as seen in this light. The freedom of the confessors is as little important, as little the basis of authority, as is the general humanity revealed in their limitation. But if by the test of Holy Scripture and therefore of the Word and will of God this confession has that character of obedience or rather of sin-forgiving grace and therefore of the perception of truth which breaks through human error and falsehood, their enthusiasm can be understood as an outward aspect of the fact that the confession arose under the compulsion of a necessity, which as such was also a permission, that the limit of its insight is that marked out by the Word of God and therefore does not merely humble the confessors but strengthens and encourages them in the human venture of their *credimus, confitemur, docemus*[EN193], and also their *damnamus*[EN194]. If this venture to con- [637] fess took place in the joy of obedience which is grounded in this way, how can it in any way diminish its authority? On the contrary, why should it not serve to confirm it?

(*e*) We have defined the Church's confession as "a formulation and proclamation reached on the basis of common deliberation and decision." In so doing we have described the mode of its origination and ratification.

First of all, the mode of its origination. The subject of a Church confession is the Church. There must always therefore be a majority. It is not necessary that

---

[EN193] we believe, we confess, we teach
[EN194] we condemn

185

they should all be the authors of the confession. It is also not necessary that they should have deliberated and resolved like a Parliament. We can seldom interpret the concept "Synod" or "Council," or the normal functioning of such an assembly, with sufficient strictness in relation to a confession which is just arising. Once it has arisen we have to give it a very generous interpretation. At the same time, it is not a Church confession unless a majority of Church members are responsible for it, and have taken part in the discussion and acceptance of its content at least in principle—by virtue of the fact of their obvious confessional position previously, or in the form of a subsequent express agreement. Is it not inevitable that the first promoters and authors of a Church confession should make every effort not merely to prove that their undertaking is that of the Church but as far as human possibility allows actually to assure that it is so by trying to put the discussion and conclusion in relation to it on the widest possible basis, by finding as many as possible instructed and committed co-confessors, and by seeking to make the whole proceeding as orderly and controllable as possible? Even if in fact only a single individual is the author of the confession, it is necessary that he should not be alone and speak only for himself, but that several, as many as possible, stand behind and with him sharing the responsibility. A confession has to speak in the name of the Church and to the Church. Therefore two or three must be gathered together—with some order and willingly and publicly—if what is said is to be a confession.

It is on this presupposition and to establish this point that the Augsburg Confession begins with the words: *Ecclesiae magno consensu apud nos docent …* [EN195] We must not press this expression. Obviously, the Saxon congregations and the great majority of the then preachers had no direct part in what Melanchthon and a few other theologians did at Augsburg with the distant help of Luther. Yet it was right and fitting and necessary that what was said should be solemnly said in their name: *Ecclesiae … docent* [EN196]. The case was much the same with the Basel Confession of 1534. Composed by Oswald Myconius, it still has the superscription: "Confession of our holy Christian faith, as held by the Church of Basel." Like that of Geneva, drawn up two years later by Farel and Calvin, it was publicly affirmed by the assembled citizens of Basel, and the view that the congregation was its author was kept alive until 1821 by the fact that every year in Passion Week it was solemnly read in divine service. The *Conf.*

[638]

helv. post. of 1561 was originally a purely private work of Heinrich Bullinger. It then appeared as the confession of the preachers of Zurich, Berne, Schaffhausen, St. Gallen, Chur, Mülhausen, Biel and Geneva, was later accepted expressly by almost all the Reformed Churches of the time, and finally with the *Heidelberg Catechism* became *the* Reformed confessional work, as it still is to this day, particularly in Eastern Europe. Similarly the Gallican Confession of 1559 did not win confessional status as the work of Calvin but as the *Confession de Foi des églises reformées du royaume de France* [EN197], and it was not as the work of Ursin and Olevian, but as "Christian instruction as given in the churches and schools of the Palatinate," and later on the basis of the willing assent of other Reformed Churches, that the *Heidelberg Catechism* of 1563 attained the same rank. As against that, the same status certainly cannot be ascribed to

---

[EN195] the churches teach with great agreement among us
[EN196] the churches teach
[EN197] Confession of Faith of the Reformed Churches of the Kingdom of France

writings like the so-called *Staffort Book* of the Margrave Ernst Friedrich of Baden-Durlach in 1599 or the so-called *Confessio Sigismundi* of 1614. When at the beginning of the latter it says that "His princely grace graciously and christianly remembers what the Holy Ghost … would have noted" in spite of the well-meant intention that "His princely grace would have the gates opened wide to the King of Glory in their land," the result was only a private concern of the prince, i.e., a landowner's declaration of his will, not the confessional writing of the Reformed Church, and it ought never to have been represented as such. If there is no *consensus ecclesiae*[EN198] there is no *ecclesia*[EN199], and therefore no *confessio ecclesiastica*[EN200]. The Brandenburg-Prussian Church has had to suffer a great deal right up to the present time because it was thought that the gates could be opened to the King of Glory in this way.

Of course, in almost all ecclesiastical confessions the theological preparation as well as the way in which the decision was made is open to question and dispute.

Most of all, perhaps, when as at the Council of Trent or the Synod of Dort, the arrangement of the advisory and legislative bodies, the order of business, the formality and explicitness of the theological pronouncements was most highly regular and controlled. What took place at Nicaea has often enough been described and deplored. And even at other Councils it is seldom or never that the opposing faction either present or absent from these consultative and legislative bodies has no reason to complain at the composition of the body in question or the lack of theological preparation or even arbitrariness and violence in the conduct of business, and to dispute the formal validity of the conclusions reached from some standpoint which can only in part be contested.

But it is not the level and content of the theological debates directly preceding its proclamation which decides the authority of a confession, although often they have failed notoriously to reach the height which is to be desired. Nor is it legal correctness nor the human "decorum" observed or not observed in reaching the decision, although it is to be deplored when the latter is wanting. What really decides its authority is simply its content as scriptural exposition, which is necessarily confirmed or judged by Scripture itself. This content can impart something of its own value and significance even to a confession which is open to question on formal grounds. A confession which stands at this point has authority even if it was adopted in the most disorderly tumult. On the other hand, a confession which arose soberly in every respect may have no authority, or only the negative authority of a divine warning and deterrent, if it does not stand at this point. There is no confession whose authority might not [639] seem endangered by the history of its origination. But there is none whose authority might not have the testimony of the Holy Spirit in spite of that history. This is not to excuse the mistakes made in consultation and decision. Where there has been too little concern about Church order in the making of a confession, that has always been avenged in its history, in spite of the sin-forgiving witness of the Holy Ghost. How much of the ineffectiveness of many a confession which is good in itself has perhaps to be ascribed to known or

---

[EN198] agreement of the church
[EN199] church
[EN200] ecclesiastical confession

unknown sins in the history of its formation! Again, when a confession is being made, we cannot be too careful about the greatest possible universality, regularity and fairness of all the proceedings. Speaking in the name of the whole Church to the whole Church we owe this—not merely to a moral scrupulosity, but to the fact itself. But when we have done all that it is our duty to do for the fact's sake, we have still to confess that we are unprofitable servants. The result of our efforts in this direction will always have obvious and concealed limits. But if this limitation will certainly not go unpunished, those to whom the completed confession comes, who are challenged to decision by it, by its content, have no right to point to this limitation in order to evade that decision. The only thing which they have to ask is whether in this limitation—however regrettable—the completed confession has for or against it the judgment of Holy Scripture, which means the testimony of the Holy Spirit. And now concerning the mode of the ratification of a Church confession the following has to be said. To make a confession, *confiteri*EN201, is to proclaim its content, to publish it, to make it known, to make it known as widely and universally as possible. A confession demands publicity. This derives from its nature as the word of the whole Church to the whole Church. It derives from its purpose to reply to the question raised in the Church by the emergence of the counter-doctrine. But it derives primarily from its basis and object: from the witness of divine revelation directed to the Church and through the Church to the world. What the confession has to say does not allow of either a complete or a partial silence. A confession cannot be spoken *mezzo forte*EN202. It cannot be spoken merely to individuals. A confession is quite different from a programme or line, by means of which the adherents of a group try to make their wishes clear without wanting to come too near to those outside the group, which, where possible, they may want to keep secret from others. A confession can only be spoken out loud and with the intention of being heard by everyone. If the claim involved in it is conditioned by a right knowledge of the Word of God, it is not presumption but the most profound and only true humility that this claim should be made without fear. In the desire to publish the confession, which can only be related to the visible sphere of human society, we

[640] have a visible representation of the consciousness that it is made before God and His holy angels, and also before the eyes and ears of the devil and all demons, in the one case with praise and thanksgiving and worship, in the other with defiance and triumph. For that reason we here stand again before the responsible seriousness of the undertaking of making confession. Should we go on, or would it be better to make peace and return? This question arises again with all its force. But where the confession is obedience, the anxiety implied in this question is removed, for it is self-evident that the confession should be made public.

EN201 confessing
EN202 with moderate loudness

In this sense most of the confessional documents of the Reformation must be regarded not so much as theological ordinances but rather as the trumpet call of a herald which is sounded out in order to assemble again in the Church all who are bound by this knowledge, giving a new account of it to its opponents and extending to them again that missionary invitation. In this respect the Augsburg Confession occupies a unique position. It is no mere imagination but an actual fact that in the ecclesiastical and confessional politics of older and more recent, and the most recent, Lutheranism the dignity of this confession has played a part which cannot possibly be explained only by the weight or scriptural character of its content. Theologically it could not satisfy for very long the needs of 16th century Lutheranism. But in spite of all the trouble it gave it had to be *the* Lutheran Confession—and as "invariata"EN203 it acquired that flavour of something holy, which cannot be changed or improved, that it has partly retained even to the present day—because it could be ranked under the saying in Ps. 119⁴⁶: *Et loquebar de testimoniis tuis in conspectu regum et non confundebar*EN204, because, as the prefaces to the Book of Concord and the Formula of Concord ceaselessly emphasised, it was laid before the emperor Charles V and the Imperial Estates at the Diet of Augsburg in 1530. Why is this so important ? There is no unequivocal answer. And modern Lutherans would do well to reflect that to recognise the Augsburg Confession was to put oneself under the protection and shadow of the religious peace promised to Protestants of the Augsburg Confession in 1555. Looked at from this standpoint, the *Augustana*EN205 is simply and soberly the guarantee of the outward right to exist given to the Lutherans by the emperor and the empire. But unfortunately, of course, it also guarantees their renunciation of evangelising the rest of the empire and therefore of the missionary character of their confession. But it would be wrong not to see the other side of the matter to which the Lutheranism of the Formula of Concord expressly held at any rate in theory. According to what we are told in the preface to the Formula of Concord (*Bekenntnisschriften der ev.-luth. Kirche*, 1930, 741, 8), the fact that the *Augustana*EN206 was laid before the emperor and empire gives to it the special value that occasioned in this way this particular confession *publice ad omnes homines Christianam doctrinam profitentes adeoque in totum terrarum orbem sparsa ubique percrebuit et in ore et sermone omnium esse coepit*EN207. We should add by way of understanding that the authors of the Formula of Concord regarded not merely the Reformation as such, but the Augsburg Confession in particular, as a direct work of God Himself (*ib.*, 740, 5, 14), and in such a way that, like Luther, they saw in the Reformation the last demonstration of the grace of God before the imminent end of all things (*postremis temporibus et in hac mundi senecta*EN208, *ib.*, 740, 6). Therefore—and we must weigh the significance of this passage in relation to the history of missionary thinking—they believed that in the *Augustana*EN209, as delivered to the emperor and empire, and in that way acquiring a modified publicity, the last and necessary call to all men had already taken place as wrought by God Himself. In the short interval between this and the end of the world they rejoiced in the advantages of the religious peace assured by the Augsburg Confession. That is certainly a strange conception, and its easy balancing of eschatology and ecclesiastical politics lays it [641] open to suspicion. All the same, it has this eschatological side, and from this point, accord-

---

EN203 unaltered

EN204 And I will speak of your testimonies before kings and I will not be confounded

EN205 Augsburg Confession

EN206 Augsburg Confession

EN207 publicly to all men who confess Christian teaching, and furthermore, it has been scattered throughout the whole world, and spread abroad everywhere, and begins to be in the mouths and conversation of all

EN208 at the last times, and in the dotage of the world

EN209 Augsburg Confession

ing to the Lutheran view, the accomplished confession is identical with an accomplished world mission. It is in this extravagant sense of a kind of an ultimate or penultimate trumpet—loud enough to make all further missions superfluous and also to give the confessors a last earthly assurance—that Lutheranism has wanted its confession to be understood.

The necessary publicity of the confession undoubtedly gives rise to certain criteria in respect of its form and content. What is to be proclaimed by a herald has to be not only right but important. It must accept responsibility and think it worth while to go before the whole Christian public and the world and to claim the hearing and attention of everybody. There are some right and necessary decisions which have to be made by the Church or individuals in the Church quietly and without having to be confessed *urbi et orbi*[EN210]. What is important or unimportant in this sense is not, of course, immediately apparent. What seems to be unimportant may *in statu confessionis*[EN211] suddenly become important and therefore a necessary object of public expression. What seems to be important may in a certain situation be unimportant, and its solemn expression an evasion of the real decision which has to be made. In a confession all have to hear that which calls all to decision. Therefore in a confession there can be no statements which are determined or instructive only on a local or regional basis. There can be no decisions which do not recognisably affect faith. It cannot be the theorems of an individual theology which are stated, for now (and we learn from Athanasius and Augustine and Luther that this can happen) the Church can and must on its own responsibility take over these particular elements as its own witness. Again, a confession has to set out its statements in such a way that their basis and inward context is revealed. There can therefore be no confession without the background of solid, theological work. But because of its publicity the confession cannot develop into a summarised dogmatics. It must speak concisely and in thesis form. And it must speak in such a way that without any knowledge of technical theology the whole Church can understand it.

Of many Reformed confessions—at any rate those that are second-class and of doubtful status—we may ask whether these rules concerning the publicity of confession were sufficiently observed when they were drawn up. In the confessions of Hungarian origin we find astonishing differentiations from superstition and local usage. Again, in the German-Reformed there are curiously minute theological and cultic demarcations from Lutheranism and a remarkable prominence of theological jargon. And in the Swiss Formula of Consent of 1675 we find distinctions of which we can only think that they were those of different theological schools, but not a matter of the faith or error of the Church. But we will do well to pronounce such verdicts with reserve. For a long time now many of the definitions in the early symbols, which not only then but even to-day are a matter of life or death for the Church, have been regarded as unnecessary ballast. We must admit that there have been [642] faults in this respect. Yet we must also admit that detailed decisions expressed perhaps in very technical language were once a call to the whole Church, and even though we cannot see in them this quality now, the day may come when they will have it again.

[EN210] to all and sundry
[EN211] where confession is at issue

But this publicity also involves that every confession will exert pressure on the rest of the Church and through the Church on the world. Therefore every confession can expect a reaction on the part of the Church or the world or both. If it is a genuine confession it challenges to decision, i.e., it challenges the others to hear its witness to a definite understanding of Scripture, and in that way to test their own understanding of Scripture by its accuracy, i.e., to test it anew, perhaps to realise for the first time that the doctrine and life of the Church must be tested by Scripture, that there is a Holy Scripture whose witness means judgment on the thought and speech and life of the whole world. The confession presents this challenge in the form of a simple Yes and No with which it questions the Yes and No of others: not only incidentally, but in the most definite way, not *disputandi causa*[EN212], but in a judgment whether their Yes and No is really of the Church, and their appeal to divine revelation is in order. This questioning means pressure. And pressure begets counter-pressure. It would be too cheap and meaningless a confession, or the confessors of a really important confession would have far too little knowledge of themselves and men generally, if there was the expectation that the confession would find a facile welcome. It is the fact that the confession "only" demands decision, that it "only" challenges others before the judgment seat of Holy Scripture—but inexorably before it—which necessarily makes it pressing. Men, even in the Church, prefer to leave open the question how they stand before this judgment seat, postponing their account before this seat to an indefinite future. If a new doctrine or movement arises in the Church, or an established one is predominant, then its representatives and adherents will not be disturbed in the presupposition that they are confirmed and protected or at any rate not attacked by the Holy Spirit. And the less active majority in and outside the Church prefer the rest of an open question to the unrest of a choice between truth and untruth. For them the danger of perhaps living in an environment in which we only appear to live but have in fact fallen victim to death seems much smaller than that which threatens when we are forced perhaps into a complete change of environment. And it is by this danger that the Church and the world are threatened by a confession. It threatens them by the fact that the question of the environment in which we can live may be decided quite differently from what their presuppositions demand by the One who has the knowledge and power to do so as the Lord of life and death. Therefore a confession demands that they come back to these presuppositions, asking whether they are right, choosing again where they think that they have already chosen rightly and satisfactorily. For that reason a confession presses and gives [643] rise to counter-pressure. If a confession were a mere change of mind, it could be adopted by the representatives of other views with friendly interest, perhaps being regarded as a welcome addition to the series of the many other open possibilities. But it says Yes and No—not as God says Yes and No, but in the

---

[EN212] for the sake of argument

human sphere, and yet in that sphere with an appeal to God Himself, and therefore with a definite assertion and denial of the unity of the Church, and with a definite indication in what sense and within what limits there is or is not fellowship in God. It cannot and does not try to anticipate the judgment of God. But in a way which cannot be ignored, it says that there is a judgment of God. It imperatively demands that we submit to this judgment. It is not because it opposes to human statements other human statements, but because in doing this it makes this demand, that a confession is necessarily a challenge, an unsettling factor, a disturbing of the environment, so that that environment inevitably wishes to silence it. For those who confess, therefore, a confession necessarily means, because of its publicity, that they are led by that environment into a struggle, into suffering and therefore into temptation. It not only can but must be so. Men in the Church and in the world, if they want to avoid the decision to which a confession summons them, may pretend that they do not see the danger of it. But in reality the fact that they do this shows that they have seen it very well. However it may be in detail, basically and in general they always see it. In some sense—as long as the Church is not completed and heaven and earth are not made new and the new order of the relationship of God and man based on Jesus Christ is not carried out by him in His own person—a confession will always bring those who confess it under counter-pressure and in that way lead them into temptation.

At this point we come face to face with the connexion made in the early Church between the concepts *confiteri, confessio, confessor*EN213, and that dangerous, costly and testing, but also hopeful conflict which the Church waged with a heathen world-power which persecuted and aimed to destroy it, and which at the time of the Reformation became identical with the might of a secular Church, which rejected the true Church because it had fallen away from it. In the measure that the confession ceased to make use of its publicity, this conflict became latent and for a long time now it has been seen only in certain peripheral phenomena and on the mission fields. But to-day, when confession is coming back to life, it looks as if this conflict will also flare up again. *Confiteri*EN214 means to enter into this conflict and to accept its hardship and also its promise. There are many forms of this conflict. It is not serious only when it is a matter of the opposition silencing confession with physical force, i.e., in some way robbing the confessors of life or external freedom. Then, of course, it becomes dramatic. The publicity of confession demands that it should reckon with this form of counter-pressure, that it should not shrink from engaging in this dramatic form in certain cases. But we can always count on it that the conflict against confession is either in an unripe and impotent stage and will soon take a worse course, or else that it is already coming to an end with the defeat of the enemy, when the latter thinks it necessary to take to the *prima*EN215 or *ultima ratio*EN216 of force. From the standpoint of confession itself there are greater and more intensive dangers than that enemies might kill the body. If they do, they are no longer able to do that worse thing which they might do to confession and confessors. From the standpoint of confession, we are, then, forced to be always on the watch, or we have already

[644]

EN213 confessing, confession, confessor
EN214 confessing
EN215 first
EN216 last means

found relief. The worst attempts to silence a confession consist in making it impossible on its own ground, the intellectual and spiritual. Another confession may be opposed to it which has perhaps a greater appeal, a superior theological technique, or a greater show of legal validity, and is far more impressive by reason of these qualities. Or it may have to sound out in the sphere of a philosophy and way of life in which all its presupposition and conclusions cannot be understood, in which its opponent finds it only too easy to slander and ridicule it as an arbitrary innovation, or an obstinate reaction, or the expression of an uncharitable spirit, or an attack on certain generally accepted sacred interests. It may even happen that the juridical and statistical uncertainty in which it has to move is noted and exploited, that it is triumphantly "seen through" on every hand, that it can be abandoned in the nullity of its claim to speak to the whole Church in the name of the whole Church, in the arrogance of its appeal to the Word of God, in the hierarchical pride of its attempt to assert and state the sole justification of this or that perception, in the uncharitable severity of its No, its *anathema*EN217 and *damnamus*EN218. It may be objected that the environment, being deaf and indifferent to confessions of every kind, has no ear for its Yes and No, that the question of truth is dead or apparently dead, that the apparent practical effects of some cheap-working religious enterprise can easily destroy the interest in the decision which it demands. But it may also happen that it is stripped of its character as a call and challenge, that it is given a friendly recognition and hearing, by being guaranteed in a religious peace or concordat as the manifesto of the decision of a recognised group or trend or party in the Church, or as a declaration of the principles of a Church which is itself regarded only as a group or trend or party, and in that way limited and set aside. And the very worst may happen that somebody or something or other has an instinct that it is better not to resist it openly and directly, or simply to put it on one side with those who confess it. On the contrary, it is adopted and affirmed. The leaders and perhaps the masses of the Church (and even of the world) recognise some advantage in accepting it, at any rate officially. It is therefore brought into a context, it is hemmed in by the rest of the Church and possibly the world, it is surrounded and overlaid by presuppositions, which do not "touch" it, which perhaps give it a new ecclesiastical and temporal glory, but—and this is the supreme cunning of the devil—it is made completely sterile by the fact that state and society, school and university all say what it says, as an allocution which demands a response. What are all the weapons of violence compared with the intellectual and spiritual enclosing and suppressing which a confession may suffer at the hands of the Church and the world?

If a confession is to stand, everything depends on whether the temptation produced by this counter-pressure (indirectly therefore by its own pressure) is recognised and overcome as such. The temptation naturally consists in the possibility of abandoning the confession. And the basic form of this abandonment is always to deny to ourselves and others the character of the confession as a challenge, question and attack on the world around. Its proclamation is renounced. It is regarded once again only as a theory and collection of propositions. With all the loyalty we might still show it in this immanent character, with all our zeal for the integrity of the theory and statements as such, there is now linked another zeal, to spare our environment the collision on the transcendent character of the confession. And it is this second zeal which—although the confession remains "untouched"—now determines our practical [645]

EN217 anathema
EN218 we condemn

attitude in word and action, in our own initiative and our response to the initiative of our environment. In this practical relationship the confessors no longer stand where they must stand if it really were their confession, that is, in the venture and responsibility of its transcendent character. Now that they have experienced what it means for its pressure to create counter-pressure, they no longer desire publicity. They want it to be their confession without this publicity. But this simply means that the confessors have in fact accepted the standpoint of the enemies of the confession. Confession without the desire for publicity, confession without the practical attitude which corresponds to it, is already a confutation of the confession, however "untouched" this may be as a theory and statement, however great may still be their zeal for the maintaining of its immanent character. For what is the meaning and purpose of the hostility and conflict in relation to the confession? As a theory and statement it will not have to suffer attack, whatever may be its content and however definitely it may be maintained and affirmed. As a theory it does not exert any pressure. As a theory it is quite harmless, indeed it is comforting even to those who do not agree with it. Behind the intention of its opponents to suppress it, there definitely does not stand any ill-will to those statements in the confession which are contrary to their own. Ultimately there stands only the desire that the confession should be a mere theory, that it should not raise the question of the correctness of their presuppositions, that it should not bring them before the judgment seat of Holy Scripture and of God Himself and in that way force them to decision. This is what takes place by means of publicity. A confession has publicity when it has confessors in the Church and the world who in their own person and practical attitude embody the venture and responsibility of its transcendent character as a challenge, question and attack, who in their existence represent what the confession says in words, and in that way consummate its proclamation. But if this does not happen, or no longer happens, even the best confession exerts no further pressure. The desire of its enemies is accomplished. Its confessors have no counter-pressure to suffer. But the confession itself has become so much paper. That it is not is the basis of all hostility to the confession, and that it should be is the purpose of the whole attack upon it. We help this attack, we participate most actively in it, when we think that we can retreat in this way. That there is no venture for the confession means that there is a venture—on the part of the confessors—against the confession. It involves treachery against the confession—pure treachery—if we are again concerned [646] with that distinction between its immanent and transcendent character. It is a great gain, therefore, if this distinction is soberly recognised for the treachery it is: not merely as surrender, but as agreement and co-operation with the enemy. It is a great gain if to justify it we no longer appeal to humility before the mysteries of God, to which no confession can do justice, or to the love with which we have to spare and carry the weak, or the necessary maintenance of the Church in its existing state, but openly and honestly—and this makes everything else superfluous—to fear of the expected or already present counter-pressure. This fear is in fact the temptation which is inevitably bound up with the publicity of a confession. And it can only be overcome in the conflict between this fear and the other fear, whether the Word of God—to which the confessors have appealed with their confession—commands or permits them to be enemies of the confession because of that first fear. Where the fear of God is greater than fear of men, the temptation has already been overcome. It is recognised that the confession is a demand primarily upon the confessors. Account is taken of that demand, i.e., they no longer yield to the expected or present counter-pressure, but resist it—for that is the demand made upon confessors. This resistance is the true ratification of a confession. The yielding of a confession by the above way of surrendering the practical attitude which puts it into effect always has the result sooner or later of making it impossible and destroying it and rendering it obsolete even as a theory or collection of propositions. The great defeats of the Church have been and are when it has wanted to honour its confession in theory but not in practice, when the living form becomes a mummy, and the mummy unnecessary lumber, and the gift of God is frustrated, when, deprived of its confession and delivered up to every possible force, the Church does not hear the Word of God and has no more to say of it. The great danger in the inevitable conflicts against a confession of the Church is that it may be taken away from it if it yields to temptation and surrenders. But there is also an even greater promise. Even the most modest and inadequate resistance which meets the counter-pressure of an alien church and world, not with surrender, but with new pressure, or rather with the old pressure of the old confession, means the ratification of the confession, and it has the promise that there will be a victory for the confession and new life for the Church.

A confession of faith is always stronger than even the most correct and profound and religious confession of error. Sooner or later a confession of faith will be accepted as superior in every philosophy and way of life in spite of misunderstandings and suspicions. A confession of faith can survive the nullity of its claim being "seen through" by the wise and its arrogance and uncharitableness being condemned by the righteous. A confession of faith has the power to summon to life again that dead or apparently dead question of the truth, and to unmask as such those cheap solutions which are placed in juxtaposition or opposition to it. A confession of faith can allow itself to be tolerated. It can make its voice heard even within a concordat or religious peace. A confession of faith can ultimately break through [647] and demonstrate the power which is proper to it alone, and not to its imitators, even where the Church and world try to enslave and suppress it by apparently accepting and adopting it. And a confession of faith has always triumphed in the long run where attempts have been made to suppress it by force. If only it is really a confession of faith—not necessarily of a heroic and inspired faith, but of a faith lived out and revealed in practical decisions! This faith does not need any special work and achievements or any special inward qualities. It needs only that it should not merely formulate the confession but also proclaim it. It needs only that it should not be forced back into the sphere of a purely theoretical agreement with the confession. It needs only the fact that the fear of God should be a little greater than the fear of men. In this "little" the pressure of a confession continues even under the most overwhelming counter-pressure. And that is what must happen. It is in this continually exerted pressure that the Church lives in the Church, even in a destroyed and apostate Church—and the Church in the world, even in a world which resists it in every possible way.

Of the Church confession which fulfils all these conditions we have to say that it has Church authority, i.e., it can and it must be distinctively heard in the Church as the distinctively articulated voice of the fathers and brethren in faith. When we say this, we do not formulate a postulate, but describe a reality: where the Church really lives, real Church confession is heard in this distinctive way. Or negatively expressed: the Church does not really live where real Church confession is not heard in this distinctive way. It is not possible that where Church confession has been made we can ignore this event, i.e., ignore its binding and imperative and authoritative character. That would be to obscure and destroy the continuity between the Church then and now, the connexion between the Church there and here. Now in practice, of course, that does happen often enough. Not every Church confession which has been adopted in some place at some time has this character always and everywhere. What we said about the geographical and temporal and material limitation of every confession works itself out in the actual limitation of the authority of every confession. But with all the mutual strangeness and division in the Church, where there is a real Church there is also an unbroken continuity between the Church then and now and an unbroken connexion between the Church there and here. There is no Church where fellowship is completely lacking in even one of these two dimensions, where in what appears to be a Church there are no fathers behind us and no brethren beside us. But having both, in both directions we hear the voice of a Church confession, within definite limits and on a definite road we take part in the story of the exposition and application of Holy Scripture, and we have therefore a definite responsibility to definite decisions made earlier and elsewhere in the Church. This responsibility can be confirmed and codified in Church law. But it does not arise because a corresponding decision is made in Church law. Nor may it be annulled or even weakened by the failure or flouting of that law. The authority [648] of a Church confession is a spiritual authority. That is, it is based on its character as correct exposition of Scripture. As such it is a self-attesting authority, to which nothing can be added and from which nothing can be taken away by Church law.

Thus the early dogma of the Trinity did not in any sense depend on the authority with which it was invested for the Roman State Church in 380 by the edict of the emperors Gratian, Valentinian and Theodosius, as later incorporated in the *Codex Justiniani*. Again, the Confession of Augsburg did not depend only on the authority ascribed to it in Lutheran territories by the religious peace of 1555. Even where the ecclesiastical establishment of a confession took place by the free decision of the Church independently of political powers, it does not depend on the authority created for it by this codification. Conversely, the authority of the confessions with whose formulation and proclamation the Swiss Churches were re-founded in the 16th century is not abolished or weakened by the fact that the liberal

19th century state revoked their canonical validity, that the Churches at that period lacked the inward resources to reaffirm them of themselves, and that they have therefore been obliterated from the present-day law of the Church. What has at one time and place been known and confessed, as was the trinitarian belief of the 4th century Church or the Scripture principle and doctrine of justification of the Reformation, may at another time and place have to suffer at the hands of all kinds of spiritual insensibility and insubordination. It may be ignored and misunderstood or overlooked and forgotten over long epochs or in large sections of the Church. But it does not derive its claim to be authority and the power to assert it from its consistent establishment in the law of the Church, nor does it lose it when the latter is weak. But where there is the Church and therefore that continuity and connexion of Church life, there genuine knowledge speaks through genuine confession, and it is always heard as an authority with or without Church law. The fact that they are not assured by Church law does not prevent the trinitarian confession of the early Church or the Reformation confessions from speaking and being heard again in our own days, and perhaps more effectively than if they still had their former guarantees in Church law. It could not and cannot diminish the undeniable factual importance, at any rate in Germany, of the unique witness of the so-called *renitenten Kirche* of Hesse in matters of the right relationship of Church and State, that it is the witness of a small free Church which hardly merits external notice. Again it would not be right for us outside Germany to try to ignore the factual significance of the confessional decisions taken there since 1934, because formally they are only the decisions of the German Evangelical Church, or of a small minority in this Church. The authority of a confession and therefore our necessary responsibility towards it is decided, not by any outward legitimation, but within the actual continuity and relation between Church and Church by its own importance, by the perception confessed in it.

Where the Church is, it does stand in this responsibility. It is to that extent a confessional Church, i.e., a Church determined by its responsibility to Church confession. It would be an unconfessional Church only if it could repudiate and actually deny this responsibility. Where this is not the case, we can distinguish only between Churches which are confessional in different ways and to different degrees. It is the case, then, that the concept responsibility describes and denotes what we have called the binding and imperative and authoritative character of the Church's confession. We have seen that confession cannot in any sense stand beside Holy Scripture, claiming the same divine [649] authority, the same character as the source and norm of Church proclamation. In substance, no express or tacit obligation to a confession can ever be anything but an obligation to Holy Scripture. But wherever the Church really is, this obligation to Holy Scripture will have a form determined by the particular guidance and history of the Church (through its continuity with the earlier Church and its connexion with Churches elsewhere). Responsibility to the fathers and brethren involves responsibility before God. It is a question of responsibility before God and this alone. But how can there be this responsibility if we try to evade responsibility before the fathers and brethren? Can we hear them as we hear God Himself in the witnesses to His revelation: that is, in all their words and statements and with a readiness to subject ourselves entirely to them? Certainly not. But obviously we cannot hear them with the impartiality and neutrality with which we hear various other human voices. *Tertium datur*[EN219]. This third thing—which is not a middle term between the Word of God and the word of man, but a human word figuratively ranked before all other human words—is the confession or dogma of the Church.

In the sphere in which it has validity, Church confession is an authority to which we must always give a prior recognition. Its authority consists primarily (and at bottom decisively) in the fact that for responsible representatives of the Church's life it is not one of the many old and new texts which we may have read or not read, read thoroughly or cursorily, read many times or only once and then never again, but it is one which has to be read, and read seriously and constantly.

It will be noted that this basic form of the recognition of its authority does not involve any *sacrificium intellectus*[EN220]—the same can be said of the authority of the Church's Canon and the Church's fathers. We may accept and follow the discipline demanded as binding without being guilty of any kind of neglect of responsibility for our own thinking and deciding. How can it harm this responsibility that these texts are recommended for our particularly intensive and persevering study?

But why this particular study? The Church's confession—and this is the second form in which its authority must be respected—is meant to be read as a first commentary on Holy Scripture. We repeat: as a commentary. It cannot replace Holy Scripture itself. It cannot replace our own exposition and application of Holy Scripture. It cannot be the only commentary which—because we have to read Scripture in the Church—we allow between ourselves and Scripture. But as the voice of the fathers and brethren it can and should be the first of commentaries. It can and should be the leader of the chorus or the key witness in that series.

We can hardly object to this as a wresting of Holy Scripture or our own conscience. No one has ever read the Bible only with his own eyes and no one ever should. The only question is what interpreters we allow and in what order we let them speak. It is a pure superstition that [650] the systematising of a so-called historico-critical theology has as such a greater affinity to Holy Scripture itself and has therefore in some sense to be heard before the Apostles' Creed or the *Heidelberg Catechism* as a more convincing exposition of the biblical witness. What we have there is simply the commentary of a theology, if not a mythology. The only thing is that this commentary has not been affirmed by a Church, that so far the theology or mythology has wisely hesitated to claim the character of a real decision. Obviously we cannot choose between the biblical text and a Church confession. We are definitely pointed and bound to the text, and not to the commentary. Again, we cannot choose between the possibility of using all available commentaries for an understanding of the text, including that of the historico-critical theology—or that of using only a few more convenient ones, including, of course, the Church confession. But we have the possibility of giving first place among all the voices which have to be heard to that of the Church confession, i.e., to listen to it first on the assumption that it has something particular to say to us as the solemnly gathered deposit of the significant existing experience of the Church with Holy Scripture. We then have to be constantly ready for corrections of its view either by other voices or by our own insight. But it

---

[EN219] There is a third option (thing)
[EN220] sacrifice of the intellect

is hard to see why its view should not be heard with the attention it deserves without having to disturb or destroy the objectivity of our relation to Holy Scripture.

After this, as it were, privileged hearing of the Church confession, we have to go and tread our own way in the understanding, exposition and application of Holy Scripture. The confession cannot and will not deprive us of our own responsibility to Scripture. We shall enter that way "confessionally determined." But fundamentally that can only mean that we have dealt with the confession as an authority of first rank and taken the direction indicated by it.

If we cannot do this, if we have to reject as contrary to Scripture the direction indicated by the confession, we then have to face the difficult problem of an exchange of confessions, that is, an alteration of our ecclesiastical position. Of course, our dealings with the confession may end in this way. They can do so legitimately only in the light of Holy Scripture. But they may also end by our having quite freely to move further in the direction indicated.

That does not mean that we have to make our own its particular theology and the details of its biblical exposition. We can be loyal to its direction and still think that in detail and even as a whole, as our confession, we would rather have it put otherwise. We can still think that we have definitely to repudiate certain of its detailed and perhaps not unimportant statements. Even a positive attitude to the confession can be a genuinely critical one. And moving in the direction it indicates, and therefore a positive attitude to it, means even less that we have to make the content of the confession the content of our own proclamation. For again: the confession cannot in any way constrain the Word of God attested in Scripture, which as such alone can and will be the content of our proclamation.

A confessional proclamation in this sense would not correspond to the meaning of the confession itself, which, as we saw, is not an exposition of the Christian faith *in abstracto*[EN221], but a weapon of faith against error in the form of individual concrete decisions. There is certainly no reason why for the purpose of instructing the Church on the antitheses of faith and error we should not occasionally make the confession as such a direct key to the exposition of Scripture, as was obviously done for centuries and to some extent is still done to-day   [651] with the *Heidelberg Catechism*, which offers itself at once for this purpose with its division into fifty-two Sundays. But the confession never has the pretension of wanting to become the theme of Church proclamation, which must be provided only by Holy Scripture.

The way of understanding the Bible must be pursued, then, as our own way. We cannot allow this understanding to be prescribed by the confession. We cannot allow ourselves to be bound by the confession as by a law. Does that mean an end of its authority and respect for it? Not at all—we might say rather that it only begins at this point. For at this point it takes a third and genuinely spiritual form. It becomes a constant antithesis, the horizon of our own thinking and speaking. Naturally, within this horizon it is a question of our own free

---

EN221 in the abstract

thinking and speaking, for which we must bear the responsibility, which is not bound by any law except that of its object, and therefore only by Holy Scripture. Our study of the confession, our hearing of it as leader and key witness, is now behind. We must now take the Word itself—but in the sphere of the Church, and now as previously this sphere is denoted by the obtaining confession. It is still, and will continue to be (if no new events intervene), the sphere determined by the trinitarian witness of the early Church and by the Reformation witness to the lordship of God in His Word and the free grace of God. It is not only we who speak in this sphere but also the fathers and brethren. Therefore in this sphere we are not sovereign in the sense that we are alone, with no antithesis, no horizon. We cannot think and speak as in the absence, but only as in the presence of the confession.

We can make this plain by the external fact that the Christian worship in which our own exposition and application of Holy Scripture is most solemnly expressed usually takes place not freely or in a neutral place, but in a "church" which even by its architecture and furnishings more or less directly and faithfully reminds those who gather in it, including the one who speaks, of their "confessional position." Even if it is mainly a witness to the helplessness of the 19th century the "Church" confronts us with Church history. And what happens in it happens not only in the presence of God and His angels, not only in the presence of the departed spirits of the past, but also—with whatever freedom and responsibility—in the presence of the confession, by which in strength or weakness, in loyalty or apostasy, our "Church" is this particular "Church." In the same way the hymn-book which, good or bad, is always used in worship, confronts us with Church history. Together with the text of the Bible our own exposition and application of the word of the Church's praise is a third trigonometrical point, and at a varying distance behind it there always stands the Church's confession. Finally, even the order of worship can more or less definitely play the same role.

We cannot avoid this fact of the—noted or unnoted—presence of the Church's confession in every present aspect of the Church's life. If we think that we are so free or so committed that after hearing the confession we must go our own way independently of it, the confession does not cease, directly or [652] indirectly to speak, tacitly opposing its word to our word, not as any kind of voice, but as the voice which has been peculiar to our Church from its inception and still characterises its being to this day. Neither the greatest liberalism nor the boldest catholicising which may be permitted in the Church can alter the fact that the sphere in which it can be disseminated is still and will continue to be the spiritual sphere of the Evangelical, Lutheran or Reformed Church, which, whether we like it or not, opposes the Evangelical confession to all extravaganzas. It is perhaps in this inflexible if non-authoritative antithesis, in a confrontation in which it has, as it were, to be a silent disputant, that the Church confession perhaps speaks most explicitly, even if only in the form of an immanent but irresistible criticism of those who stop their ears against it. In this confrontation we have to recognise and respect its genuine spiritual authority. As we ourselves confront it in a necessary freedom, it retains its own complete freedom as well. If in relation to it we think, rightly or wrongly, that we have to make certain reservations or omissions, if we interpret it critically under the guidance of the Holy Scripture to which it emphatically directs us—side by side with the form, in which we have altered it and made it our own, it still stands in its own original form, in the integrity of its propositions, in the uniqueness of its theology and language, in the historical limitation but also the peculiar greatness of its origin, in its own direct appeal to Holy Scripture. Just as freely as we confront it the confession confronts us, speaking and demanding that we should listen, still intact and including all that we have rightly or wrongly freed ourselves from, all our reservations and omissions. The spiritual authority which it exercises is that it continues to exist in its own form, so that whatever may be our attitude to it as a whole or in detail, because it is the voice of the fathers and brethren in the Church, we can never have done with it. And a spiritual respect for its authority is that we are conscious of this confrontation, that it has been given to us to realise our freedom only in this confrontation or within this horizon, that the realisation of our freedom is always a reckoning or a responsibility which we owe to it. It may be a critical, even a very critical, responsibility: but it is still a responsibility.

Even when we feel we must hold something apparently or actually opposed to a statement of the confession, this statement is still before us with all its weight as the confession of the fathers and brethren and with what is perhaps a very galling definiteness. It cannot be forgotten even though at the time we cannot accept and repeat it. As that which also opposes us, it deserves respect, even though we cannot allow its opposition; it does not cease to occupy us. We can never have done with it, because as a statement of the Church's confession it has not done with us.

This and this alone is the imperative and binding normative authority of a Church confession. Anything more: the elevation of a dogma to the rank of revelation or a law or the content of the Church's proclamation would bring us back ineluctably to Roman Catholic immanentism in which Church and revelation are equated, violating the divine authority of Holy Scripture and therefore returning the Church to that solitariness in which ultimately there can be no Church life at all and therefore no genuine Church authority. Dogma has genuine Church authority only as a word of the fathers and brethren, whose authority is in the strict sense spiritual and has to be respected spiritually. It would be to distrust the power of the Holy Spirit if we were to regard this authority and respect as inadequate. If a confession or dogma, as this word of the fathers and brethren which has authority and has to be respected spiritually, does not oppose any justifiable claim to freedom, if its claim to be heard as such cannot be refused in any justifiable liberty, there is no justifiable claim to be noticed and heard and accepted and obeyed which it cannot proclaim and make good to the extent that it is genuine witness: the genuine counter-witness of the Church to divine revelation and to that extent a genuinely spiritual word. If that is so—or quite simply, if it is a real confession of faith—it will have the power to continue speaking even at a great distance from its own geographical and temporal and historical place in the Church, to make itself directly intelligible and instructive in its application to the faith of a Church in

[653]

some quite different place, in spite of and even in the particularity of its theses and positions and negations, or even to awaken to new life the dead faith of a Church in some quite different place. It is obviously not the power of an in every way limited and fallible human word, nor is it its canonical recognition, nor is it the fact that it is divine revelation, that explains this. What can explain it except that it is a document of obedience to the Holy Spirit of the Word of God and therefore an instrument of His power and His ruling? How can it not have and be authority as such, and how else can it have and be authority? To have and be authority in this sense and therefore to confirm its imperative and binding and normative character, it needs only—but very earnestly—to be seen and understood as the silent but present antithesis of the Church's daily life, as the horizon within which—under the lordship of the Word of God—it is conducted. In this free confrontation faith speaks to faith, and faith awakens new faith, and in the witness which men bear to other men, the Holy Spirit Himself acts and works.

If we are to evaluate rightly the authority of a Church confession, we must hold apart as well as together what we have called its direction and its detailed statements as such. It may well be that the false statements against which the confession was then and there directed are no longer or not yet familiar to the Church here and now in their original form, or at any rate in their actual significance.

[654] What is the significance to us of those statements of Arius or Nestorius to which the christological dogma of the early Church was the reply? What is the significance to us of the statements of the later mediaeval doctrine of penance to which the Reformers opposed their doctrine of justification by faith alone? Or again we may ask: What is the significance to us in Switzerland or Holland or England of the statements, to us the very strange and peculiar statements, of the German Christians against which the Confessional Church in Germany must set its own statements? Or again the missionary Churches of India and China may ask: What have they to do with all the heresies to which all the dogma of the European Churches is an answer?

Similarly, it may be the case that the answering statements of the faith of the Church then and there as laid down in the confession do not strike the Church here and now as a necessary expression of its own faith. But it is still true that the confession of that time and place does constitute the antithesis and horizon of our Church life which we have to hear and regard. And we can confidently expect what will happen when this confrontation takes place. For there is a notorious connexion, even a unity, between the heresies of every age and place.

The assertion that 2nd century Gnosticism or Anus and Nestorius or Occamism have nothing to do with us is perhaps a very short-sighted one. It may be that these teachings do not have any obvious relevance and we are concerned with other errors. But although heresy has altered its form, its content is still the same. And it would be premature for us to dismiss as unimportant the dogma which opposed a strange form of error because in that form it corresponds to a teaching which no longer occupies or does not yet occupy us.

2. *Authority Under the Word*

It may be that in the assertion of the present irrelevance of the statements and counter-statements presupposed and expressed in dogma we have a fatal insinuation, an attempt on the part of modern error, to conceal and withhold from the Church the experience it has already gained and the decision it has already taken in relation to it in an earlier and different form, so as to force itself all the more surely upon it in its new and present form.

The orthodox rational theology of about 1700 knew what it was doing when it made the Church of that time suspect the Reformation doctrine of predestination and justification as the superfluous relic of the Scholasticism of a former age, thus rejecting the confessional writings as a horizon. Verbally, this was a campaign against Scholasticism. But in fact it meant the introduction of a half-stoical, half-pietistic semi-Pelagianism. They knew well enough why they did not want Luther and Calvin as witnesses against what they themselves were bringing in, although not in the formulae and expressions of later mediaeval nominalism. Similarly, it sounded well enough when in the 19th century the school of Ritschl purported to be able to perceive and unmask the Greek philosophical thinking which lay behind the dogma of the early Church, and a period began when scholars could never be sufficiently astonished at the iota of Nicaea and the prickliness and rigidity of the Chalcedonian Definition, or emphasise too much the remoteness of our own "piety" and morality and way of thinking from those distant epochs and controversies of the Church, or relativise sufficiently the significance of the trinitarian-christological dogma. Historically, the result was that many true discoveries were made. But can we doubt that objectively all this was only a pretext to create a free course for thinking and teaching about God and Christ and the Holy Spirit, which, if not in words and statements, all the more certainly in matter, was exactly the same as that of the early heretics, and against which the continuing presence of early dogma formed an unwelcome barrier. According to Ritschl, Jesus Christ is a great man who on the basis of our value-judgment is found to be the Son of God. For that reason Harnack has to call the ancient dogma a self-expression of the Greek spirit in the sphere of the Gospel. And we must look carefully to see what is really at stake when we are assured to-day that the Reformation confession was right when it opposed the sacramentalism and monkish moralism of the Catholicism of the period, but that we in the present-day Church are concerned with quite different questions and problems. We are not interested in the question of the grace of God, but the question whether there is a God at all, as was often said thirty years ago. The Christian answer to social and national questions, war, the status of women, is more important than the Scripture principle and the doctrine of justification, as was said later. And to-day, it is not the righteousness of works which is the enemy of the Gospel, but the indifference and the secularism of the masses who are only nominally Christian. Why should there not be much that is right in these assertions? But we have to note that directly or indirectly they may be aimed at the confession, that their purpose may be to obscure the confession as the horizon of the Church and make it ineffective. We have to note that they may be simply the wings behind which the old enemy, against whom the Reformation drew up its confession, will make a triumphant return into the Church in a new form. Similarly, it may be of fatal significance if the young missionary Churches of Asia think that they can let go the *Apostolicum*[EN222] because it is only the document of the Church's conflict with a Gnosticism which even in Europe has for a long time been known only historically, a conflict whose results can have no possible interest for modern Japanese and Chinese Christians. Does not Gnosticism always lurk where the Gospel begins to emerge in all its novelty from the background of thousands of years of traditional heathendom? Is it not there that it is

[655]

[EN222] Apostles' Creed

always better to close the doors against it with the formula: *Credo in Deum patrem, omnipotentem creaiorem coeli et terrae, et in Jesum Christum, filium eius unicum, Dominum nostrum?*[EN223] Is it not a very questionable proceeding if we try to slide them open on the pretext that they are too Western?

Primarily and decisively it is not the wording of a Church's confession, not its form as geographically and temporally and historically limited, but its direction (which is, of course, only real and recognisable in its statements and form), whose exposition can constitute the necessary horizon of the present-day Church and as such have and be authority. The confession of the Church then and there confronts the Church now and here with its statements. In doing this, it questions it concerning its faith, concerning the obedience of its exposition and application of Scripture. Just as there is a connexion, indeed a unity in heresy, so there is a connexion and unity of faith. The confession speaks to us of this unity of faith. What it desires of us is that we should find ourselves with it in this unity. Its statements give us the direction in which it itself, the Church then and there, has sought and found it. It is not by agreeing with these statements and appropriating them, but by learning the direction from these statements that we respect the authority of the confession. For that reason it may well be that in learning that direction from it we have to oppose critically certain or even many of its statements.

[656] This criticism will mean, therefore, that going in the direction indicated and respecting the authority of the confession we think we ought to prefer other statements as better following that direction. A certain positive criticism of the confession cannot be avoided when we respect its authority, when therefore we go further in the direction indicated by it, and therefore in our own responsibility in relation to the Church here and now. Even if there is no cause to oppose them directly, its statements have at all points to be extensively interpreted. They have to be read with underlinings and emphases and accentuations which they never had then, which they do not have when considered "historically," but which they necessarily acquire when they are the antithesis and the horizon of the present-day Church. The necessity of this positive criticism of the confession may lead to the emergence of a new confession, i.e., a confession which repeats the old one according to the new knowledge of the present-day Church. This is not merely reconcilable with the authority of the confession, but may even be demanded in some way by the authority of the confession as rightly understood, in that it does not bind us to itself but to Holy Scripture, in that it does not challenge us primarily to agreement with its statements, but to persistence in the unity of faith and only for that reason and in that sense to agreement with its statements.

But we must not forget that it does not do this formlessly, but in the very definite form of its statements. Its statements constitute the horizon within which we find ourselves in the Church. They give us the direction to the unity of faith. With their Yes and No they constitute the concrete form which questions us concerning our faith. It is not, therefore, that we can reverently listen to the confession as an attestation of any faith and therefore faith in general,

---

[EN223] I believe in God, the Father almighty, maker of heaven and earth, and in Jesus Christ, his only Son, our Lord

so that we for our part can then enjoy faith in general and therefore any faith, thinking that in that way we meet its call to the unity of faith. No, the call takes place in the form of statements. And it is in this form or not at all that it is the object of our discussion with it. Let those who think they have to oppose the confession oppose its statements. Let them do so in obedience to the Scripture to which it itself points us. Let them do so by continuing in the direction for which it claims us. Let them see to it that their criticism or interpretation does not perhaps lead them in quite a different direction and perhaps out of their Church, or that it is not perhaps based and pursued quite otherwise than in obedience to Holy Scripture. All criticism and interpretation of dogmas is dangerous in both these ways, inevitable though it may be. The dogma stands before us again after we have dealt with it, demanding a reckoning. We must see to it that we give this reckoning. Yet the worst mistake we might make in this respect is at least better than a relation to dogma in which its statements as such are no longer heard, in which they cannot speak concretely or be taken up in some way into our own thinking and speaking. That there is a dogma attesting the Church faith of the fathers and brethren is only of significance because this faith speaks in dogma. But it does so in the statements of dogma. If its statements as such remain or become alien, how can we find ourselves in the direction in which it would point us? If we find ourselves in this direction, then we necessarily also find ourselves in a definite agreement with its statements which remains even in spite of and in all our criticism and interpret- [657] ation. We can then understand these statements as statements of faith and accept them with complete freedom. With complete freedom: that is, as our own statements in the sense and understanding in which they have now imposed themselves upon us as true, with the reservations in respect of earlier interpretations (perhaps even of the original understanding) which are the necessary result of our own relation to Holy Scripture, but all the same as the confession of our own faith. In the questions which it answered then and there we recognise the questions which occupy us, and in its answers we see what we have to say here and now in obedience to Scripture. Perhaps we could say it differently. But we must not say it differently. And perhaps we cannot say it any better. What was said there and then is perhaps in its own unaltered form the most clear and definite thing that we can still say here and now even according to our insight. And in order that we too may point to the unity of faith, unless there are compelling reasons to the contrary, we will gladly say exactly what was said there and then, appropriating not only the content but also the form of the dogma, not only the direction but with the direction statements, maintaining not only faith in general but the particular faith of the dogma as defined in its wording. It is only in this way that we can continue discussion with it; that it retains its critical power over against us; that the possibility remains that the meaning and the understanding in which we have affirmed it can be corrected by it; that the faith of the fathers and brethren has more than ever before to say to our own faith.

This brings us to the last point in our deliberations. As a Church authority the authority of the confession, too, cannot be an absolute, but only a relative one. The infallible and therefore final and unalterable confession is the praise which the Church as the body eternally united to its Head will offer to its Lord in this its own eternal consummation; it is thus an eschatological concept, to which no present actualisation corresponds, to which every reality of Church confession, everything we now know as dogma old or new, can only approximate. What we know as dogma is in principle fallible and is therefore neither final nor unalterable.

Here again the ways of Roman Catholic and Evangelical doctrine obviously diverge. Dogma in the Roman Catholic sense is the witness of revelation like Holy Scripture itself. Dogma in the Evangelical sense is the Church counter-witness to this witness of revelation. This means there can never be a final word, but only a word which is imperative and binding and authoritative until it is succeeded by something else. The Church confesses, and it also appropriates earlier and other confessions. But even as it does so. it remains open to the possibility that it may be better instructed by the Word of God, that it may know it better and therefore confess it better. In its confessing it has always before it the *eschaton*[EN224] of the praise of God in its consummation. For that reason, on earth and therefore recognising its incompleteness, it must always be ready to receive such better instruction from the Word of

[658] God. In the 16th century it was the Reformed Churches which stated with particular clarity the provisional nature of their confessions and all confession. We confess the Old Church symbols only with the reservation: *pource qu'ilz sont conformes à la Parole de Dieu*[EN225] (*Conf. Gallic.*, 1559, *Art.* 5). In the official introduction to the Synod of Berne in 1532 it says even of the Reformation Confession: "But if ought is adduced by our pastors or others, which leads us closer to Christ, and according to God's Word is more profitable to fellowship and Christian love than the opinion now recorded, the same we gladly receive, not hindering the Holy Ghost, who does not lead us back to the flesh but forward to the image of Christ Jesus our Lord." And in the introduction to the *Conf. Scotica* 1560: *protestantes, quod si quis in hac nostra confessione articulum vel sententiam repugnantem sancto Dei verbo notaverit ... promittimus Dei gratia ex Dei ore id est ex sacris scripturis nos illi satisfacturos aut correcturos si quis quid erroris inesse probaverit*[EN226]. That even Councils may err, and that God will maintain His truth against the error of a Council (Calvin, *Instit.* IV, 9, 13), was a presupposition in the doctrine of all the Reformation Churches, deriving from the recognition of the divine authority of Scripture alone. It was not always and everywhere, especially on the Lutheran side, that the relativity of their own present decisions and therefore of the Reformation confessional writings was so clearly stated as at Berne and Edinburgh, or by Calvin in his work against Pighius (*C.R.* 6, 250) in relation to Luther, Melanchthon and himself. The only meaning we can give to the German text of the passage already quoted from the introduction to the Formula of Concord concerning the *Augustana*[EN227] is that in these last days (after He allowed the Reformation to happen), Almighty God Himself "composed out of the divine prophetic and apostolic writings" the confession laid before emperor and empire in 1530. And at any rate

---

[EN224] end time
[EN225] because they are conformed to the Word of God
[EN226] protesting that if anyone finds in this confession of ours an article or statement which verbally opposes the Word of God, we promise that, by the grace of God, we will satisfy ourselves with it, or correct it by the mouth of God, that it, by the Holy Scriptures ... if anyone proves that there is any error in it
[EN227] Augsburg Confession

in the later Lutheran dogmatics (cf. Hollaz, *Ex. theol. acroam.*, 1707, *Prol.* II, *qu.* 27) we can find pronouncements on the *specialis concursus Dei*[EN228] under which the symbolic books of the Lutheran Church arose, and on the divine nature of their content, etc., which appear almost to assert their inspiration and canonicity. But on a closer reading we cannot rightly speak of more than an appearance, more than a special emphasis on the ecclesiastical authority of these books, even in Lutheranism. Hollaz does not go further on this point than to say: *periculosum est, sine adiecta declaratione libros symbolicos humana scripta appellare*[EN229]. We can interpret this statement in *meliorem partem*[EN230]: it is indeed dangerous to call the dogma of the Church a human word, without adding that as the word of the fathers and brethren whom God has put before us in the Church it is to be read and received as an imperative and binding and authoritative witness to the Word of God. It would have been a fundamental abandonment of the Reformation if there had been any attempt to obscure or remove the line between the divine Word and the human. The only question we can put to Lutheranism in this connexion is whether in speaking so sacrally of "symbolic books," although it is not guilty of any theoretical error, it does not carry this emphasis too far with its strange fancies concerning the *Augustana*[EN231] and its noticeable magnifying of its own historical form generally? whether with all the undiminished theoretical support which it unquestionably gives to the Scripture principle it does not in practice exalt itself in its origin and normative form to the level of a second source of revelation, especially treating its confession (and the person of Luther) in this way? In so far as this is the case, it is also necessarily the case that in practice it has abandoned the Reformation and punished itself with the certain inflexibility and reserve towards new items of knowledge which inevitably results from such practice. We have to remember, of course, that we have here only a specifically Lutheran form of what in other forms has been the fault and fate of Protestantism as a whole.

If divine infallibility cannot be ascribed to any Church confession, then in practice we have to recognise that every Church confession can be regarded [659] only as a stage on a road which as such can be relativised and succeeded by a further stage in the form of an altered confession. Therefore respect for its authority has necessarily to be conjoined with a basic readiness to envisage a possible alteration of this kind.

Indirectly even the Roman Catholic Church has recognised this. It does not admit any perfectibility of dogma, but it does admit a perfectibility of the Church proclamation of dogma. And this is confirmed in its history and practice in which there are obviously dated and antiquated and corrected dogmas and also those which are new and obviously clearer and more definite.

But what is true of a change in the judgment of the Church regarding the extent of the Canon and the definition of fathers and brethren is also true of an alteration of the confession. We cannot regard the process as any easier or less responsible than that of drawing up the confession. It is not for any abstract reason, but recognising the Word of God in Holy Scripture, that we have now to speak as we do—and therefore differently from the fathers and brethren. There has to be an occasion important enough to justify as necessary

---

[EN228] special action of God
[EN229] it is dangerous to call the symbolic books human writings without further qualification
[EN230] charitably
[EN231] Augsburg Confession

the undertaking to speak differently from them. What we have to say on this occasion has to be so fresh and different from what they said that it will be worth disturbing the unity of faith to speak differently from them. In some recognisable and compelling way—decisive by reason of the inner weight of what is stated, in virtue of its agreement with Scripture—it has to be the Church which undertakes to speak in another way. Before the work goes forward, in addition to Holy Scripture all the voices of the now effective confession have to be seriously heard, so that nothing is lost of what it has perhaps to say, in spite of and in our new situation and task. Our own undertaking has then to prove its sincerity by its courage in laying it before the rest of the Church as a decision which we ourselves believe to be grounded in a divine decision, and therefore with the claim that a decision has to be made concerning it, and therefore without fear of a definite Yes or a definite No. And then a corresponding practical attitude has to accompany the altered confession from its inception as the indispensable means of its proclamation.

It must arise out of an ultimate human certainty and an ultimate human necessity. We have to speak of it, therefore, as Luther does in relation to the Articles of Schmalkald: "These are the Articles on which I will and must stand to my death, if God will, and I know not how to alter or yield ought that is therein. If any wish to concede ought, let him do so upon his own conscience"; and especially in relation to the doctrine of justification (at the beginning of part 2): "Of this article nought can be conceded or withdrawn, though heaven and earth fall and all that doth not endure: for there is none other name, whereby we must be saved, saith St. Peter in Ac. 4. And by His wounds we are healed. And on this article hangs all that we teach and live against the Pope, the devil and the world. Therefore we must be certain and not doubt. Otherwise all is lost, and the Pope and the devil and everything that is against us will conquer and prevail."

[660] We cannot have a new confession on any easier conditions than these—or with the omission of any one of them. If these conditions are present, we not only can but must venture a new confession. But we can also regard all these conditions as the presuppositions on which a new confession must be attempted and the problem of whether we can and ought ceases to be a problem. Attempted on these conditions, it will definitely create for itself authority and respect.

We can only close by asserting that since the Reformation and the time immediately after there has never been a new confession in the Protestant sphere (bracketing the latest developments, whose importance has still to be seen), although there has been no lack of revolutionary movements in this sphere. Neo-Protestantism in particular, which was sufficiently conscious of itself in relation to all prior development even including the Bible itself, has not produced a new confession. It has not had the confidence seriously and consistently to lay before the Church the challenge even of a confession of the non-confessionalism which it has taught and demanded, of a decision in favour of the lack of decision which alone can save. As is well known, it has never done more than obscure the old confession theologically and to some extent overthrow its canonical legality. The Unitarian Church in Hungary, Siebenbürgen and Poland is an exception which deserves honourable mention. But the question of Julius Kaftan, "Do we need a new dogma?" (1890), sounded strange, or at any rate impracticable. With many sighs and outcries the old dogma was maintained through every theological development, just as the old Canon was maintained in spite of all the criticism of it. And Neo-Protestantism never went beyond a compromise with the old dogma. Why? Presumably just because Neo-Protestantism could not fulfil the conditions of a new dogma, because it could not really claim Church authority for its dogmas and therefore with a right insight did not dare to claim it.

§ 21

FREEDOM IN THE CHURCH

A member of the Church claims direct, absolute and material freedom not for himself, but only for Scripture as the Word of God. But obedience to the free Word of God in Holy Scripture is subjectively conditioned by the fact that each individual who confesses his acceptance of the testimony of Scripture must be willing and prepared to undertake the responsibility for its interpretation and application. Freedom in the Church is limited as an indirect, relative and formal freedom by the freedom of Holy Scripture in which it is grounded.

1. THE FREEDOM OF THE WORD

To understand what it means that God has a Word for the Church, we must think of the freedom as well as of the authority of the Church. The Church, called and grounded in the Word of God, is a *communio sanctorum*^{EN1} not only in the sense that here men are gathered into a *communio*^{EN2} and as such are ruled and determined by the *sancta*^{EN3}, i.e., by the sanctuary of the evangelical faith set up in their midst, but—just because of this—in the further sense: that here men participate in this sanctuary, that it is therefore entrusted to their hands and committed to their keeping, that they themselves now become this *communio*^{EN4} of the *sancti*^{EN5} in virtue of the *communicatio*^{EN6} of *sancta*^{EN7} which takes place in this very *communio*^{EN8}, being called to be not hearers only, but also doers of the Word. Authority and respect for authority is only the objective side of the obedience that is demanded, created and implanted within the Church by the Word of God. Had we spoken only of authority, we should have spoken equivocally of the sovereignty of the God of Abraham, Isaac and Jacob, who is not a God of the dead but of the living. His authority is divinely majestic just because it has nothing in common with tyranny, because its true likeness is not the power of a natural catastrophe which annihilates all human response, but rather the power of an appeal, command and blessing

---

^{EN1} communion of saints
^{EN2} communion
^{EN3} holy things
^{EN4} communion
^{EN5} saints
^{EN6} communication
^{EN7} holy things
^{EN8} communication

which not only recognises human response but creates it. To obey it does not mean to be overrun by it, to be overwhelmed and eliminated in one's standing as a human being. Obedience to God is genuine precisely in that it is both spontaneous and receptive, that it not only is unconditional obedience but even as such is obedience from the heart. God's authority is truly recognised only within the sphere of freedom: only where conscience exists, where there [662] exists a sympathetic understanding of its lofty righteousness and a whole-hearted assent to its demands—only where a man allows himself to be humbled and raised up, comforted and warmed by its voice. Exactly the same is true of the various forms of ecclesiastical authority and the reverence due to them. If we refuse to see the equally necessary subjective side of obedience as freedom, or see it only as an incidental factor, if we evade the task of doing justice to this aspect of the problem as well as to the other, we have to consider whether we are not involved in a philosophico-political systematisation of theological insights which, though correct in themselves, are partial, and because they are so, ought not to be thus systematised as if they were a totality. Otherwise not only do they lose their character and power as theological truth, but in being thus presented as though they were the rounded whole of Christian knowledge, they hinder and disturb the recognition and victory of the truth by a one-sidedness which does not arise from the mystery of God but from the mystery of the arbitrary human will. They then produce reactions by which they are rightly affected in their philosophico-political systematisation, but which at the same time are usually found to injure the abbreviated and misused truth which they contain. The man who is merely mastered and compelled will certainly not be the man who is reached and born again by the Word of God; he will not be mastered and compelled as the Word of God masters and compels. He is mastered and compelled by powers of a very different sort, up to and including that of death. Yet there is not a single one of all these powers which so brings him under its authority as really to remove the possibility of his rebelling and therefore to make him truly obedient. He can still be like the Stoic overwhelmed by fate: *si fractus illabatur orbis, impavidum ferient ruinae*EN9. In the Church the Word of God works differently. Neither the divine authority governing the Church, nor valid authority within the Church, is exerted in the manner of these merely mastering and compelling powers. This is only possible through human misunderstanding and misuse. For this reason those reactions are superfluous in the Church because pointless. The man mastered and compelled is precisely the man whom God loves, who is therefore set upon his own feet and made truly responsible. To recognise and respect authority as a member of the Church means to love God in return and therefore to be willing and prepared to assume responsibility—real co-operative responsibility. The Christian is not a stone that is pushed, or a ball that is made to roll. The Christian is the man who through the Word and love

---

EN9 if the world shatters, and passes away, its ruins will strike me yet fearless

of God has been made alive, the real man, able to love God in return, standing erect just because he has been humbled, humbling himself because he has been raised up. Just because in the Church there is no mere mastery and compulsion, there is in it a real mastery and compulsion. Just because there is [663] authority in the Church, there is also freedom. This aspect of the problem also demands attention, and not merely cursory but serious attention.

There is reason to state all this with special emphasis to-day. The Evangelical Church and its theology, in all those countries where it is again beginning to be conscious of its task and mission, is calling to account and analysing the Neo-Protestantism or intermediate stage upon which it entered soon after the Reformation, to which it then almost completely succumbed. If appearances do not deceive, the last term of this development now lies behind us. It is no longer able to satisfy the essence and obligation of this Church and theology as seen from the standpoint of Scripture and the Reformation itself. In this process of analysis the rediscovery of the reality and concept of both divine and ecclesiastical authority is playing an important part at every point. That God is in heaven and man on the earth, that God rules and man must obey, that the Word of God makes a total claim upon men—we have had to learn anew to accustom ourselves again to these simple truths, in contradiction to a theological liberalism which would have nothing to do with them. But this new reference to the authority of God cannot be made without reference above all to its concrete manifestation in the authority of the ecclesiastical Canon, to the authority of the Reformation as something which gives a new basis to the Church, and to the authority of the confession as the documentary form of this new basis. And now of all times all this cannot be formulated or reformulated without exciting to more passionate opposition than ever the same theological liberalism against which, in fact, it must be said. But from the beginning, and to-day more than ever, this theological process of reconstruction is heavily burdened and compromised by the fact that at the same time we are in the middle of a period of philosophico-political reconstruction where similarly authority and freedom are at stake or seem to be so. Apart from the question of divine and ecclesiastical authority, in the world outside the great attempt has been made to oppose to the absolutism of an ostensibly autonomous reason, and therewith to the absolutism of the individual and humanity, the absolutism of a state authority which claims to control men singly and collectively in body and soul, and the basis and justification of which are supposed to have been discovered newly and very impressively in the idea of race. Authority has thus become a favourite secular term, while at the same time liberalism has degenerated into a term of secular abuse. A worse disturbance of the task of ecclesiastical and theological reconstruction to which we have referred can hardly be imagined. How can the life of the Church be more gravely upset than by such an *alter ego*EN10 (in this connexion we may think of the story of Pharaoh's magicians) doing apparently what it does with a parallelism which extends even to details? At an earlier time the Reformation must have been similarly disturbed by the fact that simultaneously and side by side with it there was a movement of renaissance humanism waging war against mediaeval culture; a powerful striving for independence on the part of nationalist monarchies, princes and cities against the imperial power; a rising of the peasantry against their feudal overlords; a general attempt to seize ecclesiastical property. How many alive at that time may have understood the Reformation primarily from the standpoint of one of these contemporary movements? How easy it was to affirm and support it from the standpoint of one of these secular movements and in that way to bring strange fire to its altar! How easy, on the other hand, where a man was opposed to any of these secular movements, to reject and fight against the Reforma-

---

EN10 second identity

tion because of its association with them! So to-day we must expect the theological and ecclesiastical revival to be viewed in connexion with the nationalist-authoritarian movement, to be derived from the latter in its motives or, the other way round, to be regarded as the religious source of its inspiration, or to be traced back with it to a common root. And obviously it is equally fatal to it whether it is affirmed and supported or refused and opposed by reason of this association. Every word that can and must be spoken in the Church and theology on behalf of true authority and against the abuse of freedom can obviously be both intended and understood in an utterly false sense when brought even into the remotest connexion with the parallel slogans of the contemporary movement. Of course, these parallelisms between Church history and world history are never the result of chance. The Church and the world stand so close together that it is no wonder if events in the Church are always accompanied, whether secretly or openly, by shadows and copies in the events of world history. But it is in the sovereign power of God's wisdom and might that the Church and the world thus belong to each other, and that by the appearance of this parallelism we are reminded of this interdependence and thereby of Himself. If we believe in the providence of God, this cannot mean that we are to think of ourselves as occupying a point of view from which we can systematically perceive and master this interdependence and also this parallelism. Belief in divine providence means rather that we shall not justify and legitimate the way, which the Church must follow in obedience to its mission and to the Word of God, by reference to the ways which we see the world follow. And again, we shall not try to justify and legitimate the course of world-history, about whose meaning and goal we can at most have only suppositions, by reference to the ways of the Church. It is just the obvious system of thought, the obvious connexion between these two apparently parallel things, which constitutes the danger that must be recognised as such and avoided. If it is not recognised and avoided in this way, the Church becomes involved in exertions, antitheses and consequences, to which precisely because its message is intended for the whole world, it ought to stand opposed and superior. Then it loses its authenticity; for in the very fact that it does not recognise and avoid this danger, but attends to the affairs of others instead of holding fast to its mission and the Word of God, it has shown failure to stand in that obedience which demanded from it nothing but fidelity to its own course. If I am not mistaken, this fidelity to the Church's own path was at the basis of Luther's attitude in the Peasants' War. Yet in other respects neither he nor the other Reformers always recognised and avoided clearly enough this threatening danger. And to the extent in which this did not happen, it turned speedily enough to the ill of the Reformation Church. Therefore we have every reason to make to-day the uncompromising assertion: Whatever in the divine counsels may be the connexion between the process of reconstruction now going on in the Church and theology concerning authority and freedom, and that other crisis which impressively enough is now proceeding in the realm of politics and philosophy—we cannot and must not interpret either by the other. In the present connexion, this means in practice that, when we are concerned to re-establish the authority of God and of the Church, we will have nothing to do with the current proclamation of a secular authoritarianism. We expect as little from it as we should from a new proclamation of a secular liberalism. We are most certainly grateful for all the approval and assistance which may come to us from this source. But we will make no use at all of the arguments and the emotions which it may lend us. Nor, on the other hand, do we have any cause to take part in those secular exertions from the Church point of view, or to offer ecclesiastical arguments and emotions as weapons in that conflict. When the authoritarian state-philosophy of to-day feels that it must fight against the enemy of the human race which it finds in the spirit of 1789 and 1848 and in Marxism, it may or may not be right. But in any case the opposition in which the Gospel finds itself to a false doctrine of freedom is

[664]

213

not this opposition. On the contrary, there can be no question that this modern state philosophy will itself be affected by the opposition of the Gospel. With all its authoritarianism it, too, belongs to the doctrine of freedom against which the Gospel is struggling. In just the same way, the idealism of yesterday made itself responsible for what, from the standpoint of the Gospel, is to be opposed as tyranny. We shall find that the Church in its behaviour and discourse before the world must interest itself in that idea of freedom which is now oppressed and persecuted in the worldly sphere, and protect the relative justification of its demands; not for the sake of freedom in itself, nor because the Gospel is interchangeable with a metaphysic of freedom, but rather that, in the compromising proximity in which it finds itself, it cannot be made interchangeable with a metaphysic of authority. In the period of liberalism the Church quite rightly did not become simply liberal. In spite of quite regrettable concessions to the spirit of the age, and much against its own will, it remained under constant attack from the liberal world as the refuge of the idea of authority. Similarly to-day it does not merely go along with the spirit of the day, nor does it neglect to become the asylum of the truth which to-day is on the losing side—and that is the truth of the idea of freedom. The power and authenticity of its struggle against a philosophy of pseudo-freedom depend wholly upon its refusal to take part in the secular attack on secular liberalism, upon its not being affected by the relatively justifiable criticisms with which liberalism opposes authoritarianism, and, in so far as it has to address itself to a world locked in party conflicts, upon its throwing a compensating counterpoise into the scales in favour of freedom so that justice is done. Its own struggle is too serious and bitter for it to wage except, legitimately, with unburdened back, and good conscience. This legitimacy, unburdened back and good conscience are conditioned by its holding itself "unspotted from the world" even while it keeps an open and attentive mind for what is going on in the world, that is, by its refusing to become a partisan and maintaining the superiority of the Gospel over against all worldly conflicts. For these reasons its own fight against Neo-Protestantism cannot and must not on any account be fought in a common front "on behalf of authority." To be legitimate, it must not be waged at all as a one-sided struggle "on behalf of authority." The Reformation was everywhere spiritually lost and ineffective, becoming a mild or extreme fanaticism, where it turned to its own profit and advantage the general opposition to the Papacy, Scholasticism and mediaevalism, or where it understood and presented itself one-sidedly within the terms of this opposition. Similarly, to-day, we at once weaken ourselves spiritually if we go so much as a finger's-breadth with contemporary authoritarianism, or even advance with it only along the line on which we seem to run parallel with it. It is, therefore, of supreme importance to pay attention to the other aspect of our problem, that there is freedom in the Church as well as authority. If we refuse to see this, how can we recognise and avoid the great danger presented to us by our environment to-day? How can we be free from the suspicion of serving the new spirit of the age more than the Holy Ghost? How can we be trustworthy? Let it be clearly understood: we must not pay attention to this side of the problem in order to be trustworthy. This attention is required by the nature of our objective. It is required supremely by the fact that God's revelation is revelation in the Word and also by the Spirit. "In the Word" certainly implies that the Church and theology cannot be made over to a subjectivist system. "In the Word" undoubtedly means authority in the Church. But just as certainly "by the Spirit" implies the impossibility of an objectivist system. The other side must be observed: freedom in the Church. Taking God's Word and therefore God's revelation as the point of departure, we find ourselves in fact on the other side of these antitheses. We can no longer play off freedom against authority or authority against freedom. We are not to be concerned about either the one or the other of these two principles as such, but in both only about the will of God. Therefore we must always be prepared to oppose divine authority to every human idea of freedom, and equally prepared to restrict every human idea of authority by reference to the freedom of God. We are, then, compelled by a real and not merely a [666] tactical necessity to make this second affirmation. But it may be useful to us to remember that in the present-day situation (for the sake of the trustworthiness of the Church and its message) it is also tactically necessary to be relevant and therefore actually to make this second affirmation.

That there is also freedom in the Church must be taken seriously because here, too, in this aspect of the matter, it is clearly a question of the totality. To the question: How does God's Word come to us men in Holy Scripture and how does it exercise sway in the Church of Jesus Christ? we give this second answer, that it happens through free obedience. In making such a statement we say fully what is to be said to that question. Just as God in His revelation is the Holy Spirit no less than the Son, so God's Word in Scripture is Spirit no less than Word. And we err no less in refusing to appreciate its freedom than if its authority remains hidden from us. The real relationship is this. As the Son can be revealed only by the Spirit, and in the Spirit only the Son is revealed, so authority must necessarily be interpreted by freedom, and freedom by authority. In the Church neither authority nor freedom can claim to be a principle of ultimate validity and power. In the Church both can be understood and considered only as predicates of God's Word, and therefore in the light of this which is their proper subject, and therefore only in the light which they cast upon each other.

This must be particularly remembered in the polemical use of these ideas. It is a temptation, too great a temptation, to say that in the reference to freedom we have the specifically Protestant answer to that question, in direct opposition to Catholicism. We can only issue a warning against this idea. It will fare ill with the Protestant Church if it is more protestant to speak of freedom than of authority, if the demagogic notion is true that in the last resort the aim of the Reformers was to enthrone the reason and conscience of the individual as opposed to the authority and judgment of the Church, that they were, therefore, the forerunners of Pietism, the Enlightenment and Idealism. It is true that, confronted by an authority that was no longer a real, divine or genuinely ecclesiastical authority, they proclaimed the freedom of the Christian man as a free lord of all things and subject to no one. But how can one fail to see that by this very proclamation they were, in fact, fighting on precisely the opposite front? As though Luther did not see in the enthusiasm of his time, to which all the later forms of liberalism are traceable, the same enemy as in the Papacy! How can we fail to observe that, according to Luther, the same Christian man is the slave of all things and subject to everyone? As though Calvin did not do more for the recognition of the authority of God and the Church than all the mediaeval popes and Scholastics put together! The Church of the Reformation, provided it does not allow itself to be confused by that demagogic apologetic, need not wait to be reminded by Roman Catholic polemical writers that through an ill-considered affirmation of the principle of freedom it will inevitably fall into heresy and become a sect. Neither in origin nor in essence is it in any way involved in the impasse in which the free individual is suddenly to be the measure of all things. To go no further, how can this optimism be combined with the Reformers' insight into the wretchedness of man, and his incapacity to know God and to do the good? This part of Reformation theology has had to be prudently erased for the Reformers to be represented and extolled as the fathers of the modern aspirations after freedom. Still more fundamentally, the Evangel- [667] ical view of the unique glory and saving power of the divine Word excludes the possibility of attaching to Protestantism even the intention or preparation of those aspirations after freedom. By all means let Catholicism fight for authority against freedom in its opposition to all kinds of other heresies. But in opposition to Catholicism itself we do not have to espouse first the cause of freedom, but of authority, and only then and from that standpoint freedom. For with its doctrine of the unity of the Church and revelation (together with its doctrine of nature and grace), it has attributed to man a freedom and capacity side by side with God and over God. So, then, it has really given birth to all the other heresies—however hostile it may be to them. It has made them necessary as opponents on its own level. It has destroyed the recognition of the authority of God, and in so doing—in spite of clericalism—it has destroyed that of a genuine ecclesiastical authority. That is our decisive charge against it. It is also true that with this destruction of authority it has also destroyed the freedom of the mind and conscience, the necessary freedom offered to the individual member of the Church. But how can this be understood and seriously maintained if it is not perceived and maintained first that Roman Catholicism is rebellion against the authority of the Word of God, rebellion against canonical Scripture, rebellion against the fathers too, and against every genuine confession? When at the Reformation the Word of God re-established its rule in the tottering Church, "Catholicism" refused to obey it, and continued to destroy the Church; not by knowing too much, but by knowing too little about authority, by making new opportunities and new forms for the arbitrary freedom of man to manipulate the Word of God according to its convenience. Therefore the Evangelical Church must not take its stand where according to Roman Catholic theory it ought to be, especially when it has to represent true evangelical freedom over against that theory. It must not define this *libertas Christiana*[EN11] as the inner independence of the soul which is bound immediately and exclusively to God, as though it did not realise how short a step it is from this independence to its counterpart in the form of papal infallibility. But it must define freedom, as it in truth is, as man's real dependence on the God who has mediately addressed and dealt with us. It must define freedom as the faithfulness with which we can and should trace the divine testimonies. It must define it as a cleaving to canonical Scripture, to the fathers and to the confession, and therefore to ecclesiastical authority. It must define it as the unique proud independence which as real submission to real authority is attributed to every individual member of the Church, or rather is conferred by the Holy Spirit of the Word of God. It is only in this way, that is, by a complete reversal of the front on which Catholicism would like to see us stand and where modern heresies would like to push us, that the strong and clear contrast between it and us can be made manifest, as is needful and also hopeful. Again, this must be done in the interests of the truth itself. But again, we must not fail to recognise that Roman Catholicism can listen to us, that a renewal of conversation between us, and at least a common outlook upon the *una sancta catholica*[EN12] can be achieved, only when it sees that in regard to the recognition and assertion of authority we are not inferior to it but rather superior, that with the proclamation of evangelical freedom we do not aim at a worse but at a better obedience.

The converse is true on the opposite front against Neo-Protestantism. Here the temptation on our side is to commit ourselves to the idea and reality of authority. And, again, a warning is in place. It is true and has already been said that from this angle it is in fact a question of authority: the authority of God, of the Bible and of the confession. It was so already in the struggle of the Reformers against the fanatics and humanists who were the fathers of Neo-Protestantism. But on this side, too, we cannot overlook the fact that for the

---

EN11 Christian liberty
EN12 one holy catholic (Church)

Reformers this enemy on the left stood very close to that on the right, that is, to the Papacy. [668] They reproached the former no less than the latter with legalism, monkery and the enslavement of conscience, in spite of all their appeals to the Spirit, conscience or immediate revelation. They were right to do so. They were right to oppose to its message of freedom an authority which it rejected, and to oppose it in the shape of the true message of freedom which it was really rejecting. For what did Erasmus or Carlstadt or later Servetus or Sebastian Franck know of the real freedom of a Christian man? What has the tragic seriousness with which we see all these figures take themselves, what has the portentousness with which in all later Neo-Protestantism man regards the inmost depths of his being and his experience as final reality and highest law—what has all this to do with the real evangelical freedom of the children of God? Has not Calvin himself with his inexorable proclamation of authority done more for the cause of freedom than all the forerunners of modern ideas who flourished in his day? When the Reformation Church rightly understands itself, it need not wait to be reminded by Neo-Protestantism that there is perhaps an ill-considered assertion of the idea of authority, by which the Church itself will necessarily become the victim of heresy and degenerate into a sect. Neither the origin nor the essence of the Church is to be found in the blind alley where man would like to be his own lord and law. An absolute principle of authority and an absolute principle of freedom both derive, do they not, from one and the same root, namely, an optimism which is impossible where the thought and effort of the human heart are recognised to be evil from youth upwards, and the sovereign power of the divine Word is discerned and recognised? With just such an absolute and therefore false principle of authority the Reformers reproached not merely the enemy on the right but also the enemy on the left—that is, the fathers of Neo-Protestantism. This adversary of the left may, then, be allowed to continue to fight for freedom against authority. But he must not be allowed to dictate our own attitude. In his case, too, it is safer and more hopeful if we espouse the cause of which he regards himself as champion. However blatantly and energetically he seems to maintain the cause of freedom, it is not in fact true that with him this cause is in good hands. Is there a worse threat to freedom itself than the establishment of man as his own lord and lawgiver? Who can exercise a worse tyranny over us than the god in our own breast? And what further tyrannies does not this first and decisive one drag in its train? It is inevitable that the man who claims to be directly in communion with God, and free from all concrete forms of authority, will all the more certainly be delivered over to the powers of nature and history, to the spirit of the age and of contemporary movements, to the demons of his situation and environment. If you wish to see man enslaved, you have only to free him in the manner in which Erasmus and Carlstadt once wished to see him free. If you wish to awake in him a wild longing for at least an appearance of order and authority, if you want to make him ripe for conversion, then bring him up in the kind of freedom which Neo-Protestantism preaches. Catholic authoritarianism is the inevitable counterpart of this freedom. And that is just the complaint which is to be made from this point of view. Here we are on ground where, as there is no genuine authority, so there is no genuine freedom. There is only action and reaction between a despotic arrogance and an equally despotic despair. We have here the disobedience which wished to evade the reformation of the Church by the Word of God, and does evade it, only to succumb all the more surely to the slavery which, outside the dominion of the Word of God, is in one form or another unavoidable. And therefore we oppose to Neo-Protestantism the very thing which it claims to have and which in reality it does not have, namely, freedom in the Church. Certainly, authority in the Church. Certainly God and the Bible and the Creed. But note well: all this gains validity, not as one of the inventions of the human mind which Neo-Protestantism knows only too well in its own sphere and which it will receive only with obduracy, but as the power which, unlike [669] the powers which man sets up over himself, does not lead him from one tyranny to another, but at last puts him on his own feet, and lifts him into an air in which he can breathe. Therefore, we must not please modern Protestantism by placing ourselves in the position where its own slogans aim at putting us. In face of it—and again the front is completely reversed—the message of the freedom of the Christian man, which it has so astonishingly misconceived, is the victorious truth. Here, too, we do not have to do it in the interests of any sort of strategy, but in the interests of the truth itself. Here, too, we can hardly expect a hearing and discussion and the hope of agreement, until it is clear that the accusation is not of too much but of too little freedom, and that in the representation of its own cause, it is not being underbidden but overbidden.

We have to discuss the question of freedom in the Church, which primarily and properly means the freedom of the Word of God. We have to show that there is not only authority but also freedom in the Church, that there is not only authority but also freedom under the Word. We have to show that this is a genuine freedom which comes to man in the Church, which is not merely allowed him, but conferred upon him, which is not merely permitted but commanded, which is not fortuitous but necessary. This being the case, we obviously have to understand freedom primarily and essentially in concrete terms, that is, as the freedom of the Word of God. Only as such is it truly freedom, immediate, absolute and meaningful. By it the freedom assigned to us men in the Church is established. As human freedom, it is genuine just because it is limited by the former as an indirect, relative and formal freedom. Human freedom, like human authority, means nothing if the Word of God is not primary and basic, containing and exercising both authority and freedom in itself. Because the Word of God has and exercises freedom in itself, for this reason and on this ground, where it is heeded, that is, in the Church where like evokes like, there is also a human freedom. Since this human freedom is thus evoked, it will neither evade the freedom of the Word, nor degenerate into freedom apart from the Word or without the Word or in contradiction to the Word. It can be freedom only under the Word. Again, it is as such, and only as such, that it will be a genuine human freedom.

When we speak of freedom in the Church, in the first instance we mean generally that in the Church, without prejudice to its authority, that is, order, normativeness, guidance and direction, there is also man's own choice and decision, his own determination and resolve. Since the Church consists of men, there is freedom in the Church. Where there is no choice and decision, no determination and resolve, there are no men. Even when we presuppose at once that this freedom can primarily and properly be only the freedom of the Word of God, in view of this primary and proper meaning of the idea, we must first think generally of men in the Church. It is in them and for them that the Word of God has its freedom, although their human freedom is certainly to be distinguished from the freedom of the Word of God itself. We are not speaking, of course, of the eternal Logos as such, but concretely of the Word made flesh which is believed and attested by men. Where men thus believe and attest

[670]

the Word of God, they are not merely subjected and obedient to it, but because they are so, they participate in its freedom.

In thinking of these men in the Church, we think chiefly of the apostles and prophets themselves. They certainly belong—and indeed as the oldest and first—to the succession of men who have believed and attested the Word of God, and thus, by becoming subject and obedient to it, they have gained a share in its freedom. As apostles and prophets they do not only stand in a succession with all the other men of whom the same may in general be said. As prophets and apostles they stand over against this succession with their word which is the Word of Holy Scripture. To this extent they are also bearers of the Word of God itself, with the direct, absolute and material freedom which is proper to it. But how can they become intelligible to us, if they do not also and as such stand in the succession in which we also may stand as members of the Church founded upon their word, which is the Word of Holy Scripture? Even in the indirect, relative and formal freedom which is proper to their faith and witness also, it must become clear to us that not only this kind of freedom is characteristic of their word, which is the Word of Holy Scripture; the direct, absolute and material freedom of the Word of God must also become clear to us. Otherwise they will not be intelligible to us. Therefore we affirm first of all that the relationship of the prophets and apostles to Jesus Christ, since it has the character of obedience, has also the character of choice and decision. Not a choice and decision of such a kind that in it these men can have control, or by it they can gain control, over that which they chose and for which they decided. This is excluded by the fact that Jesus Christ, the Lord, confronted them, and that they stood to Him in a relation of obedience which could not be reversed. But while there was no reversal in this relation, it was still a relation in which Jesus Christ had in these men something real to confront, in which they really responded to Him, in which, in so far as they gave Him their faith and witness, He was chosen by them, and in which they made a decision for Him. Even obedience is choice and decision, although it is essentially a choice and decision in which the obedient man surrenders his own power to Him whom he obeys. Thus even obedience is freedom. In this sense, the freedom no less than the obedience of the prophets and apostles stands at the beginning of the Church: the freedom which became actual only in the obligations of obedience, only on the basis of the transcendent freedom of Jesus Christ, but still the freedom. There cannot be a Church of Jesus Christ apart from a repetition of this freedom. The existence of Jesus Christ stands or falls [671] by the fact that Jesus Christ makes of such men something real to confront— men who respond to Him in that they choose Him as He has chosen them, who decide for Him as He has decided for them, disciples who follow Him because they are called by Him.

But we must go on to affirm that, even interpreted as freedom, the relationship between prophets and apostles and their Lord is a unique relationship— as unique as revelation itself at the centre of the ages. Therefore, although the continued life of the Church is not possible without a repetition of this free-dom, it does not mean a continual succession of prophets and apostles. In the directness of their encounter with Jesus Christ, it is impossible for the disciples of Jesus to have real successors, or for that freedom to be repeatable. Again, everything depends on whether the unique revelation of God in Jesus Christ and the prophetic-apostolic encounter with Him in its uniqueness is futile, or whether the promise: Ye shall be my witnesses, and: Lo, I am with you always, is true and has been fulfilled. If it is true and has been fulfilled, then in the freedom of their faith and witness the prophets and apostles are copies attest-ing the freedom of Jesus Christ Himself, but at the same time they are proto-types attesting the freedom of all human faith and witness in the Church founded by their Word. In their freedom, the Church must recognise and hon-our the freedom of their Lord in which the freedom of its members, as mem-bers of His body, is grounded. From this point of view also the Church cannot ignore Scripture. Scripture cannot be truly authoritative for it, unless, because it is its authority, it shares in its freedom, that is, in that choice and decision in which the prophets and apostles, on the ground of the choice and decision which befell them, became and were prophets and apostles. Scripture rules within the Church and its members only if they—the Church and those within the Church—share in the movement in which Scripture was born and in virtue of which even to-day Scripture is not mere writing but in its written character is Spirit and life. This is true especially in the narrower sense of these ideas in which they denote the movement of faith and witness in which under the guid-ance of the Holy Ghost the biblical Word became possible, and was effected and declared not only to bind, but both to bind and also to free. Scripture is a document which does not spring only from obedience as such, but from the obedience of prophets and apostles discharged in this movement. And if that promise is true and fulfilled, the movement is not now dormant and petrified in this document; rather, in that movement fulfilled in obedience, this docu-ment exists as witness to revelation. The Church comes into existence in genu-ine submission to this authority, but it cannot allow the revelation attested by Scripture to flow over itself as a waterfall flows over a cliff. Rather, because God's revelation is attested by Scripture and because Scripture furnishes the [672] documentary evidence of this movement of revelation and exists only within it, the Church for its part must allow itself to be set in movement through Scripture.

Luther has called Scripture master and judge. "Holy Scripture and the Word of God ought to be regarded as an empress, whom one should immediately follow, obeying what she com-mands" (*W.A. Ti.* 1, 186, 20) ... "it is truly the spiritual body of Christ" (*Grund und Ursach aller Artikel,* 1521, *W.A.* 7, 315, 24). It is certainly not a merely metaphorical but a literal meaning that is intended when these expressions attribute to Scripture an independent and even personal life of its own in the exercise of its functions with regard to the Church.

If we have to speak of freedom as well as of authority in the Church, there can be no question of setting up a second principle beside Holy Scripture, or of demanding a hearing for a second voice beside that of Holy Scripture. On the contrary, Holy Scripture alone has to be heard in the Church. Therefore it must be heard as the principle and voice of both authority and freedom. For it has both aspects unseparated and inseparably. It has authority as the Word of God, and freedom as man's witness to God's Word—a freedom which does not originate from below, that is, from the humanity of the biblical witnesses, but like authority from above, that is, from the divine Word by which these men were roused to faith and witness. Because they were to testify to God's Word, they were endowed and equipped with authority. Because they were to do this as men, they were endowed and equipped with freedom. And so their testimony in Holy Scripture—because it is the testimony of God's Word—meets us with the claim to be heard and accepted as authentic. But this authenticity is not that of a rigid prescription inscribed, as it were, on a stone tablet, which the Church and its members have to read off mechanically and translate into their own mode of thought and speech. It is a living authenticity; for Scripture itself is a really truly living, acting and speaking subject which only as such can be truly heard and received by the Church and in the Church. In Scripture we have to see the motivation in which prophets and apostles believed and witnessed. We have to understand this motivation as the life and operation of the Word of God Himself. We have to yield to and follow this motivation of the Word of God which takes place in Scripture. We have to be stirred up and to stir up ourselves by it in our own faith and witness. This is the problem we have to see side by side with that of the authority of Scripture, not as a distinct problem, but as the problem of the concrete understanding of this authority. It is, therefore, really a question of the freedom of the Word, and only then and on this basis, and in the interests of the Word itself, a question of human freedom in the Church—the freedom under the Word which is demanded and at the same time created and bestowed by the Word. The freedom of the Word cannot imply any limitation of the authority of the Word. On the contrary, we have obviously failed to understand its authority, and therefore its [673] loftiness, dignity, value, validity and power, and we are not honouring it as it ought to be honoured, if we do not understand and honour it as the effectual working of Scripture as the present living Word of God in accordance with His true and fulfilled promise, i.e., as a deciding, willing, guiding, governing, determining action talking place in the Church, whose concrete subject is precisely Scripture itself. Thus the superiority of Scripture over against the Church is not the idolatrous calm of icy mountain peaks towering motionlessly above a blossoming valley. The argument of life cannot be played off against the authority of Scripture. Nor can the latter be questioned and assailed in the name of a struggle for the spirit as opposed to the letter. The reason for this is that Scripture is itself spirit and life in the comprehensive and profound sense of these ideas—the Spirit and life of the living God Himself, who draws near to us in its faith and witness, who need not wait until spirit and life are subsequently breathed into the document of His revelation in virtue of the acceptance it finds in the Church or the insight, sympathy, and congeniality which its readers bring to it, but who with His own Spirit and life always anticipates the reactions of all its readers, who in this book really exercises that government in the Church which human church government can only follow by interpreting and applying His Word, by recognising the mighty acts done by Him, by preaching the truth He proclaims, by serving His revealed will. The true freedom of man in the Church, freedom under the Word, consists in this following of the God who at all times precedes us all in Holy Scripture, and in adherence to the action which He takes by Scripture. It will be our next task to illustrate and explain the freedom of the Word itself and as such.

1. The freedom of the Word of God and therefore of Holy Scripture consists primarily in the simple fact that, in contrast to all other elements in the life of the Church and the world, as a direct witness to the revelation of God in Jesus Christ, it has a theme of ineffaceable distinctiveness and uniqueness. This theme—because it has been given to it by God Himself, and because its witnesses are God's own witnesses—constitutes Scripture as a subject which distinguishes itself from all other subjects, and has its own position and activity in relation to them.

At this point we can and must think at once of Mt. 16^{16-19}: It was in the ineffaceable but representative singularity of his existence as this man that Peter uttered his confession of the Lord's Messiahship which is the alpha and omega of all biblical testimony. How did he arrive at this? He did not arrive at it—flesh and blood did not reveal it to him—but he is extolled as blessed because the confession which he makes was imparted to him by direct revelation, by Jesus' Father in heaven. As the one so blessed, he now receives the promise: "Upon this rock I will build my church." In his singularity as the man Peter which as such is representative of the attitude and function of all who bear witness to direct revelation, he thus becomes a subject distinct from both Jesus Christ and His Church, but mediating between them. He attains independence and a function of his own. This function is obviously the one which he

[674]   has already exercised in his confession (anticipating, so to speak, the content of the promise). Note how here, distinctively reversed, all the important elements appear: God's revelation, a concrete man, his institution to the ministry of the revelation, his function in that ministry. Note, too, how closely the latter two elements of institution and function are connected with and dependent on the first, God's revelation. An analogous situation occurs in the case of Paul. He is not called by man (Gal. 1^1). He is not naturally fitted to be an apostle (nor can one say of Peter that he was fitted to be that rock). But by the grace of God he is what he is (1 Cor. 15^{10}). Jesus Christ Himself has made him so. The God who raised Jesus Christ from the dead (Gal. 1^1) also separated Paul from his mother's womb, when it pleased Him to reveal His Son in him, that he might preach Him among the heathen (Gal. 1^{15-16}). This grace has sufficed him (2 Cor. 12^9). This grace was not given him in vain (1 Cor. 15^{10}). Christ is the One who is alive in him (Gal. 2^{20}) and at work in him (Phil. 4^{13}). This grace and this Christ are the content of his apostolate. According to all his Epistles, Paul cannot be an apostle, or exercise his apostolate, without continually remembering how he has arrived at it, or rather how the apostolate has come to him from Jesus Christ, as "the grace given to him" (1 Cor. 3^{10}). Therefore it is by his theme that the apostle, like Holy Scripture, is constituted a distinctive subject, differing from and contrasting with all others. It must be under-

stood that in this connexion it is meaningless to emphasise that in Holy Scripture there are, of course, many human subjects. This is true; but it is more important to realise that in virtue of the unity of their theme the many human subjects of Scripture are visible and operative both to themselves and others as a single subject—of his fulness have we all received (Jn. 1 [16]).

Therefore, to recognise the freedom of God's Word means primarily to recognise the subject created by God's revelation, the biblical witness. This subject meets us in the most varied forms as a single and unique being who requires to be heard in a single and unitary way. It is a human being. *In concreto* [EN13] it is always an individual man, a Peter or Paul. But even as a human being it is determined and characterised by the one thing which is said to it and which it has to say. The freedom of God's Word is to be recognised especially in the fact that this subject as such appears and remains ineffaceably and unforgettably before us.

2. The next and really decisive insight may be comprehensively defined as the insight into the peculiar power of this subject in its opposition and relation to all other subjects. Freedom means ability, possibility, power—power in its illimitability or its equality over against other powers. It is such power that the subject has which we find constituted by the theme of Holy Scripture—by God's revelation in Jesus Christ. Because it is the subject constituted by this theme, it has the power of the Word of God.

Let us immediately explain that this power is not to be understood as the power of the religious, cultic, ethical, aesthetical, theological daemonism which is no doubt naturally proper to the individual biblical subjects and to the biblical subject as a whole, in its humanity—the distinctive characteristic humanity determined by its theme. Both in the Old Testament and the New Testament there is a magic of biblical thought and language, of biblical perspicuity and argumentation, to which we must not on any account remain insensible, but which we can and must allow to have its due effect. As the essential pre-requisite for a biblical [675] exegesis which does not remain confined to grammatical-historical matters, there is needed an intuition, an ability to detect the daemonic magic of the Bible. But we must not forget that this is still not the power and freedom of the divine Word, however inseparable it may be from its human manifestation, and however important it may be not to overlook this factor. Mt. 11 [9] is relevant here: "What went ye out for to see? A prophet? Yea, I say unto you, and more than a prophet." Likewise the warning of John the Baptist, Jn. 5 [35]: "He was a burning and a shining light: and ye were willing for a season to rejoice in his light." We may add the warning of Paul in regard to himself, 1 Cor. 2 [1]: he has come to them οὐ καθ' ὑπεροχὴν λόγου ἢ σοφίας [EN14], but to announce the testimony of God. Daemonism and magic as such constitute a power which is, of course, characteristic of Scripture, but which at bottom it has in common with other writings, and which, therefore, does not basically distinguish this subject from others. To feel this power is still not to recognise the freedom of God's Word. This freedom is not recognised, and the daemonic magic of Holy Scripture is not correctly appraised, until in these evidences of its human and therefore not unique power (we need not be ascetic and narrow in this respect) the power of the theme, that is of God's revelation in Jesus Christ, is recognised. If the full potency imparted to the biblical testimony by its

---

[EN13] concretely
[EN14] not with excellence of speech or wisdom

theme is not to be missed, if a truly inspiring and uplifting power, majesty and profundity characterise it, if it is truly "spirit," even in the human sense of all these notions, then this mighty power is governed by the law: "Without me ye can do nothing" (Jn. 15⁵), and by the confession of Paul in 2 Cor. 3⁵ᶠ·: "Not that we are sufficient of ourselves to think anything as of ourselves; but our sufficiency is of God; who also hath made (ἱκάνωσεν) us able ministers of the new testament." Everything depends on the recognition of this ἱκανοῦν EN15, whereas if we interpret, appreciate and defend the Bible from the standpoint of its immanent human qualities regarded *in abstracto* EN16, we necessarily remain on a level on which the characteristic power of this subject cannot be unequivocally displayed, and on which it can be rivalled if not surpassed by similar powers.

We are concerned with the power of the Word of God, but, of course, the power of the Word made flesh, believed and attested by men. Therefore not even *in abstracto* EN17 with the power which the Word of God has in itself, in its glory as the eternal Logos of the Father, where no powers exist beside it, where it simply is the Lord above and utterly beyond all powers. No, our concern is with the Word of God in the humiliation of its majesty, the Word of God in the world where there are powers beside and against it, where it stands until the end of time confronting and opposing these other powers. Many other heavenly and earthly levers will constantly be effective and operative in the sphere of our human world and existence. There seems to be much power and freedom there. Recognition of the freedom of the divine Word will consist chiefly in the simple but not self-explanatory realisation that, in the midst of all other subjects, this subject which is Holy Scripture has, in fact, a real and therefore a concretely limiting and competing power. The Word of God did not remain content with its eternal and in eternity unassailed and unassailable power over all things. It has entered the terrible dialectic of these things. It has become a subject among others. Amongst other things this means that these other subjects are not now left to themselves. They do not have to reckon only with [676] themselves, but also with this new subject, Holy Scripture, by which they are really confronted.

We are reminded of Jer. 23²⁸ᶠ· where the Word of Yahweh is set over against the prophets who have dreams to tell, and it is compared to a fire and a hammer that breaks in pieces the rocks. Also Heb. 4¹²ᶠ·, where it is said of God's Word that it is living and powerful, sharper than any two-edged sword, critically piercing the entire and most hidden existence of man, "neither is there any creature that is not manifest in his sight: but all things are naked and opened unto the eyes of him." "With whom we have to do," the author expressly adds. The opposite of this Word is obviously an imagined Word of God, but, however well and truly imagined, as a mere dream it remains outside the real world and existence of man, leaving the other subjects in the sphere of our world and existence unmolested, but also unillumined and unconsoled in the depths of their creaturely existence. But now God has become man, and therefore Himself a creaturely being, in His Son, and in this human world of ours His Son lives on in the form of His instruments and their witness. So His power in this

---

EN15 making
EN16 in the abstract
EN17 in the abstract

testimony is also a concrete power at the heart of this sphere, consoling and healing, but also judging and assailing. Therefore no matter how vivid and lifelike it may be, that imagined word which remains aloof is not as such the true Word of God. In all circumstances we must conceive the real Word of God as one among the many subjects which have freedom and power in the same way as others do in this sphere.

But the new subject which in Holy Scripture confronts other subjects—and this is how we must at once characterise its power—involves a radical compromising of the power of all other subjects. We cannot say more. It does not mean their suspension in the sense of destruction. It is not that other powers do not continue really to confront the power of Holy Scripture. It is not that there does not have to be constant opposition and conflict. In God's revelation as such, in the death and resurrection of Jesus Christ, that suspension and destruction have, of course, been completed, and completed once for all. Our age, however, is not itself the age of this revelation, but the age which is encompassed by its beginning and its ending, that is, by the ascension and by the return of Jesus Christ, by the time of this revelation and by the final victory of the Word of God, and the annulment of all other powers. Our world rests in the light of this victory because we have its attestation, but it is not itself the bearer of this Light. Jesus Christ Himself and He alone is the bearer of this light. The power of the attestation of this victory, and therefore of God's revelation, consists in the opposition and conflict with the power of the other subjects in the sphere of our world and existence—a power which here and now is still left to them, although they are already threatened with its ultimate cancellation and destruction. It involves the relapse into a comfortable quietism if we see things otherwise, if in the light of the death and resurrection of Jesus Christ we act as though the dominion of the Word of God is opposed by no other dominions, and therefore by no trials, obstacles, adversaries or perils.

It is impossible to understand the special insistence with which the New Testament proclaims God's victory over all other powers, as it is already revealed and is still to be revealed in Jesus Christ, if we do not bring into the closest connexion with it the fact that this message is most emphatically given in the midst of the relativity of this world, with a constant awareness of the present operation of its forces, and a full consciousness of their dangerous character. Through this victory the eyes of those who are its messengers are opened to the fact that in their own human time and situation the Word of God is provisional, assaulted and menaced, and that the conflict in which it is involved is a genuine conflict. Although the divine revelation is complete in regard to its content, it is no less surely incomplete in regard to its effective power as a word addressed in time by men to other men. Precisely in virtue of the absolute content of this testimony, there can be no question of quietism in the sphere of Holy Scripture. This content is identical with the time, action and person of Jesus Christ, set in relief against all other times, actions and persons, so that at the heart of all other times, actions and persons the testimony which has this content will necessarily be an unsettled and unsettling, a suffering and a struggling testimony. The Word of God (or rather what is in this case called the "Word of God") can be understood in a quietistic sense only if it derives from an absolute which is not identical with Jesus Christ, which is not therefore realised in and by Him alone, but surreptitiously introduced along mystical lines. It is only in this way that there can be a relapse into the view that the Word of God is a transcendent authority above

[677]

and beyond the dialectic of actual reality and therefore not a fire and a hammer, as in the saying of the prophet, but the telling of a dream.

It belongs, therefore, to the recognition of the freedom of God's Word that we appreciate its exposed position, understanding Scripture as the sign which can be and is spoken against. But it belongs even more to this recognition to realise that its own offensive power is greater (and qualitatively infinitely greater) than the offensive which is mounted against it and from which it has to suffer. If it is true that in the sphere of our world and existence it is actually challenged, it is even more true that it constitutes itself the fundamental challenge to the subjects and powers which exist in this realm and on this level. When it confronts them, it may be that many penultimate words have still to be spoken, but the ultimate word has been already spoken, so that whatever else can and must be said, however serious and difficult it may be in face of the contradiction raised, can, so to speak, be said only in retrospect and by way of recapitulation. Self-evidently, it is by virtue of the content of Scripture that, while it is the sign which can be spoken against, it is at the same time the sign which can never be really and effectually spoken against, which in all its lowliness and assailability confronts all other signs with a decisive because qualitative superiority. The freedom of the Word of God consists in this secret but decisive superiority which it has in face of the totality of world principles, and the recognition of this freedom consists in the quiet and steadfast realisation of this superiority. The outward aspect of the relation between the power of Holy Scripture and other powers will never disclose this intrinsic superiority.

In great things and small, Holy Scripture will always be like the leaven which is really hidden in three measures of meal (Lk. 13^{21}). Note well: hidden. It is not a painful and tragic [678] destiny which overtakes the Word of God, when in face of its enemies, and perhaps still more in the company of its friends, always and everywhere in the world, it has to be worsted, pushed into a corner, repulsed, denied, distorted and spurned as the weaker principle. On the contrary, as in the passion and death of Jesus Christ Himself, this is the divine plan and will. Jesus Himself ordained that His disciples should have no silver and gold (Ac. 3^6, cf. Mt. 10^9). "Behold, I send you forth as sheep in the midst of wolves" (Mt. 10^{16}). "The disciple is not above his master, nor the servant above his lord" (Mt. 10^{24}). "And he that taketh not his cross and followeth after me, is not worthy of me" (Mt. 10^{38}). It would therefore be stupid to bear ill-will to the world, to reproach it, so to speak, because confronted by Holy Scripture it appears to possess and exercise victorious power.

But this external aspect does not disclose the whole truth. The whole truth is that in spite of all appearances to the contrary, Holy Scripture has more power than all the rest of the world together. The whole truth is that all other world-principles are already unmasked and delimited in Holy Scripture, that they are already overcome for all supposedly final and absolute validity, that their power is already surpassed and their triumph outstripped.

The whole truth—hidden but complete—is that of the story of the young David (1 Sam. $17^{23f.}$). It was not in the helmet and armour of Saul, but with his shepherd's sling, that he overcame Goliath. Very rashly, from a human point of view, he confronted Goliath in the name of Yahweh Sabaoth. "Because the foolishness of God is wiser than men, and the weakness of God is stronger than men" (1 Cor. 1²⁵). And therefore: "If any man among you seemeth to be wise in this world, let him become a fool, that he may be wise" (1 Cor. 3¹⁸). The whole truth is what the "loud voices" in heaven cry at the sound of the trumpet of the seventh angel: "The kingdoms of the world are become the kingdoms of our Lord, and of his Christ; and he shall reign for ever and ever" (Rev. 11¹⁵).

The recognition of this full but hidden truth is the recognition of the freedom of God's Word. It will be immediately apparent that this recognition is not possible apart from faith in the resurrection of Jesus Christ. It will also be apparent that we cannot believe in the resurrection without recognising that, in face and in spite of all appearances to the contrary, the world is not victorious over Scripture but Scripture over the world. The Church lives in this faith and in this recognition. But it can only do this by cleaving to the law of revelation, that the Jesus Christ who rose again is He who previously in this world suffered *sub Pontio Pilato*ᴱᴺ¹⁸, was crucified, dead and buried. The Church will really live in this faith and in this recognition when it realises that it is a question of the freedom and transcendence of the Word of God, when, therefore, it does not seek and does not hope to find the truth of that hidden kingdom in the reality of its own being as a Church.

A deep insight and a weighty project were fulfilled in the Augustinian antithesis between the *civitas terrena*ᴱᴺ¹⁹ and *civitas Dei*ᴱᴺ²⁰, which for many centuries became a norm and pattern for the Christian interpretation of history. It is a pity that they did not remain freer from the clerical and secular taint acquired from the fact that the victorious *civitas Dei*ᴱᴺ²¹ was fused with the suffering, struggling and triumphant Catholic Church, and that as a result the transcendence of God's Word became the justification and argument for a specific outlook and policy, the supposed superiority of the cause of one human party over that of another. The comfort, encouragement and hope, which the Church can and should derive from the truth that the Word of God abides for ever, are all quite impossible if it purports and intends to try to actualise and represent this abidingness in itself. if it looks at itself and affirms it instead of looking at the Word of God and believing it. The cross of Jesus Christ is lacking in the Augustinian conception, and therefore it lacks the true divine trustworthiness. The real *civitas Dei*ᴱᴺ²² on earth, which is invincible, and can therefore be proclaimed with confidence, is not the rule of the Church, but the rule of Him who in this world had to be nailed to the cross. And for His followers this means the rule of Scripture and the faith in which such a rule finds obedience. Obedience to this rule cannot mean a triumph at the point where prophets and apostles were defeated and slain and where Jesus died on the cross. Therefore faith will not rest for support on its works, nor appeal to its works and therefore to the human structure of the Church, as though the latter as such is the kingdom of God over against the kingdoms of this world, and in its invincibility in contradistinction, to them the manifestation of the superiority of the Word of God. On the contrary, faith will expect this structure to be always in jeopardy, always liable to be destroyed, and at the end definitely to

[679]

ᴱᴺ¹⁸ under Pontius Pilate
ᴱᴺ¹⁹ earthly city
ᴱᴺ²⁰ city of God
ᴱᴺ²¹ city of God
ᴱᴺ²² city of God

be destroyed like Israel's temple: for in order to enter into its glory, the body of Christ had to die and be buried. The Church must really be content to recognise the hiddenness of the truth of the freedom and transcendence of God's Word, and, through all its visible forms, to believe in its invisibility. Only so can this truth be the comfort of the Church and the inexhaustible source of its life.

Again, the secrecy in which the Word of God is free and transcendent must not be interpreted quietistically. It is true that we cannot expect to see its victory in events, forms and ordinances which are unequivocally recognisable in this sense. The leaven is really hidden. The grain of wheat must really die. All that is humanly visible must always be a picture of this dying and not the picture of a triumphant, divine, world principle. Our faith alone will thus be the victory that has overcome the world (1 Jn. 5^4). But all the same, it must not be forgotten that with this faith of ours we stand in the midst of the world. Scripture is in the world. Therefore concrete relationships subsist between the Word of God and the powers of this world. Real contacts and reactions take place in which the freedom of the Word of God, which we recognise by faith, demonstrates and establishes its reality. If it is in accordance with the character of the revelation, and therefore provided for, that the war declared upon the world by the testimony of Jesus Christ will constantly assume the visible form of human defeats, human sinning and failure, human suffering and dying, this testimony is nevertheless a challenge to battle, and not the telling of a dream which at the end necessarily leaves everything in the real world exactly as it was before.

If the disciple is not above his Master, we cannot expect that in virtue of the transcendence of the Word we will be led along a different path from that which is definitively prescribed for us in the path of Jesus Christ from the cross to the resurrection. The prophets and apostles and even more so ourselves as their pupils can expect least of all that, as favoured and resolute citizens of a visible *civitas Dei*[EN23], we are destined suddenly or gradually to trample down, overcome and destroy the powers of this world. Yet we have to remember that beyond all chiliastic errors we also have the true but obviously not contradictory sayings: "Think not that I am come to send peace on earth: I came not to send peace, but a sword" (Mt. 10^{34}). And: "I am come to send fire on the earth; and what will I, if it be already kindled?" (Lk. 12$^{49f.}$). And it continues: "But I have a baptism to be baptised with; and how am I straitened till it be accomplished!" This continuation shows that, in the word about fire on the earth, the great boundary constituted by the cross is not forgotten, but considered and reckoned with. But since it is the continuation of just this word, it shows also that the cross as a boundary must not be made a pretext for quietism.

[680]

The real world is attacked by Jesus Christ and the testimony of Jesus Christ. It is victoriously attacked. We can say positively that it is under a promise which cannot fail. It is dark in itself and therefore the arena of the crucifixion of Christ; but it is also placed in the light of His resurrection. It is the same world, yet not the same. In itself it is the same. Yet it is not the same in that in the

---

[EN23] city of God

Word of God it is now confronted by a superior power. It is the same in that its ruling powers, in accordance with their nature, have to withstand the power of the Word, and the Word has to suffer in it. It is not the same in that the Word on its own account offers resistance to these powers, challenging and disputing their claim to be divine, announcing and preparing their destruction, affirming a new heaven and a new earth as the final truth. Since Scripture confronts the world with faith in God's revelation in Jesus Christ, it cannot simply treat the world as though it is still entirely the same. It reckons soberly with this outward aspect. And events will, of course, always give fresh confirmation that it is right, and that the world is still the world. Therefore the way of Scripture in the world will undoubtedly and in all circumstances be the way in which the disciples have to bear the cross like their Master. But beyond this they will know that God is God, and therefore that although the world is the same, now, in the light of the resurrection of Jesus Christ, it is also not the same. They will know that the lie of the world has been contradicted, that its pretended divinity has been contested, and that its end is near. Faith in the resurrection of Jesus Christ will not, therefore, be an aimless, illusionary faith. As an eschatological faith, that is, the faith which sees in Jesus Christ the beginning and the end of our age and its history, it will have quite concrete content, which a reference to Holy Scripture as the witness of this beginning and end enables us concretely to specify and describe.

First, the Word of God demonstrates its freedom and supremacy in the world in the fact that it has the power to maintain itself in face of the open and secret, direct and indirect attacks made upon it.

Men with their various (but by nature unanimously hostile) attitudes towards it come and go. Their political and spiritual systems (all of which to some extent have an anti-Christian character) stand and fall. The Church itself (in which somewhere the crucifixion of Christ is always being repeated) is to-day faithful and to-morrow unfaithful, to-day strong and to-morrow weak. But although Scripture may be rejected by its enemies and disowned and betrayed by its friends, it does not cease to remain true to itself, to say the same thing on all sides and in all situations. It does not cease to present the message that God so loved the world that He gave His only begotten Son. If its voice is drowned to-day, it becomes audible again to-morrow. If it is misunderstood and distorted here, it again bears witness to its true meaning there. If it seems to lose its position, hearers and form in this locality or period, it acquires them afresh elsewhere. The promise is true, and it is fulfilled in the existence of the biblical prophets and apostles in virtue of what is said to them and what they have to say: "I have set watchmen upon thy walls, O Jerusalem, which shall never hold their peace day nor night: ye that make mention of the Lord, keep not silence, and give him no rest, till he establish, and till he make Jerusalem a praise in the earth" (Is. 62⁶ᶠ·). The maintaining of the Word of God against the attacks to which it is exposed cannot be our concern, and therefore we do not need to worry about it. Watchmen are appointed and they wait in their office. The maintaining of the Word of God takes place as a self-affirmation which we can never do more than acknowledge to our own comfort and disquiet. We can be most seriously concerned about Christianity and Christians, about the future of the Church and theology, about the establishment in the world of the Christian outlook and Christian ethic. But there is nothing about whose solidity we need be less troubled than the testimonies of God in Holy Scripture.

[681]

For a power which can annul these testimonies is quite unthinkable. "If these should hold their peace, the stones would immediately cry out" (Lk. 19⁴⁰).

Further, the Word of God demonstrates its freedom and supremacy in the fact that it possesses the power continually to isolate and distinguish itself from the elements of the world which crowd upon it and affix themselves to it.

The history of the Word of God in the world is not merely the history of the attacks but supremely of the temptations to which it is exposed. Just as the prophets and apostles themselves were not mechanically secured against error, so the Word of God, in its humanness as the prophetic and apostolic Word, is, of course, not beyond the reach of temptation, that is, not absolutely secured against the danger, which is worse than opposition and rejection, of distortion and therefore of falsification under the influence of human ideas alien to it. It cannot be disputed that in this sense, too, it is involved in a struggle as long as it remains the Word of God in and to this world. Every new language into which it is translated, every new mode or system of thought in whose framework and ways it is affirmed and received, the new spirit of each new epoch which in its own way tries to hear it and preach it, each new individual who in one way or another takes possession of it—all these are phases and problems of this perilous struggle in which the purity and therefore the power of Scripture and therefore the salvation of mankind are at stake, in which it has to guard itself against alienation on the part of the men into whose hands it is delivered as their own and in regard to whom—if it is to be appropriated by them for their salvation—it must remain undeviatingly faithful to itself. Church history is the history of the exegesis of the Word of God and therefore of the ever recurrent menace of doing violence to it. But it is also and still more the history of the criticism which it brings and always will bring to bear on all its interpreters. As the orthodox Protestants were fond of saying. Holy Scripture was the *facultas semetipsam interpretandi*EN24 which at any rate means the power sooner or later to throw off every foreign sense attributed to it, to mark and expose its perversity, and in contrast to assert itself in its own characteristic meaning. If this is in fact a matter of history, of a struggle where there must always be a [682] victorious outcome, then there is no cause for the scepticism according to which anything and everything may be proved from the Bible, as expressed in the epigram of S. Werenfels:

> *Hic liber est, in quo sua quaerit dogmata quisque*
> *Invenit et pariter dogmata quisque sua.* EN25

If this is a correct account of what might be called the natural law of all biblical exegesis, even the sincerest and best, it must also and even more be noticed with what remarkable independence this book comes through all its better and worst criticism, how carefully it is provided that its serious misinterpretations inevitably cancel each other out, how the occasional arbitrary and one-sided exegesis usually has a short lease of life, how quickly and thoroughly these texts are usually able to free themselves even from the worst bondage under which they may be confined. There is, therefore, good reason to ask whether, side by side with and superior to this fatal natural law of biblical interpretation, there may not be a spiritual law which the Bible itself dictates, which it sets and maintains in force, to which in the end all good and even bad Bible criticism is subjected, which neither the good nor the bad exegete can avoid any more than he can the natural law that can only be the reflection of human laziness or arrogance, but never the living law of the Bible itself. Scripture is exposed but not delivered over to the understanding and misunderstanding of the world.

EN24 means of interpreting itself
EN25 Here is a book in which everyone looks for his own doctrines, and where, similarly, everyone finds his own doctrines.

1. The Freedom of the Word

Scripture is in the hands but not in the power of the Church. It speaks as it is translated, interpreted and applied. But always in and even in spite of all these human efforts, it is Scripture itself which speaks.

Further, Scripture demonstrates its freedom and supremacy in the fact that, above and beyond the power of resistance and criticism, it has the power of assimilating and making serviceable to itself the alien elements it encounters.

To these alien elements, which may be open enemies or secret tempters, there belong in the first place all the historical factors which Holy Scripture opposes as the testimony of God's unique revelation in the midst of a sinful world: peoples and their languages, political and philosophical systems, the passing movements of history, the consequent situations of one sort or another, all kinds of human individuals with their secrets. But as there is nothing in this universe which of itself cannot prove inimical and insidious, so there is nothing which has of itself the power to escape the control exercised over it by Scripture. Nothing human is alien to Scripture. It can speak with original force in every language. It can express itself in the language of the most varied political and intellectual systems and win a hearing. It can make the most diverse situations and movements effective and useful, and appropriate to its service the most diverse races and individual personalities. Note well, this does not mean that these natural factors which the Word of God in the course of its history assimilates and makes serviceable have innately a secret affinity and fitness to this end, so that the Word of God uses them as ready-made instruments. The truth is rather that their original character as alien elements has first to be removed, that they have first to receive a new nature, and be awakened and newly created for this service. It is not, therefore, a question of the character native to them, but of the choice which comes upon them, of the grace which meets them and makes of them what they could not be in themselves. And this is just the history of the Word of God in the world. It is not only a history of struggle, but also one of election and grace. It is a history of remarkable transmutations, in virtue of which, even in the midst of the hostile and corrupting world—and certainly not without fatal traces of it—there is still a genuine translation, interpretation and application of Scripture. In this the affirmation and unfolding of its original sense takes place in such a way that human language, institutions [683] and personalities really come into their own in this use and service. This is not because of any particular character of their own. But their particular character is not effaced and suppressed. They are not, so to speak, put into uniform. They are genuinely affirmed. This does not mean a divinisation of historical and natural forces. This is unthinkable even in the case of the human word of the Bible, or the human nature of Jesus Christ Himself. What it does mean is a share in the typological character of the human word in the Bible and of the human nature of Jesus Christ, an inclusion in their characteristic functions, and so a widening, a differentiation and an enrichment, an expansion of the effectual working of the historical forms of God's Word. On the other hand, no enslavement of the Word is implied in this process. It is ensured that the Word is never identical with any of its symbols, and is not itself transformed into a natural factor. There is no absolute necessity or definable universal law on the basis of which these particular transformations must be effected or these particular connexions set up. Where these transformations and connexions are found, they always have the character of special events, not of universal relationships. They never have more than a locally and temporally limited significance. The symbolical value which may attach to a natural historical factor in one place may be wanting in another. If it is appropriate to-day it may be withdrawn to-morrow. There is dissimilation as well as assimilation, dismissal from as well as appointment to service, judgments as well as blessing and consecration upon the various houses of God. The freedom of God's Word would not be freedom if it did not have also a negative significance. But all the same, it still has the positive value that it is not only freedom to repel, but also freedom to attract and accept. The disquieting contact of the Word with the world does not have only a critical but also an atoning and pregnant character. Either way it points to the beginning and end of the world to which testimony is borne by Holy Scripture in the midst of the world.

Finally, and above all, the Word of God demonstrates its freedom and supremacy in the fact that it can change its own form and therefore its effect upon the world.

We understand Holy Scripture falsely, that is, not as Holy Scripture, if we regard it as a fixed, inflexible, self-contained quantity. God is the living God. He is this from everlasting to everlasting. Therefore He is it also as the Lord of our temporal world, as the One who once revealed Himself to prophets and apostles, who once placed His testimonies in their mouth. But this means that He is not buried in this "once," in the writings of these men. They are not a kind of stone mausoleum, in which, so long as it does not crumble and vanish from the earth as is ultimately the way with these structures. He can be known by historical scholars and honoured by other men under their guidance. The Holy Scriptures of the Old and New Testament are to be understood strictly as the Word of God, which means as the forward and backward looking testimony to Jesus Christ. And Jesus Christ is the living Lord of the Church and of the world. But if this is true, the form assumed by the Word of God in the human word of prophets and apostles is not His grave, but the organ of His rule, moved by the living hand of His Spirit and therefore itself alive. Thus we have not only to expect that, by deeper, more precise, more serious, more believing research into Scripture on our part, many a hidden meaning and connexion in these documents will be brought to light; just as by dint of excavations many important and interesting conclusions are to be expected about the life of those who have lived in the near or distant past. For this expectation is naturally limited by the fact that, however hard we try, more cannot be dug up than was originally there. But the [684] investigation of the Bible does not have to reckon with this natural limitation. For the Bible is a living, indeed, in the light of its content, an eternally living thing, so that from the study of it we can expect new truths to meet us—truths which were not accessible to the most conscientious inquiry of yesterday or the day before yesterday, because the Bible itself has not yet brought them to light. What is true of the content of Scripture, that it is unique in essence, is true also of its form. The word of prophets and apostles was uttered once for all. But while it remains unaltered, this does not in any way prevent it from changing and renewing its form and therefore its range and effectiveness, continually presenting itself to different ages and men from new angles, in new dimensions and with a new aspect. What we call the investigation of Holy Scripture and its results is not at bottom our efforts and their conclusions, of which we usually think in this connexion, but rather the self-initiating movements of the Word of God Himself. In its repudiation of Gnosticism, the early Church wrestled for a simultaneous recognition of the unity of God and the divinity of Christ and the Holy Ghost. The Reformation championed the understanding of man as a sinner saved by grace alone. To-day we have to defend against barbarians, and at the same time and above all to realise ourselves, the contingence of the divine revelation, that is, *in concreto*[EN26], the revelational character of the Old Testament on the one hand, and on the other, the independence of the Church and its message. To all these processes the contemporary ecclesiastical and non-ecclesiastical movement of ideas in its immanentist evolution has formed the musical accompaniment, but this is quite inexplicable apart from the initiative which proceeded and still proceeds from the Bible itself. The same will have to be said of ages and

---

[EN26] concretely

situations in which we perhaps have to speak more of the suffering than the effective working of God's Word—of its neglect and rejection, its non-recognition and distortion. The sin and error of mankind in times and circumstances like this are as much in place as are at other periods their belief and openness to the truth. For at these times as well it is proper to seek the true motive power, not in the surrounding world, but in the Word of God itself, that is, in the judgments executed in these times and situations. The Word of God hides and withdraws itself from the Church when the latter permits itself to regard and treat itself and its tradition or nature, or the being and history of mankind, as the source of its knowledge of God. The Word of God itself is silent, and yet it speaks even by its silence, when the Church wishes to hear only the human word of prophets and apostles as such and therefore the voice of a distant historical occurrence which does not really concern it or lay any obligation upon it. The Word of God itself veils itself in darkness when the Bible is interpreted with violent and capricious one-sidedness according to the promptings of various spirits instead of under the leading of its own Holy Spirit. We do not truly appreciate either the light which the Church receives from the Bible, or the darkness which enshrouds it from the same source, until we recognise in both, beyond all the human effort and human refusal which is also present, the over-ruling power of the Word of God itself, either to exalt or to abase. Only then do we realise that we cannot read and understand Holy Scripture without prayer, that is, without invoking the grace of God. And it is only on the presupposition of prayer that all human effort in this matter, and penitence for human failure in this effort, will become serious and effective. The Word of God can change its human expression. In different times and circumstances it is the same and not the same. It produces the same effect in continually new forms. Therefore man's encounter and dealings with it have a history which is not the history of a solitary man standing by himself, nor the history of a self-contained, self-centred Church, but a history which on the side of the Church and individual members in the Church has the character of a response, the initiative being always with the Word of God as the first and truly acting Subject. It is no metaphor when we say that the Word of God speaks, acts and rules; we denote thereby the characteristic and essential feature of the whole move- [685] ment called Church history. This is the characteristic and essential thing to which the life and deeds and opinions, all the insights and errors, the ways and aberrations, not only of the men who are gathered in power or weakness within the Church, but of the world which surrounds the Church with its good will, hatred or indifference, necessarily have to refer and respond. The Word of God in the form of Holy Scripture is, therefore, the object of the acting, thinking and speaking of the Church and the world—but, of course, only because and so far as it has the initiative, only because and so far as it is the real Subject of this acting, thinking and speaking. All that has hitherto been said about the self-affirmative, critical and assimilative power of the Word of God can be properly understood only when it is realised that the Word is first the Subject and only then the object of history.

We remind ourselves that all this is the content of faith in the resurrection of Jesus Christ as the revelation of the controlling beginning and end of the Church and the world. As the mere statement of a philosophy of Church history and world history these things can all be said or not said, affirmed or contradicted. We say no more than what phenomenologically can be said of the history of the *Iliad* or the Platonic dialogues. But we are not making phenomenological affirmations. We are asserting and developing the promise: Ye shall be my witnesses, and: Lo, I am with you always. What we say is true because Jesus Christ is risen and therefore this promise is true. It is from this point of view that all this about the freedom and supremacy of the divine Word has to be said and heard. But from this point of view it does have to be said and heard.

3. We have seen how in virtue of its theme Scripture becomes a subject. And we have seen something of its power as such. This power of Scripture has a special sphere of influence—the Church. This does not imply a limitation of its power. It constitutes it as free power in contradistinction to a blind, universal, automatically working force of nature. Its operation takes place on the basis of choice, not of necessity. It has, therefore, the form of a decisive, not of a general, event. So long as God is not all in all—and the fact that God is not all in all is the negative sign of this world of ours—it will certainly not be a sign of the divinity of Holy Scripture if its power is that of a universally operative necessity, or if the sphere of its operation is co-extensive with the sphere of this world. The sign of its divinity is rather the fact that its power within this world has its own peculiar sphere. It is not a sphere which is assigned or resigned to it according to the order of nature. It is not a sphere which is conceded to it by the world. It is the sphere of the Church which it has chosen, defined, claimed and conquered itself. Side by side with this sphere there is the sphere of that which is not the Church. The division is provisional in a double sense. It is provisional because of the provisional nature of the whole present state of the world, in which it is not yet identical with the kingdom of God, but only limited and relativised by the now imminent Kingdom. It is also provisional because of the provisional character of the present, visible demarcation between the Church and that which is not the Church. The Word of God chooses, defines, claims and conquers the Church as the special sphere of its effective power, not for the sake of the Church itself, but for the sake of God and, in His service, for the sake of the world. And it is not an absolute and rigid, but a flexible boundary which divides it off from that which is not His Church. In His Word God speaks to the Church and in the Church. But He does so in order that through the Church—in the concrete antithesis which arises from the fact that He addresses Himself primarily to the Church and in the Church—He may speak to the world and cause His Church to grow in the world. Again, God is not bound to the sphere which at any one time is created by His Word. On the contrary, this sphere is bound to Him and to His Word. At this point its boundaries may fall back so that there is again no Church where formerly there was the Church. Or they may expand so that now there is the Church where formerly there was none. All the same, as long as this world lasts, the concrete antithesis between the Church and that which is not the Church can as little be removed as, in spite of its fluidity, the relationship between Israel and the Gentiles. In this antithesis of two peoples, God speaks with the world. He speaks with it in such a way that His Word creates the Church first, and then by the ministry of the Church, it becomes a Word to the world.

[686]

There is, therefore, no occasion for the impatience which despises and bypasses the Church for the sake of the kingdom of God, or demands of the Church what can be demanded only of the kingdom of God, if we can demand anything at all of the kingdom of

God. The Church can and must have a continual awareness of the relativity of its boundaries and therefore of its whole existence in antithesis to what is not the Church. It can and must have a continual awareness that within its boundaries and in its special existence it is not called to serve itself, but to serve God and in the service of God the world. The Church cannot do all this unless within its boundaries and in its special existence it hopes for the consummation of the kingdom of God and, for that reason, really and selflessly discharges its ministry in the world. But it cannot wish to change or remove, in virtue of its own insight and power, the boundaries that separate it from that which is not the Church, the boundaries over against state and society, for example, or over against every kind of heathenism old and new. It is not in virtue of its own insight and authority that it has been chosen, defined, claimed and conquered as the Church, but by the free Word of God, which according to its own good pleasure called it out of nothingness into existence, into this determinate existence as the Church. It must now leave it to this Word, to which it owes its existence and which it can only serve, to move the boundaries between the Church and that which is not the Church nearer or further away, and eventually, when God will be all in all, to remove them completely. The kingdom of God is really the kingdom of God, and therefore its establishment is not surrendered to the power and control of men. Not even the most passionate missionary spirit, not even the deepest sensitiveness to the need and longing of the world, can alter in the very slightest the dividing line between belief and unbelief, obedience and disobedience, which in this world separates the sphere of God's lordship from a world which is not yet reconciled with Him. Nor can it alter the fact that for our human eyes this boundary is determined by the distinction between the service and contempt of the Gospel, between clear and distorted proclamation, between a willing and an impenitent hearing of its message, so that, humanly speaking, it is defined by the boundaries of the Church. We may try to deny this boundary. We may try to unite the world and the Church in another way than by ourselves serving and not despising the Gospel, anxious and ready to hear its message ourselves and to declare it in its purity. In the interests of the kingdom of God, or our missionary spirit, or our understanding of the need and longing of the world, we may want something other than that there should be a Church and we ourselves members of it. But if we do, how can it be in anything but arrogance, in secret or open opposition to the freedom of God's Word? And how can the kingdom of God really be served by this arrogance and opposition? The freedom of God's Word to which we will submit (if we are really waiting for the Kingdom in which God will be all in all) is not a general possibility which we are free to choose. Nor is it the sum of what we consider possible, or an extract from it. It is the freedom which God has actually assumed in His revelation, of which He has told us that He has actually assumed it. We simply do not know of any other boundary between belief and unbelief, between obedience and disobedience, and therefore between the kingdom of God and the kingdom of the world, than that which He Himself has drawn through His revelation in Jesus Christ and its apostolic testimony. If we think we do, it can only be a presumptuous surmise. But if we do not, we have to keep to the boundary which has been plainly marked out for us. We will realise its impermanence and its final cancellation. But we will also realise its provisional validity. We will realise that, on this side of its final cancellation and before any of its possible changes in detail, it is within this frontier that we have to serve God if we are going to serve Him at all.

[687]

The freedom of God's Word is its freedom to found for itself a Church. This means that it unites with itself and among themselves men of every time and place, of every type and destiny and training, of every kind of natural and spiritual disposition, and in it all of every form of sinfulness and mortality. It does so in such a way that it procures from them a hearing, the hearing of obedience, i.e., the hearing by which, for better or worse, for grace or disfavour, for life or death, they are bound to Jesus Christ. It does so in such a way that in all their sinfulness and sickness and its varied manifestations they have to recognise in Him their Lord. This hearing in obedience is Christian faith and the sphere of Christian faith is the sphere in which God's Word exercises its power. Even if this alters in its outer aspect towards the world, if it contracts or expands, it will always be the sphere of Christian faith. Even its suspension as a separate sphere can only signify that there will not then be any other sphere than that of the Christian faith now elevated to become sight. We know of no other freedom of the Word of God than that which summons us to Christian faith. It is even part of the content of this Word that it has in fact assumed this freedom and this freedom alone: the freedom to create for itself the hearing of obedience. In its founding of the Church, the activity of the Word of God is free in a double sense. It is free, i.e., powerful, over against the sinfulness and sickness of mankind which make the hearing of obedience and therefore Christian faith in itself impossible. It is free also, i.e., powerful, over against the natural diversity of men which has been made disruptive by sin and

[688] death, rendering it impossible for them to be at one with God and among themselves by faith. The Word of God is free, and exercises this freedom in the founding of the Church, in overcoming the double limitation of this impossibility, and in imparting to us the possibility of faith.

"The wind bloweth where it listeth" (Jn. 3^8). "The Son quickeneth whom he will" (Jn. 5^{21}). "Father, I will that they also, whom thou hast given me, be with me where I am" (Jn. 17^{24}). On this will that ignores present obstacles the Church rests. In this will we have to recognise at once the freedom of the Word of God. It would be more exact to describe it as its freedom to arouse attention, belief and trust in itself, which means in the biblical testimonies, and therefore to raise up disciples and followers. The Church comes to be because this testimony is accepted and assimilated. This happens in spite of its strangeness, which is both the strangeness of its content as it strives against every man, the strangeness of the form which the content assumes in claiming every man. It is not a matter of course that men will believe the prophets and apostles. The reality and unity of the faith which this witness requires, the power of illuminating to faith and the power of gathering in faith—this is the first secret of the freedom of God's Word.

But this freedom goes further. It is not the case that, when the Word of God has once been conveyed and handed over to the biblical witness of the Church, the Church is left alone like a widow with her deceased husband's legacy.

From this false conception of the biblical revelation as a *depositum*^{EN27} committed to the Church and left to its disposal, the Roman Catholic error has possibly arisen, which claims for the Church the power of ruling itself out of its

---

^{EN27} deposit

own resources. It is clear that such a conception involves both the possibility and the need to constitute tradition alongside Scripture as a second ostensible *depositum*EN28. It is also clear that the teaching office of the Church, and its head, will inevitably have to be given the most powerful possible voice as the administrator of these *deposita*EN29. Such a view obviously overlooks the whole uniqueness of the distinction, equipment and authority in which those who stand at the beginning of the Church's history are clothed. Of these it is said: "There be some standing here, which shall not taste of death, till they see the Son of man coming in his kingdom" (Mt. 16²⁸), and: "This generation shall not pass, till all these things be fulfilled. Heaven and earth shall pass away, but my words shall not pass away" (Mt. 24³⁴ᶠ·). They obviously have a function which does not simply pass over into that of the Church. For while the Church is created by their testimony, and their testimony is received and accepted by the Church, it retains its own independent function as distinct from all the functions of the Church. Their testimony is not a *depositum*EN30, but it continues as an event, and in and with this event the Word of God exercises its freedom.

The Word of God does not effect only the founding of the Church, but also its continual preservation. The freedom of Scripture gives evidence that it is divine freedom, the sovereignty of the Creator, in the fact that by it, and by it alone, the Church is what it is. Without Scripture it would inevitably dissolve at once into nothingness, perishing from the impossibility of the actuality and unity of faith. The Church, like the created world as a whole, lives by the divine *creatio continua*EN31. But in its application to the Church this does not mean the [689] patience with which the Word of God holds the created world as such in the being in which it has been created. It means rather the grace of rebirth and new creation spoken by the Word in the midst of the created world. It means the effectiveness of this Word in its continuous attestation from the faith of the prophets and apostles to the faith of the Church. Without this Word and without its continuous attestation, human religions, philosophies and systems, and the human institutions and societies founded upon them, may well live, as in fact they do: on the basis of the universal divine maintenance of all created things. But they live in the shadow of the death to which the whole created order is as such hastening. For the same reason, an erroneous and deformed Christianity, i.e., one which approximates to the form of these human systems, can also live without the Word. It can do so the more easily in proportion as, in virtue of this approximation, it is erroneous and deformed. It is the true Church which, as the sphere of revelation and faith, denies itself this purely natural vitality. Called into existence by the Word of rebirth and new creation, it cannot remain alive except by this Word. What is it profited by any natural

---

EN28 deposit
EN29 deposits
EN30 deposit
EN31 continuous creation

237

will and power to exist? What is it profited even if they are so great that with their help it gains the whole world? As one of the human systems which hasten to death, it can maintain a sort of life by such means. But as the Church of truth and of eternal life, even in the most prosperous development which it can enjoy on this plane, it will be already dead if the Word of truth withdraws itself from it.

It hardly needs to be added, and yet it is one of the things which most need emphasising, that prayer for the maintenance of the Church's life ought never to cease. The Church lives and moves solely on the basis which continually has to be offered to it by the living Word. Apart from this basis, it might live like other systems, but never as the Church of truth. And concern for the maintenance of the Church on this strength alone, and therefore for the continual offering of it, will necessarily be the proper criterion of all ecclesiastical action, of all attempts to strengthen and defend the Church, of all apologetic and ecclesiastico-political measures. No concern for the Church can rank above this in importance, or will not have to be brushed aside if it means that the Church will by it escape the living Word. Again, no concern for the Church will not be gladly subordinated to this or allowed to be dissolved in it. If the Church commits itself to the Word of truth, then, and then alone, but confidently and legitimately, it can hope and trust that the universal grace and patience of God to His creation will in some way accrue to its advantage.

The preservation of the Church by the Word of God is accomplished quite simply in the exercise of the freedom of the Word in the manner already described. In the power of the resurrection of Jesus Christ the Word has power to affirm itself in this world and to maintain itself unspotted from the world. But it also has power to draw the world to itself, and continually to express and give itself in new forms. From this inner life of the Word flows the life of the Church. The Church is alive because it is the theatre of this life of the Word, because it participates in the movements of this life, because by faith it says Yes to these movements, seeking its own salvation only in the fact that they take place, imitating them in so far as its worship and fellowship, preaching and confession occur in the following of these movements. Because this happens, the Church can as little perish as the Word of God itself. In its discipleship of the Word, it shares in its imperishability in the transitory world.

[690]

From a human point of view, the preservation of the Church therefore depends upon the selfless attention with which the Church has to accompany the course of the Word of God. It cannot be its business to desire to assert itself as the Church. Let it assert itself by promoting the self-assertion of the Word. Let it not allow itself any criticism of the world on the basis of its own polemical insight. Let it not allow itself any assimilation of secular elements on the basis of its own synthetic wisdom. But let it believe and announce the declarations of war and the conclusions of peace made by the Word of God itself. Let it not allow itself either to cling to the old or to introduce the new unless it be commanded and obliged to do so by the changing form of the Word of God which guides it. Any step away from this path will be a step into the abyss of death. Not that it will immediately reveal and avenge itself as such. It will often enough appear that only a tiny step aside is required, only a little ecclesiastical self-will, for the Church to prosper wonderfully, perhaps after a heavy trial, and for its preservation in the world to God's glory and the salvation of man actually to be guaranteed. On all hands there exist in obvious health and abounding vitality the other human structures of which this selfless attention is apparently not expected, the life of which does not rest upon the grace of rebirth and new creation, and is therefore from the human point of view to be had at a cheaper price than the life of faith. It is only for the Church of truth that what the rest of the world calls life is the abyss of death. Will it see this, although as yet it cannot be seen? Will it recognise death in what the rest of the world calls life? Will it choose the life which must inevitably appear to the rest of the world as death? Plainly everything depends on whether the Church is in fact what it is supposed to be, that is, the sphere in which man has confidence in the Word alone, and therefore in faith alone, acquiring in this confidence the capacity for that self-forgetful attention which with its will to live, its aggressiveness and wisdom, its conservatism and radicalism, the world as a whole does not have. But the Church's being what it is supposed to be depends upon its living in the strength of the Word itself. It depends upon the Word continuing to live in its midst in all its power. It depends, therefore, on the real freedom of the Word for which the Church can only pray and be thankful.

The preservation of the Church by the active freedom of the Word of God means concretely that it is unceasingly under the authoritative claim of Scripture. It is the history of the continuing witness which is given it by Scripture and which it has to receive from Scripture. In place of the sustaining Word of God, if this is not identifiable with Scripture, or if Scripture is a mere "deposit" and not a continuing witness, there can easily enter what the Church has to say to itself or to the world: the Christian idea, outlook and ethic, Christianity or the Gospel in one of the complicated or simplified forms in which man has constantly adjusted it to his needs; the content, perhaps, of a good or a bad dogmatics or ethics. It is clear that this so-called Word of God is not free but [691] dependent upon the ecclesiastical and therefore human conceptions in question. To such a Word would belong the animating, inspiring and edifying power which can be and is in fact proper to such conceptions at least at certain times and in certain situations. But to it would not belong the power to maintain the Church, to maintain it, that is, through the revolutions of epochs and situations, through the disillusionments and disappointments which are the inevitable consequence of these vicissitudes. The promise given to Scripture and only to Scripture would be lost. It would not be that Word of truth which alone has power to preserve the Church of truth from death. The Church lives, and it lives also with what it has itself to say, by what is said to it, by the Word which continually comes to it from without, the Word which it hears in Scripture. Because the Word of God is Scripture, it exercises the concrete guidance, government and education of the Church, in virtue of which it is not left to itself, but is continually touched by saving truth and made alive.

From a human standpoint the preservation of the Church depends, therefore, on the fact that Scripture is read, assimilated, expounded and applied in the Church, that this happens tirelessly and repeatedly, that the whole way of the Church consists in its striving to hear this concrete witness. As a rule the step aside which means a step into the abyss of death, the fatal lack of this self-forgetful attention, will scarcely betray itself as such at once. It will normally take the form of great fidelity (to what the Church has said) and great zeal (for what the Church believes that it must itself say). In this way it will apparently bear the seal of divine justification and necessity. Whenever life is exchanged for death, or death for life, in the

Church, this fidelity and zeal are usually operative: much good will, much serious piety, wide vision, deep movements, and in it all the sincere conviction of not being in any way self-willed but rather obedient to the Word of God. What is not noted is that this so-called Word of God is only a conception of the Word of God. It may be created freely. More probably and frequently it will take the shape of an old (no longer newly tested), or new (not yet seriously examined) interpretation of Scripture itself, but not the Word of God as it actually lets itself be heard in Scripture. As such, conceptions of the Word of God may be very good, as also, for example, recognised dogmas and confessions, luminous and helpful theological systems, deep, bold and stimulating insights into biblical truth. But in themselves these things are not the Word of God itself and cannot sustain the life of the Church. Similarly, conservatism and radicalism can only deceive and endanger the Church if they try to outshine this and claim it for their conceptions. The criterion whether it is following the Word of God with this self-forgetful attention consists in whether through everything that it says itself, or thinks it has or can receive from Scripture, it is able and willing to hear the voice of Scripture itself as the final verdict which pronounces true death and true life. The continued life of the Church depends, therefore, on whether Scripture remains open to it, whether all its conceptions, even the best, remain transparent to its content—so that it can itself confirm and legitimate, or qualify, or even completely set them aside. But Scripture cannot be the breath of life to the Church apart from this freedom. If the Church is true to itself, it will allow this sovereign freedom to Scripture, and if it departs from Scripture, it will continually have to return to it. We must again conclude that the Church's being true to itself depends on whether Scripture wins and maintains for itself this freedom within it, and whether Scripture compels the Church continually to return to it. How can we give to Scripture this freedom, however faithful we are to it? Here again we are confronted by the actuality, and we can only give thanks that it is given and pray that it will be continually given.

[692]

Looking at the same thing from another angle, we maintain that the freedom of the Word of God is its freedom to rule the Church. It is not for nothing that the Church has been founded, and it is not for nothing that it is sustained. Both things happen that it may serve a purpose, the purpose of the divine revelation, and therefore the glory of God and the salvation of mankind. In the time between the ascension and the second coming, the Church as the communion of those who have been summoned by the Word and have believed the Word is the sign of God's revelation, the sign of the incarnation of the Son of God and the sign of the new humanity redeemed by the Son of God in His coming kingdom. As such a sign, the Church must serve. It must testify in this world to the already accomplished atonement and the coming redemption of its own members and of all mankind in the power of the testimony of Jesus Christ its Lord, who is also Lord over all. But it must not, and cannot, do this in its own strength. It is not the case that the time between the ascension and the second coming is to some extent the kingdom of the believing man autonomous in and by virtue of his faith.

We can only say that this is the mistake especially of Neo-Protestantism. For it sets man on a plane which dispenses with the horizons of the accomplished atonement and the coming redemption. The former has become a dim historical memory and the latter the equally vague goal of a gradual progress in the direction of this memory; neither of them has any real significance for those who exist in the interval. All that is left to them is faith. But without this twofold reference to the Lord as its proper object, and deprived of the power of the

1. The Freedom of the Word

"Glory alone to God on high," this faith can only be a special mode of human capacity, will and activity, and therefore, in comparison with Christian faith, only a false faith. Faith can then be understood only as religion. It is the type of religion in which man is influenced by that historical memory and by that specially coloured expectation of progress. But he is only influenced. At the heart and basis, lacking that horizon, as is the case in all "religions," he is his own master, the master of his own deepest impulses. In this type of religion the fellowship of religious people, what is called the Church, can be only a society with a particular object, a club, which individual believers join for certain enterprises and common endeavours and with the greatest possible mutual forbearance towards the wishes and claims of each individual. The error in this outlook is twofold. It consists in the optical illusion that the plane on which the believer exists is unbounded, and without horizons; he does not notice the direct proximity of the hills before and behind him, whence comes his help. And it is also the acoustic error that the word "faith" still means Christian faith even though the trust and hope and daring of the human heart which it signifies has lost its direction to these hills, instead of being a promising trust and hope and daring in this direction. In substance an error of this kind must be the same as that of the heretical teachers of 2 Peter, which seems to have consisted in the decisive fact that they no longer understood that a day in the Lord's sight is as a thousand years and a thousand years as a day (2 Pet. 3^8), so that impudently and obstinately, without respect for the majesty of God, they raised themselves above angels "to speak evil of dignities" (κυριότητος καταφρονοῦντες, 2^{10}). The authority with which these heretics are confronted is: "the words which were spoken before by the holy prophets, and the commandment of us the apostles of the Lord and Saviour" (3^2).

[693]

In the interval between the ascension and the second coming the believer is certainly responsible, but not autonomous. As a believer he is a member of the body of Christ. And the body of Christ, the Church, has its Head in heaven, and therefore on earth it is not left to the insight and caprice of its members. Although it consists entirely of human beings, the Church is not a human polity, monarchical, aristocratic or democratic, in which the discharge of the witness to Jesus Christ committed to it is left to the good pleasure of its members. The Church is governed. And as it is created and maintained by the Word of God, it is also governed by the Word of God: by the Word of God in the form of the testimony to the revelation of God in Jesus Christ set down in Scripture. To say that Jesus Christ rules the Church is equivalent to saying that Holy Scripture rules the Church. The one explains the other, the one can be understood only through the other. The Son of God in His human nature, and therefore as God revealed, allows this revelation of Himself, this prophetic office of His, to be continued in the prophetic and apostolic witness to His lordship. In the same way His sovereignty, and therefore the sovereignty of God Himself, confronts the Church in and through this witness. The Holy Spirit, too, is the Spirit of this witness, the Spirit who certifies this witness to be true, the Spirit through whom this witness wins the hearts of men. How else, then, can the Church be ruled except by this witness? Any other rule can only turn the Church into that which is not the Church. Any other rule can only lead the Church back to the sovereignty of man as he is autonomous in the strength of his false faith. It can consist only in a denial of the character of our time as the time between the ascension and the second coming. We have no other time but this. The only other time is the time of sin and death, which is overcome by the irruption of this time of salvation. If we are not to live again in this time, if the salt of the Church, which is the salt of the earth, is not to lose its savour, it must not be denied that its time has the character of an intervening time. But this intervening time is a time which is determined by the Word of God in the prophetic and apostolic witness, and the government of the Church in this time is, therefore, the business of this Word.

[694]

All other forms of Church government are, therefore, false. In some cases the rule of Jesus Christ may assume merely the role of a decorative flower of speech, while in truth real control is exercised by the spurious, horizonless faith of men joined together in the Church. Or in other cases the rule of Jesus Christ may be seriously acknowledged in form, but it is represented as a direct leadership of the Spirit, and it is only a secondary question whether the point at which this leadership of the Spirit touches and seizes the Church is supposed to be an infallible Pope or Council, or the office of an authoritarian bishop, or that of a hypostatised pastor, or a free leadership or inspired individuals in the community, or finally the whole community as such. The false thing in all these types of Church government is the ambiguity with which the rule of Jesus Christ is (perhaps very seriously) asserted, but Scripture is ignored as though it were not the normative form of this government for this intervening period. If we speak of a purely heavenly lordship of Jesus Christ, and then of one of these earthly manifestations of His sovereignty, we may speak "enthusiastically," but in the last resort we are still speaking of the autonomy of human faith, and therefore not of the Church of Jesus Christ.

The horizon within which the Church of Jesus Christ exists is only seen and grasped—and we only begin to speak of the Church of Jesus Christ—when it is seen and grasped that Holy Scripture is the concrete bearer of Church government. This mediacy was instituted by Him, and made effective by His resurrection. Therefore, far from imperilling the immediacy of the relation between the Lord and His Church, it constitutes the true immediacy of this relationship. And far from resulting in any legalistic hardening of the relationship, it is the guarantee that freedom and therefore inspiration will prevail in this relationship.

Where Scripture exercises authority over the Church, all the things which under the rule of autonomous faith are either declared essential and indispensable with legalistic zeal, or avoided and rejected with a similar legalistic concern, can at different times have a place or not have a place, not merely by permission but by command, not merely because they are harmless, but for salvation: Popes and Councils, bishops and pastors, the dignity of synods and congregations, leaders and inspired teachers, the ministry of theologians and others in the congregation, the ministry of men and the ministry of women. But why this or that? And not this or that? It is only if the freedom of God's Word is suppressed, or on the presupposition of an "enthusiastic" supplanting of Scripture, that we can wish legalistically to command or to forbid.

Scripture as the proper organ of Church government will not destroy the immediacy of the relation between the Church and its Lord, and will not impose on the Church the rule of law, so long as the distinction between Scripture itself and all human conceptions of it is maintained and continually made, so long as by constant attention to Scripture, in the unbroken discipline of its reading and exegesis, we allow it to take continual precedence of all human theories in order to follow it faithfully, so long as its government and its being allowed to govern are really taken seriously in the Church.

Over-systematised and rigid conceptions of the Word of God will, of course, necessarily both imperil the immediacy of this relation, and at the same time threaten the Church positively or negatively with some kind of legalism. If it is guilty of these over-systematised and rigid conceptions the Church is not behaving obediently but very disobediently.

This does not mean that these theories may not exist and may not have their own worth and validity. We have seen in the preceding paragraphs that there are conceptions of this kind which, in the sphere under the Word, cannot be denied the highest necessity and the greatest worth. But their existence will [695] not, however, trespass upon the freedom of the Word. They must not destroy the fundamental openness of the Church to the leading of Scripture. On the contrary, they must serve it. The freedom of the Word of God in regard to the government of the Church means that in all circumstances the Church walks in the way which was yesterday indicated to it by Scripture, which has to be trodden to-day, and which to-morrow will again have to be indicated by Scripture; in a way, therefore, where to-day it is willing and ready to take fresh directions with the obedient spirit it showed yesterday. Just for this reason, exegesis in the Church cannot and must not be discontinued. Each new day its task consists in tracing out the particular freedom which the Word of God takes to-day in the course of its government of the Church. But here again we conclude with the reminder that at this focal point of the Church's action the decisive activity is prayer, the giving of thanks for the reality of this government and the petition that it may never cease to be a reality. Because it is the decisive activity prayer must take precedence even of exegesis, and in no circumstances must it be suspended.

2. FREEDOM UNDER THE WORD

In Phil. 1⁹ we hear Paul praying that the love of his readers may abound more and more ἐν ἐπιγνώσει καὶ πάσῃ αἰσθήσει εἰς τὸ δοκιμάζειν τὰ διαφέροντα EN32, so that they may be sincere and without offence at the day of Jesus Christ, filled with the fruits of righteousness which are by Jesus Christ, to the praise and glory of God. Similarly in Col. 1⁹ᶠ· (cf. 1²⁸, 2²), he writes that he prays unceasingly ἵνα πληρωθῆτε τὴν ἐπίγνωσιν τοῦ θελήματος αὐτοῦ ἐν πάσῃ σοφίᾳ καὶ συνέσει πνευματικῇ EN33, that they might walk worthy of the Lord. Rom. 15¹⁴ speaks also of the same being filled with γνῶσις EN34, this time in express connexion with the allusion to the capability which is obviously rooted in this γνῶσις EN35, to give each other mutual instruction. And in Eph. 3¹⁸ᶠ· the same gift is again solemnly represented as the

---

EN32 in knowledge and all insight, for discerning what is excellent
EN33 that you be filled with knowledge of his will in all wisdom and spiritual understanding
EN34 Knowledge
EN35 Knowledge

epitome of that for which Paul prays when he thinks of his congregation: that they "may be able to comprehend (καταλαβέσθαι) with all the saints what is the breadth, and length, and depth, and height; and to know the love of Christ which passeth knowledge." We should set alongside these passages the saying in 2 Tim. 3[7] which deplores the γυναικάρια who are constantly learning and never able to reach a knowledge of the truth. From these and similar passages we infer that there is an authentic appreciation and understanding by their followers and congregations of the revelation which they attest. This is distinct from the treasures of wisdom and knowledge hidden in Christ (Col. 2[3]), just as His love for us is distinct from our love for Him. It is also distinct from the knowledge and doctrines of the apostles themselves. By it their followers and congregations become "wise," i.e., they both show themselves and become capable of judging. Both the frequency and the urgency with which this is mentioned show the central importance which this matter that concerns the human members of the Church has for the apostles as founders of the Church. The fact that in all these passages it is an object of apostolic petition shows on the one hand that we deal here with a pneumatic-charismatic gift to man and not with a human capacity or ability. On [696] the other hand, it shows that its impartation to men in the Church does not take place apart from, but through, transmission by apostles as the original bearers of testimony to Christ, since their testimony borne to the community is also a petition for it. We shall have to think of this gift of knowledge and wisdom mediated by the ministry of the first witnesses to the members of the Church now that we come to speak of the freedom under the Word which corresponds to the freedom of the Word.

The Church as the kingdom in which the freedom of God's Word operates is an assembly of men. They have not assembled themselves together, but they were and are assembled. Nevertheless, they are men, and the divine Word which calls them is also a human word. Now if the freedom of His Church is the characteristic of this divine and human Word which gathers them, if it is true that this Word has the power to affirm itself and to keep itself pure in the world, making its way and continually re-establishing itself and in that way founding, maintaining and governing the Church, then it must also follow that, where this power as such is recognised and experienced, where it is not merely suffered as judgment but is also believed as grace and finds obedience, where then the testimony of Scripture is accepted, there arises and subsists, relatively, mediately and formally, utterly dependent upon that acceptance and related to it, but within these limits quite really, a human power and freedom corresponding to the power and freedom of the Word of God. The men assembled in this sphere cannot escape that which in virtue of the freedom of the Word of God happens in their midst. Necessarily it determines them. It concerns them. It communicates itself to them. They can and must for their part affirm and accept it. For all the distance which separates man from God and the dependence of man upon God, it becomes and is, not only God's affair, but theirs. We have seen in the previous section that the testimony of Scripture cannot be received unless the members of the Church are willing and ready, in its interpretation and application, to listen to each other. Correspondingly, we must now say that this testimony cannot be received unless those who accept it are ready and willing themselves to assume the responsibility for its interpretation and application. This readiness and willingness to make one's own the responsibility for understanding of the Word of God is freedom under the Word.

It is perhaps legitimate to define this freedom as the freedom of conscience, in opposition to the authority of the Church referred to in the earlier paragraph on this subject. According to Calvin the rule of Jesus Christ means (*Cat. Genev.*, 1545, edited E. F. K. Müller, 120, 35): *quod eius beneficio ... vindicati in libertatem conscientiarum, spiritualibusque eius divitiis instructi, potentia quoque armamur ...* EN36 In this context "conscience," συνείδησις, *conscientia*, the knowing with God of what God knows, has to be understood strictly as the conscience freed and raised by God for this purpose, and not a universal and always effective human disposition and capacity. Freedom of conscience is not, therefore, the permission, which in the 18th and 19th century sense we all have, to think what we consider fine and desirable. It is rather the power, which God imparts to those who accept His revelation, to think what in His judgment is right, and therefore true and wise. To avoid the Catholic misapprehension (in contradistinction to the prolegomena of 1927) we could accept the authority of the Church only under the title "Authority under the Word." Similarly, to avoid the misapprehension of the 18th and 19th centuries, we now set the freedom of conscience under the title "Freedom under the Word."   [697]

Let us immediately point out a fundamental presupposition of all that follows. It will have to be borne in mind in everything that we say. We have seen already that authority under the Word, that is, the authority of the Church, is not a final and absolute court of appeal, confronting the authority of the Word with its own dignity and validity. It exists and can be considered only in proper subordination to the authority of the Word, to serve its proclamation and establishment. In exactly the same way, freedom under the Word, that is, the freedom of conscience of individual members of the Church, is not a final thing which exists in its own right and therefore without boundaries. That it is contingent is already clear from the fact that it is counterbalanced by an authority under the Word, that is, by a willingness and readiness which the reception of the witness of Scripture imposes on members of the Church to listen to each other notwithstanding their individual responsibility. But this counterpoise of human freedom and authority points beyond itself to the common origin of both without which there would be neither authority nor freedom in the Church, nor indeed any Church at all. The original basis, limitation and determination of human freedom in the Church is the freedom of the Word of God. This human freedom is, therefore, neither something which is already proper to man, nor a freedom which man assumes in reaction to the Word of God. It is an event, in which the Word of God, in the freedom of God Himself, assumes the freedom to found and maintain and govern the Church. Because this happens, and happens within a human gathering, and therefore happens to men, it results in an emancipation of these men, in their being endowed with a possibility which they did not have before and which they could not have from their own resources. In discussing the freedom of the

---

EN36 through his goodness ... we have been set free into liberty of conscience, instructed in its spiritual riches, and we are also armed with its power ...

Word of God as such, we have already found it necessary to make constant allusion to prayer, since in actual fact this freedom means that the Church can be present only with thanksgiving and petition at the occurrence of the event by which it is created, maintained and ruled. Similarly, we now have to say even more emphatically that the freeing of man which takes place as a result of this event, our own share in the freedom of the Word, our own willingness and preparedness for its responsible understanding, can be only the object of our thankful prayer. As freedom under the Word, it is not a secure possession, or a merit, but a gift from the divine mercy, continually to be received as such, and only as such. We are not responsible in this matter, but we are made respon-

[698]   sible. In so far as it is really a gift, an honour which is vouchsafed to man as man, we must accept it as a portion which we have not deserved and on which we have no claim. And in that it implies at the same time a task, an obligation of care and concern laid upon man, we most accept it as a vocation in the fulfilment of which we are not our own masters, but servants. The joy, the earnestness and the dignity which it imparts to us, the duty which it enjoins upon us, the whole independence of human being and doing which it confers upon us, cannot for a single moment fall outside the framework of prayer, just as the self-determination which we carry through in the fulfilment of this being and doing cannot for a single moment fall outside the framework of divine predestination.

It was, therefore, no pious flourish, but sober affirmation of objective fact, when J. Wolleb (*Theol. Chr. comp.*, 1626, *Praecogn.* 19) placed *frequens oratio*[EN37] at the head of the *media verum Scripturae senstum investigandi*[EN38]. To pray is clearly a free act of man. Certainly the Holy Spirit intercedes for us in prayer with groanings which cannot be uttered, because we do not know how to pray as we ought (Rom. 8[26f.]). But this does not alter the fact that "it" does not pray, but we pray when we pray. The other media of scriptural exegesis which Wolleb gives in the same connexion are similar free acts of men: linguistic study, investigation of sources, etc. But prayer is the one free act of man in which he confesses that the initiative lies with the freedom of God rather than with his own freedom. In his own freedom he follows in prayer the freedom of God, and in that way relates himself to God. He knows that he cannot do this of himself, but is disposed and empowered to do it by God Himself. He therefore leaves it to the freedom of God—and this happens in the prayer of thanksgiving and petition—to bring man in his freedom into discipleship, and so, by preceding him, to lead him in the divine way. When we pray we turn to God with the confession that we are not really capable of doing it, because we are not capable of God, but also with the faith that we are invited and author-ised to do it. For these reasons, prayer is literally the archetypal form of all human acts of freedom in the Church, and as such it must be continually repeated in all other acts of freedom. Whatever else can and must happen in the special responsibility laid upon the members of the Church for the understanding of Scripture, at least there must always hap-pen in it that which actually does happen in prayer: confession and faith, awestruck shrink-ing and comforted appropriation, in which faith and appropriation are only obedience to the grace which always precedes and which only as such will constantly suggest that confes-sion and shrinking. And it hardly needs to be said that it is true everywhere that the judg-

---

[EN37] frequent prayer
[EN38] means of investigating the true sense of Scripture

ment whether all this happens rightly does not belong to us, that our freedom is only true freedom when the Holy Ghost intercedes for us to enable us to accomplish what out of our own resources we certainly cannot do.

We do not, therefore, need a subsequent safeguard against the possibility that "freedom in the Church" will become dangerous and develop into a freedom in opposition to the Word, an emancipation from the Word. This possibility is excluded from the outset and by the nature of the case. If freedom is under the Word, the possibility is precluded that it will become emancipation, arbitrariness or self-assertion. Therefore we have no need to fear this. We need not suspect that a place is thus being allotted to man which does not properly belong to him in his confrontation by God. That which by its nature is a recog- [699] nition of the freedom of the Word of God, that which by its nature can develop only within the framework of prayer and of a consciousness of divine predestination, cannot change into revolt, in spite of the fact that as submission and obedience it is also freedom, human spontaneity and activity, human dignity and action. This kind of freedom cannot come into conflict with the authority of the Church, although it is the opposite pole of the life of the Church and the process of scriptural exegesis within which it takes place. How can those who are challenged by the witness of Scripture itself to a responsible understanding of it fail to be summoned as well to a mutual listening to one another? How can they obey in the one sphere if they do not listen in the other? How can they stand in freedom if they do not also stand under authority? But their standing in freedom and under authority will both be limited by the fact that first and last they stand under the Word of God. We thought of this limitation when we spoke about authority; we have also to think of it now that we are speaking of freedom, and this in the double sense that human freedom in the Church has in the limiting function of the Word of God both its foundation and its crisis.

Our present starting-point is that at all events it has in it its foundation. God's Word comes to man as a human word. This is the process in which it exercises its freedom, in which it founds, maintains and governs the Church. The purpose of this process consists in the arousing of men so that they become believers and witnesses, believers in God's Word and witnesses to it. But this process cannot fulfil such a purpose except in the form of God's Word coming to man as a human word. Just in this form it is the continuing witness to God's revelation, i.e., to the event that God's eternal Word became flesh for us men. It is because God's eternal Word became flesh that there are prophets and apostles and Holy Scripture, and it comes to us in the form of a human word. It is because it became flesh for us men that it comes to us in this form as to men. Its condescension, self-surrender and self-humiliation begin in the fusion with the human nature in Jesus Christ, continue in the calling of His first witnesses, and are completed in the fact that by the Word of the first witnesses it comes also to us, arousing us to believe and to witness. This coming of the Word to us can be understood as a claim, a command which meets us, and a law which is laid upon us. Of ourselves we do not and cannot know the Word of God. But it is now required of us that we take knowledge of it, since it gives itself to be recognised by us. Or to put it more concretely: although our way of life is so different from that of the prophets and apostles, it is now required of us that we hear their Word and take it up into our own particular situation, seeing that in Holy Scripture it has, in fact, already entered into our situation. The same process can be understood as a gift made to us, a possibility actually opened up to us: God's Word has for our sakes stepped forth out of the unapproachable mystery of its self-contained existence into the circle of those things which we can know. Or, again, to put it even more concretely: the biblical prophets and apostles did not merely live for themselves, or speak for themselves, but they spoke to us, and because their apparently so different and distant walk of life does actually intersect ours, we have to listen to them. In the last analysis, over and above both these insights, if this whole process achieves its goal and purpose by arousing us to believe and testify, we can only understand it as a mystery which encounters us. It is by no means a matter of course that God's Word exists for us as this claim or gift, or that with all the other things we have for good or ill, we should also have Holy Scripture. And again, it is not a matter of course that we should render obedience to that claim and accept that gift. On the contrary, when all this happens, it happens in virtue of the fact that Jesus Christ intercedes for us, taking our place before His Father, and in virtue of the illuminating and purifying work of the Holy Spirit upon us. In opposition to all that we can conceive as possible, there is then completed both objectively and subjectively an incomparable renewal. But it is still the case that this claim and gift, and even this miracle, whose occurrence is always so utterly inaccessible and incomprehensible, consist concretely in the fact that we ourselves are aroused to believe and witness, i.e., that the Word of God in the form of a human word gives itself to be appropriated by us in our humanity, so that now it is not merely God's Word nor even the word of apostles and prophets, but, as appropriated to us and received and accepted by us, it is our very own word. As the word spoken to us, we now speak it to ourselves and to others. How can it have reached us, how can its condescension have been completed, if in the last resort it remains foreign to us and outside of us, if we have not affirmed and accepted it—as, of course, the word which is appropriated to us, the foreign word which comes to us from without? How can it have reached us, if this does not mean that we decide to give it our hearing, and with our hearing ourselves? How can we believe if, remaining passive, we do not say to ourselves what is spoken to us? And how can we be witnesses if again, remaining passive, we do not say to others what is said to us? Even though we can and must understand what happens here as an unheard-of claim or gift, though we can and must remember that we do not understand how this objective and subjective miracle can occur when this claim is fulfilled and this gift accepted, yet we cannot fail to reckon with the fact that it does actually happen that in our humanity we ourselves are now drawn into the process in which the Word of God exercises its freedom and as the word of the prophets and apostles takes its course through the world. That we are believers and witnesses will always be a matter for doubt, and humanly speaking even for despair. We have to remember that this is a reality for which we can never do more than give thanks and pray. But we deny this reality, and therefore the whole process of events in which God's Word comes to man as a human word, and therefore the work of the Son and of the Holy Ghost, and therefore the self-revelation of God and even God Himself, if we try to escape the fact that we ourselves in our humanity stand at the preliminary end and goal of this process, not left outside, but drawn into its orbit, not as strangers but as children of the household, not as onlookers but as those who co-operate in responsibility, not passively but actively, not in ignorance, but as participants in the divine knowledge, *conscientes*[EN39]. [701]

If we ourselves in our humanity stand at the end and goal of this process, this cannot mean only that something encounters us, that we are placed in a receptive position, that something has been decided and ordained for us. But inasmuch as all this happens, because it happens to us in our humanity, it must also and primarily mean that our self-determination, our spontaneity and our activity are engaged in the service of the Word of God. This self-determination may be limited by its creatureliness and perverted by its sinfulness, but it is the characteristic essence of the humanity by which we are distinguished from the life of nature (at least in so far as we know or presume to know the latter). This does not mean that in virtue of this humanity we have, as it were, a disposition towards the service of the Word of God, and can therefore recognise ourselves as naturally responsive to God. In the very fact that our humanity is placed in the service of the Word of God, we recognise rather its incapacity for this service, and can understand the fact that we are called in this humanity to serve the Word of God only as a claim, a gift and a miracle. How can we serve grace if we are in a position to ascribe to our human nature as such a capacity for this service? Do we not then deny it even before we enter upon this service? On the other hand, how can we and will we enter upon and exercise this service if we try to refuse and withdraw our humanity from the Word of God? We cannot even appeal to its powerlessness, its creaturely insufficiency, its sinful perversity. For we are not asked about our disposition for this service. Its realisation is not conditioned by our fitness. The completion of the divine condescension is not limited by the incapacity of our humanity. The Word of God still comes to us even as those who are not disposed for its service. Again, and this time from the other side, it is obviously rebellion against grace if we try to withhold from it our humanity because the latter is so clearly unredeemed nature, because the fact and extent that we can serve grace by it is incomprehensible to us. Its full and real incomprehensibility only appears when we know that the Word of God comes to us only by the miraculous work of the Son and of the Holy

---

[EN39] co-knowers

[702] Ghost. If we do not realise this, we shall refuse our human service by appealing to our incapacity, and this plea will be just as much a manifestation of self-will as the other in which we appeal to our natural capacity and on this basis exalt ourselves as counterparts to God. The one standpoint as much as the other is alien to the true recognition of divine grace. If we realise that it is the divine claim and gift, the miraculous work of the Son and of the Holy Ghost, that God's Word reaches us, then a pessimistic self-assertion will be just as impossible as an optimistic; we can just as little withhold our humanity from the service of grace because of its unfitness, as we can flaunt it before God to our own self-glorification. Therefore, whatever may be said about their intrinsically insurmountable limitations, our self-determination, spontaneity and freedom will be placed in the service of the Word of God. It is ourselves that the Word of God concerns, intends and meets. It gives itself to be ours, and it wills us for itself. We are sinful creatures. We are unfit for its service. We cannot in our own strength become either believers or witnesses. In the light that falls upon us when we are taken into its service we have to discover and confess that we are not only useless, but inexcusably recalcitrant. But in spite of this, it concerns ourselves, and, because we are men, our decision and assent. We are not asked whether we are in a position to give or ascribe to this decision of ours the character of obedience, of a plain, clear-cut, honest, total and indeed absolute decision. Rather, we are told by the Word for which we have to decide that we are not in this position and never will be. We are told that the truth and goodness of our decision consists and can be sought only in the fact that it is made in virtue of Jesus Christ's intervention for us in which we can believe and to which we can testify, and in virtue of the gift of the Holy Spirit by which we become believers and witnesses. But on this presupposition, we are asked about our decision, and to be asked about our decision means we are asked about ourselves. Since the fall, to exist as a human being means to exist in decision. The question put to us by the Word about ourselves or our decision does not concern our goodness or badness, but concerns the agreement of our own decision with the decision that has been made concerning us in the Word spoken to us. Can we evade this agreement? Is it possible for us to dissent from the decision made about us in the Word of God and therefore continue the alienation described in the story of the fall. Can we persist in sin? Or must we identify our own decision and ourselves in our goodness or badness with the divine decision, in order that—irrespective of our goodness and badness—in that identification and therefore under the authority of the Word, we may be what we truly are? It is about this and this alone that we are asked. It is only in this sense that we are asked about our self-determination, spontaneity and activity. But in this sense we are asked, and to the question put to us in this sense we must reply one way or another.

[703] We add a further consideration. Here at the end and goal of the process in which God's Word comes to us as a human word, it is the individual man who is what he is as a man and therefore identifies himself with the decision made

about him in the Word of God. It is not the individual without the Church. It is not the individual apart from the relation to his neighbour indicated to him by his being in the Church. It is not, therefore, the individual who has not heard other men in the Church, who has imagined that he can hear the Word of God in some abstract relation between God and the soul, and the soul and God. It is the individual as a member of the body of Christ and therefore as a member of the Church. But as such the members of the Church are not a mass of interchangeable specimens, but in the whole context of their relationships with each other they are individual men. Although the Word of God is given to them in common and although they can only receive it in common, yet this giving and receiving does not take place in any mechanical way but in a spiritual communion corresponding to the individuality of the man Jesus and of all His witnesses, i.e., in the oneness of the many who as individuals are awakened to believe and testify, through the all-embracing oneness of Jesus Christ and the Holy Ghost, the oneness of the Church and baptism. Therefore the decision which stands at the end and goal of the process must be understood concretely, *concretissime*[EN40], as our very own decision, as thine and mine. I am merely recounting a myth if I speak of the coming of the Word of God to man as of something other than the coming of the Word to me. Only as the Word which comes to me can I hear it as the Word which comes to the Church and therefore to others too.

Perhaps it sounds self-evident, but it is not really so, if we say that in the nature of the case it is only as each individual thinks of himself that we can really think through all the matters which have been put forward in this connexion: the coming of God's Word as claim and gift and miracle, the overcoming of the false dialectic of the two forms of self-assertion, and particularly the idea of that decision in which the coming of the Word of God to man reaches its present goal. Those who do not know anything of themselves in this matter can know nothing at all. The conscience that is freed through the Word of God is the personal conscience of each individual, and it is each individual who partakes of the dignity but also of the burden of this freedom under the Word. We shall seek in vain for this freedom elsewhere than in the freedom of the individual.

But here, too, a critical reservation is demanded. As we have seen, it is not the case that our humanity as such, our characteristic existence as men in decision, is something good in itself, and that we have, as it were, to bring it to the Word of God in order that in co-operation with it, as partners with God qualified by our humanity, we may help to fulfil the course of God's Word in the world. We have also seen that no disqualification of our humanity can give us the occasion or the right to evade and resist the course of the Word of God. The case is exactly the same with the second consideration, that it is always an individual who is intended and reached when the Word of God calls man to [704] identify himself with the decision it has made about him. We have said indeed that in the Church it is always this or that individual who is addressed. But it is

---

[EN40] most concretely

not at all the case that, not in virtue of our common humanity, but in virtue of our particular humanity as this or that man, we have a capacity for communion with the Word and therefore a claim to that communion. It is not the case that the mystery of the individual, or personality—"the greatest boon of the children of men"—has to be brought to the Word of God as the most precious of gifts. Nor again is it the case that in consideration of the nothingness and lostness of our individuality, in doubt or despair about our strictly personal being, we have the right or warrant to withdraw from communion with the Word of God.

It should be noticed that neither in the Old nor in the New Testament, where it has sometimes been eagerly sought, does there appear an idea of the individual in virtue of which his immediate relationship to God is to be found in his human individuality. The Bible takes no independent interest in the individuality of man determined, as it were, from below or from within. What constitutes the members of the body of Christ, the members of the Church as such and therefore as individuals, is not the peculiar quality which this or that individual brings under his personal name and as his personal contribution to the discipleship of Jesus and to the Church. The Old and New Testaments know nothing of those "biblical character sketches" which people have tried to find in them, especially in modern times. The material sought in them for the characterisation of the most important and "greatest" personalities is obviously scanty and insufficient for the purpose. The investigation of the life of Jesus has foundered because critics have been so slow to see this truth. But as in the Bible universal humanity, i.e., human decision, is of interest only as implicated in the question whether it is identical with the decision of the Word of God concerning mankind, so also the special humanity of the individual is of interest only as implicated in the question whether this individual will accept and use the divine gift conferred upon him. It is only by his conduct as a steward of the talents committed to him, and not by his prior disposition, that it is decided into which category each of the servants in the parable Matt. $25^{14f.}$ will fall. And it is only in relation to the characterisation of the various and yet inter-related *charismata*[EN41], that what we would call the problem of individuality is discussed in the Pauline Epistles (e.g., Rom. $12^{3f.}$, 1 Cor. $12^{4f.}$, Eph. $4^{7f.}$).

It is just the grace of God's Word that it always comes in a quite specific, concrete, definitely challenging and self-giving form—for it is the free Word of God—not merely to the Church as a whole, but also in the Church to this or that individual, in order that in the Church he may be this man, this particular member. Confronted by this grace, neither my justifiable self-confidence nor my equally justifiable self-despair can be of the slightest interest. I am not asked who and what I am from below or from within, who or what I may be in my natural state as an individual. I am asked solely about my relationship to the Word of God as it comes specially to me, from above or from without, annihilating my pride and covering my sin. I am addressed by the name I received in [705] my baptism, and not by the title which might be given me by others as an indication of my personality. The point is that I, very definitely I, should be what I am in this relationship and therefore in the process of that annihilation and covering. The point is that I should take myself, very definitely myself,

---

[EN41] spiritual gifts

seriously in my particular existence created by my new birth by the Word of God. The point is that I should exist only as this particular man born again by the Word of God. The point is that I should yield and surrender my earthly and inner particularity to the particularity of the gift of grace offered to me. And I am not asked about the richness or poverty of my personality, but only about the possibility or impossibility of refusing and withdrawing myself from existence as this new man.

We must bear in mind a third characteristic. We have seen that at the end and goal of the process in which God's Word comes to mankind as a human word, a man is what he is as a man, and therefore decides in his self-identification with the decision of the Word of God about him. We have also seen that in virtue of the special divine decision made about him he is precisely this man. Our third point is that as such he becomes clear to himself in the individual decision in which his self-identification with the divine Word takes place. We cannot say that he only comes to exist in this event, but we must say that in this event alone he becomes clear to himself. As the founding, maintaining and governing of the Church as a whole has a history, so the life of its members has a history. The continuity of its history, the truth that at all times and in all places it is founded, maintained and governed by God's Word, is hidden from the Church. The Church cannot see this. It cannot point to it and reconstruct it. It can only believe it to be the truth: and how can this happen except in the constant fact of its founding, maintaining and governing? That the Church can only believe in this (but, of course, may and must believe in it) as a truth of God revealed to it, is shown in the fact that, as this event takes place, the Church will both give thanks and pray for its occurrence. It is precisely the same with the calling of the individual man and his awakening to faith and witness. Certainly, his whole existence is involved, the whole span of his life from his mother's womb to his death, and also its whole breadth, that is, his psychico-physical existence in the totality of its presuppositions, effects and relationships. Only in this totality are we really ourselves. Even if only a second of my existence in time is lacking, or a hair of my head, I am no longer I, man, this man. It is either in this totality that I am a target for the Word of God, or not at all. It is either in this totality that the decision of the Word of God is taken concerning me, and I am born again by the Word, or not at all. It is either in this totality, "with body and soul, in life and death," that I belong to "my faithful Saviour Jesus Christ," and am a living member of His body, or else it is not in any sense true. It is impossible to emphasise this too strongly. Its [706] truth is compromised by every qualification. Yet while I may and must believe this truth in this totality—and I do not believe it at all except in this totality—it is still the case that I can only believe it. In faith and only in faith is it clear to me, because and in so far as my faith is faith in the Word of God and therefore in Jesus Christ. In Jesus Christ, I am revealed to myself as he who in the totality of his existence is received and accepted by Him. I shall then accept this revelation as one accepts revelation in faith: I shall accept it with thankfulness and prayer. But apart from faith, and therefore apart from Jesus Christ, this truth is always hidden from me in its totality (without which it is not this truth). But in faith we always have to do with a single event, an individual decision, in which I decide in conformity with the decision of the Word of God. If in this event we link up with the fact that we have perhaps believed before, and if in this event we receive the promise that we will again believe in the future, if there is thus a state of believing which embraces past, present and future, faith itself is not identical with this state of believing. As distinct from it, it is never something which is there already. It is always a gift which has to be seized again and again. We can have it, and the retrospect and the prospect which it gives (and what can truly be called a Christian state of believing), only as it is given to us as a gift, and as we grasp it as such.

Here again we find the same false dialectic with its twofold perversion. On the one hand, there arises the optimistic self-assertion which considers that we can know, name and describe individual events in our own lives or that of others, the actuality of whose content consists in just this gift and its appropriation by us. These events are to be described as special experiences and illuminations, internal and external turning-points. They are extraordinary events in the context of the rest of life, islands in the stream, so to speak, but in this isolation they are to be understood as identifiable happenings, on whose actuality we can definitely count and reckon. But strangely enough, their isolation cannot usually be maintained, and on this presupposition it is not at all the case that the rest of a man's life, the totality of our existence in its determination by the Word of God, is respected as a truth which is concealed from us.

Once such extraordinary events are recognised and admitted in their supposed authenticity, the presumed insights into their occurrence increases, and the corresponding statements about them group themselves into series, patterns and pictures. There arises the so-called "miracle story which we have ourselves experienced." There arises the "testimony" which is supposed to be so edifying both to ourselves and to others. Alongside the confession of the Church in which Scripture is expounded, there arises the confession of the individual Christian, of which he himself is the object, that is, as he thinks he knows himself. There arises, in its main outlines, Christian biography, which, when it is completed, will do away with that hiddenness altogether, and represent the whole life of a man as a more or less uninterrupted sequence of such events.

[707]   And again we find the complementary pessimistic form of self-assertion in which we will have nothing to do with events of which the content is the gift and appropriation of faith. We defiantly dispute the reality of such things. We scornfully interpret whatever we hear from others in this respect as illusion and ecstatic fantasy. We contentedly accept the fact that in our own lives such things never have been and never will be. It is obviously not impossible that what in the eyes of some is fire from heaven appears to others as triviality and vanity. Indeed, it often happens in the life of one and the same person that he takes first the one view of these things and then the other.

The worst pessimists in this respect are always those who have been optimists. But again, the worst scepticism and indifference are often enough only the prelude or occasion for an all the more powerful assertion of these personally experienced events, and finally for an all the more complete abolition of every kind of hiddenness of the life in God. The two forms of self-assertion are as close together as this, and as little are they protected from turning into their opposite.

To all this we can only say again that we are not asked about the thing on which both sides believe so passionately that they can hold their views. We are not asked about the faith-incidents as such, which can certainly be seen in our lives, but obviously only in the greatest ambiguity. We are not asked about any sort of humanly demonstrable actuality as such. We are asked about ourselves by the Word of God. Each individual is individually asked about himself. And this means, of course, that we are asked about certain particular events of our life in which the hidden totality of our life in God becomes visible to faith. We have seen, however, how the humanness of the decision for which we are asked, and its distinctive humanness as our own personal decision, are certainly not to be regarded as springing from us, from within and from below, but from the Word of God which alone confers reality upon them. And it is just the same with the particularity of the events of faith. It will fare ill with us if, according to the common presupposition of these two types of self-assertion, as a proof of their actuality we have to perceive and establish them as such by our own resources, from within and below. It will fare ill with us if just at this point, where our whole spiritual life is at stake, we have to rely upon facts which can, of course, be a subject for boasting, but can also very obviously be a subject for despair. It will fare ill with us if even the suspicion can arise that the facts in question have been created and perhaps only imagined by us ourselves. But this is just not the case. For the faith which forms the content of those special events, whether interpreted as a divine gift or as our own appropriation of this gift, is primarily and essentially faith in Jesus Christ. Both it and therefore also those special events of faith are primarily and essentially to be regarded only from above, from Jesus Christ, because they are only real when seen in this way from above, from Jesus Christ. Again, the fact is that both he [708] who boasts of that which is demonstrable on the human level, and he who despairs of it, are missing the mark. Why should it not be the case that at this point—even if with the fluctuating and yet factual certainty which alone is possible in this connexion—a single thing is in fact to be affirmed? It is not to be denied but rather affirmed that in certain humanly identifiable moments and situations, not simply in recollection or expectation but in the concrete present of faith, we are in fact humbly and thankfully aware in a very special way, not merely of our state of believing, but of our real faith, and therefore of our whole life as a life lived in God, and that in this sense we gladly recall such moments as certainly significant. Of course, this does not mean that we simply have to believe that this has happened. Nor does it mean that when it is a question of proving faith we have the right and duty to refer to them. For how can it be otherwise than that on the other hand at other moments—indeed perhaps already in the same moment—we are just as certainly made aware of the relativity and ambiguity of such an event when humanly affirmed, that therefore to some extent it falls from its special position into the series of other ordinary events in our life, and mingles with the stream of that totality of our life which, being our life in God, is hidden and not revealed to us, and therefore cannot be the object of our faith and witness. In their human identification these special events are obviously subjected to an interplay of light and darkness which can only damage and forbid both the absolute affirmation of the optimist and the absolute negation of the pessimist. The really outstanding events of our life, upon which our faith lives and in which our whole life is revealed to us in faith as life in God, are not those which we can affirm with this human certitude and then have to doubt again. They are not subject to this fluctuation; they can and must be discussed apart from this false dialectic. These really outstanding events of our life are simply identical with our share in the great acts of God in His revelation. The fact is that according to the testimony of Scripture God's revelation is a unique thing, and yet is completed in certain distinct and definite events. And it is this fact which forms the basis of the real distinctiveness of those moments in which faith apprehends them, and also of their significance for our whole life. We must say further and without hesitation that just those individual and definite events in which, according to the Bible, God's self-revelation is fulfilled, in that they have already happened and we here and now may share in them, constitute the reality of the faith-events of our own life. Whether certain humanly identifiable incidents of this our life remind us of this reality or not, still the reality itself continually breaks through these fluctuating possibilities, and in it these definite revelatory events have taken place in such a way that here and now we are

[709]   called to share in them. In any event, it is only in their own singularity that the identifiable and yet so insecurely identifiable events of our life have their truth. Whether we can evade participating in those biblical events or not is the question which God's Word puts to us—it does so both when we are conscious of the exalted and exalting events of our life and also when we are conscious rather of their relativity. The truth of such events is determined solely by the content of our faith which is active in them, not by the meaning which, in their fluctuating certainty as the effects of our faith, we sometimes arbitrarily like to ascribe to them, and at other times just as arbitrarily like to deny them.

It is said that H. F. Kohlbrügge once answered the question: When was he converted? by the laconic reply: On Golgotha. This answer, with all its fundamental implications, was not the witty retort of an embarrassed and unconverted man, but the only possible and straightforward answer of a truly converted Christian. The events of faith in our own life can, in fact, be none other than the birth, passion, death, ascension and resurrection of Jesus Christ, the faith of Abraham, Isaac and Jacob, the exodus of Israel from Egypt, its journey through the desert, its entrance into the land of Canaan, the outpouring of the Holy Ghost at Pentecost and the mission of the apostles to the heathen. Every verse in the Bible is virtually a concrete faith-event in my own life. Whether this is actually the case, whether with my own life I have been present at this or that event here testified to me, this and this alone is what I am asked by the Word of God which bears witness to me of God's revelation in and through all this, and in every single verse of Scripture. In comparison with this, what can be the value of the various more or less reliable insights which, apart from these testimonies, I may have in myself? Is there a miracle story that I can relate from my own life, which, especially if it is genuine, will not be totally dissolved in this divine miracle story, and which therefore will hardly be worth relating *in abstracto*? Have I anything to testify about myself which I cannot testify infinitely better if I make my own the simplest ingredient of the Old Testament or New Testament witness? Have I experienced anything more important, incisive, serious, contemporary than this, that I have been personally present and have shared in the crossing of Israel through the Red Sea but also in the adoration of the golden calf, in the baptism of Jesus but also in the denial of Peter and the treachery of Judas, that all this has happened to me here and now? If I believe, then this must be the right point of view. If this is the right point of view, what other faith-events in my life should I and could I wish to seek? What, then, becomes of the bold assertion with which I claim first this and then that crisis and turning-point, and then gradually my whole life, as a sacred history? And what becomes of the defiant and shrinking doubt and despair about all exalted and exalting moments, and finally about my whole life? However high may rise or however deep may fall the waves of life's events, as they are perceptible to us from within and below, the real movement of my life, the real events in which it is clear to me that in the whole dimension of my existence I belong to God, both at the flood and ebb, are secured from the other side, by the Word of God Himself. And we shall have to answer this question and this question alone: whether, after the Word of God has sought to provide us with this movement and meaning, we have perhaps evaded it?

All this, therefore, is human freedom under the Word based upon the freedom of the Word of God. We see that it is a question of genuine human freedom, of us ourselves in our decision, of each of us personally, in the special events of our life in which it becomes clear to us that our whole existence is at [710] stake. But we see also that this genuine human freedom is based in its entirety upon the freedom of God's Word, upon the all-embracing decision which through the Word has been pronounced upon mankind, upon the particular grace with which the Word comes to this or that man, upon the uniqueness of the events which form the content of the Word. Therefore, human freedom cannot encroach upon divine freedom. Always and in every respect the latter precedes the former. Yet, on the other hand, divine freedom cannot destroy and suspend human freedom. Always and in every respect the former draws the latter to and after itself. We ourselves are rooted in this genuine human freedom under the Word, prayerfully and thankfully, recognising this reality as it wills to be recognised—we ourselves in our humanity—as the present end and goal of the process whereby God's Word comes to man as a human word; not as ignorant but as sharing in the divine knowledge, as *conscientes*[EN42].

We have still to make clear to ourselves the fundamental scope of this cognisance and of our freedom under the Word. How far is it a fact that God's Word does not remain God's Word, or even the word of apostles and prophets, but

---

[EN42] co-knowers

gives itself to be appropriated by the Church and therefore is received and accepted by the members of the Church and becomes their own word? What is the place of interpretation and application of the Word of God under the freedom of the Word? Here we have to answer the fundamental question, and we must give a fundamental answer. We presuppose that an interpretation and application of the Word actually comes to pass in human freedom under the Word, just as we previously assumed that there was really under the Word a human authority—that of the Church. But as in the former case, in view of the indissoluble connexion of genuine human authority with the authority of the Word, we could not presume to present a system of ecclesiastical authority operating as though it were not the result of the authoritative Word of God itself seen in actual lordship over the Church, so now we may not venture to advance and systematically to represent freedom under the Word, i.e., genuine effective interpretation and application based upon and connected indissolubly with the Word of God, as though this were not the act of the free Word of God itself which is always beyond our control and inscrutable to us. Assuming this act, and also assuming that true interpretation and application of the divine Word is a real event, the one thing which we can—and must now—do is to mention and discuss some of the human possibilities in which it becomes evident that human freedom is actively engaged in this event, and in what sense it is engaged.

1. We have already characterised freedom under the Word, that is, human freedom in the Church, as the assumption of responsibility for the interpretation and application of Holy Scripture. Let us now seek to grasp generally [711] what this means. If the members of the Church have a responsibility towards Scripture, this clearly means that the founding, maintaining and governing of the Church by Scripture does not happen in such a way that the members of the Church are only spectators or even objects of this happening. It takes place rather in such a way that in their specific place and function they become subjects of it. To be a member of the Church in relation to Scripture which founds, maintains and rules the Church, means not only to hear, receive and believe the Word of God, and so in one's own life to become a man directed and consecrated by the Word; more than all this it means to take seriously and understand as one's own responsibility the effective operation of the Word, its being continuously expressed and heard, its being continuously proclaimed and made fruitful. The Word of God wills always to be newly and more widely heard in the Church, and beyond the Church lies the world, where by the Church it also wills to be always heard. Because of his freedom which is grounded in this Word, a member of the Church cannot retain a passive, indifferent and merely waiting role in face of this will of the divine Word, as though anyway, in its own time what has to happen will happen. Certainly, it will happen, but not without us. We have seen that we ourselves stand at the present end and goal of the way which the Word of God takes in approaching men. We ourselves are thus present when the way leads on into the Church and the

world. Called by the Church into the Church, we ourselves become the Church into which we are called. Yet we cannot merely note that the Church is calling and wait to see whether and how far the Church will continue to call. Rather we ourselves have become the Church in person, and as such have been made responsible for its future. And this means in concrete terms that we are responsible participants in the great event by which Holy Scripture lives and rules in the Church and in the world.

It was not to all men generally, but to His disciples as witnesses, that Jesus said (Mt. 5¹³ᶠ): Ye are the salt of the earth; ye are the light of the world. It follows that, where the original witness of the revelation performs its proper task, it does not function as fructifying salt simply for the private enjoyment and use of those who happen to be called and illuminated; but in principle the same task is laid upon them, too, differing from that of the prophets and apostles only in the fact that for them Jesus is now the One to whom prophets and apostles bear witness, so that their task has this witness as concrete content. The prayer of Peter in Ac. 4²⁹: "Grant unto thy servants that with all boldness (μετὰ παρρησίας πάσης) they may speak thy Word," must now be their prayer too, *mutatis mutandis*ᴱᴺ⁴³. And it is certainly not only in a moral sense that Paul speaks concerning the public and private speech of Christians, but (perhaps not without allusion to Mt. 5¹³) he is referring to their commission in the Church, when in Col. 4⁶ he writes: "Let your speech be always with grace, seasoned with salt, that ye may know how ye ought to answer every man," or when again in Eph. 4²⁹ he requires that the speech of Christians be "good to the use of edifying (ἀγαθὸς πρὸς οἰκοδομὴν τῆς χρείας), that it may minister grace unto the hearers." There is a very clear connexion with 1 Pet. 3¹⁵ where the persecuted Christians are told that if they would sanctify the Lord Christ in their hearts, they must be ready to answer (πρὸς ἀπολογίαν) every man who may ask them to justify the hope they entertain. Again, it is in this and not merely a generally moralistic sense that we must understand what is said in the famous passage in Jas. 3¹ᶠ concerning the judgment under which they stand who have not dedicated their tongue to the service of teaching.

[712]

We must always bear in mind how far from self-explanatory it is that there can be any sort of human participation and responsibility in this matter. At this point we have good cause to consider again the whole secret and mystery of the incarnation, of the existence of the man Jesus, and His decisive prophetic office, and the whole riddle of the existence of His plenipotentiary witnesses. It is indeed true that we ourselves with our word are included in this circle; but what an incomprehensible condescension of God, what an incomprehensible elevation of man is to be observed in this truth! We have to realise and accept it in all its mystery and incomprehensibility. We are not asked whether we of ourselves hold it to be possible or can make it possible; we have to observe and accept it in its reality, and then to prove its possibility by the exercise of the freedom which is thereby promised to us. That the responsibility laid upon us is too exalted and wonderful is an aspect of the matter to be considered and pondered. But, on the other hand, it is to be noted that we are asked whether we can well evade such a responsibility. If we accept the fact that we cannot, then we must consider in what exactly this responsibility consists. In order to

---

ᴱᴺ⁴³ in different circumstances

be proclaimed and heard again and again both in the Church and the world, Holy Scripture requires to be explained. As the Word of God it needs no explanation, of course, since as such it is clear in itself. The Holy Ghost knows very well what He has said to the prophets and apostles and what through them He wills also to say to us. This clarity which Scripture has in itself as God's Word, this objective *perspicuitas*EN44 which it possesses, is subject to no human responsibility or care. On the contrary, it is the presupposition of all human responsibility in this matter. All the explanation of Scripture for which we are responsible can be undertaken only on the presupposition that Scripture is clear in itself as God's Word; otherwise it will at once disintegrate. And all scriptural exegesis for which we are responsible can lead only to the threshold beyond which Scripture is clear in itself as God's Word. But this Word in Scripture assumes the form of a human word. Human words need interpretation because as such they are ambiguous, not usually, of course, in the intention of those who speak, but always for those who hear. Among the various possibilities, the sense intended by the speaker has to be conveyed, and as the sense which they have for the speaker, it has to be communicated to the thinking of the hearer, so that the words have now a meaning for him, and indeed the meaning intended by the speaker. Perhaps this twofold interpretation, which can be distinguished as exegesis and application, can be made at once by the hearer; perhaps the speaker himself is in a position to offer this twofold interpretation of his words, or, if not their application, at least their exegesis; perhaps a third party must intervene and perform this service of interpretation for speaker and hearer. All human words without exception need one of these interpretations. Now, since God's Word in Scripture has taken the form of a human word, it has itself incurred the need of such interpretation. Our human responsibility is related to this need of interpretation, and thus to Scripture expressed in human words. When we take into consideration all that is comprised by the term "interpretation," it can be only a partial responsibility. Why should not the prophets and apostles always be heard directly in the interpretation which the hearers themselves are enabled to give? And why should they not always be in a position to offer an explanation themselves? It is not, then, the case that by the very fact that it has assumed the form of Scripture, and therefore of human words, God's Word is, so to speak, defencelessly exposed to the need of human interpretation for which we as members of the Church have been made responsible. It is good that in the life of the Church these first possibilities of interpretation in their mutual relatedness both continue to play their part. It is good that, alongside of the clarity which the Word of God has in itself, there is also a self-interpretation of its form as a human word.

[713]

This, too, forms a presupposition of the scriptural exegesis in the narrower sense which is incumbent upon us, and without which it cannot itself be realised. All the same, the first two

---

EN44 perspicuity

possibilities have their limits. Not every one, and no one at all times and in all circumstances, can be his own interpreter of Scripture, affirming the meaning of the biblical word from his own resources, and affirming it in such a way that it has meaning for him, and indeed its original meaning. We must also add that not always and not to everyone are the biblical authors, who speak from the point of view of their own circle and reveal to us only a small excerpt from that circle, in a position to make the meaning of their words clear and also to communicate it to the thinking of the modern reader. We are thinking of the man (Ac. 8²⁶ᶠ·) who was reading Is. 53 in his chariot—it was not quite unprepared that he had gone to Jerusalem to worship—and who to the question: "Understandest thou what thou readest?" had to answer: "How can I, except some man should guide me?" (ἐὰν μή τις ὁδηγήσει με).

At this point there commences what we may call the need of interpretation in the narrower sense, and at this point, too, there also commences the responsibility laid on the members of the Church. A member of the Church is as such called upon to be the third party who, in order to help on both sides, intervenes between the speaker and the hearer, and therefore between the human word of Scripture and the other members of the Church, but also between the biblical word and the men of the world. On the side of Scripture, he helps by attempting to illuminate its sense, on the side of the hearing or reading man, by attempting to suggest to him the fact and extent that Scripture has a meaning for him. The former task has also to be understood, of course, as a service to men, the latter as a service to Scripture. [714]

We might glance at this point at the excellent definition which Polanus has given of biblical interpretation: *Interpretatio sacrae Scripturae est explicatio veri sensus et usus illius, verbis perspicuis instituta ad gloriam Dei et aedificationem ecclesiae*EN45 (*Synt. Theol. chr.*, 1609, 635 f.). From this we see that it is a question of (1) the *verus sensus*EN46 and (2) the *verus usus*EN47 of Scripture. Both remain obviously clear in and by themselves. Both can also speak for themselves, and both do so. Yet both need *explicatio*EN48; hence there is a need of interpretation and application. The region of the *verba*EN49, lying between the two, is problematical. Here there is a need, and there arises a responsibility. It is a question of the *verba perspicua*EN50 in regard both to the *sensus*EN51 and also the *usus*EN52 of Scripture. That the necessary work of communication should be done: *ad gloriam Dei et aedificationem ecclesiae*EN53, is the task of *interpretatio*EN54, and therefore a matter of the responsibility laid upon members of the Church.

It will be good to emphasise more strongly than was done in the 16th and 17th centuries that fundamentally this responsibility is laid upon all members of the Church and not upon a specialised class of biblical scholars. The need

---

EN45 The interpretation of sacred Scripture is the exposition of the true sense and use of it, organised in clear words for the glory of God and for the edification of His church
EN46 true sense
EN47 true use
EN48 explanation
EN49 words
EN50 clear words
EN51 sense
EN52 use
EN53 to the glory of God and the edification of the church
EN54 interpretation

for the interpreting third party is not an isolated or occasional thing. There are the two first possibilities of interpretation, as a result of which the Word of God, quite apart from the clarity which it has in itself, may even as a human word, so to speak, go its own way on its own feet, so that there is always a direct relationship and possibility of understanding between the biblical authors and their modern readers. Yet despite this, the life of Scripture in the Church and in the world never rests solely upon these two possibilities, and the Word of God has surrendered itself so fully to the need of interpretation that some mediation is always necessary. There is no one who as hearer of the Word does not also and necessarily live by the service of such mediators. They may perhaps be remote from him. They may not be known to him as such. But they are in fact effectual, and they have intervened between the scriptural word and himself, and performed for him the service of interpretation and application. We can declare positively that the Church as a whole is an organisation which exists for this mediatorial work. For this reason no member of the Church can remain unconcerned, idle and inactive in face of this duty. If the interpretation of Scripture is not the concern of a special office but of the whole Church, no member of the Church can remain a mere spectator of what is or is not undertaken by this office to this end. Only when every member of the Church realises that the responsibility in this matter devolves upon him too can there be an intelligent critical appreciation of what is or is not done in this regard. If a part—and probably much the greater part—of the Church declines its responsibility for this task, it signifies nothing more nor less than that this section of the Church is renouncing the freedom which it is offered under the Word, and wishes to live only by authority in the Church. In this

[715] case, how soon it will be manifest that for this party there is no ecclesiastical authority either. Those who are silent in deference to scriptural learning, the congregation which is passive in matters of biblical exegesis, is committed already to secret rebellion. It is emancipated from the Canon and confession, and therefore from the Word of God and from faith. Therefore it is no longer a true congregation of Jesus Christ. Whoever will have nothing to do with this secret and one day open rebellion, whoever wants ecclesiastical authority for the sake of the authority of God's Word, must affirm freedom under the Word as the freedom of all Christian men, and must wish the congregation to participate in scriptural exegesis with real responsibility.

2. The necessary and fundamental form of all scriptural exegesis that is responsibly undertaken and practised in this sense must consist in all circumstances in the freely performed act of subordinating all human concepts, ideas and convictions to the witness of revelation supplied to us in Scripture. Subordination is not opposed to freedom. Freedom means spontaneous activity in relation to an object, such as is characteristic of human conduct and decision, as opposed to merely passive conduct determined from without and subject to necessary development. But freedom does not necessarily mean the divine sovereignty over the object, nor as human freedom does it necessarily mean a

relation of reciprocal influence between the object and the freely acting self over against the object. If there is an object in regard to which any other appropriate reaction is excluded, why should not human spontaneity in face of it consist in man's putting himself under it without at the same time putting himself over it? We may ask whether there is such an object. Even if there is, we can and must also ask the question whether in fact such a subordination of man over against it will be so realised that all impulses to superiority are effectively excluded. It is easy enough to show that, in point of fact, even in face of such an object man lapses into a relation of reciprocity and further into the presumption of his being divinely and sovereignly controlled, so that, even in the most willing subordination, superiority makes itself felt. But all this does not alter the fact that if there is an object which requires activity in relation to it, and permits no other kind of activity but that of subordination, then the only freedom possible to man consists in the fulfilment of this subordination—and this without its ceasing to be freedom, or being less really freedom than in activity over against objects which evoke the relation of reciprocal activity. He comes to take himself seriously in the exercise of this freedom; he comes to exercise his freedom in this way, without even asking about the result, about which in the moment of decision he must not ask; or he comes in this way to discharge the task. In that God's Word is given to us in Holy Scripture, an object is given to us which requires our spontaneous activity, but this activity of subordination.

In Holy Scripture we are dealing with a Word of God coming to us in the [716] form of human words, and, in the activity the Word demands of us, we are dealing with the explanation of this Word, in so far as in its human form it needs an explanation. That the essential form of its explanation must be subordination is based, of course, on the circumstance that it is God's Word in human form. What make the Word of God, in the form in which we encounter it, obscure and in need of interpretation are the ideas, thoughts and convictions which man always and everywhere brings to this Word from his own resources. When the Word of God meets us, we are laden with the images, ideas and certainties which we ourselves have formed about God, the world and ourselves. In the fog of this intellectual life of ours the Word of God, which is clear in itself, always becomes obscure. It can become clear to us only when this fog breaks and dissolves. This is what is meant by the subordination of our ideas, thoughts and convictions. If the Word of God is to become clear to us, we cannot ascribe to them the same worth as we do to it. We cannot try to appraise the Word of God by reference to them; or to cling to them in face of the Word of God. The movement which we have to make in relation to it—and quite freely, of course—can be only that of yielding, surrender and withdrawal.

Is. 40[12ff.] certainly contains the suggestion of a theory of knowledge: "Who hath measured the waters in the hollow of his hand, and meted out heaven with the span, and comprehended the dust of the earth in a measure, and weighed the mountains in scales, and the hills in a balance? Who hath directed the Spirit of the Lord, or being his counsellor hath taught him? With whom took he counsel, and who instructed him, and taught him in the path of judgment, and taught him knowledge, and shewed to him the way of understanding?" Similarly Is. 55⁷ᶠᶠ: "Let the wicked forsake his way, and the unrighteous man his thoughts: and let him return unto the Lord, and he will have mercy upon him; and to our God, for he will abundantly pardon. For my thoughts are not your thoughts, neither are your ways my ways, saith the Lord. For as the heavens are higher than the earth, so are my ways higher than your ways, and my thoughts than your thoughts."

The matter seems further complicated by the fact that God's thoughts in His Word do not come to us *in abstracto*ᴱᴺ⁵⁵ but *in concreto*ᴱᴺ⁵⁶ in the form of the human word of prophets and apostles, which as such is not only the expression of God's thoughts but also the expression of their own. It is the case, then, that the divine Word itself meets us right in the thick of that fog of our own intellectual life, as having taken the same form as our own ideas, thoughts and convictions. It is "a light that shineth in a dark place" (2 Pet. 1¹⁹). But in fact this apparent complication makes it all simple and easy to understand. The pure Word of God as such needs, of course, no explanation because, like the light of the sun above our atmosphere, it is clear in itself. But as such it would not have come to us, and we could have nothing to do with it. In fact, however, without [717] ceasing to be clear in itself—clear always by reason of the clarity which it possesses in itself—it has come down to us through the testimony of apostles and prophets. For that reason it has come to need interpretation in so far as it has assumed the mode of our intellectual world and is thus exposed to the risk of being understood, or rather not understood, by us according to the habits of our mentality, in the relationship of reciprocal activity by which we are normally accustomed to understand human words. But just because it has compromised itself in this way, it has become capable of explanation; not only of fundamental self-explanation in virtue of its intrinsic clarity, but also of the interpretation which its human witnesses are at least partially capable of giving, of the interpretation which the human hearers and readers of these witnesses, again at least partially, are also in a position to give, and finally of interpretation in the narrowest sense of the term, by which the members of the Church serve the Word of God and each man his brother. All this is possible because the Word of God is not given to us *in abstracto*ᴱᴺ⁵⁷, because it is real light, not merely in the for us inaccessible stratosphere of its inner existence, but also, thanks to the resurrection of Jesus Christ in the witness of the prophets and apostles, in the atmosphere of our own intellectual world. This means that this subordination to the Word, which is the basis for its interpretation in so far as this is our responsibility, is no mere idea or empty postulate, in face of which the only possible actuality is that we set ourselves above the

---

ᴱᴺ⁵⁵ in the abstract
ᴱᴺ⁵⁶ concretely
ᴱᴺ⁵⁷ in the abstract

Word of God, and in the end probably in an absolute sense, as we are accustomed to do in regard to other objects.

Such a relation would obtain if we had to do with the eternal Logos of God as such, and with the world as its form of manifestation. As we can see from every form of heathenism, and every philosophy which looses itself even relatively from the revelation of God in Jesus Christ, subordination to it would then simply take the form of a reciprocity of subordinate and superior, behind which it would appear that the real meaning is the attempt to express divine sovereignty over the object. But this is not the true relationship, seeing the eternal Logos has become incarnate, has risen in the flesh, and in the flesh has established a witness for Himself.

Just because we have to do with God's Word in the form of definite human words, the realisation of this subordinate relationship becomes a concrete task. Certainly we are not concerned with its final accomplishment ; but it can be seen and understood concretely as a task imposed upon us. To interpret God's Word must and can now mean to interpret Holy Scripture. And because the interpretation of the Word of God can take place only through man's subordination, this subordination now comes concretely to mean that we have to subordinate ourselves to the word of the prophets and apostles; not as one subordinates oneself to God, but rather as one subordinates oneself for the sake of God and in His love and fear to the witnesses and messengers which He Himself has constituted and empowered. In the real contrast between the [718] ideas, thoughts and convictions which we meet in the words of the biblical witnesses and our own ideas, thoughts and conceptions, there can and must be practised that proper subordination in which alone the illumination of the Word of God can take place at least for us. It is true that in the last resort this clarity is intrinsic to the Word. It is true that every interpretation of Scripture consists substantially in the interpretation which the Word gives of itself. It is true that all the clarity which the words of the apostles and prophets can have in themselves and for us without special explanation, and therefore all the clarity which we can lend to the Word and to the brethren through interpretation in the narrowest sense of the term, rests ultimately upon the clarity which the Word of God has in itself. But it is still the case that this self-illumination does not take place without us, and therefore terminates in that freedom to which as members of the Church we are called, and therefore in a human activity in the service of the Word of God. This activity becomes necessary and possible, is commanded and permitted, by the fact that we have the Word in the form of its human witnesses. It is over against them that this subordination as the essential form of human interpretation must take place; not in regard to the divine Word in general, but in regard to its human witnesses. Otherwise it does not take place at all. But in what must it then consist? It is not as though we had simply to abandon and forget our ideas, thoughts and convictions. We certainly cannot do that, just as little as we can free ourselves from our own shadow. Nor should we try to do it; for that would be arrogance rather than humility. Subordination does not mean the elimination and annihilation

of our own resources. Subordination implies that the subordinate is there as such and remains there. It means placing oneself behind, following, complying as subordinate to superior. This is what is required in subordinating our ideas, thoughts and convictions to the witness which confronts us in Scripture. It cannot mean that we have to allow our ideas, thoughts and convictions to be supplanted, so to speak, by those of the prophets and apostles, or that we have to begin to speak the language of Canaan instead of our own tongue. In that case we should not have subordinated ourselves to them, but at most adorned ourselves with their feathers. In that case nothing would have been done in the interpretation of their words, for we should merely have repeated them parrot-like. Subordination, if it is to be sincere, must concern the purpose and meaning indicated in the ideas, thoughts and convictions of the prophets and apostles, that is, the testimony which, by what they say as human beings like ourselves, they wish to bear. To this testimony of their words we must subordinate ourselves—and this is the essential form of scriptural exegesis—with what we for our own part hold to be true, beautiful and good. With the whole weight of our reason and experience we have to follow in the path of this
[719]   testimony and become compliant to it. It is another matter that in the process elements in the stock of our experience will be set aside as superfluous and discordant, others receive quite a new form and yet others be newly added to this stock. The decisive point is that in scriptural exegesis Scripture itself as a witness to revelation must have unconditional precedence of all the evidence of our own being and becoming, our own thoughts and endeavours, hope and suffering, of all the evidence of intellect and senses, of all axioms and theorems, which we inherit and as such bear with us.

Scriptural exegesis rests on the assumption that the message which Scripture has to give us, even in its apparently most debatable and least assimilable parts, is in all circumstances truer and more important than the best and most necessary things that we ourselves have said or can say. In that it is the divinely ordained and authorised witness to revelation, it has the claim to be interpreted in this sense, and if this claim be not duly heeded, it remains at bottom inexplicable. The Bible is outwardly, so to speak, accessible only from a certain point below. Therefore we must take our stand at that point below, in order to look up to the corresponding point above. In this connexion we are reminded of Jas. 1 25: ὁ δὲ παρακύψας εἰς νόμον τέλειον τὸν τῆς ἐλευθερίας καὶ παραμείνας ... EN58. Of course, humanly speaking, no one can be obliged or compelled to this παρακύπτειν EN59: it must be an act of human freedom. But if we cannot decide for it, then from the standpoint of our own unshaken intellectual world we can perceive the outlines of the apparently equally unshaken world of the Bible; and there may then arise the relative understanding which is possible between representatives of different worlds. This may lead on to the corresponding interpretation of the Bible. It cannot in this case be explained as a witness to revelation, not even by one who understands it supremely well in this way. It can be explained as a witness to revelation only to a human intellectual world the inner security of which has been shaken, and which has become yielding and responsive to the biblical world; and then it will be

---

EN58 the one who looks intently into the whole law of freedom, and continues ...
EN59 intent looking

manifest at once that the biblical intellectual world is not an unshaken quantity, but a moving, living organ existing and functioning in a very definite service. In order that it should perform this service for us, and only for this reason, we must bring to it that subordination. Because it performs this service, it speaks in all its parts with greater correctness and weight than we ourselves can speak to ourselves. We cannot perform this service for ourselves, but only allow it to be performed by the Bible. This service consists precisely in the communication of the witness to revelation which is proper, not to our world, but to the Bible and its world. This is the deeper meaning of the only apparently tautological exegetical rule of the older Protestant orthodoxy, whereby an interpretation of Scripture is to be recognised as true or false by the fact that, if it is true, it is in accord with Scripture so far as this is the Word of God: *Norma interpretandi scripturam et iudicandi de interpretatione scripturae sacrae verane sit an falsa, est ipsamet scriptura sacra, quae vox Dei est. Quaecunque enim interpretatio consentit cum scriptura, illa est vera et ex Deo; quaecungue ab ea dissentit, est falsa et non est ex Deo*EN60. To this is added the citation, Is. 8^{20}: "(Hold) to the law and to the testimony: if they speak not according to this word, it is because there is no light in them;" and Lk. 16^{29}: "They have Moses and the prophets; let them hear them;" and 1 Jn. 4^6: "We are of God; he that knoweth God heareth us; he that is not of God heareth not us. Hereby know we the spirit of truth, and the spirit of error" (Polanus, *ib.*, 683).

The decisive basis of this fundamental rule of all scriptural exegesis can be inferred, of course, only from the content of Scripture, and only from there [720] can it become really intelligible. Why must we subordinate the testimony of our own spirit to the testimony of the spirit of Scripture? Why do we have this peculiar assumption which is so obviously out of accord with the technique of interpretation generally? Why is it that in this case interpretation is not a conversation *inter pares*EN61, but *inter impares*EN62, although here, too, we have one man confronting another man, and one human intellectual world another? We will leave aside for the moment what we have already established earlier in another connexion—that perhaps the technique of interpretation generally, in so far as it does not seem to go beyond that conversation *inter pares*EN63, has every cause to learn from the special biblical science of interpretation which in the last resort is perhaps the only possible one. There will be reasons for the fact that it does not desire, and is not able, to do this. But it is certain that biblical hermeneutics must be controlled by this special fundamental principle because the content of the Bible imperatively requires it. The content of the Bible, and the object of its witness, is Jesus Christ as the name of the God who deals graciously with man the sinner. To heed and understand its witness is to realise the fact that the relation between God and man is such that God is gracious to man: to man who needs Him, who as a sinner is thrown wholly

---

EN60 The rule for interpreting Scripture and judging whether an interpretation of sacred Scripture is true or false is sacred Scripture itself, which is the voice of God. For whichever interpretation agrees with Scripture, is truly from God; whichever dissents from it, is false and is not from God

EN61 among equals

EN62 among unequals

EN63 among equals

upon God's grace, who cannot earn God's grace, and for whom it is indissolubly connected with God's gracious action towards him, for whom therefore it is decisively one with the name of Jesus Christ as the name of the God who acts graciously towards him. To hear this is to hear the Bible—both as a whole and in each one of its separate parts. Not to hear this means *eo ipso*[EN64] not to hear the Bible, neither as a whole, nor therefore in its parts. The Bible says all sorts of things, certainly; but in all this multiplicity and variety, it says in truth only one thing—just this: the name of Jesus Christ, concealed under the name Israel in the Old Testament, revealed under His own name in the New Testament, which therefore can be understood only as it has understood itself, as a commentary on the Old Testament. The Bible becomes clear when it is clear that it says this one thing: that it proclaims the name Jesus Christ and therefore proclaims God in His richness and mercy, and man in his need and helplessness, yet living on what God's mercy has given and will give him. The Bible remains dark to us if we do not hear in it this sovereign name, and if, therefore, we think we perceive God and man in some other relation than the one determined once for all by this name. Interpretation stands in the service of the clarity which the Bible as God's Word makes for itself; and we can properly interpret the Bible, in whole or part, only when we perceive and show that what it says is said from the point of view of that concealed and revealed name of Jesus Christ, and therefore in testimony to the grace of which we as men stand in need, of which as men we are incapable and of which we are made

[721] participants by God. From this is to be inferred the basic principle of the subordination of our ideas, thoughts and convictions to the testimony of Scripture itself. Our own ideas, thoughts and convictions as such, as ours, certainly do not run in the direction of the testimony which has this particular content. From the standpoint of what the biblical witness says, the fog and darkness of the human world of thought consist in the fact that, while it arises and subsists as our world, it constantly exposes our nature, the nature of sinful man, without the name of Jesus Christ, and therefore without the God who deals graciously with us. The nature of this man is a striving to justify himself from his own resources in face of a God whose image he has fashioned in his own heart, to make himself as great as possible and therefore at the same time to make God as small as possible. But if the Word of God has actually come into its own, and if it is to be clearly seen, the only thing which can happen to the world of thought which exposes the nature of man is that it should at least give ground (for we cannot simply free ourselves from it, nor ought we to try to do so, since emancipation from it is identical with the resurrection of the flesh), that it should become fluid, losing its absoluteness, subordinating itself and following the Word as a tamed beast of prey must follow its master. To try to hold together and accept *pari passu*[EN65] both the testimony of the Bible which has

---

[EN64] thereby
[EN65] in the same moment

this content and the autonomy of our own world of thought is an impossible hermeneutic programme. Its execution founders on the task of scriptural exegesis. To maintain the dualism of this programme implies the renunciation of this task. If we cannot evade this task, we must renounce the dualism of this programme. The fulfilment of the task will then consist necessarily and fundamentally in the surrender of that autonomy. With our whole fund of reason and experience we will let ourselves be led and taught and corrected by the Word of God and therefore by Scripture, that is, by its testimony to Jesus Christ, of which the biblical authors in all their humanity are the instruments. In short, we will concede to Scripture the prescribed primacy and precedence.

We can again refer to some words of Polanus. Immediately after the passage already adduced, he goes on at once to speak very illuminatingly about the continuity between the principle that Scripture is to be interpreted by Scripture, on the one hand, and the special content of Scripture on the other: *Doctrina prophetarum et apostolorum est certus sermo Dei, quem universis totius mundi suffragiis secure opponere necesse est et inde veritatem a mendacio distinguere. Sermo autem ille absque ulla dubitatione est in sacra scriptura*[EN66]. (Thus: God's speech in Scripture in the form of prophetic and apostolic doctrine is, as such, confidently to be distinguished from all other voices. This distinction must be made and the speech of God must be appreciated as the criterion for the recognition of the true and false.) There now follows the allusion to the question of scriptural exegesis: *Quaecunque igitur interpretatio loci alicuius scripturae consentit cum sacra scriptura, illa est vera; quae dissentit a sacra scriptura est falsa et repudianda*[EN67]. (It ought to be clear from the previous discussion that when Polanus insists that a true interpretation of Scripture must agree with Scripture itself he is not thinking only [722] of the basic principle of all hermeneutics, that each passage must be understood and explained in the light of its parallels, obscure passages by clear ones, etc. What he obviously has in mind is a rule which is valid only for biblical hermeneutics, that if it is to be true an interpretation must agree with the Scripture in Scripture, i.e., obviously with the *sermo Dei*[EN68] contained in the *doctrina prophetarum et apostolorum*[EN69], and that it is false if it deviates from this Scripture in Scripture, that is from this *sermo Dei*[EN70].) Is there a material definition of this *consentire*[EN71] or *dissentire*[EN72] and therefore of the *sermo Dei*[EN73] by which all scriptural exegesis is to be measured? Polanus thinks he knows such a definition, and here, too, he comes to speak of the special content of the Bible as the very palpable criterion of its interpretation: *Illa autem (interpretatio) consentit cum sacra scriptura, quae omnem laudem salutis nostrae aeternae in solidum Deo tribuit et homini prorsus adimit: illa vero non consentit cum sacra*

[EN66] The teaching of the prophets and the apostles is the certain speech of God, which one must fearlessly set against all the judgments of the whole world, and thereby distinguish truth from falsehood. For that speech is without any doubt in sacred Scripture

[EN67] Therefore, whichever interpretation of some part of Scripture agrees with sacred Scripture, it is true. Whichever dissents from sacred Scripture is false and must be rejected.

[EN68] voice of God

[EN69] teaching of the prophets and apostles

[EN70] voice of God

[EN71] agreeing

[EN72] dissenting

[EN73] voice of God

scriptura, quaecunque vel minimam partem gloriae salutis aeternae homini adscribit[EN74]. He quotes on this point Jn. 7[18]: "He that speaketh of himself seeketh his own glory; but he that seeketh his glory that sent him, the same is true, and no unrighteousness is in him." It is to be noted that Polanus draws here the extreme conclusion that because the content of the Word of God spoken to us in Scripture is that in matters concerning our eternal salvation the glory belongs only to God and not in any sense to man, this is also the criterion for all scriptural exegesis. Exegesis is true or false according as it makes this clear or not. I see no possibility of disagreeing. Of course, we have to understand clearly that this does not put into our hands a convenient master-key which will open every door. But in relation to every individual text there is given us the serious and specific task of recognising that in every verse the whole glory is given to God. Understood as a fundamental rule, this statement of Polanus is unsurpassable.

3. From the establishment of this basic rule, we come to the individual phases of the process of scriptural interpretation. The first plainly distinguishable aspect of the process is the act of observation. In this phase, exegesis is entirely concerned with the *sensus*[EN75] of the word of Scripture as such; it is still entirely a question of *explicatio*[EN76], explanation, i.e., as the very word suggests, the unravelling or unfolding of the scriptural word which comes to us in a, so to speak, rolled-up form, thus concealing its meaning, that is, what it has to say to us. We remind ourselves that what is concealed is objectively a self-concealment of the divine Word only in so far as in the form of the scriptural word the latter has adjusted itself to our human world of thought, thus exposing itself to the darkening prism of our human understanding, although, of course, clear in itself (even in the form of the scriptural word). Yet even in this darkening, it still retains its power to explain itself, which means above all to present itself. And as it does this, there arises the corresponding human task: to follow this self-presentation, to repeat it and, as it were, to copy it. Interpretation as presentation is an introductory attempt to follow the sense of the words of Scripture. If interpretation cannot be exhausted by presentation—as the self-explanation of God's Word is not exhausted in its self-presentation— nevertheless it must in all circumstances begin with this attempt. If we ourselves or others are to be in a position to follow the sense of the words of Scripture, they must first be put before us clearly, that is, as in themselves intel-
[723] ligible, in contrast to mere noises. This presentation of the scriptural word as something intrinsically intelligible is the problem of scriptural interpretation as presentation. Its presupposition and its most important instrument is, of course, literary-historical investigation. I must try to hear the words of the prophets and apostles in exactly the same freedom in which I attempt to hear the words of others who speak to me or have written for me as in the main

---

[EN74] And that interpretation agrees with sacred Scripture which ascribes all praise of our eternal salvation in its entirety to God and removes it entirely from men. But whatever ascribes even the smallest part of the glory of eternal salvation to man does not agree with sacred Scripture
[EN75] sense
[EN76] explanation

intelligible words. That means that I must try to hear them as documents of their concrete historical situation. They speak through it; I must see them in that situation, if I am to hear them speaking intelligibly. It must become for me a speaking situation. At the start of this attempt we still find ourselves wholly upon the plane of general hermeneutics. Obviously, then, the task of investigation will have to be twofold. In the first place we have the documents in their concrete historical situation—the text, as opposed to what is said through it. In this connexion we have to consider the prophets and apostles themselves as speakers.

This is the distinctively literary side of the process, and it may be described in detail as follows. I attempt to bring into the most likely inner connexion the words and phrases of which a certain biblical text is composed. For this purpose I use the methods of source-criticism, lexicography, grammar, syntax and appreciation of style. My aim is to convey the subject-matter or reference of what the author says in this particular text. In this way I obtain a picture of his expression, and I then compare this with other things which the same author has said about the same thing and with what he has said on other matters. To obtain further standards for insight into what he wishes to say in this text I go on to compare what is said on the matter by other authors, who are contemporary or who in other ways stand in a close positive or negative relationship. On the basis of the insight thus gained into the relation of what is said in this text with what has been said elsewhere by the same author or by others, if there seem to be any lacunae in the text—as though the text itself forbade me—I can then try to complete and round off its presentation. Finally, I shall then try to establish how far in what he says the author has perhaps been dependent upon others, or with others upon a third, and how far again this is perhaps the case of others in regard to him. This will enable me to see clearly how far in what he says I am dealing with his own original, perhaps very original, ideas, and how far I have to do with what is held in common. To grasp the meaning of what is said in any given text, it is basically necessary that I should use all these ways of trying to unfold its meaning as a text.

But investigation is obviously incomplete even in the sense of general hermeneutics, indeed it has not yet reached its decisive stage, if the matter is allowed to rest there. I have to see the prophets and apostles in a concrete historical situation if I am to appreciate the meaning of their words. But to this situation there does not belong only the speaking of the prophets and apostles. As its decisive determination there belongs also that which is spoken by them. The image which their words conjure up reflects a certain object. Again, therefore, exactly as I do in regard to the words of other men, I shall try to reproduce and copy the theme whose image is reflected in the picture of the prophetic-apostolic words and controls those words—for they relate to it. [724]

So we come to the distinctively historical aspect of the process. I now seek to form an idea of what is said in the text—the outward or inner history which it reports or to which it is related. This means that with the help of what I can conjure up, I try to form a picture of what has taken place on the spot to which the words of the author refer, and of what has occasioned the author to use these particular words of his text. To form a picture of this happening means, however, that as it comes to me in the mirror of these words by means of the literary examination, I shall fit it into the series of other pictures which are at my disposal through reconstructing the objective historical situation of the author and of what he has seen. These will include pictures of his own time, its events and typical manifestations, its circumstances and aspirations, its natural and intellectual conception, its objective and subjective assumptions and problems. They will also include pictures of the periods which immediately precede and follow, in the sequence of which the happening which he reports takes its place, and within the process of which it forms an essential member, linking what goes before with what follows. It is not to be forgotten—and here the matter becomes critical—that I have, of course, a more or less definite picture of historical realities generally, and of the whole epoch which forms the framework of the observable process in which the event referred to in the text has its special place. This general picture will certainly determine my picture of the time in which the event referred to in the text falls, my picture of the preceding and succeeding periods, and of the whole historical process. And this applies necessarily also to the particular picture which I form of this event in the narrowest of those various circles. Alternatively, it is possible that this particular picture—not because it is my picture, but because it is the representation of the object spoken of to me—will be so strong that it will determine and modify, shatter and remould my previous picture of that time, then of the whole historical process, and in the end perhaps even of historical reality generally. Even within the framework of general hermeneutics I shall obviously have to reckon with both possibilities. In my attempt to picture to myself the image of what is said to me, I may actually begin with what I could imagine already. But I must not refuse to widen my circle of conceptions, perhaps even to allow it to be widened in a very unexpected fashion. In forming this picture, I cannot and must not fail to exhaust all the possibilities at my disposal. At the same time I must not exclude in principle the idea that what is said, i.e., the object which the words to be interpreted offer for my consideration, might suggest other possibilities than those hitherto known to me, and I might not be able to resist these if I am not to give up the task of interpretation.

In this phase of presentation in the process of scriptural exegesis everything will immediately depend on whether, in the literary and historical examination which underlies the presentation, we really form an accurate picture of the object mirrored in the prophetic-apostolic word. That is to say, it all depends whether as interpreters we are able to allow the text to speak to us, and to take account of the message and its contents, fully prepared, on the one hand, to mobilise and employ in the formation of that picture as the picture of a real occurrence all the possibilities we know from history, world-history and the philosophy of history, but fully prepared, on the other hand, to allow the circle of these possibilities, if need be, to be newly defined and broadened and [725] eventually shattered and re-moulded, and in certain circumstances even to bring and apply to the task of faithful understanding possibilities which hitherto and in other circumstances we regarded as impossibilities.

Do the methods of general and those of biblical hermeneutics separate inevitably at this point? We cannot admit this. That they diverge in fact is, of course, obvious. It is only within definite limits that general hermeneutics is accustomed to take seriously the idea that what is said in a text, that is, the object which we have to reproduce, might bring into play other possibilities than those known to the interpreter. To be sure, it realises that the hitherto accepted picture of a certain epoch, and even the picture of the historical process as a whole, can be changed in detail and even very radically by what is said in a text. But it holds fast all the more definitely to a certain preconceived picture of actual occurrence itself. It thinks it has a basic knowledge of what is generally possible, of what can have happened, and from this point of view it assesses the statement of the text, and the picture of the object reflected in it as the picture of a real, or unreal, or doubtful happening. It is surely plain that at this point an alien factor is exercising a disturbing influence upon observation. Strict observation obviously requires that the force of a picture meeting us in a text shall exercise its due effect in accordance with its intrinsic character, that it shall itself decide what real facts are appropriate to it, that absolutely no prejudgment shall be made, and that it shall not be a foregone conclusion what is possible. If general hermeneutics does, in fact, hold this different point of view and work with a conception of what is generally possible as the limit which will be self-evidently presupposed for what can really have happened, it has to be said that this point of view is by no means inevitable and is not required by the essential character of hermeneutics. Biblical hermeneutics is not guilty of an arbitrary exception when it takes a different line. On the contrary, it follows the path of strict observation to the very end. Certainly, it does this because of its own definite presupposition. But it is to be noted that this presupposition does enable it to be consistent as hermeneutics. The same cannot be said of the presupposition of general hermeneutics.

The idea with which scriptural exegesis must begin is that of fidelity in all circumstances to the object reflected in the words of the prophets and apostles. This is the fidelity which this object in itself requires. It also requires all the fidelity which we owe to the object of every human word if it is to be interpreted. This fidelity does not imply a necessary suspension of historical orientation and criticism. In so far as this is essential to its observation and representation, it must be applied; and it is not possible to lay down for it in advance any general limits. How can we appreciate the concrete historical situation of the prophets and apostles, with regard either to their speaking or to what is spoken by them, unless we freely survey their historical existence as speakers, or the existence of that of which they speak? How can it be appreciated without critical questions and answers on both sides? To observe undoubtedly means to establish the facts, and so distinguish the real from the unreal or the certain from the uncertain. And it is in order if we address ourselves to this task with the presupposition of all that we otherwise know to be real or think we know to be possible. But, on the other hand, we must leave to this object, as to any other with which we might have to do. the freedom to [726] assert and affirm itself over against these presuppositions of ours, and in certain cases to compel us to adopt new presuppositions, as in fact it can do. Our representation of it must be determined by its form, not by the laws of form which we bring with us. Biblical hermeneutics does actually reckon with an object in its texts that claims this freedom. In regard to this object our own presuppositions are not adequate and if we wish to represent it we must be prepared to alter our own ideas of the laws of form. The necessary historical orientation and criticism is not suspended. On the contrary, it is made essential in a qualified form. But unavoidably this object prescribes its own law for our activity, so that we must be prepared to submit to its law if we are not to renounce the task of observation and presentation. How can the freedom of orientation and criticism be in any way limited by this fact? Indeed, how can it be otherwise exercised than as the freedom of loyalty to this object? How can it degenerate into freedom from this object, that is, from the text and its contents? In the freedom of loyalty, therefore, the examination of the biblical texts must do justice both to the texts themselves and also to their object, whatever conclusions and distinctions it may then be necessary to make. From this standpoint it will have to allow itself in certain circumstances to be corrected even on the literary side, because on the assumption of fidelity to the object all the problems may present themselves in a new way. And only in so far as it takes into account the texts in their whole scope and meaning will it be capable of representing what they are trying to say and therefore of drawing out their sense. A representation based on such an examination will allow even the detailed words of the texts to speak exactly as they stand. It will not take away anything from the concrete historical contingency of their origin and their relation to their object. It will not suppress, silence or distort anything which is fitted to illuminate this contingency. It will include the methods of observation used in general hermeneutics. It will have considered all the questions, without exception, which arise from that point of view in forming its general picture of the text. Therefore it will not have to fear any inquiry in respect of historical orientation and criticism. On the other hand, it will not tolerate any restrictions. It will allow the text to speak for itself in the sense that it will give full scope to its controlling object. It will not seek to conceal its ultimate determination for the sake of any preconceived notion of what is possible. It will not distort the text by trying to obscure and level down and render innocuous its real object. It will allow the text to say what, controlled by its object, it does actually say in its historical contingence. In doing this and to this extent, in so far as it can happen in fulfilment of the human task posed, it will explain, unfold and affirm its real historical sense, and thus make it possible to follow the sense of the text itself, what it does actually say.

[727]   In conclusion, we must again emphasise that in taking this line biblical, theological hermeneutics is not claiming for itself a mysterious special privilege. The object of the biblical texts is quite simply the name Jesus Christ, and these texts can be understood only when understood as determined by this object. But this insight is not a privilege of theologians. It could also be an insight of the interpreter as such, and biblical hermenentics might then be only a special case of general hermeneutics, within which it might acquire an instructive significance in the exposition of very different texts. In fact, this insight is not that of the interpreter as such. But this again must not hinder the task of biblical hermeneutics from being undertaken where the insight does exist, and, if possible, carried through quite irrespective of the protest of a general hermeneutics which has not yet been better informed in this regard.

4. The second plainly distinguishable moment in the process of scriptural exegesis is the act of reflection on what Scripture declares to us. What is meant is not, of course, an act which follows the first in time, nor a second act which takes place independently of the first, but the one act of scriptural exegesis considered now in the moment of the transition of what is said into the thinking of the reader or hearer. We are now just at the middle point between

sensus[EN77] and *usus, explicatio*[EN78] and *applicatio*[EN79]. Even in the moment of transition, scriptural interpretation, in which Scripture is primarily explaining itself, is an act of our human freedom and to be valued as such. It is inevitable, as we have already seen, that the way and manner of this transmission will influence and limit our observation and representation of Scripture. Even in the act of observing and representing, no interpreter is merely an observer and exponent. No one is in a position, objectively and abstractly, merely to observe and present what is there. For how can he do so without at the same time reflecting upon and interpreting what is there? No one copies without making this transition. In affirming and representing what is written, and what is because of what is written, we accompany what is written, and what is because of what is written, with our own thinking.

This is self-evident, and it has been formulated by A. Ritschl (*Rechtf. u. Vers.*, edn. 4, III, 25), but it is still necessary to state it: "As we only hear with our own ears and see with our own eyes, we can apprehend by means only of our own understanding, not of that of another." Naturally, for if we do not do so, we do not understand at all.

Above the picture observed, like the second rainbow which is distinct from the first, although related to and dependent upon it, there inevitably arises the picture contemplated, in which the reader or hearer tries, as it were, to assimilate the former. It is at this point that we see that it is really quite impossible for us to free ourselves of our own shadow, that is, to make the so-called *sacrificium intellectus*[EN80]. How can we objectively understand the text without realising it subjectively, in our own thinking? How can we let it speak to us without at least moving our lips (as the readers of antiquity did visibly and audibly) and ourselves speaking with it. The interpreter cannot help this. Even in what he says [728] as an observer and exponent, he will everywhere betray the fact that, consciously or unconsciously, in cultured or primitive fashion, consistently or inconsistently, he has approached the text from the standpoint of a particular epistemology, logic or ethics, of definite ideas and ideals concerning the relations of God, the world and man, and that in reading and expounding the text he cannot simply deny these. Everyone has some sort of philosophy, i.e., a personal view of the fundamental nature and relationship of things—however popular, aphoristic, irregular and eclectically vacillating. This is true even of the simplest Bible reader (and of him perhaps with particular force and tenacity). But it is definitely true of the educated Bible student, who in appearance and intention is wholly given up to observation.

We have to describe as a philosophy the systematised commonsense with which at first the rationalists of the 18th century thought that they could read and understand the Bible, and later, corrected by Kant, the school of A. Ritschl, which was supposed to be so averse to every

---

[EN77] sense
[EN78] use, explanation
[EN79] application
[EN80] sacrifice of the intellect

type of speculation and metaphysics. It is all very well to renounce the Platonism of the Greek fathers, but if that means that we throw ourselves all the more unconditionally into the arms of the positivists and agnostics of the 19th century, we have no right to look for the mote in the eye of those ancient fathers, as though on their side there is a sheer hellenisation of the Gospel, and on ours a sheer honest exegetical sense for facts. There has never yet been an expositor who has allowed only Scripture alone to speak. Even a biblicist like J. T. Beck patently failed to do this. For, while he let Scripture speak, he also gave very powerful and sometimes very fateful expression to what he had assimilated from the philosophers F. C. Oetinger, Schelling and Baader. In the same way, it is obvious that the famous biblical realism of the older and more recent Swabian schools was not merely a biblical, but also a philosophical and theosophical realism, strangely consistent with the idiosyncrasy of that region. The Scholastics of the Middle Ages and the orthodox Protestants since 1600 openly appropriated in the most open manner the luminous conceptuality of Aristotle. But from a philosophical point of view, Luther and Calvin were equally unmistakeable Platonists: Luther probably more of a Neo-Platonist, Calvin a classical Platonist. And Zwingli, in this respect more modern than either, would not have been Zwingli without the Renaissance pantheism of Pico della Mirandola, for which reason he could become not unjustifiably the special favourite of W. Dilthey. The most important historical and exegetical school of the 19th century, the Tübingen school of F. C. Baur, made no less powerful use of the illumination of Hegelian philosophy than the Scholastics did once of that of the Aristotelian. But behind the exegesis of the Form-criticism school of to-day there stands unmistakably the presupposition of the phenomenology of Husserl and Scheler. Again, if we elevate the anti-Hegelianism of Kierkegaard into a principle, believing that the key to the mystery of the old and new covenant is to be found in anxiety about the limitation of human existence by its subjection to death, or in its relationship to the Thou stabilised in ordinances, we must remember that we are definitely ranging ourselves with those who "explain" the Bible, i.e., read it through the spectacles of a definite system of ideas, which has the character of a "world-view" and will in some way make itself felt as such when we read and explain the Bible. If we hold up hands of horror at the very idea, we must not forget that without such systems of explanation, without such spectacles, we cannot read the Bible at all. It is, therefore, a grotesque comedy, in which it is better not to take part, that again and again there are

[729]   those who think that they can point with outstretched finger to all others past and present, accusing them of falling victim to this or that philosophy, while they themselves abide wholly by the facts, relying on their two sound eyes. No one does that, for no one can. It is no more true of anyone that he does not mingle the Gospel with some philosophy, than that here and now he is free from all sin except through faith.

In reading the Bible, as in all other reading and hearing, we use some sort of key or scheme of thought as a "vehicle" in which to "accompany" it. In an exploratory way we attribute to that which confronts us, to the image arising through our observation (we attribute this to it already as it emerges in the act of observation), one or other of the possibilities of meaning already known to us through our philosophy. In the process we think of something—something which we can think in terms of the standard of our philosophy—without regard to the fact that this something as such is not already there in the text and as such is not the object of our observation, but is very properly added in our own mind if in the act of observation we are not to fail completely to find possible dues for interpretation—for after all it is we who observe. This process must certainly be undertaken with great care and circumspection. But it cannot as such be rejected with horror. There would be no sense in wishing to interdict it. It is not only unavoidable as such, but legitimate, just as it was not only unavoidable but legitimate when, just as he was, in his poverty and rags, the prodigal son arose and went to his father.

There is, therefore, not much point in a theological criticism if it rests only on the affirmation that the theological statement under consideration betrays more or less obvious traces of the philosophical culture of its author, and that it makes use of a certain philosophical system of ideas. If a criticism of this kind invites the reader or hearer of the statement to beware and be on his guard, he will have to confess at once that he himself is very definitely involved in a similar system, and as an inhabitant of this glass house he certainly has no cause to throw stones. If he wants to criticise others, he will have to examine himself to see whether he is not perhaps engaged only in the conflict of one philosophy with another—a conflict which has, of course, nothing to do with the interpretation of Scripture. The proper course is first to listen to what the other, using his system of ideas, has to say about the subject itself, i.e., as an exponent of Scripture, and to pass on to criticism only if objections have to be raised on the basis of the subject. If, then, the criticism is to be a positive contribution to scriptural exegesis, in the philosopher-theologian it is not the philosopher but the theologian who will have to be criticised.

In attempting to reflect on what is said to us in the biblical text, we must first make use of the system of thought we bring with us, that is, of some philosophy or other. Fundamentally to question the legitimacy of this necessity would be to question whether sinful man as such, and therefore with such possibilities of thought as are given to him, is called to understand and interpret the Word of God which encounters us in Scripture. If we cannot and must not dispute this, if we are not to dispute the grace and finally the incarnation of the Word of God, we cannot basically contest the use of philosophy in scriptural exegesis [730] Where the question of legitimacy arises is in regard to the How of this use. In this connexion the following points are to be noted.

First, when the interpreter uses the scheme of thought he brings with him for the apprehension and explanation of what is said to us in Scripture, he must have a fundamental awareness of what he is doing. We must be clear that every scheme of thought which we bring with us is different from that of the scriptural word which we have to interpret, for the object of the latter is God's revelation in Jesus Christ, it is the testimony of this revelation inspired by the Holy Ghost, and it can become luminous for us only through the same Holy Ghost. Our philosophy as such—as the philosophy of those who are not themselves prophets and apostles—stands always in contrast to the philosophy of Scripture. Of whatever kind our system of thought may be, as our own thought, in and by itself, it is certainly not identical with biblical thought. It cannot do more than participate in the biblical mode of thought as with its help we seek to pursue what the biblical word has to say to us. Therefore we must not think any of our own schemes of thought is of itself fitted, or even peculiarly fitted, to apprehend and explain the word of Scripture. On the contrary, we should assume from the outset that it is not in itself fitted for this purpose, that at best it can only acquire this fitness through its encounter with and pursuit of the scriptural word. Therefore it can never be a matter of course that we will apply this or that scheme of thought for the apprehension and contemplation of Scripture. It is true that in obedience to our calling we may not refuse to do this. But we must be clear that we can do so only in the venture of obedience, not on the ground of the value, or indeed the special value, of our scheme of thought. Therefore, we have to maintain a constant awareness of the essential distance between the determinative thought of Scripture and our own imitative thought determined as it is by our own philosophy. This imitation must never cease to bear the character of obedience, and indeed of the venturesome obedience which relies solely upon the grace of the Word.

Secondly, the use of the manner of thought we bring with us in reflecting upon what Scripture has to say can have only the fundamental character of an essay, and the use of our philosophy for this end can have only the fundamental character of a hypothesis. On the assumption that I, with my particular mode of thought—not on account of and in virtue of this mode of thought, but in spite of it and with it—am a member of the Church, and that as a member I am invited to undertake the task of scriptural exegesis, I can and must apply this way of thought to the problems of Scripture, in an exploratory and experimental and provisional manner. It is a false asceticism if I am unwilling to do this, if I try to suppress and deny my mode of thought. For this can only [731] mean either that I have to choose another human system of thought, or that I withdraw from the task imposed upon me. But as I apply myself to this task, it will be decided under the Word what becomes of my mode of thought, whether and to what extent it will be serviceable to me in this activity—the activity of interpreting Scripture. If it becomes serviceable, then it will be in the service and under the control of the Word whose explanation lies in itself, and it will be in virtue of the light which falls upon my thinking from the object of my thinking, from above. My mode of thought may not be of any use in and by itself, but by the grace of the Word of God why should it not be able to become useful in His service? In itself, as such, it is a hypothesis: the hypothesis upon which I must venture in obedience, because I have only the alternative either of risking some other hypothesis or of not obeying at all. But it is a hypothesis. In and by itself it is not a form which is adequate to apprehend and interpret the scriptural word. And therefore in itself my undertaking to apprehend and interpret the scriptural word with the help of my mode of thought is never more than the attempt to perform the necessary task of reflection. It is not the already successful and completed performance of this reflection. I shall have to bear in mind the difference between my mode of thought and that of Scripture, the essential unfitness of the means employed by me. I shall have to remember that grace is implied if my attempt and therefore my mode of thought can become useful to this end. After each attempt I shall also have to be willing and ready to proceed to new attempts. And I cannot exclude the possibility that the same attempt can and must be ventured with the application of quite other philosophies than mine. Therefore I shall not radically deny to other philosophies than my own the character of useful hypotheses in the service of the same end. I ought not to allow the existence of my special hypothesis necessarily to restrain me from paying heed, for the sake of the task, of the matter itself, to what is said in the interpretation of Scripture when hypotheses quite other than my own are applied. I cannot radically exclude even the possibility that in certain circumstances, and for the better interpretation of Scripture, I myself will decide to use some quite different hypothesis, and even have to become a more or less consistent "convert" to a different philosophy.

Thirdly, the use of a specific mode of thought and philosophy brought to the task of scriptural exegesis can claim no independent interest in itself. It cannot in any way become an end in itself. At this point we have to remember the danger which philosophy has always involved, and always can involve, in the matter of scriptural exegesis.

We must remember Col. 2⁸ in this connexion: Βλέπετε μή τις ὑμᾶς ἔσται ὁ συλαγωγῶν διὰ τῆς φιλοσοφίας καὶ κενῆς ἀπάτης κατὰ τὴν παράδοσιν τῶν ἀνθρώπων, κατὰ τὰ στοιχεῖα τοῦ κόσμου καὶ οὐ κατὰ Χριστόν[EN81]. Similarly, we must recall Tertullian's savage elucidation of these words of Paul: *Fuerat Athenis, et istam sapientiam* [732] *humanam, affectatricem et interpolatricem veritatis de congressibus noverat, ipsam quoque in suas haereses multipartitam varietate sectarum in vicem repugnantium. Quid ergo Athenis et Hierosolymis? Quid academiae et ecclesiae? Quid haereticis et Christianis? Nostra institutio de porticu Solomonis est, qui et ipse tradiderat Dominum in simplicitate cordis esse quaerendum. Viderint qui Stoicum et Platonicum et dialecticum christianismum protulerunt. Nobis curiositate opus non est post Christum Jesum, nec inquisitione post evangelium. Cum credimus, nihil desideramus ultra credere. Hoc enim prius credimus, non esse quod ultra credere debeamus*[EN82] (*De praescr.* 7).

When and under what circumstances can the use of an imported mode of thought become dangerous in scriptural exegesis? It obviously becomes dangerous when in using it we cease to be aware of its difference from the biblical way of thought and its original unfitness for the apprehension and interpretation of the latter. It becomes dangerous when we consider it to be a fit and adequate instrument for this purpose. It becomes dangerous, therefore, when—even with the best intention, that of doing justice to Scripture—we posit it absolutely over against Scripture, expecting that by placing it, as it were, on the same high level as Scripture, we can use it to control Scripture.

[EN81] See that no-one takes you captive through philosophy, and empty deception which is in accordance with the tradition of men, in accordance with the elements of this world and not in accordance with Christ

[EN82] He had been in Athens, and he knew from his debates that human wisdom, that meddler and falsifier of the truth, that she was also divided in many parts among the heresies, in turn, of her repugnant sects. What then has Athens to do with Jerusalem? What has the academy to do with the church? What have heretics to do with Christians? Our institution is by the portico of Solomon, who himself passed down that the Lord is to be sought in simplicity of heart. Let those who offer Platonism, Stoicism, and dialectical Christianity note this. After Christ Jesus we need have no curiosity, and no inquisitiveness after the Gospel. When we believe, we long for nothing beyond believing. For we have already believed that it is such that we ought not believe anything beyond it

Again, it becomes dangerous when we view its consistent presentation as an end in itself, or when we consider ourselves strictly obliged to be exponents not only of Scripture but also of our own mode of thought, and to remain absolutely loyal to it. In such a use, philosophy becomes κενὴ ἀπάτη EN83, an *affectatrix*EN84 and *interpolatrix veritatis*EN85. Scripture is necessarily distorted. The Word of God is not confronted by man as a man, but as a second God, overruling and controlling the Word of the first God, who as such can no longer be the true God. What is said in Scripture is now considered *inter pares*EN86. In the whole history of the Church there is no error or heresy which has not arisen from this *curiositas*EN87 which is excluded *post Christum*EN88, from this reversal of the right attitude of the interpreter of Scripture, from this over-valuation of the human mode of thought, from this concession of autonomy to the philosophical interest and therefore from philosophy generally. Every philosophy which is posited absolutely leads necessarily to a falsification of Scripture because to posit absolutely what is man's own and is brought by him to the Word is an act of unbelief which makes impossible the insights of faith and therefore a true interpretation of the Word. In this connexion it is hardly relevant to distinguish between good and bad, between the philosophies of this or that school. Nor is it relevant to seek a philosophy which cannot become dangerous in this way. There is none which must become dangerous, because there is none which we cannot have without positing it absolutely. There is none which cannot possibly become dangerous, because there is none which we cannot posit absolutely, that is, in disloyalty to Scripture erect its presentation into a principle and an end in itself. This, then, is the thing [733] which must not in any circumstances happen when we use our mode of thought in meditating on the word of Scripture. Independent interest can be claimed only by the scriptural mode of thought which takes precedence of ours. Following it, every human mode of thought can be good; not following it, but affirming and asserting itself over against it, every human mode of thought will necessarily be bad. This is the test, and always will be the test, whether we have assimilated this fundamental rule concerning the subordin-ation of our own thought to the alien thought of Scripture.

Fourthly, in the necessary use of some scheme of thought for reflection upon what Scripture has to say, there is no essential reason for preferring one of these schemes to another. Of course, it can never be a matter of chance for the individual whether his thought takes this or that particular direction; and it would be stupid to dispute the immanental significance of the difference of philosophical schools and tendencies. Yet it is hard to see how far there follows

---

EN83 empty deception
EN84 meddler
EN85 falsifier
EN86 among equals
EN87 curiosity
EN88 after Christ

from this the universal necessity of a definite choice among these various possibilities. The necessity which there is is particular: in a specific situation this or that particular mode of thought can be particularly useful in scriptural exegesis, and it can then become a command to avail oneself of it in this particular instance. But it has always proved fatal when this particular necessity is elevated at once into a general one, when this or that mode of thought is enjoined upon all, when by means of this particular mode of thought it is hoped to apprehend and interpret all the words of Scripture, or even one such word fully, and when it is treated as normative for all situations and times. The freedom of the Word of God then reveals itself in the fact that in defiance of the presumed necessity of what is thought to be a selected philosophy, it will usually acquire at once a new and greater clarity in the language of what is perhaps a diametrically antithetic philosophy. As exponents of Scripture, we should not allow any understanding of reality to impose itself as the normal presupposition for the understanding of the reality of the Word of God. How can we bind ourselves to one philosophy as the only philosophy, and ascribe to it a universal necessity, without actually positing it as something absolute as the necessary partner of the Word of God and in that way imprisoning and falsifying the Word of God? Thus from the point of view of scriptural exegesis the relevance of the inner conflicts and debates and the whole history of philosophy as the history of human modes of thought can only be contingent and provisional, not basic and ultimate. It is true that in this history there has hardly been a single possible mode of thought which has not been dangerous in itself and as such to the task of scriptural exposition, but has still become fruitful through the grace of the Word. It is also true that it will not be otherwise in the future and that therefore there is every reason, from the point of view of scriptural exposition, to interest ourselves in this history. Yet there is [734] not the slightest ground for the opinion or expectation that in this history the decision either has been, or will be, made, which alone, for purposes of the task, will lead to the establishment of one mode of thought as adapted to the Word of God, thus releasing the expositor from the venture of obedience because it is itself equipped with the *potentia oboedientialis*[EN89] and can therefore be recommended as universally necessary. This decision is not to be expected from philosophy because according to Scripture itself it is not to be expected from man at all. For true reflection on Scripture as the Word of God cannot be bought under a rule of thought definable by men, and the choice of a particular mode of thought for its serviceableness in this reflection is the business of grace and therefore cannot be our business. In this connexion we have to guard ourselves most carefully against just those representations which are made most eagerly and those possibilities which seem the most attractive.

Fifthly, the use of a scheme of thought in the service of scriptural exegesis is legitimate and fruitful when it is determined and controlled by the text and

---

[EN89] authority to be obeyed

the object mirrored in the text. We might simply say: when it really becomes contributory to reflection. At this point, therefore, we come to grips with the decisive thing which has to be said in regard to the problem of observation and representation. The truth of our reflection is determined by the object mirrored in the text as the master of our thinking; as is also on our side the measure of our fitness and adaptability in thinking of this object. The meaning of reflection on what is said to us is that we "go along with" it. But since it is the Word of God that here speaks to us, what can this mean except that with our human thought we are carried along by the Word of God, and therefore that we allow ourselves to be carried along by it, not resisting or evading the movement to which it gives rise, but allowing it to be communicated to our own thinking. We can say, therefore, that the use of a human scheme of thought in the service of scriptural exegesis is legitimate and fruitful when it is a critical use, implying that the object of the criticism is not Scripture, but our own scheme of thought, and that Scripture is necessarily the subject of this criticism. It should now be plain why we had to lay so great a stress on the hypothetical, relative and incidental character of every philosophy used for this purpose. It is not really a question of replacing philosophy by a dictatorial, absolute and exclusive theology, and again discrediting philosophy as an *ancilla theologiae*[EN90]. On the contrary, our concern is that theology itself, which in itself and apart from its object can only be the fulfilment of a human way of thought, and therefore a kind of philosophy, should not forget its hypothetical, relative and incidental character in the exposition of Scripture, or become guilty of opposing and resisting its object. It will certainly do this if it

[735] fails to heed these warnings in regard to the use of philosophy, if the use which it makes of it is dictatorial, absolute and exclusive. In face of its object, theology itself can only wish to be *ancilla*[EN91]. That is why it cannot assign any other role to philosophy. Scripture alone can be the *domina*[EN92]. Hence there is no real cause for disputes about prestige. What must never happen in any circumstances is that some scheme of thought should affirm and assert itself over against Scripture. The mode of thought we bring will automatically become a source of error if we use it to argue against Scripture, if we impose it upon Scripture, if we take Scripture captive by it, if we try to make it a measure of Scripture, if it becomes the ground and nerve of our affirmation and also of our reservations over against Scripture. When this happens, Scripture eludes our interpretation; it evades and passes it; its freedom becomes a judgment upon the false freedom which we have wrongly assumed in relation to it. We do not perform the service to Scripture and the Church which as interpreters we ought to perform, and it passes to others who are not guilty of this infidelity. That is why so solemn a warning has to be issued at this point. If the warning is

---

[EN90] hand-maid to theology
[EN91] hand-maid
[EN92] mistress

heeded, there is no question of the danger of philosophy for scriptural exegesis, but only of its necessity. Philosophy—and fundamentally any philosophy—can be criticised in the service of the Word of God, and it can then gain a legitimate critical power. It can be elucidated and then elucidate. It can be set in motion and then have power to move. If as exponents of Scripture we do not give it more confidence than we can give to ourselves in our humanity (and this can be confidence in the power of the vocation which comes to us as men), we will not and may not refuse it this confidence (which is always the confidence for which we can answer in Scripture). If we do not commit ourselves unreservedly and finally to any specific philosophy, we will not need totally or finally to fear any philosophy. As interpreters of Scripture, perhaps not in practice but in principle, we will be able to adopt a more friendly and understanding attitude to the various possibilities which have manifested themselves or are still manifesting themselves in the history of philosophy, and to make a more appropriate use of them, if the object on which we reflect has put us on our guard against their particular genius. Even from a human point of view, it is possible to regard scriptural exposition as the best and perhaps the only school of truly free human thinking—freed, that is, from all the conflicts and tyranny of systems in favour of this object. But, however that may be, the task of scriptural exposition demands both caution and also openness with regard to all the possibilities of human thought, because no limits may be set to the freedom and sovereign power of its object. If made with this caution and openness, this transition of the Word of God from the thought of the apostles and prophets into our own—wherever and whenever the Word of God wills to pass over into our own thinking—will become the inevitable and right step to exposition from which no one, if he is to be true to his vocation, may withdraw. [736]

5. The third individual moment in the process of scriptural exposition is the act of appropriation. From *explicatio*[EN93] we must pass over the bridge of *meditatio*[EN94] to *applicatio*[EN95]. The *sensus*[EN96] must also show itself to be the *usus scripturae*[EN97]. Again, it is not a question of an act which is to be viewed in abstraction as complete in itself, but of the one totality of scriptural interpretation. No appropriation of the Word of God is possible without critical examination and reflection. But similarly, of course, there is no possibility of a valid and fruitful examination of what is said to us in Scripture or reflection upon it, unless, proceeding further, it develops into appropriation of them. Without this, observation can be only a historically aesthetic survey, and reflection only idle speculation, in spite of all the supposed openness to the object in both cases. The proof of our openness to the object is that our observation and

---

[EN93] observation
[EN94] meditation
[EN95] assimilation
[EN96] sense
[EN97] use of Scripture

reflection on what is said leads to its assimilation. Or, put the other way round, our openness to the object, through which alone assimilation can properly be carried out, is to be tested by whether it really springs from observation and reflection. By "assimilation" is to be understood that what is declared to us must become our very own, and indeed in such a way that now we really do become *conscientes*EN98, those who in virtue of what is said to them know themselves, and can, therefore, say to themselves and to others what is said to them, those who not only reflect on it but think it themselves. Think it from inner impulse and necessity, just as we think something because we must, because we cannot not think it, because it has become a fundamental orientation of our whole existence. Because the Word of God meets us in the form of the scriptural word, assimilation means the contemporaneity, homogeneity and indirect identification of the reader and hearer of Scripture with the witness of the revelation. Assimilation means assuming this witness into our own responsibility. How can we have heard it, and how can we be its hearers if and so long as we still distinguish our own concern from its concern? How can we have heard its Word if we do not feel compelled to speak it as our own word to ourselves and pass it on to others? Thus assimilation is not a third act which will have to be added to the already complete exposition of Scripture and might possibly not be added. Exposition has not properly taken place so long as it stops short of assimilation, so long as assimilation has the appearance of a work of supererogation by means of which we have to make exposition fruitful by making something for ourselves of the Word of God as already expounded. This act of ours which we call assimilation can only be our activity in view of the free, and indeed the most proper and the most intimate activity of the Word of God itself in the form of impartation.

[737]   What is it, then, that the object reflected in the image visible in the biblical text wills in order to become the master of our thinking concerning what is said in the biblical text? It wills not to be without us, but to be in communion with us, and in this communion to be what it is for us. It wills to be appropriated by us. It wills not merely to master our thinking about it, but our thinking and life generally, and our whole existence. If it is envisaged only as a so-called theory into which our practice has to breathe the necessary life, it has not been properly seen at all. And our observation and reflection on Scripture have been not merely useless but false. False scriptural exegesis at the two first stages usually betrays itself and is avenged at the third stage in the fact that our attitude to Scripture now assumes the dualistic form of this unholy doctrine of "theory and practice," disintegrating into an ostensible righteousness of faith and a suddenly triumphant righteousness of works. From the point of view of the biblical text and its object, concern about a so-called practice limping behind a so-called theory is not only superfluous but impossible.

Ὅσα γὰρ προεγράφη, εἰς τὴν ἡμετέραν διδασκαλίαν ἐγράφη, ἵνα διὰ τῆς ὑπομονῆς

EN98 co-knowers

καὶ διὰ τῆς παρακλήσεως τῶν γραφῶν τὴν ἐλπίδα ἔχωμεν[EN99] (Rom. 15⁴). Πᾶσα γραφὴ θεόπνευστος καὶ ὠφέλιμος πρὸς διδασκαλίαν, πρὸς ἐλεγμόν, πρός ἐπανόρθωσιν, πρός παιδείαν τὴν ἐν δικαιοσύνῃ[EN100] (2 Tim. 3¹⁶). This is the *usus scripturae*[EN101]. It is to be noted how in these two passages it is not described as something which we have to make out of Scripture, but as a necessary function inseparable from the existence and therefore from the explanation of Scripture.

We have to concern ourselves about this function of Scripture itself if we want to understand the office which at this point again, in freedom under the Word and in the service of scriptural exegesis, devolves upon ourselves. The Word of God remains the Word of God even as that which gives itself to be, and is, appropriated by us. It wills to control us, as it takes up its abode within us. It crosses our threshold as the Lord. This is the state of affairs for which we have to make allowance in every way. It will certainly be the case that we on our side encounter the Word of God with all kinds of specific wishes and needs, hopes and fears. Not man alone in respect of his thinking, but each of us in virtue of our whole fate and character, is a specific system of presuppositions, expectations and restraints. When we assimilate something, this implies that we make it a part of this system. We consume it. We assimilate it to ourselves. We begin to do something with it. We utilise it in accordance with what we are and what we are not, with what we like and what we do not like. The Word of God, however, cannot be used along these lines. When the Word of God is appropriated, it means that each individual who hears or reads it relates what is said to himself as something which is not spoken generally or to others, but to himself in particular, and therefore as something which is to be used by him. If the Church is the assembly of those who hear the Word of God, in the last resort this necessarily means (for what would the hearing amount to otherwise?) the assembly of those who make use of it. But this, too, can mean only the assembly of those who are ready and willing that the Word of God on its part should make use of them. The customary inverted act of assimilation clearly cannot come into consideration in this context. Or rather, we have to reverse that kind of assimilation at every stage; instead of our making use of Scripture at every stage, it is Scripture itself which uses us—the *usus scripturae*[EN102] in which *scriptura*[EN103] is not object but subject, and the hearer and reader is not subject but object. Man is certainly right to expect something from the Word of God— indeed, something decisive, central and fundamentally necessary for himself and his life: instruction and guidance, consolation and reproof, strengthening and joy. But he is far from right if he stubbornly insists on trying to know for himself in what everything will consist if it is imparted to him. He is far from

[738]

[EN99] For whatever has been written in the past was written for our instruction, so that through perseverance and through the encouragement of the Scriptures, we might have hope

[EN100] All Scripture is God-breathed, and useful for teaching, for rebuking, for correcting, and for training in righteousness

[EN101] use of Scripture

[EN102] use of Scripture

[EN103] Scripture

right if he wants to insist on the feelings and ideas with which he views it. On the contrary, he will have to be prepared for the fact that it may be imparted to him, but in a very different way, one which is perhaps quite contrary to his feelings and ideas, a way which is grounded in the Word of God itself. He will have to have the confidence that the decision, what is good for him and how this good is to be imparted to him, is not his business, but is contained and determined in what is said to him, that in this form it is well determined, and that in this form it is to be accepted by him. Therefore the use which is to be made of Scripture must consist in the fact that man allows the scriptural declaration as such to penetrate his life, executing its own counsel and not that of man, and conveying its own "patience" and its own "consolation," so that man finds satisfaction and endowed in this way can venture to hope.

Therefore it is not the case that in this third and last stage of exposition, the Word is to be conveyed to man (actual, contemporary man) according to the statement of his special claims and hopes, so that *applicatio*[EN104] means the adaptation of the Word of God to the service of this man. It is not the case that the exposition of Holy Scripture must finally issue in the answering of the so-called burning questions of the present day, that if possible it will acquire meaning and force as it is able to give an illuminating answer to the questions of the present generation. It should and must be carried out in serene confidence that it will in fact do this; but it must be left to Holy Scripture to decide how far it does so. We cannot try to lay down impatient conditions or ultimata in this respect. We cannot boast about a present-day point of view which it must under all circumstances take into account or to which it must correspond. We must not wish to determine what is interesting, salutary and understandable to the modern man, what he "expects" and so forth. If we do, it can mean only that although we may appear to be eagerly laying ourselves open to it, in fact we are shutting ourselves off from it. And the inevitable result will be that in turn it will conceal itself from us, evading and escaping us as it did when we insisted on apprehending it according to the pattern of some philosophical preconception. In this respect, too, we cannot trifle with the freedom of the Word of God. In face of it, we cannot know beforehand what the real present is, what are its burning questions, who and what we are, "our generation," "the modern man," etc. In a very real sense this will not appear until the Bible opens up before us, to give us correct and infallible information concerning ourselves and our real questions, concerns and needs.

[739]

Precisely in order that he may really appropriate what Scripture has to say, the reader and hearer must be willing to transpose the centre of his attention from himself, from the system of his own concerns and questions (even if he thinks he can give them the character of concerns and questions typical of his whole epoch) to the scriptural word itself. He must allow himself to be lifted out of himself into this word and its concerns and questions. It is only from this that light can ever fall upon his own life, and therewith the help which he needs for his life. How can that happen if, on the contrary, he insists on remaining rigidly at the focal point of his own life (or that of the life of his time, as he thinks to know it), as though this could give any illumination? How can he live out his faith if he repudiates faith itself, that is, a looking away from

---

[EN104] assimilation

self and to the word? Everything depends on the fact that this looking away from self and to Scripture should not be a preliminary stage which we have to leave behind us, but that for the sake of redeeming our life we abide by faith and therefore by this looking away from self and looking to Scripture. This assimilation of Scripture cannot be split again into two parts, of which the first consists in faith and therefore in this looking away from self and to Scripture, and the second, in which we turn our backs on Scripture, because we have now been taught and comforted by it, involves the transition to an independent answering of our own concerns and questions. The impatient question: And now?, with which we now so easily think that we can finally come to grips with the matter, can only be a sign that in reality we have not got down to the matter at all. The issue in question can only be the unconditional sovereignty of the Word, or, from our standpoint, an unconditional confidence in the goodness of its sovereignty. But this question, and its impatience, is the surest token that in reality we have already evaded the *usus scripturae*[EN105] in which *scriptura*[EN106] is the subject, and that we propose to make of Scripture that profane, because arbitrary, use which we are accustomed to make of all other things, but which we cannot make of Scripture. The confidence which we apparently accorded it at the first stage will be shown to be spurious, if later we tire of faith at a second stage. We have failed in advance to expect from its sovereignty everything that we ourselves need. We have failed in advance to give scope to its true sovereignty. We have reserved to ourselves the right to be wise and just again at this later point, and to be able to comfort and exhort ourselves. If there is to be a real appropriation of the Word of Scripture, we must believe wholeheartedly. For always we either believe wholeheartedly or not at all. When we look away from ourselves and to the scriptural word, when we transfer to Scripture the focal point, the centre of gravity of our attention, this cannot be merely an [740] episode. It cannot be followed by a second act under a different rule. Necessarily everything has already happened and will continually happen in this first and single act. Necessarily this first and single act will have been performed and will continually be performed with perfect confidence; not in an abstract confidence in its salutariness as our act, but in a concrete confidence in its object—the object we encounter in the image reflected in Scripture. This object requires and justifies our confidence as perfect confidence. Jesus Christ is this object. Only when this is forgotten can this act remain undone, or become an act in which we wish to consume instead of allowing ourselves to be consumed, to rule instead of to be ruled, or become merely a first act alongside which we have to place a second in which we have something better to do than believe. Only if Jesus Christ is forgotten can we understand the assimilation of Scripture which we have to make as something other than the continual adoption by us of an attitude to the act of appropriation by which in its own

---

[EN105] use of Scripture
[EN106] Scripture

wisdom and power it claims us. And only if we forget Jesus Christ can we understand by this attitude something other than faith. By faith we ourselves think
what Scripture says to us, and in such a way that we must think it because it has
become the determining force of our whole existence. By faith we come to the
contemporaneity, homogeneity and indirect identification of the reader or
hearer of Scripture with the witnesses of revelation. By faith their testimony
becomes a matter of our own responsibility. Faith itself, obedient faith, but
faith, and in the last resort obedient faith alone, is the activity which is
demanded of us as members of the Church, the exercise of the freedom which
is granted to us under the Word.

INDEX OF SCRIPTURE REFERENCES

INDEX OF SUBJECTS

INDEX OF NAMES